OXFORD STUDIES
IN MODERN EUROPEAN HISTORY

General Editors
SIMON DIXON, MARK MAZOWER,
and
JAMES RETALLACK

Russia in the Microphone Age

A History of Soviet Radio, 1919–1970

STEPHEN LOVELL

OXFORD
UNIVERSITY PRESS

OXFORD
UNIVERSITY PRESS

Great Clarendon Street, Oxford, OX2 6DP,
United Kingdom

Oxford University Press is a department of the University of Oxford.
It furthers the University's objective of excellence in research, scholarship,
and education by publishing worldwide. Oxford is a registered trade mark of
Oxford University Press in the UK and in certain other countries

© Stephen Lovell 2015

The moral rights of the author have been asserted

First Edition published in 2015

Impression: 1

Published in the United States of America by Oxford University Press
198 Madison Avenue, New York, NY 10016, United States of America

British Library Cataloguing in Publication Data
Data available

Library of Congress Control Number: 2014956891

ISBN 978–0–19–872526–8

Printed and bound by
CPI Group (UK) Ltd, Croydon, CR0 4YY

Links to third party websites are provided by Oxford in good faith and
for information only. Oxford disclaims any responsibility for the materials
contained in any third party website referenced in this work.

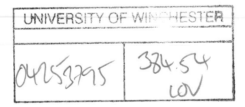

Acknowledgments

My first steps with this topic were taken during leave funded by a Philip Leverhulme Prize in 2005–6. After some interruption, the project was then sustained by the award of an AHRC Research Fellowship in 2010–11. The book was mostly written in the idyllic environment of the Kulturwissenschaftliches Kolleg at the University of Konstanz in 2012–13. I offer my warm appreciation to all these institutions, as well as to my home department at King's College London.

Many sympathetic colleagues have helped me along the way. At the risk of terrible omission, I should mention especially the following people: Emma Gray, for sharing with me her own research on Soviet radio as I was just getting started; Evgeny Dobrenko, for serving up juicy morsels of information from his vast store of knowledge of Stalin-era culture; Jurij Murašov, a fellow radio enthusiast, for his warm welcome in Konstanz; and Catriona Kelly, for supplying references and documents from her own encyclopedic store and for reading the entire manuscript with her unfailingly keen eye.

In Russia, several people were kind enough to share with me their experience of and insights into Soviet radio: thanks especially to Aleksandr Ivanovich Akhtyrskii, Liudmila Dem'ianovna Bolotova, Ekaterina Bolotova, Lev Solomonovich Markhasev, and Iraida Fedorovna Sukhonina. My work was further assisted by a great many librarians and archivists, among whom I should single out the wonderful staff of the A. S. Popov Museum of Communications, St Petersburg.

I also extend my warm thanks to Robert Faber, Cathryn Steele, and Christopher Wheeler, my patient and insightful editors at OUP; to Simon Dixon, the no less patient series editor; and to the two anonymous readers.

In the latter stages of this project my family was growing at a faster rate than my manuscript, and doing considerably more to enrich my life. Natasha, Matthew, and Nina have my gratitude and much else besides.

I dedicate this book to the memory of my father, William Lovell, who should have been granted time to read many more books.

I gratefully acknowledge permission to draw on some material already published in the following places:

'How Russia Learned to Listen: Radio and the Making of Soviet Culture', *Kritika: Explorations in Russian and Eurasian History*, 12/3 (2011).

'Broadcasting Bolshevik: The Radio Voice of Soviet Culture, 1920s–1950s', *Journal of Contemporary History*, 48/1 (2013).

'The *Magnitofon* and the Rhetoric of Soviet Culture', in Riccardo Nicolosi and Tanja Zimmermann (eds.), *Ethos und Pathos in den Medien* (Böhlau-Verlag, 2015).

Finally, a word on transliteration: I have adopted the Library of Congress system with the occasional exception for well-known names (thus 'Gorky', not 'Gor'kii').

Contents

List of Illustrations   ix
Abbreviations of Sources   xi

Introduction: Why Radio?   1

1. Institutionalizing Soviet Radio   13

2. Radio and the Making of Soviet Society   43

3. How Russia Learned to Broadcast   71

4. Mobilizing Radio: The War   107

5. From Wire to *Efir*: Radiofication and Beyond   135

6. The *Magnitofon* and the Art of Soviet Broadcasting   161

7. Radio Genres and Their Audiences in the Post-War Era   181

Epilogue: Beyond the Microphone Age   211

Note on Sources   217
Glossary   221
Bibliography   223
Index   233

List of Illustrations

0.1 Grave of Iurii Levitan. Author: Kwdavids 5
Source: Wikimedia Commons,
http://commons.wikimedia.org/wiki/File:Yuri_Borisovich_Levitan.JPG

0.2 Village children with *tarelka* 9
Source: A. S. Popov Central Museum of Communications

1.1 Postage stamp (1989) depicting Popov's first demonstration of his invention 17
Source: Wikimedia Commons,
http://commons.wikimedia.org/wiki/File:1989_CPA_6117.jpg

1.2 The 'Shukhov Tower' at Shabolovka. Photo: Sergei Arsenyev, 2006 22
Source: Wikimedia Commons,
http://commons.wikimedia.org/wiki/Shukhov_tower#mediaviewer/File:Shukhov_Tower_
photo_by_Sergei_Arsenyev_2006.JPG

1.3 Map of active and projected broadcasting stations in the USSR, 1925 24
Source: *Radio vsem*, no. 5 (1925)

1.4 An amateur radio club under the auspices of the union of workers
in the catering industry (Narpit), Moscow, 1931 28
Source: A. S. Popov Central Museum of Communications

1.5 Radio as tool of the Red Army 35
Source: Front cover of *Radioslushatel'*, no. 5 (1931)

2.1 The Soviet broadcasting dream: Shukhov Tower superimposed on Kremlin
and mass meeting 44
Source: Cover of *Radioslushatel'*, no. 9 (1928)

2.2 Radio audience gathered in peasant assembly room, Georgia, 1925 55
Source: A. S. Popov Central Museum of Communications

2.3 'Listening to Moscow' (*Slushaiut Moskvu*), 1927–1928. A typical 1920s
image of rural radiofication. 57
Source: A. S. Popov Central Museum of Communications

2.4 Image of 1930s middle-class listening 65
Source: A. S. Popov Central Museum of Communications

2.5 The *tarelka* at the other venue for Soviet domesticity: the dacha, 1931 65
Source: A. S. Popov Central Museum of Communications

2.6 Listeners take notes from a radio lecture, 1930s 68
Source: A. S. Popov Central Museum of Communications

3.1 An early indication of the coming symbiosis of radio and literature: Gorky
in headphones 92
Source: Cover of *Radioslushatel'*, no. 8 (1928)

5.1 A listener in Leningrad region enjoys the new Rodina model, 1947–1948 144
Source: A. S. Popov Central Museum of Communications

7.1 Transistor radio in a Russian village, 1970s.   204
       Source: © Viktor Akhlomov/Photosoyuz
7.2 Agniia Barto in the studio during a broadcast of 'Find a Person', 1969.   209
       Source: © Nikolai Bobrov/Photosoyuz

Abbreviations of Sources

ERAF	Estonian Historical Archives (former party archive)
ERA.R	Estonian Historical Archives (former state archive)
GANO	Gosudarstvennyi arkhiv Nizhegorodskoi oblasti
GARF	Gosudarstvennyi arkhiv Rossiiskoi Federatsii
GOPANO	Gosudarstvennyi obshchestvenno-politicheskii arkhiv Nizhegorodskoi oblasti
HP	The Harvard Project on the Soviet Social System
LG	*Literaturnaia gazeta*
Oxf/Lev	Life history interviews conducted for a project sponsored by the Leverhulme Trust under grant no. F/08736/A 'Childhood in Russia, 1890–1991: A Social and Cultural History' (2003–2006)*
Popov Museum	A. S. Popov Central Museum of Communications, St Petersburg
RGAE	Rossiiskii gosudarstvennyi arkhiv ekonomiki
RGAFD	Rossiiskii gosudarstvennyi arkhiv fonodokumentov
RGALI	Rossiiskii gosudarstvennyi arkhiv literatury i iskusstva
RGANI	Rossiiskii gosudarstvennyi arkhiv noveishei istorii
RGASPI	Rossiiskii gosudarstvennyi arkhiv sotsial'no-politicheskoi informatsii
RGASPI-M	RGASPI, Komsomol collection
RR	T. M. Goriaeva, *Radio Rossii: Politicheskii kontrol' sovetskogo radioveshchaniia v 1920–1930-kh godakh. Dokumentirovannaia istoriia* (Moscow, 2000)
Sovradiotel	*Sovetskoe radio i televidenie*
TsAOPIM	Tsentral'nyi arkhiv obshchestvenno-politicheskoi istorii Moskvy
TsGAIPD SPb	Tsentral'nyi gosudarstvennyi arkhiv istoriko-politicheskikh dokumentov Sankt-Peterburga
TsGALI SPb	Tsentral'nyi gosudarstvennyi arkhiv literatury i iskusstva Sankt-Peterburga
TsGAMO	Tsentral'nyi gosudarstvennyi arkhiv Moskovskoi oblasti
VKD	T. M. Goriaeva (ed.), *'Velikaia kniga dnia…': Radio v SSSR. Dokumenty i materialy* (Moscow, 2007)

* See Note on Sources for more detail.

Introduction
Why Radio?

The underlying conviction of this book is that a media-centred approach has much to add to our understanding of Soviet history. This is not an obvious or uncontroversial contention. It might seem that technologies of communication played an illustrative rather than formative role in the Soviet era. All branches of cultural production were closely supervised, and none more so than radio, which was minutely censored and conceived as the mouthpiece of power. But culture was not simply the handmaiden of politics; it was more akin to a valued senior employee. If this was a mass-media dictatorship, some of the media in question were of recent origin and hence still uncharted territory for Bolshevik rhetoricians. Perhaps the greatest success story in pre-war Soviet culture was cinema, identified by Lenin as the 'most important' of the Soviet arts, which in the 1930s became the flagship of Stalinist popular entertainment. But this rise to eminence was not automatic or easy. Cinema had to make the leap from commercial to state socialist film industry. It also had to negotiate the perilous passage from silent film to sound. Even in the late 1930s, all Soviet films were released in silent and spoken versions, given the lack of audio equipment in many cinemas outside the cities.[1]

Sound broadcasting was to an even greater extent a work in progress in the early Soviet period. Unlike cinema, it had no pre-revolutionary history. To begin with, no one was quite sure what it should be called. The subsequently standard term *radioveshchanie* was brought into currency by the radio press only in 1924; before then, the words *radiotelefoniia* and *shirokoveshchanie* (the literal Russian equivalent of 'broadcasting') had been used.[2] Even when terminological matters had been settled, it remained unclear exactly what radio could be expected to *do*. Developments came thick and fast. The first wireless transmission of the human voice took place on 27 February 1919, when an engineer in the Civil War headquarters of radio research tried his luck in the ether with an experimental transmitter: the phrase he uttered, 'Hello, this is the Nizhnii Novgorod Radio Laboratory speaking', has acquired canonical status.[3] By early 1920, the inventor M. A. Bonch-Bruevich

---

[1] Oksana Bulgakova, *Sovetskii slukhoglaz: Kino i ego organy chuvstv* (Moscow, 2010), 98.

[2] *RR*, 7.

[3] The moment is given its due, for example, in the chronologies of broadcasting history presented on two authoritative websites: http://www.tvmuseum.ru and http://www.rustelecom.ru (checked 20 June 2014). As with most stories of technological innovation, however, we should not exaggerate its significance. In the account later published by the leading light of the radio laboratory, the test transmission

and his team in Nizhnii Novgorod had developed a usable transmitter that was deployed in Moscow later that year. In June 1921, loudspeakers were set up in Moscow to broadcast a 'spoken newspaper'. In September 1922 came the first radio concert, and in autumn 1924 the start of regular programming under the auspices of a newly created broadcasting company that was soon renamed Radio-peredacha. Eight years on from the Revolution, in November 1925, came Russia's first ever outside broadcast—suitably enough, from Red Square.[4] Most fundamental of all, the Soviet Union, like other states in the interwar period, had a big decision to make about the kind of radio infrastructure it wanted to build. In the late 1920s, it opted for wired networks as opposed to mass production of wireless sets, and this decision profoundly shaped Soviet political communication for the following twenty years. In the post-war era, however, the authorities changed their priorities and started investing in production of wireless radio sets, many of them with short-wave capacity. Broadcasters were affected just as much as listeners by technological change: in the 1920s, and for the most part the 1930s too, they lived through an era of live broadcasting, but with the introduction in the mid-1940s of better-quality and more usable recording technology—otherwise known as the tape recorder, or *magnitofon*—they entered a new era of pre-recording and editing.

As Rick Altman has noted in his prehistory of sound cinema, 'new technologies are always born nameless'.[5] New media are conceived by analogy with existing media until their newness fully crystallizes: until it becomes clear that, as well as doing the old things better or faster, they can do new things that were previously unimaginable. Even as they claim to innovate and supersede, they gain kudos and formal coherence from association with their antecedents.[6] As we shall see in later chapters, broadcasters in the 1920s and 1930s spent a good deal of their time explaining how 'radio' was, or was not, different from existing media such as the press, theatre, and film. Was radio a spoken version of the newspaper, theatre for the blind, or something else entirely? Even broadcasting hardware could drastically change its function and meaning over time. The radio station at Khodynka Field in northern Moscow was built speedily at the start of World War I for wireless telegraph communication with Russia's Western allies. Taken over by the Bolsheviks,

---

of 27 February is not even mentioned: see M. A. Bonch-Bruevich, 'K istorii radioveshchaniia v SSSR' (1st pub. 1927), in Bonch-Bruevich, *Sobranie trudov* (Moscow and Leningrad, 1956), 241–6. For Bonch-Bruevich, the key task at that moment was to develop a transmitter that would be powerful and reliable enough for wireless telephony; this had in the main been achieved by the end of 1919. A later account by local radio historians similarly downplays the significance of 27 February 1919, pointing out that a reliable wireless voice connection to Moscow was demonstrated only in January 1920. See V. E. Batakov and V. A. Ukhin, *Govorit gorod Gor'kii* (Gorky, 1978), ch. 4 (accessed on 20 June 2014 at http://www.museum.unn.ru/managfs/index.phtml?id=13_6_01).

[4] The milestones are laid out in, for example, V. B. Dubrovin, *K istorii sovetskogo radioveshchaniia: Posobie dlia studentov-zaochnikov fakul'tetov zhurnalistiki gosudarstvennykh universitetov* (Leningrad, 1972).

[5] Rick Altman, *Silent Film Sound* (New York, 2004), 19.

[6] On this 'dialectic of remediation', see Jay David Bolter and Richard Grusin, *Remediation: Understanding New Media* (Cambridge, Mass., 1999). The argument in the book pertains primarily to contemporary digital media, but the authors rightly see it as having much broader applicability.

it was soon established as a centre for the new technology of wireless telephony (and renamed the 'October' radio station). During World War II it was used for broadcasting to the front line and the partisan movement, while in the Cold War era it played a full part in jamming Western radio. In autumn 1991, in a further twist, it became the home of the first non-state broadcasting company.[7]

Yet it still ostensibly makes sense to see the story of Soviet broadcasting as a fall from grace. Having been the vanguard of experimentation and technological utopianism in the 1920s, radio was converted into a kind of Stalinist oracle; the magical headphones of the early days turned into the plate-shaped wired receiver point, colloquially known as the *tarelka* and more formally as the *tochka*, which by the late 1930s was pumping out the main national channel for 20 hours per day. Improvisation at the microphone, still possible in the mid-1920s, turned into rigid preliminary censorship. As the satirical writer Il'ia Il'f observed in one of his aphoristic jottings, things had once been different. 'Radio' had been everywhere in science-fiction writing of the early twentieth century, serving as an emblem of the capacity of technology to remake human life for the better. But, as Il'f continued in the best-known bon mot on Soviet radio: 'Now we have radio, but there's still no happiness' (*Vot radio est', a schast'ia net*).[8] By the late 1930s, a time of terror and war scares, radio was perhaps the most pervasive and intrusive medium of public communication for Soviet urbanites. Whether at the workplace or at home in barracks or communal flats, it had become difficult to escape the *tarelka*.

All the same, Soviet radio cannot be reduced to the themes of totalitarian ideology and political control—if nothing else, because its history did not end with the late 1930s or even with the death of Stalin. The evolving forms and practices of Soviet broadcasting provide a revealing accompaniment to the mainstream history of Soviet politics and ideology. As historians of socialist realism in literature and the other arts have shown, it was one thing to have an ideological agenda, quite another to translate that agenda into cultural form. Even a repressive and doctrinaire regime had to rely on the expertise of its writers, painters, and musicians. This distinction between message and medium is even more worth making when we speak of a technology of communication that was brand new when the Bolsheviks came to power and required colossal investment in complex new infrastructure as well as the efforts of thousands of—often harassed and undereducated—broadcasting proto-professionals. There is no medium that so closely matches the trajectory of the regime that sought to control it. Long-range transmission of the human voice first occurred in Russia in 1919, a year and a half after the Bolshevik takeover. By the seventh anniversary of the revolution, regular broadcasts had started. Radio would then play its part in the trials and triumphs of Soviet history—polar expeditions and show trials in the 1930s, the supreme ordeal of the war, Sputnik in 1957 and Gagarin in 1961—before

---

[7] There is an informative and well-illustrated account at http://sontucio.livejournal.com/17780. html (checked 5 May 2013).

[8] Il'ia Il'f, *Zapisnye knizhki 1925–1937*, ed. A. I. Il'f (Moscow, 2000), 311. This witticism was written down in summer 1930.

ceding its primacy to television at more or less the moment the Soviet regime began to lose its own vigour (around 1970).

The number of different possible functions of broadcasting can be illustrated not only by its evolution in the Soviet period but also by its complex ancestry. What we now call 'radio'—sound broadcasting—can been seen as the heir of several earlier modes of communication. First, it represented an amplification of various forms and practices of public speaking that predated sound reproduction: lectures, speeches, meetings, and theatre. Second, it can be seen as the latest in a series of technologies to overcome distance and allow the ever more rapid spread of information: above all, the telegraph, which from the mid-nineteenth century revolutionized—in this case the word is appropriate—the global knowledge economy. Third, radio served to speed up 'news' and give it a real-time immediacy; in this sense, it transcended the print newspaper. Fourth, radio took its place in an emerging history of sound reproduction; its most prominent ancestor here was the gramophone. Fifth, radio should be considered in the context of the main existing method of sound transmission—the telephone; not for nothing was it known as 'radiotelephony' in the early days.

REMEMBERING RADIO

By now, however, Soviet radio has itself become part of Russia's cultural ancestry.[9] Despite its obvious function as organ of state propaganda, many people brought up in the Soviet period have fond recollections of their listening experiences. To this day, Russians of various age groups wax nostalgic about their favourite programmes—often theatre broadcasts or children's programmes such as 'The Club of the Famous Captains' (*Klub znamenitykh kapitanov*, first broadcast at the end of 1945), *KOAPP* (beloved of the 1960s generation), and 'Radio Nanny' (*Radioniania*, a 1970s phenomenon).[10] Older listeners regularly cite radio's role in providing positive models for emulation and setting high linguistic and cultural standards; more often than not, they compare the Soviet era favourably with the fragmented and undisciplined media system that replaced it.[11] Radio memories also quite often arouse local pride. Gorky, Kazan, Voronezh, and many other cities had their own broadcasting organizations and, by the 1960s if not before, their own well-loved studio actors and annnouncers. This regional dimension of Soviet broadcasting culture is reflected in the wave of dissertations in recent years on radio in various parts of the USSR from the Caucasus to Vladivostok.[12] Radio has also benefited from the

---

[9] An important caveat: this book will be concerned almost exclusively with broadcasting in Russian. A study of radio in other languages—especially in the Baltic republics, which had a pre-Soviet broadcasting pedigree and a reputation for formal innovation in the post-Stalin era—would surely yield interesting results.

[10] For more on all these examples, see Chapter 7.

[11] A typical example comes in an interview with a 70-year-old Leningrad schoolteacher (b. 1933): see Oxf/Lev SPb-02 PF 20 (A), p. 40.

[12] See the Bibliography for a significant sample.

Russian cult of the Great Patriotic War. From the front line to the evacuated factories in the east, the *tochka* became a crucial interface between the individual citizen and the patriotic cause. In besieged Leningrad, the most celebrated site of home front heroism, radio is remembered as a virtual lifeline, a cultural equivalent of the Road of Life that brought food to the city across Lake Ladoga.

The main broadcasting hero of the war, and indeed the most famous voice in Soviet history, is without doubt Iurii Levitan (see Figure 0.1), who read out thousands of rousing announcements during the war in his inimitable momentous style. Decades later, he could move audiences to tears just by delivering his trademark opening line: 'Attention! Moscow speaking!' Yet, just a few years earlier, Levitan had been giving similar oratorical treatment to reports on the show trials of

Figure 0.1. Grave of Iurii Levitan. Author: Kwdavids.
Source: Wikimedia Commons,
http://commons.wikimedia.org/wiki/File:Yuri_Borisovich_Levitan.JPG

1936–8. To consider Levitan complicit in the Terror would be to shoot the messenger—in 1934 he was effectively appointed Stalin's voice, and no one could have refused such an assignment—but his earlier career does at least cast a shadow over heroic treatments of wartime broadcasting: maybe the war was the apotheosis of Stalinist mobilization rather than a breakthrough to popular patriotism.[13] A recent biographer of Levitan seeks to overcome the resulting cognitive dissonance by turning the newsreader into a closet dissident.[14]

In writing the history of Soviet radio, the difficulty is not only that memory is selective, but also that the sources are themselves fragmented and unbalanced. Even historians of broadcasting who work on relatively well-documented places (such as the United States) tend to find that radio, as an inherently fleeting medium, is extraordinarily difficult to remember accurately and describe historically.[15] For the Soviet Union, the situation is even less promising. The administration of Soviet radio in the 1920s and 1930s has not left a lengthy paper trail: the archives of the main organizations in charge of broadcasting between 1924 and 1941 were severely depleted by a bonfire of documents in Moscow as the Germans drew near in October 1941. Texts of broadcasts for the 1930s are in especially short supply, as these were considered non-essential by the authorities as they prepared frantically for evacuation. Sound recordings of pre-war broadcasts are vanishingly few. Although the Soviet Union from the late 1920s had a technology for recording onto tape, and in 1932 even established a central state archive for sound recordings, only a few dozen broadcasts from the 1930s have survived, due to a combination of inadequate storage facilities and politically motivated purges of the archive in the period 1939–41.[16] Although the record for the post-war era is much fuller—there are tens of thousands of surviving recordings—here too the sound archive was routinely purged. Aural memory could be as politicized as every other kind in the Soviet Union. In the late 1940s, the Leningrad radio correspondent Lazar' Magrachev only preserved his priceless footage of the Blockade by smuggling tapes out of broadcasting headquarters; otherwise, they would certainly have fallen victim to the purge unleashed by the 'Leningrad Affair'.[17] In the later Soviet period, the principles of selection were perhaps less rigidly ideological than in the 1930s and 1940s, and the Soviets were no different from large broadcasting organizations in the West in pruning their archive so as to save storage space, but the effects were to emphasize the official and triumphalist dimension of media coverage.[18]

---

[13] Most likely it was both, as I suggest in Chapter 4.

[14] Ella Taranova, *Levitan: Golos Stalina* (St Petersburg, 2010), 82 (for Levitan's role in reading out death sentences), 84–6 (for a seizure Levitan apparently suffered in the studio after reading out a *Pravda* denunciation of Tukhachevskii in June 1937), 131 (for critical sentiments Levitan purportedly entertained after the war).

[15] See for example Susan J. Douglas, *Listening In: Radio and the American Imagination, from Amos 'n' Andy and Edward R. Murrow to Wolfman Jack and Howard Stern* (New York, 1999), 9.

[16] *RR*, 36–40. The first documentary recording on Red Square took place on 7 November 1931 (according to the sleeve notes of the LP *Govorit Krasnaia ploshchad'*, Melodiia, 1987). The few recordings preserved from the 1930s can be found in the Rossiiskii gosudarstvennyi arkhiv fonodokumentov, Moscow (RGAFD).

[17] Lev Markhasev, *Belki v kolese: Zapiski iz Doma radio* (St Petersburg, 2004), 153.

[18] *VKD*, 19.

Yet, for all the gaps in the documentary record, there is plenty of material with which to write the history of Soviet broadcasting even for the pre-war period. The radio journals of the 1920s–30s provide an essential foundation. The pre-war holdings of the Radio Committee archive are severely depleted but not by any means negligible, and radio left traces in the records of other institutions (trade unions, party committees, Komsomol) as well as in the personal archives of various broadcasting luminaries (writers, composers, actors). I have further attempted to round out the archival picture by using material from the Leningrad party archive and the records of the radio committee in Nizhnii Novgorod/Gorky. Leningrad was the most important broadcasting centre outside Moscow. Gorky had a proud radio tradition thanks to Bonch-Bruevich's Radio Laboratory, it established one of the earliest Russian broadcasting stations outside the capitals, and its archive was not subject to the same wartime depredations as that of the All-Union Radio Committee in Moscow. For the post-war era the sources are much richer. The archive of the State Committee for Television and Radio (Gosteleradio) has tens of thousands of pages of programme transcripts from the 1940s, 1950s, and 1960s as well as a much fuller record of editorial decision-making than exists for the 1930s. The pre-war drought turns into a post-war glut: it is easy to drown in the amount of material, especially given that existing histories of Soviet radio tend to concentrate on the interwar period and have hardly begun to assimilate the vast documentation of the later era. Nor should the historian of Soviet radio rely exclusively on the archival record: we can also draw on a handy stock of published memoirs by broadcasters as well as a number of high-quality websites. Radio enthusiasts are very often technophiles, and it is not surprising that many of them have adapted with gusto to the Internet age.[19]

This is the first full history of Soviet radio in English, though there have been good treatments of particular aspects of the subject.[20] In Russian, as one might expect, the literature is much more extensive. Towards the end of the Soviet period came the first reliable general histories.[21] In post-Soviet times a great deal of new material has come out, but two prolific historians of Soviet broadcasting are especially worthy of mention. The first is Aleksandr Sherel' (1937–2005), a broadcaster,

---

[19] Here I mention the three that I have found most useful (also because they are nicely complementary): http://www.tvmuseum.ru (which has a large collective of biographies and historical surveys of particular programmes and rubrics, mainly written by veterans of Soviet broadcasting); http://www.staroeradio.ru (which offers the opportunity actually to hear samples of many famous and not-so-famous Soviet radio programmes); and the virtual museum 'Otechestvennaia radiotekhnika 20 veka', at http://rw6ase.narod.ru.

[20] Particularly worthy of mention are the following works: the perceptive chapter on wartime broadcasting by James von Geldern, 'Radio Moscow: The Voice from the Center', in Richard Stites (ed.), *Culture and Entertainment in Wartime Russia* (Bloomington, Ind., 1995), 44–61; the contrasting, archivally based treatment of the same subject in Karel C. Berkhoff, *Motherland in Danger: Soviet Propaganda during World War II* (Cambridge, Mass., 2012)—though this work has more to say about newspapers than about radio; and Kristin Roth-Ey's fine general account of radio in the post-Stalin era in her *Moscow Prime Time: How the Soviet Union Built the Media Empire That Lost the Cultural Cold War* (Ithaca, NY, 2011), ch. 3.

[21] Dubrovin, *K istorii sovetskogo radioveshchaniia*; P. S. Gurevich and V. N. Ruzhnikov, *Sovetskoe radioveshchanie: Stranitsy istorii* (Moscow, 1976); V. N. Ruzhnikov, *Tak nachinalos': Istoriko-teoreticheskii ocherk sovetskogo radioveshchaniia 1917–1928* (Moscow, 1987).

teacher, and writer who spent twenty years of his career working in Soviet radio and later wrote extensively on the subject.[22] Although his books repeat themselves to an extent and in places lack scholarly apparatus, they are an important resource. An extremely well-informed observer-participant, Sherel' could evidently draw on first-hand accounts he accumulated from colleagues as well as on the documentary record. The second major figure is Tat'iana Mikhailovna Goriaeva, currently the director of the Russian State Archive for Literature and the Arts, who has produced a valuable study of the institutional history of pre-war Soviet broadcasting as well as two voluminous document collections.[23]

The history of Soviet radio, then, is far from being terra incognita. Until now, however, the territory has been mapped in very particular ways. Russian accounts have tended to focus on broadcasting technology and institutional history (with, in Goriaeva's case, a particular emphasis on censorship). Broadcasting content has rarely been subject to the same level of analysis, while reception and social impact have hardly received any attention. The aim of this book is to weave together these various aspects, granting more prominence to the social and cultural dimensions of broadcasting than has previously been the case, and giving the post-war era—hitherto less well understood than the 1920s and 1930s—its due.

THE SIGNIFICANCE OF RADIO

Before embarking on the story of Soviet broadcasting, we should reflect briefly on why that story might be interesting—on how it might help us to understand Soviet culture in a broader sense. Radio was unrivalled among media in what it seemed to offer the early Bolsheviks. First, it made possible the almost instantaneous dissemination of politicized information over huge distances. Second, it held out huge promise as a collective organizer: even the most charismatic and resonant orator could not hope to reach more than a few thousand people at once, but radio had every prospect of creating an audience of several million. Third, radio was the epitome of modernity: it would accelerate progress from darkness to light, from ignorance to enlightenment. The bearded *muzhik* in headphones or with receiver was one of the iconic images of the 1920s (see Figure 0.2).

That was theory, but the practice fell some way short. Although the technology of sound broadcasting was developed in the early 1920s, radio did not reach anything approaching a national audience until a decade after that. For all the Bolshevik asseverations (dating back to Lenin himself) of radio's importance, its cultural impact in the pre-war era was limited by the poverty and underdevelopment of the USSR. Historians can point to innumerable occasions when party

---

[22] See the profile at http://www.tvmuseum.ru/catalog.asp?ob_no=6864 (checked 6 May 2013). Sherel''s main works are: *Rampa u mikrofona* (Moscow, 1985); *Tam, na nevidimykh podmostkakh...: Radioiskusstvo: problemy istorii i teorii. 1922–1941* (Moscow 1993); and *Audiokul'tura XX veka. Istoriia, esteticheskie zakonomernosti, osobennosti vliianiia na auditoriiu: Ocherki* (Moscow, 2004).

[23] Goriaeva (ed.), *Istoriia sovetskoi radio-zhurnalistiki: Dokumenty. Teksty. Vospominaniia. 1917–1945* (Moscow, 1991); *RR*; *VKD*.

Figure 0.2. Village children with *tarelka*. In Soviet propaganda of the 1920s radio could invade even the most bucolic scene.

Source: A. S. Popov Central Museum of Communications

and state agencies bemoaned their inability to harness radio as a significant force for cultural construction.[24] Comparisons with Nazi Germany are unflattering to the Soviet propaganda machine. In August 1933, Goebbels declared that 'What the press was to the nineteenth century, radio will be to the twentieth'. Even at the start of 1933, before the Nazis came to power, 4.3 million receivers were registered in Germany. By 1934, following the launch of the cheap *Volksempfänger*, the figure had risen to 8.2 million.[25] At the end of the same year, the USSR could boast only 2.5 million reception points.[26] The two dictatorships can likewise be differentiated by examining the rhetorical styles of their leaders: Hitler's gift for charismatic oratory contrasts starkly with Stalin's readiness to remain in the shadows and let Iurii Levitan do his talking for him.[27] The position of radio would seem to be further weakened by the well-attested scriptorial bias of Stalin-era culture, and by the existence of an overbearing leader cult that was overwhelmingly visual in its communication strategies.[28] The already overpowering

[24] This is largely the approach taken in Stefan Plaggenborg, *Revoliutsiia i kul'tura: Kul'turnye orientiry v period mezhdu Oktiabr'skoi revoliutsiei i epokhoi stalinizma* (St Petersburg, 2000), ch. 4.

[25] Horst J. P. Bergmeier and Rainer E. Lotz, *Hitler's Airwaves: The Inside Story of Nazi Radio Broadcasting and Propaganda Swing* (New Haven, 1997), 6, 9.

[26] Alex Inkeles, *Public Opinion in Soviet Russia: A Study in Mass Persuasion* (Cambridge, Mass., 1950), 274–5.

[27] On Hitler as speaker, see Josef Kopperschmidt (ed.), *Hitler der Redner* (Munich, 2003), which among other things explores the notion of a 'rhetorical Sonderweg' that made German society especially susceptible to Hitler's style of oratory.

[28] On the reader as imagined addressee of Soviet culture, see especially Evgenii Dobrenko, *Formovka sovetskogo chitatelia: Sotsial'nye i esteticheskie predposylki retseptsii sovetskoi literatury* (St Petersburg, 1997). On the scripted character of Soviet culture in the 1930s and the role of Stalin as 'the

sense of Soviet radio's inadequacy is further heightened by the fact that, in the post-war era, Soviet broadcasting found itself fighting a losing battle against much more effective aural propaganda from abroad. In the Anglophone world, far more has been written on Western broadcasting into the USSR than on broadcasting within the Soviet Union.[29]

The fact remains, however, that radio was a major technological innovation that coincided with, and underscored, social change. Living in Bolshevik Russia not only felt and looked different, it also sounded different. This point has long been understood by film-makers, who go to great trouble to create an authentic sound-scape for cinematic depictions of the 1930s or 1940s: Aleksei German's *My Friend Ivan Lapshin* (1984), Nikita Mikhalkov's *Burnt by the Sun* (1994), and Gleb Pan-filov's recent serialization of Solzhenitsyn's *The First Circle* (2006) would be less compelling and plausible without their aural backdrops.[30]

It is certainly true that pre-war Soviet broadcasting suffered from a shortage of resources and struggled to reach its addressee outside the major cities—but other, ostensibly more established, Soviet media had similar problems to confront. The press went through a period of crisis in the 1920s before it made the crucial decision to address itself to an audience of activists.[31] Yet, while this turned the Soviet newspaper into an effective means of mobilization for the younger urban audience, it did not by any means turn the entire Soviet population into a nation of readers. It is also true that Soviet broadcasters and administrators spent much of the 1920s and 1930s castigating themselves for the failure to achieve satisfactory 'radiofica-tion'. But this was an era of self-castigation, and the same discourse of failure to achieve the Party's goals could be heard in almost all areas of Soviet life.

Radio had one crucial distinctive attribute relative to the other main media: orality. Even when the campaign to 'liquidate' illiteracy began to make headway in the 1930s, this remained a society where the spoken word mattered enormously. In one sense, Soviet society had become more oral even as it became more literate: people from many different walks of life were now called on to speak publicly at all manner of meetings, and oral 'agitation' was at least as important as its written partner, 'propaganda'. In the late 1930s, canonical Stalinist texts such as the *Short Course on the History of the Communist Party*, or even the less arcane *Short Course on the History of the USSR*, clearly went over the heads of most of their intended audience; to the extent that they did reach the mass public, they did so not on the

origin of the sacral word', see Katerina Clark, *Moscow, the Fourth Rome: Stalinism, Cosmopolitanism, and the Evolution of Soviet Culture, 1931–1941* (Cambridge, Mass., 2011), ch. 2, quotation 89. On the leader cult, see Jan Plamper, *The Stalin Cult: A Study in the Alchemy of Power* (New Haven, 2012).

[29] For example: Walter L. Hixson, *Parting the Curtain: Propaganda, Culture and the Cold War 1945–1961* (Basingstoke, 1997); Michael Nelson, *War of the Black Heavens: The Battles of Western Broadcasting in the Cold War* (Syracuse, NY, 1997); Arch Puddington, *Broadcasting Freedom: The Cold War Triumph of Radio Free Europe and Radio Liberty* (Lexington, Ky., 2000).

[30] On the capacity of sound to trigger historical memory, see also *VKD*, 10.

[31] On the crisis, see Jeffrey Brooks, 'The Breakdown in the Production and Distribution of Printed Material', in Abbott Gleason et al. (eds.), *Bolshevik Culture* (Bloomington, Ind., 1985), 151–74; on the shift to Stalininist newspapers, see Matthew Lenoe, *Closer to the Masses: Stalinist Culture, Social Revolution, and Soviet Newspapers* (Cambridge, Mass., 2004).

page but in the retelling by poorly educated propagandists.[32] As late as the 1970s, Soviet citizens outside the major cities could be remarkably ignorant of the content of newspapers, continuing to draw much of their information from hearsay; face-to-face oral communication was still considered one of the most effective methods of propaganda.[33]

These examples draw our attention to the double-sided nature of Soviet broadcasting. On the one hand, radio was the voice of power, a powerful tool of totalitarian brainwashing, a medium that could impose itself on the consciousness of even the most recalcitrant citizen. This dimension of Soviet radio was memorably satirized in Iulii Daniel' 's novella *Moscow Speaking!* (published abroad in the early 1960s), in which Soviet radio announces an upcoming 'Murder Day' when citizens will be permitted to kill each other without facing punishment.[34] On the other hand, radio was a medium uniquely well suited to the mobilizational, participatory culture of Soviet socialism in the period *c*.1930–*c*.1970. Its mission was to broadcast not only the voice of authority but also that of 'the people'. Broadcasters, in other words, were confronted with a tricky version of the traditional Marxist conundrum of spontaneity versus consciousness. Their rhetorical task was to find a style of delivery that was both impeccably correct and plausibly popular. Under constant pressure from the censorship bureaucracy and the Central Committee, they found this a hard challenge to meet. The records of the All-Union Radio Committee are peppered with self-critical discussions of the leaden language of Soviet broadcasting, yet the participants in these meetings also routinely berate their colleagues for errors ranging from slips of the tongue to lapses in editorial judgement.

This book will suggest that, by the 1960s, Soviet broadcasters had become more successful rhetoricians. By now, political supervision, while still overbearing, was no longer paralysing, and improved broadcasting technology had substantially reduced the risk of incriminating error. 'Developed socialism' had its established idiom of 'good news' journalism as well as established and well-loved formats in areas such as literature and theatre, sport, and children's broadcasting.

In the post-Stalin era, however, yet another ambiguity of radio came to the fore. As Marshall McLuhan put it in one of his evocative formulations, twentieth-century radio was a 'tribal drum'. This quintessentially modern medium was atavistic in the sense that it built group solidarity (and shaped collective action) through aural affect: without radio, the 'somnambulism' of Hitler's followers would be

---

[32] David Brandenberger, *National Bolshevism: Stalinist Mass Culture and the Formation of Modern Russian National Identity, 1931–1956* (Cambridge, Mass., 2002), 73–5.

[33] See the account of a survey of Taganrog in 1971 in B. A. Grushin, *Chetyre zhizni Rossii v zerkale oprosov obshchestvennogo mneniia. Ocherki massovogo soznaniia rossiian vremen Khrushcheva, Brezhneva, Gorbacheva i El'tsina v 4-kh knigakh. Zhizn' 2-ia. Epokha Brezhneva (chast' 2-ia)* (Moscow, 2006), ch. 8.

[34] The theme lives on into the present. In a recent novel by contemporary Russia's most fashionable writer, the otherwise unprepossessing protagonist has a gift for imitating the voice of Iurii Levitan. He is put to use by the FSB as the voice of God, which is to be transmitted into the head of George W. Bush in order to guide the President's actions. See Viktor Pelevin, *Ananasnaia voda dlia prekrasnoi damy* (Moscow, 2011).

impossible to explain.[35] Yet McLuhan also acknowledged another attribute of radio: its power to address the listener individually in 'high definition'. In certain contexts, perhaps, this made radio the weapon of totalitarian propagandists; in others, however, it served to fragment (or segment) the audience. As the Stalinist *tochka* was replaced in many Soviet households by the wireless set, perhaps even by a transistor radio, it became ever less possible to control not just how people responded to what they heard but even what they listened to. Radio had played a full part in building the Soviet nation that came to maturity sometime in the 1950s, but it was also no respecter of national boundaries. Until the arrival of the Internet, it was the most international medium of communication known to mankind. By the 1960s, Soviet urbanites were routinely getting a significant part of their news from foreign broadcasts, and radio, more than any other single phenomenon, gave the lie to the notion of the USSR as a hermetically 'closed' society.

[35] Marshall McLuhan, *Understanding Media* (1964; London, 2001), 324–7.

1

Institutionalizing Soviet Radio

The history of most communication technologies is one of slow diffusion; talk of a 'print revolution' has always tended to obscure the delays and equivocations in the adoption of Gutenberg's invention, not to mention the powers of endurance of manuscript culture.[1] In the case of radio, however, the notion of a cultural 'big bang' does not seem much of a stretch. Wireless broadcasting was indeed a remarkable, and remarkably sudden, expansion of human communicative capacity. In the space of five years or so, all the world's more or less developed regions adopted this new means of transmitting sound across virtually unlimited distances without the need for any physical infrastructure between sender and receiver. The impression of a common global phenomenon was heightened by the passion for vicarious border-crossing among radio's early practitioners. The radio ham was, at least potentially, a new kind of world citizen.

Yet the rhetoric—and in large measure the reality—of a global 'radio moment' should not lead us to overlook the extent to which the medium was shaped by its national contexts. Between 1920 and 1927, different countries took a series of formative decisions that determined at least for the medium term what 'radio' would mean on their territories: for politicians, armies, administrators, and businessmen, national borders remained every bit as tangible as before. Naturally, the decisions of these actors were conditioned by the existing political and economic order, but they also had a significant element of contingency. During a 'chaotic interregnum' in the mid-1920s, Weimar Germany became 'a strange hybrid between a capitalist business and a profit-restricted public enterprise'; the regional companies and their private investors were cleverly reeled in by the relevant ministries in Berlin, and central radio came under de facto state control in 1926.[2] The vaunted public service mission of the BBC was 'a concept grafted onto an initial pragmatic set of arrangements between the Post Office and the British radio industry': the industrialists wanted a market for their products, while the Post Office wanted a stable revenue stream without allowing chaotic competition between broadcasters. In 1922, at the moment the British Broadcasting Company was created, very little thought was given to what we might consider the main business of radio—the

---

[1] For the Russian example, see Simon Franklin, 'Mapping the Graphosphere: Cultures of Writing in Early 19th-Century Russia (and Before)', *Kritika: Explorations in Russian and Eurasian History* 12 (2011): 531–60.
[2] Karl Christian Führer, 'A Medium of Modernity? Broadcasting in Weimar Germany, 1923–1932', *Journal of Modern History* 69 (1997): 724–7.

content of programmes.[3] A very different case, and one the British authorities in the 1920s were keen to avoid emulating, was that of the United States. Although the airwaves remained in public ownership, the American licensing system brought into being a highly commercial radio culture, where advertising revenue and the consequent need to attract listeners were from an early stage uppermost in broadcasters' minds.[4] On the one hand, America could claim to have a uniquely democratic media culture, since it had few of the restrictions on broadcasters that were found in European states; on the other hand, the reality was that large corporations were from an early stage able to make enormous profits from providing access to the notionally common resource of the airwaves.[5]

It will surprise no one to hear that Soviet Russia ended up with a broadcasting system that was the polar opposite of the American. But in Russia as elsewhere, political objectives had to take into account the nature of this new technology, the peculiar economic challenges it presented, and the character of the listening public. The USSR, too, had a broadcasting 'company' to begin with, and the institutional and infrastructural contours of radio did not really start to become fixed until 1927.

But sound broadcasting was defined not just by the conjuncture of the 1920s. It also had a complex inheritance to draw on. Early thinking about broadcasting was conditioned by the experience of managing other forms of communication technology for the preceding half-century or more. Since Independence, America had created what was by European standards a remarkably decentralized media system; conversely, Germany since its unification was well practised in balancing the need for regional cultural autonomy with the imperative of strong rule from Berlin. With a view to such elements of path dependency, the first section of this chapter will investigate Russia's previous experience in the political economy of telecommunications.

A GENEALOGY OF SOVIET BROADCASTING

What came in the 1920s to be known as 'radio' was the latest in a series of technologies for overcoming distance that stretched back almost a century. In organizational and conceptual terms, the crucial inheritance came from wired telegraphy. Pioneered in the 1840s, this technology had 'dematerialized' communication, allowing information to travel far faster than people or material goods and thus transforming the world's economic geography.[6] It also developed into a crucial attribute for any ambitious state in an age of competitive imperialism.

[3] Paddy Scannell and David Cardiff, *A Social History of British Broadcasting*, i. *1922–1939: Serving the Nation* (Oxford, 1991), quotation 5.

[4] Paul Starr, *The Creation of the Media: Political Origins of Modern Communications* (New York, 2004), 329.

[5] Susan J. Douglas, *Inventing American Broadcasting, 1899–1922* (Baltimore, 1987), 315–22.

[6] Roland Wenzlhuemer, 'The Dematerialization of Telecommunication: Communication Centres and Peripheries in Europe and the World, 1850–1920', *Journal of Global History* 2 (2007): 345–72.

By the late nineteenth century, the British, with their far-flung dominions, led the way. But the other major powers were desperate to catch up: in the wake of the Fashoda incident and the Boer War, telecommunications was 'no longer just a business or a public utility but had become one of the pillars of national security'.[7]

In Russia too, the telegraph radically accelerated communications over the course of the nineteenth century. For a large territorial empire such as this, tele-communications had even greater significance than in the smaller nation states of nineteenth-century Europe, which were already more densely networked: in Russia, contrary to the central European pattern, telegraph routes often preceded the railway.[8] The first mention in government circles of any form of telegraph comes in the papers of the Main Administration for Routes of Communication (Glavnoe upravlenie putei soobshcheniia) in 1823. At this point electrical cables still lay in the future, and the subject of discussion was the 'optical telegraph', a semaphore system first developed by Claude Chappe in Revolutionary France. The first such telegraph line in Russia, built in 1824, connected St Petersburg to Shlisselburg, an important outpost at the source of the Neva on Lake Ladoga. In the following decade, various Russian and foreign inventors were active in this field. One of them, the Frenchman Jacques Chateau, was given permission in 1833 to construct an experimental line between St Petersburg and Kronstadt; a few years later, in 1839, a similar connection was completed between St Petersburg and Warsaw.[9]

Chateau's optical telegraph operated in Russia until 1854, but by then it had been made obsolete by the faster, more reliable, and cheaper cable telegraph. Russia's first demonstration of an electrical telegraph was conducted by the scientist and orientalist Pavel L'vovich Schilling (1786–1837) in St Petersburg in 1832, but his initiative remained without practical application in his lifetime. It was only in 1849, on an experimental basis, that the first underground electromagnetic cables were laid along a 10-verst stretch of the railway line from St Petersburg to Moscow; that same year, Russian engineers were sent abroad to learn more about the electrical telegraph. The first operational lines were laid in the 1850s. St Petersburg was connected to Kronstadt and Gatchina, and then to Moscow, Warsaw, Reval, and Helsingfors; a St Petersburg city telegraph followed in 1857; and a cable was laid under the Neva in 1864. Similar developments came in Moscow in 1861 and Kiev in 1881. In 1853, Nicholas I resolved that telegraph lines should be laid to connect all strategically important parts of European Russia. This decision came too late to improve Russia's performance in the Crimean War—the St Petersburg–Sevastopol line, laid by Siemens & Halske in 1855, could only be taken as far as

---

[7] Daniel R. Headrick, *The Invisible Weapon: Telecommunications and International Politics, 1851–1945* (New York, 1991), 111.

[8] Marsha Siefert, "'Chingis-Khan with the Telegraph': Communications in the Russian and Ottoman Empires', in Jörn Leonhard and Ulrike von Hirschhausen (eds.), *Comparing Empires: Encounters and Transfers in the Long Nineteenth Century* (Göttingen, 2011), 82.

[9] N. A. Mal'tseva, *Materialy po istorii sviazi v Rossii XVIII—nachalo XX vv.* (Leningrad, 1966), 67–70.

Simferopol, as Sevastopol by then had fallen to the enemy. But the impetus was now there for the creation of a high-speed communications network that would bring the centre of the Russian Empire much closer to its far-flung provinces. During the reign of Alexander II, the telegraph spread to the Caucasus, Central Asia, and the Far East. As of 1 January 1858 there were 6,364 versts of telegraph lines, and seventy-seven stations with a staff of 892. In the mid-1880s, the list of telegraph stations ran to 160 pages. By the end of the nineteenth century, all major cities in the empire were connected by telegraph.[10]

Telegraph cables were expensive to lay and maintain and vulnerable to attack or interference, especially if they went by land rather than under the sea. Radio telegraphy was the next radical extension of the communication capacity of the modern world. Its great pioneer and salesman was Marconi, who at high-profile demonstrations in the late 1890s convinced the British government that this technology was worth major investment. The stakes of technological innovation seemed as high as they had ever been. As Daniel Headrick observes, radio 'was born into a world of jittery jingoism and started life as a weapon in the commercial and military rivalries of the great powers'. Marconi soon received an order from the British War Office, which used Marconi sets and Marconi-trained operators to assist its operations in the Boer War. In the 1900s, the Marconi company skirmished with its main rival, the German Telefunken, and the quality of signals was much lower than it would be when radio made the jump from 'spark transmission' to 'continuous wave' in the 1920s. But even in the 1900s radiotelegraphy had redefined the scope of modern communications: now Morse signals were free to depart from the routes traced out by cables and could in principle reach practically anywhere (in particular, across national boundaries).[11]

The Russians have their own story to tell of the origins of radiotelegraphy. In the Soviet era, and especially from the late Stalin period onwards, they would claim to be the 'homeland of radio'. The founding myth of this alternative broadcasting tradition was the paper 'On the Relationship of Metallic Powder to Electrical Fluctuations' delivered by A. S. Popov on 25 April 1895 (new style: 7 May) at a meeting of the Russian Physico-Chemical Society in St Petersburg University (see Figure 1.1). As innumerable patriotic Russian technophiles have noted, Popov's account of a technique for registering electromagnetic waves came more than a year earlier than the meretricious Marconi's demonstration of his version of

---

[10] Information in this paragraph from: M. S. Vysokov, *Elektrosviaz' v Rossiiskoi imperii ot zarozhdeniia do nachala XX veka* (Iuzhno-Sakhalinsk, 2003), ch. 2 (for Schilling and the early electromagnetic telegraph); *Sobranie tsirkuliarov, prikazov i drugikh rasporiazhenii po telegrafnomu vedomstvu (nyne deistvuiushchikh) s 1859 po 1874 g.* (St Petersburg, 1877), pp. ii–iv; *Spisok telegrafnykh i pochtovo-telegrafnykh uchrezhdenii Rossiiskoi Imperii dlia rukovodstva pri prieme telegramm vnutrennei korrespondentsii* (St Petersburg, 1886); Mal'tseva, *Materialy po istorii sviazi*, 90–6; M. A. Bykhovskii, *Razvitie telekommunikatsii: na puti k informatsionnomu obshchestvu. Istoriia telegrafa, telefona i radio do nachala XX veka* (Moscow, 2012), 293–6.

[11] Headrick, *The Invisible Weapon*, ch. 7, quotation 116.

Figure 1.1. Postage stamp (1989) depicting Popov's first demonstration of his invention.

Source: Wikimedia Commons, http://commons.wikimedia. org/wiki/File:1989_CPA_6117.jpg

the technology. The first public 'radiotelegraph' broadcast, over a distance of 250 metres, allegedly took place on 12/24 March 1896, when Popov successfully transmitted the words 'Heinrich Hertz'.[12]

The question of primacy in the invention of radio is unlikely ever to be settled to everyone's satisfaction. Popov may be considered the first to demonstrate a means of receiving electromagnetic waves. Yet Marconi, who seems to have achieved his results quite independently, was from the beginning more interested in the next step—creating a usable device capable of transmitting and receiving sense-bearing information (i.e. Morse code). If we look forward to the practical applications of the discovery of radio waves, there is no question that Marconi was the prime mover. Conversely, if we are interested in the genealogy of radio, there is no obvious reason to start with Popov rather than going further back in time and handing the laurels to Faraday, Maxwell, or Hertz.[13] There is also a strong case to be made that the true breakthrough—the invention that superseded Morse code telegraphy and made possible broadcasting proper—was the non-obvious move from spark transmission

---

[12] For the canonical narrative, see V. B. Dubrovin, *K istorii sovetskogo radioveshchaniia: Posobie dlia studentov-zaochnikov fakul'tetov zhurnalistiki gosudarstvennykh universitetov* (Leningrad, 1972), 4. A recent restatement comes in the biography of Popov in the prestigious Lives of Remarkable People series: Moisei Radovskii, *Aleksandr Popov* (Moscow, 2009), especially the preface by Viktor Erlikhman, 'O chem ne napisano v etoi knige', 5–9, which takes a hefty swipe at Western sceptics. According to Vysokov (*Elektrosviaz' v Rossiiskoi imperii*, 209–10), however, the established Soviet account of the demonstration of March 1896 is dubious: there is nothing in the contemporary record to suggest an event of this magnitude, and the first confirmed use of Popov's device to transmit and receive Morse code came in December 1897. Radovskii acknowledges the puzzling gap in the minutes of the March 1896 meeting, but cites later witness testimony (*Aleksandr Popov*, 124–5).

[13] See the argument put forward by one of the few Russian sceptics on the question of Popov's primacy: Vysokov, *Elektrosviaz' v Rossiiskoi imperii*, ch. 5.

to continuous wave.[14] Popov, then, is perhaps best regarded as an important link in a chain rather than a point of origin. He was also operating in a completely different institutional environment from his peers in the West. Marconi was a scientist-entrepreneur who devoted his life to the cause of radiotelegraphy; Popov was a military engineer with very little opportunity or inclination for self-promotion, whose time and energies were taken up with many other projects.

Even if Popov had achieved a breakthrough that made wireless radio possible, the impact of the invention in his homeland remained limited for at least a decade. The Baltic fleet was responsible for the first practical applications of the new technology in the late 1890s; the most striking instance came in the winter of 1899–1900, when radiotelegraphy played an important part in the rescue of Battleship Apraksin from near the island of Hogland in the Gulf of Finland. In 1900, a radiotelegraphy workshop was set up on Kronstadt, though its output in the period 1901–4 was only a modest fifty-four transmitters.[15] Compared to its international competitors, Russia's performance was unimpressive. As usual, it took a war to demonstrate how debilitating the absence of a modern communications network might be. In the 1850s the lack of a rail network had turned Russia's Crimean campaign into a logistical disaster; in 1904, the Russians were comprehensively outmanoeuvred by the Japanese at least in part because the enemy had superior wireless radio connections. Establishing a radio link with the Far East accordingly became a high priority after 1905.[16]

Radio remained a naval and military preserve, and Russia fell far behind the wealthier Western countries where wireless development was at least in part commercially driven. True, foreign companies gradually started investing in this area, and by 1910 Russia had about 30 radio stations other than those for military or government use.[17] By the start of 1913, however, Russia had a mere 230 wireless transmission stations (170 on ships, only 60 on land), while Britain had more than 1,600.[18] The military network was more impressive than the civilian, though it remained very much a work in progress. In 1910, the Ministry of Defence started building a strategic network of radio stations (in Moscow, Baku, Tashkent, and Vladivostok), though the war started before this work was finished. The Khodynka broadcasting station (later to be known as the Oktiabr'skaia) was built in autumn 1914 for communication with the Entente powers. By 1917, Russia had a number of powerful strategic stations (in Tsarskoe Selo, Khodynka, Nikolaev, Tashkent, and elsewhere) as well as coastal stations under naval administration and a non-military network of stations under the control of the Main Administration for Post and Telegraph.[19]

[14] See Hugh G. J. Aitken, *The Continuous Wave: Technology and American Radio, 1900–1932* (Princeton, 1985).
[15] Vysokov, *Elektrosviaz' v Rossiiskoi imperii*, 216–17.
[16] Mal'tseva, *Materialy po istorii sviazi*, 127–8.
[17] Mal'tseva, *Materialy po istorii sviazi*, 136.
[18] Bykhovskii, *Razvitie telekommunikatsii*, 309–10.
[19] Dubrovin, *K istorii sovetskogo radioveshchaniia*, ch. 1; V. N. Ruzhnikov, *Tak nachinalos': Istoriko-teoreticheskii ocherk sovetskogo radioveshchaniia 1917–1928* (Moscow, 1987), 30–1.

The revolutions of 1917 spread so fast at least in part because Russia had since 1914 entered a new era of high-speed communication. Irkutsk, for example, got to hear of the fall of the imperial regime by radiotelegraph on 27 February, while the new government in Petrograd was soon able to gauge the response from around Russia when local authorities sent back telegrams in response to the news of revolution.[20] No political group was more aware of the importance of communications than the revolutionary party that would come to power later in the year.[21] Between February and October, the Bolsheviks did what they could to infiltrate the post and telegraph offices (even though they enjoyed little support among the largely white-collar staff of these institutions). When the time came for seizing power, the central telegraph office was taken over the day before the Bolshevik coup, and Trotsky used it to broadcast news of the storming of the Winter Palace even before that had occurred. A radio station on the Avrora was also used to spread the word about the Bolshevik takeover; radio signals about the rising were picked up in Moscow and other places on 25 October. In his memoirs, Alexander Kerensky would later write of the enormous significance of the Bolsheviks' control of the telegraph and the Tsarskoe Selo radio station (the most powerful in Russia at the time): their message of 'immediate peace' had quickly destroyed troop discipline. Lenin would continue to make good use of wireless telegrams in the weeks after the revolution, for example to communicate with soldiers over the head of the insubordinate General Dukhonin in early November. In July 1918, when the Socialist Revolutionaries took over the central telegraph, Lenin reacted instantly: he ordered that a Sovnarkom bulletin be sent out from the Khodynka radio station to decree that all telegraph communications be considered provocation until further notice.[22]

Wireless telegraphy was an indispensable tool of rule—especially in a state as enormous as Russia and at a time when political authority was violently contested. The new regime, accordingly, wasted no time in seizing the Khodynka station, even though this remained out of action for much of 1918. Radio telegraphers moved over to the side of the revolution: they held all-union congresses first in Petrograd (November–December 1917) and then in Moscow (June–July 1918).[23] By a Sovnarkom decree of 19 July 1918, the new regime centralized radiotelegraphy under the auspices of the Commissariat of Post and Telegraph (hereafter Narkompochtel).[24] The telegraph agency, ROSTA, issued a regular 'radio bulletin' (*radiovestnik*), which offered a mixture of military reports, home front news, and

[20] E. V. Shestopalova, 'Istoriia stanovleniia i razvitiia radioveshchaniia v Irkutskoi oblasti v 1920–1930-e gody' (candidate's dissertation, Irkutsk, 2008), 46; Roger Pethybridge, *The Spread of the Russian Revolution: Essays on 1917* (London, 1972), 61.

[21] For a valuable survey of Bolshevik communications policy in the founding years of the revolutionary state, see Larissa Zakharova, '"Le Socialisme sans poste, télégraphe et machine est un mot vide de sens": Les Bolcheviks en quête d'outils de communication (1917–1923)', *Revue historique* 660 (2011): 853–73.

[22] Material in this paragraph from Ruzhnikov, *Tak nachinalos'*, 34–6; Dubrovin, *K istorii sovetskogo radioveshchaniia*, 17–18; Aleksandr Kerensky, *The Kerensky Memoirs: Russia and History's Turning Point* (London, 1966), 442; Pethybridge, *The Spread of the Russian Revolution*, 64–8, 76–82.

[23] Ruzhnikov, *Tak nachinalos'*, 38.   [24] *VKD*, 967.

practical information.[25] The reach of radio communications grew steadily during the Civil War. In 1919, circulars broadcast from Khodynka were received in 81 different locations; by the end of 1920 this figure had risen to 200.[26] In 1919, the Khodynka station put out more than 3,000 issues of the news bulletin 'To Everyone, from Moscow' (*Vsem iz Moskvy*), primarily for further distribution through the local press.[27] In July 1919, moreover, the new regime issued a decree on the immediate construction of a powerful radio station in the new capital, Moscow (by this time the Khodynka station was overloaded).[28]

The adoption of radio by the new regime was, however, not just a matter of exploiting and extending the existing infrastructure. The distance-conquering capacity of the telegraph made it of paramount importance to the Bolsheviks. But the revolutionaries were also in position to capitalize on a radical expansion of the technology's information-bearing capacity: by the midpoint of the Civil War it was clear that very soon radiotelegraphy would be able to transmit and receive not just Morse code but also the human voice. The very medium of 'radio' was at a formative stage of its infancy—on the cusp of a transition from 'radiotelegraphy' to 'radiotelephony'.

The Bolsheviks already well understood the value of the only existing technology for transmitting the human voice: the telephone. Telephone networks had started to grow in the major cities of the Russian Empire from the early 1880s, when the first concessions were handed out (and soon sold on to the Bell Telephone Company). On the eve of the Revolution, there were 232,000 telephone subscribers in Russia, half of them in Moscow and Petrograd. This was a communication network of incalculable value to a revolutionary regime looking above all to establish itself in the major cities. As Anatolii Lunacharskii observed in 1924, 'the takeover of its main telephone station in the capital is an apocalyptic blow for any government'.[29] In 1905, the workers had tried but failed to take over the main telephone station in Moscow; in 1917, the Bolsheviks captured the Petrograd equivalent on 25 October as a precondition for their seizure of power. Lenin himself was a devotee of the telephone. When he took up residence in the last two years of his life on a former Mamontov estate south of Moscow, the telephone was his political lifeline; when it malfunctioned, he issued dire threats to the engineers until it was repaired.[30] Subsequently, the Lenin myth would use images and descriptions of the leader's telephone interventions to show him as active and omnipresent.[31]

[25] See the (slightly edited) example from 21 October 1918 in *VKD*, 195–201.
[26] P. S. Gurevich and V. N. Ruzhnikov, *Sovetskoe radioveshchanie: Stranitsy istorii* (Moscow, 1976), 24.
[27] Ruzhnikov, *Tak nachinalos'*, 68.
[28] Dubrovin, *K istorii sovetskogo radioveshchaniia*, ch. 2.   [29] *VKD*, 204.
[30] The telephone is on proud display in the museum now housed at Gorki Leninskie (as I saw myself on a visit in October 2010).
[31] Irina Lazarova, *'Hier spricht Lenin': Das Telefon in der russischen Literatur der 1920er und 30er Jahre* (Cologne, 2010), 31–8. For the general history of the telephone in pre-revolutionary Russia, see ibid. 23–31.

The Bolsheviks, with Lenin himself to the fore, did what they could to accelerate the fusion of telephony and wireless radio into what we would recognize as 'broadcasting'. As early as October 1918 Lenin was writing to N. P. Gorbunov about the urgency of this project, and a 'radio laboratory' was duly set up by decree of 2 December 1918.[32] Headed by the inventor M. A. Bonch-Bruevich, who had studied radiotelegraphy as a military engineer before the war, this laboratory started conducting experiments on transmitting the human voice in late February 1919 and by the start of the following year had created a usable model of wireless radio station. Lenin famously took a close personal interest in Bonch-Bruevich's work. In February 1920, he wrote to congratulate the inventor on his achievements so far, in the process introducing the greatest catchphrase of Soviet broadcasting history: 'The newspaper without paper and "without distances" that you are creating will be a great thing.' Then, in March 1920, the Nizhnii Novgorod radio laboratory was entrusted with the task of building a radiotelegraphy station with a radius of 2,000 versts within two and a half months; in autumn 1920, signals sent from this new transmitter, set up at Khodynka, were received as far away as Chita and Berlin.[33] The next step was to make the wirelessly transmitted human voice audible to a wider audience. In the summer of 1921, Lenin was excited to hear that in Kazan loudspeakers had been used for a public broadcast. This pioneering example was soon followed in Moscow: 5 million rubles were allocated to Narkompochtel for setting up loudspeaker broadcasts of a spoken newspaper in the capital. In May 1922 Lenin wrote to Stalin and other members of the Politburo to emphasize the value of radio for maximizing the impact of communist propaganda on the illiterate masses.[34] Even when Lenin was too ill to attend meetings in 1922, he continued to keep himself informed on the development of radio. On 8 December 1922 came the first broadcast of his own speeches, sixteen of which had been recorded between 1919 and 1921.[35]

That same year of 1922 had brought a significant expansion of transmitter capacity. In March a new station at Shabolovka, just south of central Moscow, had started operations; with its hyperboloid structure, designed by Vladimir Shukhov and soon to become a modernist icon, it left a lasting mark on the capital (see Figure 1.2). In September came the launch of a new, more powerful radio station located on Voznesenskaia ulitsa (now Ulitsa radio), near Kursk railway station in Moscow. Officially opened on the fifth anniversary of the October Revolution, this was known as the Komintern station. Five years later, it was supplanted by a revamped version of the Shabolovka station, colloquially known as 'Big Komintern'. The two other centres of Moscow radio in the 1920s were the Moscow trade union station (MGSPS), based in the Hall of Columns that would become the

---

[32] P. S. Gurevich and N. P. Kartsov, *Lenin o radio* (Moscow, 1973), 9; *VKD*, 968.

[33] For documents illustrating Lenin's involvement in radio, see *VKD*, 969–72. On Bonch-Bruevich's career and achievements, see A. A. Pistol'kors, 'Mikhail Aleksandrovich Bonch-Bruevich (Ocherk zhizni i deiatel'nosti)', in M. A. Bonch-Bruevich, *Sobranie trudov* (Moscow and Leningrad, 1956), 5–33.

[34] *VKD*, 970–1; Gurevich and Kartsov, *Lenin o radio*, 21, 29.

[35] Dubrovin, *K istorii sovetskogo radioveshchaniia*, ch. 2.

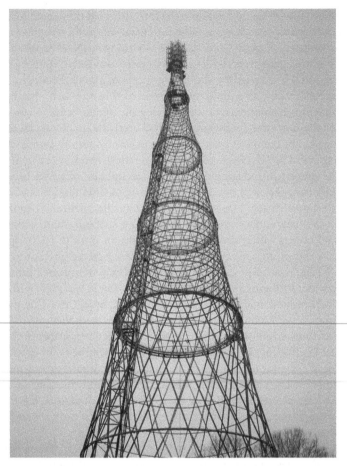

Figure 1.2. The 'Shukhov Tower' at Shabolovka. In recent times this landmark structure has fallen into a state of severe disrepair, and in early 2014 there was even talk of dismantling it for safety reasons. In summer 2014, however, the authorities responded to protests by declaring the tower a conservation site. Photo: Sergei Arsenyev, 2006.

Source: Wikimedia Commons, http://commons.wikimedia.org/wiki/Shukhov_tower#mediaviewer/File:Shukhov_Tower_photo_by_Sergei_Arsenyev_2006.JPG

venue for many of the major spectacles of the Stalin era, and the A. S. Popov station in the northern suburb of Sokol'niki, which first broadcast on 12 October 1924. The start of regular broadcasts from Komintern came a little more than a month later, on 23 November.

BUILDING A NETWORK

Which of these moments in the early broadcasting history should be considered the foundational moment of Soviet radio is a moot point. 'Radio' would continue to be a medium in flux at least until the early 1930s. The essential point is this: from almost the very beginning of their period of rule, the Bolsheviks had to reckon with the fact that existing technologies of communication would be supplemented by a means of wirelessly transmitting the human voice. This prospect threw up a number of unprecedented organizational challenges.

The first task was to set up infrastructure that would allow radio to reach beyond the handful of cities where loudspeaker networks had been established. It was not just transmission capacity in Moscow that grew during the 1920s; it was also the network of radio stations around the USSR (see Figure 1.3). Construction of these began in earnest in 1925. By 1 February 1927, the USSR had twenty-nine major broadcasting stations, of which twenty-two were in the European part of the country.[36] By this time there were already broadcasting stations in Novosibirsk (as of 1925), Vladivostok (1926), and Irkutsk (1926). Radio communications in the Far East were the only way of bringing the remoter corners of the country within reach of even a regional capital, let alone Moscow: Irkutsk region was one and a half times the size of Spain.[37] Although wire was to become the preferred means of radio diffusion in areas of reasonably concentrated population, it was manifestly too expensive for trans-Eurasian communications between Moscow and Eastern Siberia.[38] Most of the more powerful stations came under the jurisdiction of Narkompochtel. This commissariat allocated wavelengths to particular stations, though according to an inspection in 1928 it was not proving very successful at bringing order to the airwaves (unlike the Federal Radio Commission in America, which simply closed any stations that did not fit the general plan). A 2-kilowatt station had a reliable audibility range of 200 kilometres, but it generated interference over a range of 1,800 kilometres.[39]

At the same time, smaller broadcasting stations began to appear. This greatly increased listening opportunities, as most members of the Soviet radio audience did not have sets powerful enough to pick up signals from far afield. In Belorussia, for example, a radio station in Minsk was opened in November 1925, and regional stations followed in due course. In Gomel', a station was set up in a former merchant house; it used a transmitter of the 'Small Komintern' type, one of twenty-seven such produced by the Nizhnii Novgorod radio laboratory. In order to reduce reverberations in the studio, the wall and ceiling were covered in heavy black material, while carpets—mainly confiscated from churches—were laid on the floor. The studio was equipped with a reed organ (*fisgarmoniia*) brought from some nearby country estate and a Telefunken microphone that was not bad for the time. The station generally broadcast for 6–7 hours per day, from the late afternoon onwards.

[36] GARF, f. 6903, op. 3, d. 10, l. 2. According to Ruzhnikov (*Tak nachinalos'*, 62), ten stations (both transmitting and receiving) had been built by the company Radioperedacha in 1924; by 1928 there were sixty-five.

[37] Shestopalova, 'Istoriia stanovleniia', 70–1.

[38] A point made in a 1927 report on radio communication between Moscow and the Far Eastern reaches of the USSR that is stored in the files of the Worker-Peasant Inspectorate. See GARF, f. 374, op. 28, d. 2144, ll. 55–6.

[39] GARF, f. 374, op. 28, d. 2131, ll. 19–20.

Figure 1.3. Map of active and projected broadcasting stations in the USSR, 1925. The circles indicate the radius of audibility of three different stations on an ordinary crystal receiver.

Source: Radio vsem, no. 5 (1925)

The output consisted mainly of programmes received by wire from Moscow; broadcasts from Minsk were less frequent, as the quality of the line was very poor. If the wire connection was playing up, the Gomel' team improvised 'concerts' of their own on the reed organ. Liszt's *Hungarian Rhapsody*, complete with squeaky pedals, was a particular favourite.[40]

While the spread of transmission capacity to the far reaches of the socialist state was good news for the Bolshevik regime, it also presented certain political risks. Whether to the West or to the East, radio was the quintessential international medium. In the 1920s, Irkutsk radio enthusiasts established contact with China, Japan, even Hawaii.[41] Broadcasting technology was a competitive game where the Bolsheviks had to measure themselves against developments abroad. Strategically important border regions were an especially high priority for investment. In the

[40] Popov Museum, Fond Radio, op. 1 , d. 884, ll. 6–11.
[41] Shestopalova, 'Istoriia stanovleniia', 60.

Far East, for example, a radio station was ordered for Khabarovsk from the USA in 1926. Completed in summer 1927 and named after M. V. Frunze, it was the most powerful short-wave station in the country (15 kilowatts). At the time, only three long-wave stations were more powerful: Komintern, Leningrad, and Khar'kov.[42]

In the second half of the 1920s, Soviet officials worried more and more that their country's broadcasting capacity was inadequate. In December 1927, Narkompochtel representatives warned Molotov that, although Komintern was still the most powerful station on the European continent, this could not be expected to last for long given the investment in this area by 'bourgeois' countries. The government now had to confront the worrying prospect that Western powers might be able to jam Soviet broadcasts all the way to Moscow in the event of war. It was true that progress was being made: during the recent revolutionary anniversary festivities, more than twenty stations around the country had broadcast programming from Moscow (which they had received either over the airwaves or by wire), and within another two or three years Moscow radio would have the capacity to cover the entire European part of the USSR. Nonetheless, potentially hostile powers were building broadcasting stations on sensitive borders, and in view of this fact Moscow needed to build a new 300-kilowatt station that would cost 2.5 million rubles.[43] A report the following year reached similar conclusions. In absolute terms, the USSR was the country with the greatest transmission capacity in the world. As of 1 May 1928 it could boast fifty-nine stations, and radio had spread beyond the Slavic core to places such as Kazan, Ufa, Makhachkala, Nal'chik, Tashkent, Samarkand, Ashkhabad, Baku, Tiflis, and Erevan. But this was no ground for complacency: relative to territory, Germany was forty times better off than the USSR for transmitter power. The USSR needed to take special care over border regions that were vulnerable to hostile propaganda (especially from Poland); the Leningrad station was a particular priority. Another defensive tactic was to use wavelengths close to those of the powerful British or German stations, which meant these states would interfere with their own broadcasts if they attempted to conduct raids into Soviet air space.[44]

The big breakthrough in Soviet transmission capacity came in 1929 with the opening of the VTsSPS (central trade union) station in the north of Moscow. Originally, the plan had been to commission construction of the station from the German company Telefunken, but the government then decided that it would be faster and cheaper to have Soviet engineers take up the project. A group was set up for this purpose in Leningrad, and under the leadership of A. L. Mints (subsequently the Soviet Union's most celebrated radio expert) the work was completed in a matter of months. Not only that, the station was twice as powerful as Telefunken had offered: 100 kilowatts instead of 50. A few years later, in 1933, the USSR would become the first country in the world to break the 500-kilowatt

[42] V. V. Pogartsev, 'Stanovlenie i razvitie sistemy radioveshchaniia na Dal'nem vostoke Rossii (1901–1956 gg.)', candidate's dissertation (Khabarovsk, 2006), 58, 60.

[43] RGASPI, f. 17, op. 85, d. 148, ll. 78–9, 82–90.

[44] GARF, f. 374, op. 28, d. 2131, ll. 18, 24–5.

barrier; also designed by Mints, this station was called Komintern, like its predecessors of 1922 and 1927.[45] These developments seem to have had an international impact. It was no doubt gratifying for the Soviet broadcasting authorities to learn in December 1930 that the British Foreign Office had been severely put out by an English-language broadcast from the VTsSPS station in which Maxim Gorky had addressed an open letter to workers in capitalist countries apropos the recent show trial of the 'Industrial Party'. When challenged by the British ambassador, the Soviet foreign minister Litvinov claimed that the broadcast had come 'not from a station under control of the Government but from a private station which is at the full disposal of the All-Union Central Council of Trade Unions'. The British were sufficiently discomfited as to contemplate jamming but rejected the idea due to the likelihood of Soviet retaliatory action against British commercial wireless.[46]

ADMINISTERING RADIO

Whether from the international or the domestic perspective, the importance of radio was clear. Much less obvious was how this complex new technology was to be managed in institutional terms: how directly involved the state apparatus should be, and how to strike the right balance between technical expertise and bureaucratic oversight. This was a problem faced by all developed states at this time, as broadcasting was adopted across Europe and North America, and no two cases were identical.

In the USSR, the management of radio was of course a political question—a matter of ensuring that broadcasting followed the party's agenda and that the airwaves did not fall into the wrong hands—but also an economic and social one. Who, quite simply, was going to pay for the construction of the broadcasting network and the production of radio broadcasts? Which institutions in the Bolshevik party-state were to have a stake in broadcasting? And how were those institutions to establish an effective working relationship with the technophile citizens—radio hams—on whom they would willy-nilly have to rely for the spread of the new technology? In the 1920s, no state—least of all the USSR—was rich or technologically advanced enough to micromanage the spread of radio equipment. Grass-roots enthusiasts had to do much of the work.[47]

Rivalry with the West concerned not only transmission capacity but also receiver capacity. In August 1926, for example, the Central Committee was informed that radio technology had made huge strides abroad in recent years. In 1920, Americans had spent 2 million dollars on radio equipment; in 1926, the figure was 578 million dollars, and almost one-fifth of American homes now had radio. The number of

---

[45] See the account by Mints himself in *VKD*, 687–90.

[46] B. Bridges, 'A Note on the British Monitoring of Soviet Radio, 1930', *Historical Journal of Film, Radio and Television* 5 (1985): 183–9, quotation at 187.

[47] In his response to the First All-Union Radio Exhibition in 1925, Mikhail Kalinin admitted that, although Soviet technicians were already achieving great things, industrial production in this area lagged well behind the West. *VKD*, 683–4.

registered radio sets in England had risen from a few thousand to 2 million over a similar period. It was clear, moreover, that Western capitalist countries had been highly successful in harnessing the talents of radio hams.[48] From near the beginning of regular broadcasting, the Soviet authorities were aware of the need to mobilize their own radio-savvy population—the *radioliubiteli*—in the same way.[49]

The key piece of legislation in this area was a Sovnarkom decree of 28 July 1924, 'On Private Radio Receiver Stations', which established the right of Soviet citizens to acquire radio sets and catch what they could in the ether. In exchange, they had to register their radio sets and pay a fairly high licence fee.[50] By 1 February 1927, 115,896 radio sets had been registered in USSR; 102,141 were the cheap and simple crystal receivers, 13,755 the more elaborate tube radios.[51] Much was said in the 1920s about the need to crack down on 'free riders' (*radiozaitsy*) who evaded the registration fee, though campaigns to that effect seem to have had only modest impact. In Irkutsk, for example, there were reckoned to be 150 active radio enthusiasts in 1925, but there were only six registered sets. The antennas on view in many districts were visible evidence of the existence of *radiozaitsy*. By April 1928, 5,000 sets had been registered in this town of around 100,000 people, but even this was well below the true figure. In October 1930, the state gave up and substantially relaxed the rules.[52]

The organization charged with marshalling the efforts of *radioliubiteli* was the Society of Radio Lovers (Obshchestvo druzei radio, or ODR).[53] As of 1928, it was reckoned to have 170,000 members, of whom just over 50,000 were classified as 'workers'. These numbers need to be treated with caution, not least because, in the words of the Worker-Peasant Inspectorate, 'as a general rule radio clubs [*radiokruzhki*] are in a decrepit state'.[54] There were also administrative tensions. Grass-roots radio, like most other areas of early Soviet 'cultural construction', was prone to bickering between the interested parties. The Society of Radio Lovers had an unhappy relationship with the other organizations that aspired to shape and control the activities of the *radioliubiteli*. In February 1926, the ODR wrote to the Central Committee Secretariat to complain of friction with the central trade union organization (VTsSPS). The trade unions argued that the ODR was responsible merely for spreading radio to the villages; they considered urban workers their own preserve and tried to prevent the ODR from establishing grass-roots organizations in

[48] RGASPI, f. 17, op. 85, d. 148, ll. 13–14.

[49] See e.g. a report on *radioliubitel'stvo* solicited in September 1925 by the Komintern Department of Agitation and Propaganda: RGASPI, f. 495, op. 30, d. 166, ll. 22–30.

[50] Extract in *VKD*, 973–4. Implementation of the decree was discussed in the Presidium of the Moscow Soviet in May 1925. All institutions and individuals with receiving equipment were required to register within seven days. Antennas and wires on the sides of buildings required the approval of the house (residents') committee. TsGAMO, f. 66, op. 11, d. 615, ll. 103ob–104.

[51] GARF, f. 6903, op. 3, d. 10, l. 2.

[52] Shestopalova, 'Istoriia stanovleniia', 53–4.

[53] It was set up in July 1924 as the Society of Radio Lovers of the RSFSR, but was renamed the ODR in December 1924.

[54] GARF, f. 374, op. 28, d. 2131, l. 23. Suspiciously, the figure of 170,000 was also given for 1 January 1927 in GARF, f. 6903, op. 3, d. 10, l. 3.

Figure 1.4. An amateur radio club under the auspices of the union of workers in the catering industry (Narpit), Moscow, 1931.

Source: A. S. Popov Central Museum of Communications

the factories (for one such workplace radio club, see Figure 1.4).[55] The all-union ODR, for its part, kept an eye on its regional affiliates and expressed disapproval if a local 'society of radio-lovers' was insufficiently active in social outreach to rural and factory districts or was too interested in turning a profit through the sale of radio parts.[56]

The various parties were united only in their common concern at the weak development of the infrastructure for listening. As of 1928, almost 90 per cent of radio sets in the USSR were crystal receivers, and their range was considerably smaller than that of tube radios (which could be as much as ten times more expensive). About 70 per cent of Soviet radio sets were home-made. Wired transmission was starting to spread in urban and some rural areas, but in the villages especially it could not be expected to reach much of the population in the immediate future. There were only 7,000 loudspeaker points across the whole USSR, and about half of these did not work properly. Even those that had not broken down were unable to operate the whole time due to energy shortages and inadequate batteries. In the meantime, the price of radio sets had to come down, as a peasant could not be

[55] RGASPI, f. 17, op. 85, d. 148, ll. 2–2ob. The decision of the Radio Commission later that year was that the ODR could form cells at factories and institutions on a voluntary basis, but radio *kruzhki* organized at clubs, red corners, and worker dormitories should be considered the province of the trade unions. Ibid., l. 4.

[56] These criticisms were levelled at the Nizhnii Novgorod radio society in April 1927: see GOPANO, f. 1, d. 5527, ll. 11–12ob.

expected to afford more than 10 rubles. State-owned industry needed to improve its performance: as of 1927–8 it was far outstripped by the private sector.[57] Given the embryonic state of the technology, radio in rural areas needed careful administrative nurturing. In Moscow region, village soviets were instructed in 1926 to appoint supervisors to provide technical support for loudspeakers as well as to advertise the upcoming programme of broadcasts to the local population. In the interests of conserving equipment, the supervisors were also to make sure that the average time radio was used did not exceed 3 hours per day, and that it was only turned on when an audience was present.[58]

Ensuring the spread of radio technology to the Soviet 'periphery' would remain a preoccupation of the broadcasting authorities for decades; it was not deemed completed until the early 1960s. In the early days of radio, however, there was a more immediate and fundamental issue to resolve: what institution should oversee broadcasting, and from where was it to draw its funding? The Bolsheviks understood fairly well how a newspaper or publishing house might be run, but radio required an entirely new administrative structure containing a wide range of different expertise: from electrical engineers to literary editors. By making use of telegraph stations and telephone wires, moreover, it laid claim to infrastructure that already had its institutional masters.

The first specially designated broadcasting agency in Soviet history was a limited company (*aktsionernoe obshchestvo*) named Radioperedacha, which was set up in autumn 1924 just as regular broadcasts were starting in the USSR. The main shareholders in the company were not individuals or commercial interests but rather major Soviet institutions with a stake in broadcasting: Narkompochtel, the Trust for Low-Voltage Factories (Trest zavodov slabogo toka), and TASS (the Soviet telegraph agency). Each of these institutions owned 30 per cent of Radioperedacha, according to the balance sheet at 1 October 1925.[59] In the early days, Radioperedacha was also able to draw on quite generous state credits, and it was provided with a constant revenue stream through the sale and taxation of radio equipment. With this funding it was expected to produce broadcasts and maintain and expand the network of broadcasting stations.[60]

In a memo to the Central Committee of April 1926, the head of Radioperedacha was able to claim definite successes. The commercial revenues of the organization had risen to 300,000 rubles per month and the network had expanded to 300,000 receiver points (of which 80,000 were in the villages). If radio hams and unregistered 'free riders' were included, the radio audience now exceeded 1.5 million. In institutional terms, however, Radioperedacha was still weak. It lacked strong support from the party, and it had to put up with lack of cooperation and even interference from other organizations with a stake in broadcasting: Narkompochtel, the central trade union organization (VTsSPS), and the Moscow trade union organization

---

[57] GARF, f. 374, op. 28, d. 2131, ll. 20–2, 26–9.
[58] TsGAMO, f. 66, op. 19, d. 262, ll. 33–9.
[59] RGASPI, f. 17, op. 85, d. 148, l. 8. See also the statutes of Radioperedacha in *VKD*, 974–5.
[60] *RR*, 56–8.

(MGSPS). Only recently the deputy head of Narkompochtel had gone so far as to interrupt a Radioperedacha broadcast from the Komintern station and substitute one from MGSPS. Capitalist countries were already acting to put an end to 'radio chaos'; the USSR now had to do the same.[61]

The sources of tension within the administration of broadcasting were several. As a notionally autonomous and commercial enterprise, Radioperedacha was never wholeheartedly embraced by the Soviet government, and its institutional rivals evidently wished to exploit this. In radio we find the same kind of turf wars that are familiar from other fields of Soviet culture in the 1920s, as articulate and ambitious men fought unscrupulously for the ear of their political masters. But the bickering also had a hard economic edge. The question, quite simply, was who got to control the income flow from the tax on radio equipment and the registration fees that radio listeners were obliged to pay. In December 1927, for example, Sadovskii, the head editor of the workers' version of news broadcasting, wrote to Molotov to complain that Radioperedacha was preventing radio news (as presented by the *radiogazety*) from assuming its proper importance, which he considered to be fully on a par with print newspapers. His practical concern, however, was to ensure material independence for his *radiogazeta* by obtaining a fixed percentage of broadcasting revenue.[62]

Evidently, the party leadership had not yet decided on the best institutional model for broadcasting. That did not mean, however, that it was indifferent to what went out on air. While the period 1924–8 was less draconian than what followed, from 1925 onwards it became steadily less relaxed. In March 1925 came a Central Committee decree on 'radio agitation' which charged Agitprop with general supervision of the *radiogazeta*. In June 1925, a 'radio commission' containing some big party names—Lunacharskii, Krupskaia, Kosior, Kalinin, Enukidze—was set up under the auspices of Agitprop.[63] The newly created censorship administration, Glavlit, began to monitor radio more carefully. In the early days, only political broadcasts were subject to preliminary censorship, and many lecturers on radio did not speak to a script. At the end of 1925, however, the authorities called for greater discipline in the studio, and in due course the censors started demanding to receive schedules in advance. By now, Glavlit was lobbying for full preliminary censorship. Evidently, it was pushing at an open door: in November 1926, the Commissariat of Enlightenment recommended that Glavlit be especially vigilant with respect to broadcasts of 'evenings of entertainment', given that 'often what can be allowed in other places should be forbidden for broadcast on radio'.[64] In January 1927, the Secretariat of the Central Committee ordered that party committees take a close supervisory role in the work of radiotelephone stations, 'using them to the maximum for the goals of agitation and enlightenment'.[65] Three days later, a Central Committee decree established that all material for broadcast should be

---

[61] RGASPI, f. 17, op. 85, d. 148, ll. 11–11ob.   [62] RGASPI, f. 17, op. 85, d. 148, l. 37.
[63] *RR*, 60; decree in *VKD*, 976.   [64] *VKD*, 33.
[65] *RR*, 89; text of decree in *VKD*, 977.

shown in advance to Glavlit.[66] Broadcasters followed the cues and became more vigilant. In May 1926, for example, Luncharskii's contribution to a broadcast debate went out on air but not the reply from his opponent: the latter had not been approved by Glavlit, and there had been no time to clear it with Agitprop.[67] When the semi-disgraced Zinov'ev gave a speech at a meeting at the Moscow trade union Hall of Columns in May 1927, the chairman was summoned to the telephone from the podium and asked whether he considered it right to continue the broadcast. Although he said yes, when Zinov'ev moved on to international questions, the broadcast was interrupted all the same 'for technical reasons'.[68]

The imposition of preliminary censorship on the radio was formally completed in January 1928, when Radioperedacha introduced strict rules on the prior submission and approval of texts for broadcast and on the secure storage of the texts after they had been read out on air.[69] Yet, although firm political control had now been established, the struggle over the institutional structure of Soviet broadcasting was just coming to a head. The main antagonist of Radioperedacha was Narkompochtel, which had powerful leverage as it was in a position to starve the broadcasting organization of revenue from subscription fees.[70] A recommendation of the Worker-Peasant Inspectorate in May 1926 reveals how even then the financial screws were being tightened. Construction and exploitation of the network of most powerful broadcasting stations was handed over to Narkompochtel; Radioperedacha was only permitted to take part in the construction of local stations, making use of the local budget rather than drawing on central state funds, and only after securing the approval of the commissariat. Radioperedacha was told its domain was 'pure broadcasting'. It was also instructed to give up its commercial operations and to coordinate its activities closely with party, trade union, and other public organizations.[71]

In 1927–8, as the clouds gathered over Radioperedacha, that organization tried to put forward an alternative vision of broadcasting administration before it was swallowed up by Narkompochtel. Although it prophylactically liquidated its own commercial operations in September 1927 and acknowledged that some kind of restructuring of the broadcasting system was required, Radioperedacha resisted the idea of the transfer of radio to the state budget and to direct state supervision, arguing instead for a free-standing all-union broadcasting organization under the auspices of the Soviet government (Sovnarkom). The heads of Radioperedacha were against the idea of transferring radio to the Commissariat of Enlightenment (Narkompros), where in their view broadcasting would be a low priority and enjoy little financial support. It was rather the party that should oversee the propaganda dimension of radio. Narkompochtel was also an unsuitable institutional home for

---

[66] *RR*, 80; generally on the development of radio censorship, see ibid., 78–90.
[67] RGASPI, f. 17, op. 60, d. 804, l. 159.   [68] RGASPI, f. 17, op. 85, d. 22, l. 76.
[69] *RR*, 89–90.
[70] In February 1928, Radioperedacha alleged that Liubovich, representative of Narkompochtel and also of ODR, had failed to release the money due to it in the last quarter of 1926–7 and the first quarter of 1927–8. *VKD*, 44.
[71] *VKD*, 32.

Soviet radio, as the expertise of this organization lay in technical infrastructure, not in broadcasting. As concerned the financial model for broadcasting, listeners themselves should continue to fund radio through taxes on radio equipment and (less important) licence fees. The alternative proposed by Narkompochtel, to fund radio directly out of the state budget, would only serve to reduce the financial autonomy of broadcasting and further to inflate the state bureaucracy. The main problem with current arrangements was that Narkompochtel took far too large a cut from broadcasting revenues: 20 per cent of taxes and 50 per cent of registration fees.[72]

However it might protest, it was fairly clear in the spring of 1928 that Radioperedacha was losing the argument. In May it was presented with the unfavourable findings of a report by the Worker-Peasant Inspectorate, which recommended transferring control of broadcasting fully to Narkompochtel. In a response of 18 June 1928, the directors of Radioperedacha reiterated their view that their institutional rival was not competent to take on the broadcasting side of radio. They also argued that, when liquidating the limited company, the authorities should not create a broadcasting organization that was too closely allied with the state. Given the possibility of raising tensions with capitalist countries by hostile broadcasters, it was better for the state—at least notionally—to keep an arms-length relationship with broadcasters.[73]

On 20 June 1928, at a meeting of the Central Committee commission on radio and cinema, came the final showdown between Radioperedacha and Narkompochtel. By now it was generally accepted that broadcasting content and technology needed a common administration. The differences lay in what that administration should be. Radioperedacha continued to advocate a free-standing radio agency that would be answerable to the government rather than to a particular ministry or other bureaucratic interest. The spokesman for Narkompochtel poured scorn on these proposals.[74] The top party leadership took the decision the following month: broadcasting was transferred entirely to Narkompochtel.[75] Everything we know of the institutional context for this decision suggests that the defeat of Radioperedacha was preordained. The summer of 1928, an early phase of Stalin's 'Great Break', was not a good moment to be proposing the creation of a quasi-autonomous broadcasting agency.

Four and a half years later, another bout of restructuring brought into being after all an All-Union Radio Committee under the Council of People's Commissars (Sovnarkom).[76] Contrary to what Radioperedacha had proposed, however, it

---

[72] These points were made in a lengthy 'letter of information' by Guzakov and Berdnikov in February 1928 and a proposal for reorganizing Soviet broadcasting of April 1928. See *VKD*, 35–47, 47–9.

[73] GARF, f. 374, op. 28, d. 3121, ll. 5–9, 31.

[74] A lengthy extract from the stenogram of the meeting is published in *VKD*, 50–66.

[75] Goriaeva suggests that the final ruling was made by Stalin and his inner circle. Earlier on, Narkompros had appeared to be the front runner. *RR*, 143.

[76] To give it its full name: the Vsesoiuznyi komitet po radiofikatsii i radioveshchaniiu. There had also been minor restructuring in 1931–2, but until January 1933 radio had remained under the jurisdiction of the communications ministry (until 1932, this was Narkompochtel, then it became the People's Commissariat of Communications (Narkomat sviazi SSSR)).

was not 'self-financing' but rather depended on direct state funding. Under its Old Bolshevik head, Platon Kerzhentsev, Soviet broadcasting extended its technical reach and expanded its schedule. In October 1933, a Second Programme was introduced. Local transmission networks—at the factory or district level— continued to grow. Central broadcasting also made more of an effort to broadcast for the whole country: in 1936, five distinct timetables were introduced (for audiences in the European part of the country, in Central Asia, Western Siberia, Eastern Siberia, and the Far East).[77]

By 1933, moreover, radio was already a very different phenomenon from what it had been in the early days of *radioliubitel'stvo*. This was a matter not only of ever more rigorous party supervision, but also of technology. In the years of the first five-year plan, the Soviet Union firmly established wired networks as the basis of its broadcasting system. Although the notional goal was still to produce cheap crystal receivers so as to bring radio within earshot of the common listener, the millions of migrants who streamed into the construction sites and factories of the early 1930s were likely to get their radio from wired receiver points at the workplace or in their barracks and communal flats. As an American visitor of the time put it, 'the air throbs with a barrage of soviet radio messages. Our hotel room in Leningrad faced upon an open square, where a loud speaker functioned from six in the morning until eleven at night.'[78]

Wired networks of receiver points had first been set up in Moscow in 1925, and other areas (primarily urban) followed suit in due course. The Soviet state at various levels began to set up thousands of radio diffusion exchanges, which received programmes from Moscow or one of the other broadcasting centres and then sent them over a system of wires to dozens, hundreds, or even thousands of networked speakers. The process gathered momentum in the second half of the 1920s in large part because the alternatives to wire were too expensive to provide and maintain. Demand for crystal receivers far exceeded the capacity of central production to provide, which meant that prices remained too high for peasants and the state was forced to rely on the private operators that it found so distasteful.[79] A meeting of the Moscow party organization in December 1929 revealed just how poorly the alternatives to wire were performing. At present there were only about 1,200 registered short-wave users across the whole USSR, and the city of Moscow was only 30 per cent 'radiofied' (the percentage for rural areas of Moscow region was, of course, lower—22.5 per cent). To complete the job, as one speaker observed, the money the village spent on vodka would have to be diverted to radio instead. The best hope of improving the situation was to continue connecting up districts in the Moscow region by wire.[80] A similar story could be told of Nizhnii Novgorod. Batteries and experienced radio technicians were in short supply; in 1929, it was estimated that,

[77] Gurevich and Ruzhnikov, *Sovetskoe radioveshchanie*, chs. 4–5.
[78] Howard Woolston, 'Propaganda in Soviet Russia', *American Journal of Sociology* 38 (1932): 36.
[79] See e.g. the transcript of a meeting in the Moscow party organization on the state of broadcasting in June 1929, at TsAOPIM, f. 3, op. 11, d. 808, ll. 44, 46.
[80] TsAOPIM, f. 3, op. 11, d. 807, ll. 2, 4, 8, 16.

of the mere 266 tube radios in use around the region (excepting the city of Nizhnii Novgorod itself), more than a third were not working.[81] But wired radio began to compensate for these failings. By November 1928, the Nizhnii Novgorod Agit-prop department was noting the spread of wired transmission through the city and the advantages of this method for turning radio into a mass phenomenon. By that time, 7.2 kilometres of cable had been laid, five loudspeakers had been set up on the streets, and about forty in the 'Red corners' of clubs and workplaces. In the region as a whole, there were 4,667 receivers for private use and 427 for public use. The numbers would soon increase dramatically. The number of *tochki* in Nizhnii Novgorod region was reported to have risen almost ten times between October 1929 and October 1931 (from just over 4,500 to nearly 44,000), and the number of wired relay networks from 32 to 115 over the same period. On average there was one *tochka* for every thirty-five families across the region (even if the distribution was very uneven: in the backward Chuvash Autonomous Republic, the average was one for every seventy-nine families).[82]

Wire was cheap and durable, and as of the late 1920s was the only realistic means of turning radio into a 'mass' phenomenon; it also, of course, allowed greater control of content.[83] The minutes of meetings of town and district soviets in the Moscow region in 1928–9 show clearly that the priority was wired radiofication of public places (such as squares) and semi-public spaces such as worker dormitories, barracks, clubs, and 'Red corners'.[84] Crash industrialization and the consequent concentration of population gave the process greater momentum. In 1926, for example, there had been just under 1,800 receiver points in the whole of Siberia. By April 1930 in the towns of the region there were more than 20,000 receiver points, of which more than three-quarters belonged to workers.[85] In the Central Black Earth Region, one of the best connected outside the capitals, there were receiver points in 64,000 apartments by the time of the region's reorganization into oblasts in 1934.[86]

In the early days, *radioliubiteli* had had the field almost to themselves. Now, however, wired radio became the mainstream, and they were pushed to the margins. The ODR had often had a less than cordial relationship with Narkompochtel, now the state organization in charge of broadcasting infrastructure.[87] Radio enthusiasts were also inherently suspicious to the party authorities, as they were the Soviet

[81] GOPANO, f. 1, op. 1, d. 6055, ll. 75–75ob.

[82] GOPANO, f. 1, op. 1, d. 5941, ll. 11–14 (material related to discussion of radio in Nizhnii Novgorod Agitprop, November 1928); f. 2, op. 1, d. 1662, ll. 25–7 (material for the regional party conference, 1932).

[83] This is given as the rationale for the adoption of wire in the old but very good account by Alex Inkeles, *Public Opinion in Soviet Russia: A Study in Mass Persuasion* (Cambridge, Mass., 1950), 243–4.

[84] TsGAMO, f. 66, op. 11, d. 6000, ll. 7, 9. For the story in Nizhnii Novgorod, see the minutes of a meeting in the regional party committee on the subject of radio on 17 November 1928: GOPANO, f. 1, d. 5941, ll. 11–12.

[85] Shestopalova, 'Istoriia stanovleniia', 73, 86.

[86] M. I. Tsukanova, 'Stanovlenie i razvitie Voronezhskogo radioveshchaniia 1925–1991 godov (na primere VGTRK)', candidate's dissertation (Voronezh, 2007), 21.

[87] A speaker at a Moscow party meeting of June 1929 stated that the NKPT had effectively been boycotting the ODR: TsAOPIM, f. 3, op. 11, d. 808, l. 40.

Figure 1.5. Radio as tool of the Red Army.
Source: Front cover of *Radioslushatel'*, no. 5 (1931)

people best equipped to cross borders—at least virtually—and exchange information with the wider world. For this reason, although *radioliubitel'stvo* was still officially encouraged, its activities were increasingly circumscribed and it was subject to ever closer party supervision. In April 1933, the ODR was liquidated, and the Komsomol took over *radioliubitel'stvo*. Radio enthusiasts were left to forge new paths with short wave, while the better established long-wave frequencies were the preserve of state broadcasting.[88] To be sure, state production continued to deliver disappointing figures, and the *radioliubiteli* continued to be active: at the second

[88] For the example of Eastern Siberia, see Shestopalova, 'Istoriia stanovleniia', 117–18.

all-union amateur radio exhibition (*zaochnaia radiovystavka*) in 1936, more than 1,000 devices were on display in twenty-seven different locations.[89] Although Soviet transmission capacity remained impressive in absolute terms, in listening technology its performance was puny: a mere 13 receiver points per 1,000 people at the beginning of 1935 (as compared with 148 in the USA).[90] In 1940, the whole of Turkmenistan had only 28,600 *radiotochki* (of which a mere 4,500 were in the villages).[91] But by the late 1930s, as numerous memoirs attest, wired radio was becoming close to ubiquitous in the major cities. Wireless sets—especially tube radios—were the preserve of well-paid and well-connected Soviet citizens. On the eve of the Great Patriotic War, about 80 per cent of the 7 million listening devices in the USSR were wired receiver points.[92]

Radioliubitel'stvo, meanwhile, had become practically a branch of military train- ing. By 1940, as many as 90,000 people were being taught radio technology under the auspices of the Radio Committee; the thirteen largest radio stations were pro- viding distance-learning courses in Morse code. There were 240 courses for radio enthusiasts below conscription age and 560 clubs for radio operators with a total membership of 14,000 people.[93] The acquisition of radio proficiency increasingly took place within the formal structures of a state that was gearing up for war (see Figure 1.5). Conversance with radio technology was considered to be an important skill for national defence (like putting on a gas mask), and the signaller (*sviazist*) would later appear regularly as a heroic and resourceful figure on the killing fields of the Great Patriotic War.[94]

STALINISM ON THE RADIO

As radio became perhaps the key medium of urban modernity, so broadcasters became more exposed. Rigorous preliminary censorship had been introduced in the late 1920s, but in the 1930s political supervision became even more intrusive— and the penalties for error more severe. Typical was the decision of the Leningrad authorities in September 1933 to set up a group of censors to check programme content both before and after a broadcast. Censors were now to listen to radio 'sys- tematically' and check that broadcast corresponded to text.[95] In other words, as Goriaeva puts it, ' "live" broadcasting did not have a single word that was not sub- ject to preliminary control, apart from broadcasts from Red Square, which were rehearsed in advance and had a practically unchanged scenario from year to year'.[96]

[89] GARF, f. 6903, op. 1, d. 41, l. 60.

[90] *Radio v SSSR: Otchet VII s" ezdu sovetov* (Moscow, 1934), 18.

[91] T. M. Novokreshchenova, *Sozdanie i razvitie radioveshchaniia v Turkmenistane* (Ashkhabad, 1991), 22.

[92] Gurevich and Ruzhnikov, *Sovetskoe radioveshchanie*, ch. 5 (on the state of radio in the period 1936–41).

[93] GARF, f. 6903, op. 1, d. 55, l. 26.

[94] As e.g. the hero of the celebrated film by Grigorii Chukhrai, *Ballada o soldate* (1959).

[95] 'Pis'mo Lenoblgorlita v radiootdel' (28 September 1933), in *VKD*, 82.   [96] *RR*, 157.

The screws tightened further in the late 1930s, as strict rules on advance submission of texts for broadcast were imposed and the category of information classified as 'military secrets' broadened.[97]

Censors were naturally on the lookout for outright ideological violations. Odessa and Khar'kov radio, for example, were purged in 1934 on the grounds of nationalism. The authorities also intervened to reduce still further the scope for spontaneity and local initiative. In January 1935, youth and children's radio was ordered to cut down on text, while regional radio committees were told firmly not to get literary ideas above their station: the centre had a monopoly on material to do with 'current political campaigns'. Finally, in October 1937, the live link-up (*pereklichka*), perhaps the signature radio genre of the first five-year plan, was banned.[98] Like everything else in Stalinist public culture, radio was to be meticulously stage-managed. In broadcasting, as in other fields of propaganda, an important watershed was the 1937 Supreme Soviet elections. An Agitprop representative underlined in September 1937 the role radio could play in the colossal organizational task of bringing millions of Soviet citizens out to vote at 100,000 polling stations. It was especially important that radio function in rural areas: the 'illiterate or poorly literate population' was still not reading newspapers, instead 'picking things up by ear'.[99] In the cities, too, listeners were to be provided with every opportunity to follow the public script of Soviet life. In distant Irkutsk, for example, installation of radio receiver points in the region's factories was made a high priority in the late 1930s; the trade unions released money to provide radio in the apartments of Stakhanovites, while more than 1,000 new receiver points were installed in advance of the elections.[100]

The Soviet regime had vast ambitions to reset the mental horizons of its population, but it was at the same time acutely anxious that it would fail. It was attempting to communicate with a vast and far-flung population whose 'cultural level' left a great deal to be desired. The Soviet Union was a poor country with only limited spare resources even for first-order cultural tasks. It lagged far behind America and Germany not only in the spread of listening equipment but also in the adoption of technology for broadcasters such as sound recording. Although a device for recording on to 'sound film' (*tonfil'm*) was invented in the late 1920s, its effects on Soviet broadcasting in the 1930s were modest. High-quality recording on sound film was a costly business, as components needed for its manufacture were also in high demand in the defence industry; the film was also highly inflammable, so storage was expensive as well. As a result, recordings accounted for just over a quarter of all programming in 1940.[101] The preponderance of live material, and the inadequacy of the technical support, meant that glitches on air were practically

[97] See the several documents from 1938 to 1939 in *VKD*, 98–102.
[98] The relevant decrees of the Radio Committee and Glavlit can be found in *VKD*, 88–91, 98.
[99] *RR*, 166.   [100] Shestopalova, 'Istoriia stanovleniia', 95.
[101] GARF, f. 6903, op. 1, d. 55, ll. 24–5.

unavoidable. Acoustic conditions in broadcasting studios were also recognized as inadequate, with sound insulation a particular problem.[102]

Radio committees and the radio press throughout the 1930s issued a stream of complaints and accusations about botched programmes.[103] Two conferences of radio workers in September 1934 revealed the extent of technical problems. Interruptions to broadcasts were regrettably routine matters. An egregious case had come at the First Congress of Soviet Writers the previous month. The start time of Gorky's speech was wrongly announced, and when the broadcast did begin, the writer's voice was transmitted poorly because a microphone had malfunctioned. Another embarrassing case had been the triumphal return to Red Square of Otto Schmidt (the leader of an Arctic expedition that had got stranded and been dramatically rescued), where background noise had drowned out the speech of the returning hero. Another source of interference was the studio workers themselves, whose private conversations could sometimes be heard on air. Admittedly, announcers faced less than ideal working conditions. The level of technical support was inadequate, and the instructions from studio managers were last-minute or opaque. At the Congress of Soviet Writers, it had not been clear which speeches were to be broadcast and which were to be withheld from the audience. Yet, according to one speaker, there was no doubt that radio performers had become careless. Three years ago announcers were in awe of the microphone and entered the studio as if it were a 'Buddhist temple'. Now, by contrast, the studio was like 'Tverskoi boulevard' during broadcasts as people wandered about and scraped chairs. The real-life consequences of such glitches were not too far from the surface. As the concluding speaker observed, in local radio networks 'there have been cases of people being arrested and put you know where' for mistakes committed by central broadcasters.[104] For their part, announcers regularly complained that they were working under unreasonable pressure: they received the script too late to prepare properly, and 90 per cent of mistakes on air were due to poor editorial work in advance of the broadcast.[105] The memoirs of Nataliia Tolstova, perhaps the best-known Soviet radio newsreader other than Iurii Levitan, who started her career in 1929, describe early broadcasters as confronting constant technical problems—both short-term glitches and more fundamental inadequacies (such as the fact that sibilants were swallowed up in the ether).[106]

Even in the 1920s, reviewers had not hesitated to point out political 'errors' committed on air. In 1929, for example, a radio newspaper in Tver' had blithely admitted to the existence of an opposition within the party, while another in

---

[102] GARF, f. 6903, op. 1, d. 41, ll. 3, 8 (document pertaining to 1936). There appears to have been some investment in this area in the late 1930s: Khabarovsk radio, for example, acquired in 1938 a new building with three studios equipped according to the last word in technology (according to Pogartsev, 'Stanovlenie i razvitie', 75).

[103] For a regional example, see the discussions in the Nizhnii Novgorod radio committee in 1932 in GANO, f. 3630, op. 1, d. 8, ll. 1–3; d. 17, l. 2.

[104] Popov Museum, collection of V. A. Burliand, d. 12, ll. 4–5; d. 13, ll. 2–5, 9, 11ob, 28.

[105] A view expressed, for example, by E. Ia. Rabinovich in 'Diktor—tvorcheskii rabotnik', *Govorit SSSR*, no. 22 (1933), 9–10.

[106] N. A. Tolstova, *Vnimanie, vkliuchaiu mikrofon!* (Moscow 1972), 18–20.

Krasnodar had allowed unfortunate juxtapositions: an item on loans for industrialization had been followed by a waltz called 'Autumn Dreams', and a report on relations with Poland had been followed by a funeral march.[107] From the end of 1934, however, the tone of reprimands became altogether more menacing. Slips of the tongue or technical glitches were automatically interpreted as counter-revolutionary sabotage.[108] At editorial meetings and other public forums of the 1930s, broadcasters did their fair share of ritual *samokritika*. Slips of the tongue such as *politsiia* for *militsiia* or the false announcement of Lloyd George's funeral occasioned severe reprimand.[109] Thus, while announcers might enjoy a certain degree of celebrity, they were also in the firing line for public disapprobation if they erred in style or substance. As the children's writer Lev Kassil' observed at a meeting during the war, 'No form of art and propaganda gets so much harsh criticism as radio. A newspaper sits there at home and stays silent until you open it, but radio invades all the crevices of your mind and you notice even the slightest slip and find it offensive.'[110]

Because their work was inherently so public, broadcasters came under especially close scrutiny for the class origins, political beliefs, personal relationships, and professional biographies. As has often been noted, millions of Soviet people in the 1930s were forced to arm themselves against the possibility of such hostile attention—whether by concealing aspects of their past, reinventing themselves, or turning themselves into model Soviet people.[111] But if the scrutiny became too intense, even measures such as these did not guarantee survival. Broadcasting organizations contained more than their fair share of 'reactionary elements'. To the inquisitorial eye of a purge commission, they seemed capable of causing untold damage.[112] In July 1937, *Pravda* published a menacing editorial on 'enemy activity' in the Ukrainian and Belorussian radio committees, accusing the head of the radio committee, K. A. Mal'tsev, of negligence.[113] Mal'tsev was shot two years later. Even very close colleagues of Iurii Levitan, the Soviet Union's premier newsreader, were arrested in the late 1930s, while Levitan himself may have been the victim of denunciation.[114] Events in Moscow were grimly replicated in the regions.

[107] E. Riumin, 'Kak delaiutsia radiogazety na mestakh', *Radioslushatel'*, no. 3 (1929), 5.

[108] Examples are given in *RR*, 158.

[109] GARF, f. 6903, op. 1, d. 58, l. 91 (these examples from Tambov in early 1941).

[110] GARF, f. 6903, op. 1, d. 91, l. 50 (transcript of meeting on 28 September 1944).

[111] For contrasting treatments of this point, see Sheila Fitzpatrick, *Tear Off the Masks! Identity and Imposture in Twentieth-Century Russia* (Princeton, 2005) and Jochen Hellbeck, *Revolution on My Mind: Writing a Diary under Stalin* (Cambridge, Mass., 2006).

[112] This is the language of a hostile report (undated, but presumably of 1932) on the quality of broadcasters' performance. The report also found that radio was a closed 'caste' with a very limited group of performers (Lebedev, Kantsel', Zalesskii, and Abdulov were mentioned by name) and lax work discipline. The young Iurii Levitan, it alleged, was already being made to stand in for senior colleagues on important broadcasts. RGASPI, f. 135, op. 1, d. 218, ll. 48, 56, 63.

[113] 'Nanesti bol'shoi poriadok v radioveshchanii', repr. in *VKD*, 745–7.

[114] Ella Taranova, *Levitan: Golos Stalina* (St Petersburg, 2010), 79. It is very hard to assess the reliability of the latter claim, as this book is written with a good deal of literary licence (though it does apparently also draw on interviews with people who knew Levitan).

As Shestopalova shows in her study of Irkutsk, a lot of former ODR members were thrown to the wolves when terror gained momentum in 1937.[115]

Outside the capitals, working conditions were far worse than in Moscow or Leningrad, and the calibre of personnel left much to be desired. Radio workers in the 1930s, especially in the district-level networks, tended to be poorly educated and proletarian.[116] As a string of meetings in the VRK in the first half of 1941 make clear, they were also very often untrained and overworked. As of 1940, less than one in six managerial and editorial staff working on radio had higher education. Finding competent staff was close to impossible in the remote 'periphery'. In the Buryat-Mongol radio committee no fewer than thirty editors came and went during 1940 alone. Not a single staff member was competent to edit texts in the local language.[117] A journalist in the slightly less remote Komi Republic got his start in January 1941, when he knocked on the door of the modest wooden house that accommodated the local radio committee. He was given a trial as an announcer when it was ascertained that he was at least literate. Here too, personnel with basic broadcasting know-how who also spoke the local language were in vanishingly short supply. In practice, texts of broadcasts were often sent from Moscow for translation into Komi.[118] Even in the European heartland of the USSR, local broadcasting on occasion was guilty of hair-raising deviations from Soviet norms. In one village in Nizhnii Novgorod region, a local party member was reported to have held an epic drinking session in the local radio station (which was housed in the home of the miller), in the course of which he broadcast the following message to the community: 'Listen up, comrades!...we had a party member called Kirov, a good party man, but he got his neck broken, comrades [*bashku sebe slomil*].'[119]

Broadcasting in the Soviet Union was centralized and hierarchical, but in another sense it was highly dispersed. As of 1940, it was taking place in 110 radio committees around the USSR (with daily programming ranging from 1 to 15 hours) and more than 1,500 local transmission networks (*redaktsii uzlovogo veshchaniia*). The seventy broadcasting stations were transmitting material in fifty different languages of the Soviet Union. Maintaining ideological control over this range of material was an anxiety-inducing task for the authorities. In November 1935, for example, the NKVD sharply informed the head of Leningrad radio that a local transmission network in the region had been sending out 'anti-Soviet' broadcasts from foreign radio stations, as well as putting out its own unauthorized programmes.[120] At the all-union level, the authorities conducted hundreds of inspections of the output of regional broadcasters (in the process, unsurprisingly,

[115] Shestopalova, 'Istoriia Stanovleniia', ch. 2.

[116] See the lists of personnel for the Gorky region in 1932–3 in GANO, f. 3630, op. 1, d. 96.

[117] GARF, f. 6903, op. 1, d. 58, l. 35.

[118] Vasilii Krivoshein, 'Oskolki minuvshego', in *Radio: Vremia i liudi* (Syktyvkar, 2001), 18–20.

[119] GOPANO, f. 2, d. 3505, l. 11. The incident was reported to the party authorities on 24 December 1934, so three weeks after Kirov's death.

[120] TsGALI SPb, f. 9, op. 2, d. 11, l. 401. The Leningrad authorities were urged not to close down this operation but to take control of it: the network served about 100 *tochki* and thus represented a valuable channel of propaganda to workers in the nearby factories, who would otherwise have no access to radio. Thanks to Catriona Kelly for passing on the details of this file.

uncovering plenty of 'crude political errors'). They tried, where possible, to reduce the amount of text in broadcasts and feed regional stations uncontroversial musical or literary material from the Komintern station. In 1940, almost 1,500 hours worth of broadcasting was sent to regional radio committees on sound film as well as 70,000 gramophone records.[121]

Yet, for all the measures taken and the rhetorical importance attached to radio, it was clear in 1941 that the network remained unsatisfactory in all kinds of ways. The primary and inescapable failing was technological. On 6 June 1941, the Radio Committee wrote to Stalin with a sobering assessment of the wired radio network. Although wired receiver points now numbered more than 5.7 million in a total of more than 11,000 networks around the country, thus accounting for more than 80 per cent of radio listening equipment, they were in very poor condition: wires were worn out, interruptions and breakdowns were frequent. The state of wireless radio, it hardly needed saying, lagged far behind that of the West. To take the most straightforward measure of Soviet backwardness: the USA had 343 radio receivers (wired or wireless) per 1,000 population, Germany had 159, but the USSR a mere 36. Soviet radio administrators made no apologies for the heavy reliance on wire, whose value for propaganda and military preparedness was clear. There were signs that other countries, notably Britain, might be following the Soviet lead, given the resilience of wire networks in the event of war. But that did not make the current state of the Soviet radio network any more satisfactory.[122]

As we now know, the supreme challenge for the Soviet order would come a mere fortnight later, with the German invasion of the USSR. How broadcasters responded will be the subject of Chapter 4. In the meantime, however, we turn to the social and cultural dimensions of Soviet broadcasting in its first two decades.

---

[121] GARF, f. 6903, op. 1, d. 55, ll. 26, 32–4.

[122] GARF, f. 6903, op. 1, d. 56, ll. 10–12 (memo to Stalin), 13–14 (report on wired broadcasting in England), 19 (figures on radio use in USSR and other countries).

2
Radio and the Making of Soviet Society

Radio caught the imagination of early Soviet Russia like no other medium. By transcending distance, overcoming the debilitating rift between city and village, and projecting the word of Bolshevism to even the least educated Soviet people, it promised to solve several of the age-old problems of Eurasian governance. But radio was even more than a state-of-the-art tool of administration. It promised to make the country not only governable but also culturally united. One excitable foreigner summarized its role as follows: 'To make Russia one in thought, and action, nationally. To unite every part of Russia, the great city with the remotest village, so as to break down isolation, remove differences of conduct, of speech, of thought and action. To supplement the work of the theatre in space.'[1] For those with even broader horizons, wireless communication also promised to make the Soviet people as one with the rest of humanity. Radio enthusiasts set about communicating with distant lands. In the 1920s at least, they were born internationalists. Esperanto tuition was a prominent feature of early Soviet broadcasting schedules, while Soviet radio periodicals in the 1920s constantly cast their eyes in the direction of the West. An article on 'Radio in Everyday Life', for example, alleged that 'contemporary babies' abroad made use of the 'radiotelephone' even before learning to speak: 'they listen to music and melodious lullabies sung for many thousands of children from broadcasting stations'. No parent could be expected to match this repertoire of songs and stories.[2] Cartoons and caricatures further cultivated the imagination of Soviet radio enthusiasts: readers were entertained with the image of a 'radio policeman' from America or the imposing vision of a radio 'town crier of the future' (*radioglashatai budushchego*), with loudspeakers mounted on huge towers broadcasting to mass audiences.[3]

For many early Soviet observers, 'radio' was not just a means of telecommunications. It was a metaphor for the power of technology to remake human society—to make it more 'rational' and modern, but also to bring about the kind of collective society that could be firmly counterposed to the individualistic 'bourgeois' world (see Figure 2.1). Radio inspired the utopian visions of science fiction. In Aleksandr Beliaev's *Battle of the Ether* (*Bor'ba v efire*, 1927), a Muscovite finds himself relocated to the city of Radiopolis, a centre of wireless communication in the USSR of

---

[1] Huntly Carter, *The New Spirit in the Russian Theatre 1917–1928* (London, 1929), 294.
[2] Nik. I-tin, 'Radio v bytu', *Radioliubitel'*, no. 1 (1924): 3.
[3] These examples from *Radioliubitel'*, no. 1 (1924): 2 and no. 5 (1924): 66.

Figure 2.1. The Soviet broadcasting dream: Shukhov Tower superimposed on Kremlin and mass meeting.

Source: Cover of *Radioslushatel'*, no. 9 (1928)

the future. He finds not only that telecommunications permeate everyday life in Radiopolis—one of the devices used by locals is indistinguishable from our own mobile phones—but also that the continuing war of civilizations between foreign capitalists and the USSR is being fought largely by electromagnetic waves: the dastardly Americans have used radio to build a 'death ray', while the Soviets have established an effective defence.[4] Velimir Khlebnikov, the first Russian writer to elevate radio to mythic status, had gone further still in the powers he ascribed to the new medium: in his view, radio was nothing less than 'the spiritual sun of the country, a great magician and enchanter'. If radio were to stop working, the whole

---

[4] A. Beliaev, *Bor'ba v efire: Nauchno-fantasticheskii roman* (Moscow and Leningrad, 1928).

country would go into a 'spiritual faint'. Radio was the nerve centre of the modern world, but also a religion for the twentieth century.[5]

Khlebnikov set down his ideas in 1921, and his visionary exaltation would never be surpassed by later commentators. Nonetheless, radio continued to exert fascination over the revolutionary avant-garde throughout the 1920s. For Vladimir Maiakovskii, the broadcast word offered a thrilling opportunity to put into practice the two central axioms of his aesthetic credo: poetry was for speaking and hearing, not for writing and reading; and the mission of art was to speak to, and indeed create, a vast community. Maiakovskii produced a number of high-spirited poems specifically about the radio: the celebratory 'Radio Agitator' ('Radioagitator', 1925); the witty 'Without Rudder or Sail' ('Bez rulia i bez vetril', 1928), where a radio enthusiast struggles to get decent reception; and the exuberant 'Happiness of the Arts' ('Schast'e iskusstv', 1928), which observes that nineteenth-century writers could have done with the amplification that radio offers the written word. True to his principles, Maiakovskii also made a point of delivering his own poems over the airwaves. His first radio appearance was on 2 May 1925, and he would declaim his poetry from the studio on more than fifteen subsequent occasions.[6] As Maiakovskii declared in his main programmatic statement on the subject, Soviet culture had to 'broaden its verbal foundation' by exploiting to the full the oral dimension of literature: 'I am not voting against books,' he concluded. 'But I demand my fifteen minutes on the radio.'[7]

Even leading Bolsheviks were excited. On 23 November 1924, Anatolii Lunacharskii, the Commissar of Enlightenment, delivered a radio lecture to introduce the start of regular broadcasts. For Lunacharskii, radio was the latest stage in the inexorable progress of the human transfer of information that had started with rivers, continued with literacy, and culminated in telecommunications. As he explained the effects of the 'magical radio', materialist philosophy took him too in the direction of science fiction:

> The atmospheric layers hugging our planet, and indeed the very air around each person, are filled with boundless colossal psychic treasures, which transmit news and relay every human thought, and which disseminate artistic values and human emotions. This atmosphere, hitherto silent, begins to talk as soon as you put your ear to a small device: radio. All of a sudden you hear music, passionate oratory bring you tidings of catastrophes and joyful events; you hear ordinary human speech.[8]

Utopian projections of the distant future lost their hold over the Soviet imagination in the 1930s, but radio continued to symbolize modernity and the building of

---

[5] *VKD*, 680–2; for more on Khlebnikov's sense of the magic of radio, see Jurij Murašov, 'Das elektrifizierte Wort: Das Radio in der sowjetischen Literatur und Kultur der 20er und 30er Jahre', in Jurij Murašov and Georg Witte (eds.), *Die Musen der Macht: Medien in der sowjetischen Kultur der 20er und 30er Jahre* (Munich, 2003), 86–90.

[6] *RR*, 68; on radio and Maiakovskii's aesthetic mission, see Murašov, 'Das elektrifizierte Wort', 90–6.

[7] Maiakovskii, 'Rasshirenie slovesnoi bazy' (1927), in id., *Polnoe sobranie sochinenii v trinadtsati tomakh* (Moscow, 1955–61), 12: 163.

[8] *VKD*, 205.

Soviet community. The receiver box made very regular appearances on the big screen. Even in the silent era, radio set and headphones were important visual cues for the overcoming of backwardness. The standard treatment is exemplified in the film *Mzago and Gela* (1932), where radio is brought to a remote Georgian village and has a life-changing effect on the heroine Mzago, inspiring her to run away from her hot-blooded suitor Gela and start a new life in the city.[9] With the arrival of sound, radio made even better cinematic material, as the turning of knobs and the moving of lips could be accompanied by the sound of the voice joining 'centre' and 'periphery'. In *Seven of the Brave* (*Semero smelykh*, 1936), the radio connection to Moscow is a solemn ritual for a Komsomol expedition enduring the bitter winter in the far north; in more domestic vein, Grigorii Aleksandrov's *The Path of Light* (*Svetlyi put'*, 1940), opens with a scene of rhythmical housework performed by Stalinist cinema's greatest star, Liubov' Orlova, to the accompaniment of Moscow radio.

Yet radio's enthusiastic advocates never had things entirely their own way. There was also a dystopian way of looking at telecommunications. Radio threatened to bring not only the benefits but also the vices of modern civilization: exhaustion, neurosis, atomization. In the wrong (that is, capitalist) hands, it could increase and intensify, not reduce, the tensions between particular communities or entire states.[10] All the more reason, then, for the Soviet state to take firm control of the medium—which, by the end of the 1920s, it had done.

An even more pressing problem for the makers of Soviet culture was that institutional control of broadcasting did not guarantee that radio would achieve the desired impact on the population. The frustrating reality was that the mythic potential of radio far outran its actual technological capacity in the pre-war USSR. Even more fundamentally, modern telecommunications, while they apparently projected propaganda to the far corners of the Soviet nation, did not provide the means to control or measure the response of listeners. As the writer Valentin Kataev noted in a 'radio feuilleton' written for the first ever edition of *Radiogazeta* in November 1924, he could spot his readers on the street if he saw a copy of the latest journal sticking out of their pocket. His listeners, however, were harder to identify. And what those listeners made of what they heard was quite impossible to know.[11] The aim of this chapter is to make slightly less mysterious the impact of radio on Soviet society in its formative first two decades.

SOVIET RADIO IN THE HAM PHASE

The irony of radio's early adoption was that the Bolsheviks, ideologically committed both to technological progress and to concerted action on the cultural

---

[9] Gender norms are, nonetheless, observed: on arriving in the city, Mzago becomes a milkmaid, while Gela, who follows in due course, overcomes his initial disorientation to study to be a...radio engineer. Thanks to Julian Graffy for bringing this film to my attention.

[10] Lunacharskii had something to say about this too in his radio lecture.

[11] Text published in *VKD*, 212–13.

front, had to rely on the ad hoc efforts of grass-roots enthusiasts to advance the cause of 'radiofication'. This made Soviet Russia no different from any other part of the broadcasting world at the time: North America and Britain were also dependent on their radio hams in the early days. But in Russia this dependence had an uneasy relationship with the *Kulturträger* mission of the new regime.

Such lone enthusiasts, according to the radio press, began to appear in late 1923.[12] In July 1924, as we have seen in Chapter 1, the Society of Radio Lovers (ODR) was set up, and the activities of the radio hams were put on a secure legal footing. They also acquired their own periodical, *Radioliubitel'*, which had around 2,000 subscribers by March 1926.[13] By October 1924, the Moscow trade union organization claimed that 180 small clubs (*kruzhki*) existed under its auspices in factories around the city.[14] In September 1925, there were reportedly more than 500 such clubs in the capital.[15] The equivalent society in Leningrad had a greatly inflated membership figure of 38,000 in September 1924 (after only five months of existence), but by 1 April 1925 it had fallen back to a more plausible 13,000 as many passive members were weeded out.[16]

The pages of the radio ham publications bear ample witness to the high spirits and the pioneer enthusiasm of the movement. The futuristic zeal of *Radioliubitel'* shone forth from the modernist design of its front covers. As well as detailed technical articles on building radio sets and antennas, the journal carried regular reports on the spread of radio reception to ever more remote parts of the Soviet Union and kept readers informed about news and innovations from around the world. For lighter material, readers could turn to cartoons, ditties on radio themes (*radiochastushki*), cartoons, and stories (many of them translated from the Western press) such as a 'sensational American radio-detective novel'.[17] One regular source of humour was the figure of the mentally absent husband or father carried away by his radio enthusiasm into neglecting his family; another was the son whose radio mania was incomprehensible to the older generation.

The frenzied character of *radioliubitel'stvo* was also due to the inadequacies of radio production in the 1920s–30s, a time when manufactured sets were expensive and often impossible to obtain. The simplest form of listening technology was a crystal receiver (*detektornyi priemnik*), which required no battery power and involved a simple tuning circuit that a resourceful amateur could make from a small quantity of copper wire. The crystal 'detector' that gave the device

[12] 'Radioliubitel'skaia zhizn'', *Radioliubitel'*, no. 1 (1924): 7.
[13] Tsentral'nyi gosudarstvennyi arkhiv Moskovskoi oblasti (TsGAMO, f. 180 (Moskovskii Gubernskii Sovet Professional'nykh Soiuzov), op. 1, d. 2456, l. 11 (memo by editor of *Radioliubitel'*, 13 March 1926).
[14] A. V. Vinogradov, 'Lenin—kul'tura—radio', *Radioliubitel'*, no. 5 (1924): 67.
[15] TsGAMO, f. 180, op. 1, d. 1705, l. 34 (summary of meeting of *radioliubiteli* in the Moscow food industry, 8 September 1925).
[16] S. S. Derevianko, 'Obshchestvo druzei radio v Leningrade (1924–1933 gg.)', in A. P. Kupaigorodskaia (ed.), *Dobrovol'nye obshchestva v Petrograde-Leningrade v 1917–1937 gg.: Sbornik statei* (Leningrad, 1989), 115, 117.
[17] *Radioliubitel'*, no. 5 (1924).

its name concentrated the current and directed it into earphones.[18] According to a report of 1927 delivered to the Nizhnii Novgorod party committee, a crystal receiver cost 3–4 rubles to make at home and 7 rubles to buy. A more powerful tube radio (*lampovyi priemnik*) cost 35–40 rubles to make at home and 120 rubles to buy. Home-made receivers, moreover, were generally of much higher quality.[19] Nonetheless, the press regularly carried reports on the shady entrepreneurs who were taking advantage of the deficiencies in state production of radio sets by flogging poor-quality but cheap equipment to *radioliubiteli* who were desperate to get started.[20] The general position was that DIY activity should be encouraged, but that it was no substitute for mass production.[21] Yet, the need to show ingenuity in the face of technical obstacles was precisely what attracted young men to *radioliubitel'stvo*. As a sketch from *Novosti radio* makes clear, a 'real' radio ham did not buy parts and then assemble them according to a ready-made design but built everything himself.[22]

A textbook *radioliubitel'* biography was that of Aleksandr Sergeevich Balashkin, a pioneer of Tomsk radio. His interest in the subject was first aroused in 1919, when as a teenager he heard Morse signals on telegraph wires near a field where he was playing football. A student at the local technological institute then began to explain to him how telegraphy worked. In 1920, while still a schoolboy, Balashkin built the first amateur crystal receiver in Siberia. By 1922, he and a colleague had managed to pick up signals from Moscow and even Paris on a home-made tube radio. After signing up for a course on electromagnetic waves at Tomsk State University, Balashkin set about building a 10-watt transmitter. In due course, and now working under the auspices of the Tomsk ODR, Balashkin switched his attention to short wave, and in early 1927 set what was apparently a new world record by picking up a signal from an American station. In September 1927, Moscow gave permission for six amateur short-wave transmitters in Tomsk (regular broadcasts from the main Tomsk radio station began only in May 1928). In August 1928, floods in the Far East meant that regular communications between Moscow and Vladivostok and Khabarovsk were cut off. Tomsk short-wave stations had to step into the breach to transmit government communications.[23] Further east, in Irkutsk, the first head of the local branch of the ODR was a certain Vil'iam Robertovich Taigint, who worked until 1917 at the Leningrad Mechanical Factory and served

---

[18] A good layman's description is Michael Riordan and Lillian Hoddeson, *Crystal Fire: The Birth of the Information Age* (New York, 1997), 20.

[19] GOPANO, f. 1, op. 1, d. 5527, ll. 6–8. A quite high level of technical proficiency was required to build a tube receiver at home. Take for example one of the informants of the Harvard Project on the Soviet Social System, an engineer, who recalled having a home-made set with six tubes before the war (HP, vol. 32, no. 385, 40). Another approach was to buy a cheap radio in the store and fit it out with additional tubes: see HP, vol. 10, no. 131, 74.

[20] See e.g. 'Mobilizatsiia radio-promyshlennosti', *Novosti radio*, no. 3 (1925): 1.

[21] I. Veller, 'Samodel'nyi radiopriemnik ili fabrichnyi', *Novosti radio*, no. 6 (1925): 1.

[22] S. Do., 'Nastoiashchii', *Novosti radio*, no. 6 (1925): 6. The Nizhnii Novgorod radio archive is full of correspondence from *radioliubiteli* on the performance of their home-made equipment: see e.g. GANO, f. 3630, op. 1, d. 1.

[23] See Balashkin's memoir at Popov Museum, Fond Radio, op. 1, d. 1482.

in the Red Army on the Eastern front from 1917 to November 1924. His deputy, Efim Efimovich Izbushkin, was senior technician in the Irkutsk post and telegraph office. The secretary of the organization, Mikhail Dmitrievich Mittichuk, had been a private in the tsarist army before fighting for the Reds in 1920–1; he then studied at Irkutsk State University in 1921–2. Although both money and suitably qualified people were in short supply in Irkutsk, local enthusiasts chalked up notable successes. In February 1927, one of the most prominent *radioliubiteli* in the town, Vasilii Illarionovich Kokhanovich, a mechanic on the railway telegraph with only primary education, managed to pick up a performance of the opera *Ruslan and Liudmila* from Novosibirsk; the reception was clear enough for fifty or more people to listen.[24]

Listeners were fundamentally differentiated by the technology they had at their disposal. *Detektorniki* could only pick up programmes over short distances, so they were reliant on what their local station could provide.[25] In the second half of 1928, listeners reacted angrily to the suggestion (apparently aired in the local press) that it might make sense to close the Nizhnii Novgorod broadcasting station and rely instead on Moscow. Leaving aside the importance of decent coverage of local affairs, it was simply impossible, they argued, to tune in reliably to Moscow on the equipment they had available. As one correspondent argued: 'You shouldn't pay attention to tube radio owners [*lampoviki*], who on the whole belong to the well-off class and, if the [Nizhnii Novgorod] station is giving them interference, they can get themselves sets with sharp tuning [*ostroi otstroikoi*] or install filters.'[26] In 1929, according to a report delivered to the regional party conference, the Nizhnii Novgorod radio station could be picked up within a radius of 240 kilometres on a crystal receiver, but the range of a tube receiver was 3,000 kilometres. Information from registration documents suggested that three-quarters or more of listeners were using crystal radios.[27] Press reports from Voronezh at the end of January 1928 presented a similar picture: 1,148 registered *detektory*, 207 tube radios, and 64 loudspeakers.[28]

For the time being, the poorly resourced Soviet state was obliged to welcome the efforts of these passionate enthusiasts, since they offered a cheap way of developing an important new technology and extending its reach. The *radioliubiteli* also had their demographic profile in their favour. They were overwhelmingly young, male, and proletarian, thus belonging to the most prestigious category of the population in early Soviet Russia. One estimate from 1925 reckoned that only 5 per cent were

[24] E. V. Shestopalova, 'Istoriia stanovleniia i razvitiia radioveshchaniia v Irkutskoi oblasti v 1920–1930-e gody', candidate's dissertation (Irkutsk, 2008), 107, 112–14.

[25] For a disgruntled collective letter on the inadequacy of provision from the local station in Nizhnii Novgorod, see GOPANO, f. 1, op. 1, d. 5527, l. 25 (23 February 1927).

[26] GANO, f. 3630, op. 1, d. 3, l. 92. There are many other letters on the subject in this file and ibid., d. 4.

[27] GOPANO, f. 1, op. 1, d. 6055, ll. 90, 92 (report on work of Nizhnii Novgorod regional radio station, November 1927–August 1928).

[28] M. Smol'nyi, 'Vmeste so slushateliami na bor'bu za kachestvo', *Voronezhskaia kommuna*, 3 March 1928, 3.

over the age of 30, and only 0.5 per cent were female.[29] On 1 May 1925, according to a report delivered to the Moscow trade union organization, 83 per cent of radio hams were workers, and 45 per cent were under 20.[30]

These young, working-class radio enthusiasts were regularly portrayed as enthusiastic participants in cultural construction. It was thanks to their efforts that even the most benighted villages might discover the magic of the speakerless voice and lose their attachment to the priest or the bottle. In one characteristic story, a priest from the Chuvash Autonomous Republic was fined 250 rubles for agitating against the radio and opposing the attaching of an antenna to his bell tower.[31] Radio formed the auditory component of the campaign against old peasant ways.[32] There is no reason to doubt that many *radioliubiteli* themselves felt great excitement at breaking through the silence of Russia's many backwaters. As one radio technician recalled of setting up an antenna in a village 70 kilometres from Kazan in the autumn of 1927: 'By the evening the receiver started working, and the round pancake of the loudspeaker, which had been set up in a big izba, suddenly started talking. It's impossible to describe the surprise on the faces of the listeners. They sat there until the middle of the night, without fidgeting, afraid to let slip a single word.'[33]

But the *radioliubiteli* had vices as well as virtues. Radio hams, in the Soviet Union as elsewhere, were almost by definition self-motivated loners for whom the pursuit of new frequencies and the quest to transmit over ever greater distances stood far above the spread of popular enlightenment. Their most treasured achievement was to pick up signals from America.[34] In 1926, for example, seven different Japanese and Chinese stations could be heard in Irkutsk as well as some European stations, while by September 1928 this centre of radio expertise in the Far East had contact with a polar observatory, Iceland, the Philippines, Hawaii, Paris, and various other European cities.[35] The radio press of the 1920s was full of (mostly admiring) reports on developments abroad, and published listings from the mid-1920s usually included several Western European stations: Chelmsford and London in England, as well as stations in Belgium, Germany, and France. Esperanto tuition was offered both on air and in radio periodicals.[36]

By their very nature, radio hams were likely to show more interest in technology than in politics, and they were at times inclined to behave in distinctly antisocial

---

[29] Anod., 'Radioliubiteli i ikh priemniki', *Novosti radio*, no. 4 (1925): 4. Women accounted for around 10 per cent of registered *radioliubiteli*, but that was apparently because underage sons persuaded their mothers to register on their behalf.

[30] TsGAMO, f. 180, op. 1, d. 1705, l. 42.

[31] 'Radiokhronika', *Radioslushatel'*, no. 5–6 (1929): 5.

[32] Richard L. Hernandez, 'Sacred Sound and Sacred Substance: Church Bells and the Auditory Culture of Russian Villages during the Bolshevik *Velikii Perelom*', *American Historical Review*, 109 (2004): 1475–1504.

[33] Quoted in M. L. Aituganova, 'Stanovlenie sistemy radioveshchaniia v Tatarstane (1918–iiun' 1941 gg.)', candidate's dissertation (Kazan, 1996), 52.

[34] I. Kliatskin, 'Mozhno li uslyshat' Ameriku?', *Novosti radio*, no. 4 (1926): 1.

[35] Shestopalova, 'Istoriia stanovleniia', 60.

[36] As far away as Irkutsk, Esperanto broadcasts were a regular feature of the schedule in the 1920s: Shestopalova, 'Istoriia stanovleniia', 154.

ways: by evading the fee for registering their home-made equipment, or by clogging up the airwaves in their efforts to send and receive signals over ever larger distances. A list of 'Ten Commandments for the Radio Lover' gave a jokey warning of the various kinds of behaviour that were to be avoided: radio hams were not to make an 'idol' of illegal unregistered sets, to listen to their radios in an inconsiderate manner, to steal other people's telegrams from the airwaves, or to engage in other forms of 'piracy'.[37] Using radio equipment without registration might have been understandable in the old days, when radio hams existed in legal limbo, but such activities were criminalized after 1924, when clear rules for registering radio sets were published.[38] The first prosecutions of radio hackers (*radiozaitsy*) were reported in March 1925.[39] In April 1925, a staged 'trial' of these free riders took place in an experimental theatre (it opened with a poem by Dem'ian Bednyi).[40] Nevertheless, in March 1926 *radiozaitsy* numbered an estimated 100,000 in Moscow alone.[41]

Yet, as we have seen in Chapter 1, the unruly *radioliubiteli* of the 1920s would soon be reined in and their energies redirected from wilful internationalism to Soviet patriotism. They were also pushed to the margins of the Soviet listening audience by the spread of wired networks, the expansion of radio's propaganda function, and the emergence of a mass radio public. None of these developments could have occurred without a concerted effort by a range of institutions in the Soviet party-state.

REACHING THE MASS LISTENER

Comparative perspectives on radio history soon reveal how unwise it is to generalize even about so international a medium. In the USA and parts of Western Europe, radio quickly moved beyond the 'ham' phase to become an instrument and a symbol of domesticity. By the mid-1920s, for example, middle-class families in Weimar Germany were gathering around their wireless sets—which by now had become proper items of furniture, their technical apparatus decorously concealed by tasteful wooden cases.[42] The style of radio delivery became correspondingly more familiar and intimate as broadcasters moved towards a 'fireside' mode.[43]

The Soviet case was very different. In the pre-war USSR, listening was above all a collective activity. It took place in village reading rooms, in workers' clubs, in

---

[37] 'Desiat' zapovedei radioliubitelia', *Radioliubitel'*, no. 6 (1924): 82.

[38] I. Veller, 'O radio-zaitaskh', *Novosti radio*, no. 7 (1925): 1–2.

[39] See 'Radio-khronika', *Novosti radio*, no. 8 (1925): 8.

[40] 'Sud nad radiozaitsami', *Novosti radio*, no. 13 (1925): 4.

[41] 'Ugolok "radiozaitsa"', *Novosti radio*, no. 12 (1926): 6.

[42] Karl Christian Führer, 'A Medium of Modernity? Broadcasting in Weimar Germany, 1923–1932', *Journal of Modern History* 69/4 (1997): 722–53.

[43] Kate Lacey, *Feminine Frequencies: Gender, German Radio, and the Public Sphere, 1923–1945* (Ann Arbor, 1996). On the better known equivalent developments in the United States, see Douglas B. Craig, *Fireside Politics: Radio and Political Culture in the United States, 1920–1940* (Baltimore, 2000).

army barracks, or on city streets and squares. In its early days, radio can best be understood as a technologically extended branch of agitation. That, in large part, was how it was seen by the Bolsheviks themselves. In the words of one senior comrade, Lenin well understood the importance of loudspeakers, as he knew what it was like to 'deliver hour-long speeches in our halls with incredibly bad acoustic conditions, where orators used to have to burst their vocal chords in order to be heard by even half of the audience'.[44]

The year 1917, and the following civil war, saw a vast amount of speech-making and agitprop. Although the leading Bolsheviks had, for most of their careers, been creatures of the written word, they were acutely aware also of the need to *speak* effectively to their target groups (workers, soldiers, and peasants). In June 1917, for example, Bolshevik networks of oral agitation were reaching 500 regiments at the front and thirty city garrisons.[45] A year later, an estimated 50,000 activists were spreading the word of Bolshevism from the capital to the rest of the country.[46]

Old-fashioned, non-amplified public speaking remained a key means of communication for the Bolsheviks. In the 1920s, studies nervously probed the extent of popular ignorance of Marxist-Leninist terminology. A study of Red Army soldiers in Moscow examined transcripts of twelve political agitation sessions and discovered that the spoken language of these men differed wildly from the printed word that was directed at them.[47] Given the manifest failures of print culture to reach its audience, the spoken word was expected to fill the communication gap. Tens of thousands of 'agitators' went forth to spread the word of Bolshevism. More generally, public speaking was deemed to be a skill of prime importance in the new society. There were now innumerable reports (*doklady*) to be delivered and meetings at which to speak up. As one manual intoned, 'anyone who wants to be an active member of the new Soviet society must be able to speak in public and must learn the art of oratory'. A 'tongue-tied society' (*obshchestvennoe kosnoiazychie*) was the undesirable legacy of an old regime that had kept most people mute.[48]

In the proliferating advice literature of the time, budding orators were told they needed to be aware of their audience and know its 'class composition'. When they reached the podium, they should draw attention to themselves, avoid false modesty, and launch in with an arresting opening gambit. The audience must at all costs be kept quiet and attentive—if necessary by asking disruptive people to leave. It was important not to speak too early in a meeting, thereby allowing your opponents to trump your arguments. As for style and register, the recommendation was

[44] V. Bonch-Bruevich, 'V. I. Lenin i radio', *Radioslushatel'*, no. 9 (1928): 1–2.

[45] Roger Pethybridge, *The Spread of the Russian Revolution* (London, 1972), 161. For more on the extent of Bolshevik agitation in 1917 among the army and the peasantry, see ibid. 154–70.

[46] Peter Kenez, *The Birth of the Propaganda State: Soviet Methods of Mass Mobilization, 1917–1929* (Cambridge, 1985), 53–4.

[47] I. N. Shpil'rein, D. I. Reitynbarg, and G. O. Netskii, *Iazyk krasnoarmeitsa: Opyt issledovaniia slovaria krasnoarmeitsa moskovskogo garnizona* (Moscow and Leningrad, 1928). For a valuable survey of the audience research of the 1920s, see Jeffrey Brooks, 'Studies of the Reader in the 1920s', *Russian History*, 9/2–3 (1982): 187–202.

[48] A. Adzharov, *Oratorskoe iskusstvo: V pomoshch' molodomu oratoru* (Moscow and Leningrad, 1925).

to avoid pomposity and speak directly. The linguistic standard was the 'clear, resonant' language of the Moscow proletariat. Jewish, Ukrainian, Nizhnii Novgorod, or Yaroslavl accents only 'deformed' Russian pronunciation. Speakers should avoid cheap rhetorical effects and over-exuberant gestures. They should marshall their physical energy and their self-belief in order to win over their audience. Speakers should not attempt to learn their speech by heart, but might find notes useful. They should make sure they had had plenty of sleep and avoid eating anything that might challenge their digestion before taking to the platform. In short, the authoritative works on the subject were as one in their conviction that good orators were made, not born.[49]

Yet effective public speaking was less about self-empowerment than about providing an effective means of mobilizing the masses. Soviet instructional literature differed from earlier manuals on public speaking (which were published profusely in late imperial Russia) in its focus on the various forms of grass-roots political assembly that Soviet citizens were likely to encounter: *sobraniia* (ordinary meetings), *mitingi* (larger-scale meetings), *besedy* (talks), and *chitki* (readings).[50] There was, however, no question that the printed word provided the raw material and the primary point of reference for these gatherings. Potential orators needed not only to be possessed of self-assurance, concentration, and a good pair of lungs—they also needed to have studied the resolutions of the relevant party congresses.[51]

As a propaganda instrument, radio was a godsend because it spared the lungs of early Soviet orators and made their speeches accessible to an audience larger than those within earshot. In the early 1920s, this meant people round the corner or on the next street, not those in another city or region. The first instance in Russian history of technologically mediated public speech took place in Kazan in early May 1921, when loudspeakers broadcast a 'spoken newspaper' on the streets of the city. The Tatar capital, therefore, has a claim to be the birthplace of Soviet radio.[52] The following month, something similar took place in the Soviet capital: ROSTA telegrams were read out through loudspeakers on half a dozen squares in central Moscow. It was not until four years later, however, that Soviet Russia heard its first

---

[49] Adzharov, *Oratorskoe iskusstvo*, 9, 13–18, 25, 62, 65, 85; V. Rozhitsyn, *Kak vystupat' na sobraniiakh s dokladami i rechami* (Moscow, 1928), 32, 36–7. Other guides to public speaking include: A. Iaron, *Oratorskoe iskusstvo (Kak sdelat'sia khoroshim oratorom)* (Moscow, 1917); A. V. Mirtov, *Umenie govorit' publichno* (2nd edn., Moscow and Leningrad, 1925); E. Khersonskaia, *Publichnye vystupleniia: Posobie dlia nachinaiushchikh* (2nd edn., Moscow, 1923); V. Gofman, *Slovo oratora (Ritorika i politika)* (Leningrad, 1932).

[50] Besides the sources already mentioned, note the following: V. A. Kil'chevskii, *Tekhnika obshchestvennykh organizovannykh sobranii* (Yaroslavl, 1919); E. P. Medynskii, *Kak organizovat' i vesti sel'skie prosvetitel'nye obshchestva i kruzhki* (Riazan', 1918); S. Beksonov, *Zhivoe slovo kak metod propagandy i agitatsii* (Samara, 1921); E. Khersonskaia, *Kak besedovat' so vzroslymi po obshchestvennym voprosam* (Moscow, 1924); I. Rebel'skii, *Vechera voprosov i otvetov* (Moscow, 1925); R. Burshtein, *O gromkikh chitkakh v derevne* (Novosibirsk, 1926); V. D. Markov, *Zhivye doklady: Rukovodstvo dlia derevenskikh politprosvetchikov i dramaticheskikh kruzhkov* (Moscow, 1927); *Kak provodit' gromkie chitki khudozhestvennoi literatury* (Leningrad, 1936). A rare attempt to treat popular speech on its own terms, rather than as an object for remaking, is Georgii Vinogradov, *Ob izuchenii narodnogo oratorskogo iskusstva* (Irkutsk, 1925).

[51] Rozhitsyn, *Kak vystupat' na sobraniiakh*, 40.

[52] Such is the claim in Popov Museum, collection of I. V. Brenev, op. 1, d. 417, l. 9.

live media event. The occasion was the eighth anniversary of the Revolution. On 3 November 1925 came the first ever open-air broadcast in the USSR, which comprised the speeches at Frunze's funeral on Red Square. Listeners were presented with a medley of sounds: bells from the Kremlin, the firing of salutes, military bands, crowds, and speeches. The extensive musical programme over the holiday period included broadcasts of *Evgenii Onegin* from the Leningrad Mariinskii and of *Sadko* from Moscow's Bolshoi Theatre. Radio was emphatically fulfilling its mission of connecting the far-flung parts of the union to events in the 'centre'.[53]

Nowhere did this broadcasting extravaganza mean more than in Moscow itself. The still novel technologies of sound transmission and amplification meant above all that these events could be immediate and meaningful to the vast majority of Muscovites who were not in earshot. For those very close to events, eight large loudspeakers ensured that the speeches could be heard all over Red Square. Loudspeakers were also set up in some squares and a few large residential buildings. The other important listening places were worker clubs. The Moscow trade unions claimed that more than 30,000 workers had been brought together in these venues to listen to a revolutionary programme that included the operas *Carmen* and *Rusalka*, a speech by Kamenev, a trade union concert, and formal greetings from Red Square. As many as 5,000 workers might assemble in and around the larger central clubs to listen. An observer noted that listeners respected Kamenev's request to respect the memory of the victims of the Revolution by getting to their feet when the Internationale was played.[54]

In 1924, industry started to produce equipment designed for clubs and *izby-chital'ni*. Twenty-five districts around Belorussia were provided with Radiolina sets (the first Soviet model of tube radio) along with amplifiers to make possible collective listening.[55] Newspapers of the time were full of reports on the installation of loudspeakers. In December 1924 and January 1925, for example, Radioperedacha had set up around 400 loudspeakers for audiences of between 160 and 1,500.[56] Broadcasts of meetings and concerts seem to have been major public events in the mid-1920s—and not just in Moscow (for an example from Georgia, see Figure 2.2). On 15 March 1926, for example, the First Congress of Soviets of the Far East was broadcast outdoors in central Khabarovsk; people came with their families to listen. In October of that year, on Freedom Square, four loudspeakers broadcast a concert from Osaka, which drew an 'enormous' audience: this was the first ever international broadcast in the Far East.[57]

[53] See the description of the schedule in A. Mints, 'Radioveshchanie v oktiabr'skuiu nedeliu 1925 g.', *Radio vsem*, no. 4–5 (1925): 67.

[54] TsGAMO, f. 180, op. 1, d. 1709, ll. 1, 190–1.

[55] Memoir by V. A. Solov'ev on the development of radio in Belorussia, 1917–29, in Popov Museum, Fond Radio, op. 1, d. 884, l. 5. For a brief description of the Radiolina, see http://www.rustelecom-museum.ru/objects/?ContainerID=11502&containerType=60&objectID=660&langID=57 (7 May 2013).

[56] GARF, f. 6903, op. 3, d. 7, l. 27. This file is a day-by-day chronicle of the press in 1925.

[57] V. V. Pogartsev, 'Stanovlenie i razvitie sistemy radioveshchaniia na Dal'nem vostoke Rossii (1901–1956 gg.)', candidate's dissertation (Khabarovsk, 2006), 55.

Figure 2.2. Radio audience gathered in peasant assembly room, Georgia, 1925.
Source: A. S. Popov Central Museum of Communications

The main Bolshevik festivals—May Day and Revolution Day—became fixed points in the radio calendar in the interwar period. From 1 May 1928, the radio team had their own special box on Red Square so that they could provide live commentary.[58] The atmosphere of such occasions is well captured by Dziga Vertov's *Entuziazm* (1930), which shows the continuing close link between broadcasting and face-to-face agitation by constantly switching the camera between the two, and by the surviving sound recordings of holiday broadcasts in the 1930s, where the presenters' high-flown commentary is regularly punctuated by hurrahs, salutes, songs, and sheer background hum.[59] By the mid-1930s, loudspeakers blaring out rhymed slogans from the studio were an important component in the carefully orchestrated May Day festivities.[60] At less ceremonial times, listening facilities were valued by the authorities as a symbol of public order. A trade union report of June 1927 noted that the Danilov market urgently needed loudspeakers to counter

[58] P. S. Gurevich and V. N. Ruzhnikov, *Sovetskoe radioveshchanie: Stranity istorii* (Moscow: Iskusstvo), 64.

[59] The earliest example I have found is a report on May Day 1932, 'Velikii den'', directed by Viktor Geiman, RGAFD, call number PN-33 (1–3). A *locus classicus* is the 'radio film' (i.e. non-live broadcast) 'Priezd cheliuskintsev v Moskvu', RGAFD, P100 (1–5).

[60] S. Korev, 'Zametki o pervomaiskom veshchanii', *Govorit SSSR*, no. 10 (1935): 6. This review, while noting that the loudspeaker broadcasts had in general been better coordinated than in previous years, found that the reliance on rhymed material was cloying.

its accordions, dancing, bazaar, and general squalidness.[61] Loudspeakers in public spaces warned listeners to beware of pickpockets.[62]

The new medium continued to extend its reach on the national level. In June 1927, Radioperedacha reported that the USSR could now boast eighteen radio stations extending from Gomel' and Minsk to Novosibirsk. Radio coverage had now extended to the whole of European Russia, the Caucasus, and Western Siberia. As of 1 April 1927 there were over 150,000 radio sets (excluding the Transcaucasus and Central Asia), which was almost double the number six months earlier. The total radio audience at this time was estimated at 1.5–2 million. By 1926–7, then, it appeared that radio had come to play an important part in the Agitprop network.[63]

The spread of broadcasting technology was an important issue for the Bolsheviks, but it was not the only issue. They were concerned not only that radio should theoretically be available but that Soviet people should actually pay attention to it. Reports from agitators clearly indicated the difficulties in ensuring that the radio was received in the ways that broadcasters hoped. The Moscow trade union organization observed in 1927 that the radio needed to be brought from the background to the foreground: loudspeakers were often set up in intermediate spaces such as corridors and canteens, and radio was used as a filler before more important events such as meetings or lectures.[64] A worker at a Yaroslavl factory observed that the radio in his factory club had been moved to the bar, where it served merely as a resting place for empty beer bottles.[65]

The problem of holding the attention of the target audience was writ large in the Russian village, where simple incomprehension was deepened by technological inadequacies. Reports streamed in on the phenomenon of 'silent' or malfunctioning loudspeakers in rural areas. A party member from a Zaporozhian village wrote to Viacheslav Molotov in November 1927 to explain how radio was failing to fulfil its mission. When radio had first been set up in his district, 'the audience had rushed to it as something new and extraordinary', but enthusiasm had soon waned in the face of transmission glitches: 'when we turned on the radio at the first plenum of our village soviet, to begin with you could have heard a pin drop, everyone was expecting something elevated, on the achievements of science and technology in the twentieth century, but after an hour everyone had given up and gone, and this has happened more than once'. At a 'radio meeting' at the end of the same year, the microphone was handed to a rural inhabitant of Tambov region, who let rip: 'only we, the inhabitants of remote corners, can understand how unpleasant and frustrating it is when radio turns into some kind of Punch and Judy, I can't find any other word to describe what's been going on in the last little

[61] TsGAMO, f. 180, op. 1, d. 2461, l. 403.

[62] N. A. Tolstova, *Vnimanie, vkliuchaiu mikrofon!* (Moscow, 1972), 147.

[63] GARF, f. 5508, op. 1, d. 1028, ll. 22–3. The estimate of the radio audience can also be found in RGASPI, f. 17, op. 85, d. 148, l. 11 (report to Central Committee from chairman of Radioperedacha, 14 April 1926).

[64] TsGAMO, f. 180, op. 1, d. 1168, ll. 2–3.

[65] RGASPI, f. 17, op. 85, d. 148, l. 74 (text of *radiomiting*, 1927).

while. Komintern interferes with Popov, Popov interrupts a Komintern broadcast. During the intervals you can hear Moscow telephone conversations.'[66]

All the same, radio was the most accessible wonder of the modern world for the Russian village in the 1920s (see Figure 2.3). Many peasant listeners quite literally could not believe their ears. To begin with, they imagined they must be hearing a version of the gramophone, or else there must be a telephone hidden in the next room.[67] Even a young member of a *radiokruzhok* in the Belorussian town of Bobruisk recalled his astonishment at donning the earphones for the first time in 1924: 'We listened rapt to a concert...from Moscow, it made a powerful impression on us. We couldn't believe that it was coming from Moscow, without any wires.'[68] The radio enthusiasts who brought antennas and loudspeakers to the village took to their task with missionary zeal. One young technician from Nizhnii Novgorod was sent to Kostroma region in April 1924 to install a five-tube set as a gift from the laboratory to a rural district the radio laboratory was 'sponsoring'.

Figure 2.3. 'Listening to Moscow' (*Slushaiut Moskvu*), 1927–1928. A typical 1920s image of rural radiofication.

Source: A. S. Popov Central Museum of Communications

[66] RGASPI, f. 17, op. 85, d. 148, ll. 68, 73. For similar examples, see: N. Lebedev, 'Gromkogovoritel' molchit! Antenna dlia vorob'ev', *Voronezhskaia kommuna*, 3 April 1928, 3; TsGAMO, f. 180, op. 1, d. 1709, ll. 15–17 (report on radiofication in Moscow region, 1 March 1926).

[67] The conflation of radio and gramophone was a story often told in the radio press of the 1920s, and archival material shows that it was by no means apocryphal: see e.g. GARF, f. 6903, op. 3, d. 7, l. 44 (report of 17 April 1925); Aituganova, 'Stanovlenie sistemy', 61; GANO, f. 3630, op. 1, d. 1, l. 54 (listener's letter, May 1928). For the theory of the hidden telephone, see GARF, f. 6903, op. 3, d. 7, l. 44 (a report from Tsaritsyn, April 1925).

[68] Memoir of V. A. Solov'ev, Popov Museum, Fond Radio, op. 1, d. 884, ll. 4–5.

With the assistance of the village party organization and Komsomol, he erected a 20-metre radio mast. The antenna was suspended between the bell tower of the church and the mast. All the while, local people bombarded those responsible with questions about the purpose of this new structure. Finally, on the eve of 1 May, the radio finally 'spoke', as a ceremonial meeting and concert were broadcast from the Komintern station. The audience listened through headphones, and perfect quiet had to be maintained for them to hear anything. The first listeners were the 'leading people' of the village: Komsomol members, representatives of the village party organization and soviet, the local intelligentsia that consisted of foresters, a doctor and a teacher, and the village policeman: 'Pressing their faces to the window of the room and following avidly the flickering lamps (electrification of the village was back then still a dream), they tried to catch something through the glass.'[69] In Kazan region, radio was of limited interest while it broadcast only in Russian. But when Tatar broadcasts started, the number of radio sets in the village increased sharply, and those villages with radio became 'sites of pilgrimage' for the surrounding population.[70]

As the language of the last quotation hints, radio was a key element in the anti-religious campaign. In a typical scenario, radio hams and Komsomol members would set up a loudspeaker in the centre of village in direct competition with the priest. In Ivanovo-Voznesensk in 1925, according to one report, activists were successful in thus distracting the local population from their Easter celebrations.[71] A stock story in the atheistic press was the priest who vainly tried to fight back by taking down the antenna.[72] Yet infrastructural problems were such that radio was in no position to perform its full anti-religious mission.[73] Even just before World War II, rural Russia had only 82,000 functioning radio sets.[74] The quality of equipment in many villages was so poor that even at a distance of three paces from the speaker it was hard to make out what language was being spoken: Russian might sound like 'a mixture of Gypsy and Aramaic'.[75]

Given all these difficulties, radio periodicals and handbooks on agitation advocated special methods of 'organizing' listening. Once the novelty of broadcasting had worn off, Soviet people—especially in rural areas—needed convincing that it was worth their while to gather by the loudspeaker for the latest news. In cases where settlements were a long way from the nearest loudspeaker, it was imperative to create a 'radio wall newspaper': one comrade would be entrusted with listening to the full TASS broadcasts and then writing down the main points for public display.[76] The Moscow trade union recommendation was if necessary to build up a mass audience gradually by assembling small groups of five to ten listeners interested

[69] Letter with recollections of Andrei Alekseevich Vendrikh, Popov Museum, Fond Radio, op. 1, d. 784, ll. 1–2.

[70] Popov Museum, Brenev collection, op. 1, d. 417, l. 10.

[71] GARF, f. 6903, op. 3, d. 7, l. 44.   [72] See e.g. GARF, f. 5407, op. 2, d. 46, l. 32.

[73] GARF, f. 5407, op. 1, d. 90 (materials on role of radio in anti-religious campaign, 1931).

[74] GARF, f. 6903, op. 1, d. 55, l. 2.

[75] Ia. F. Pogodin, 'Mikrofon v derevne' (1929), *VKD*, 700.

[76] M. N. Kallan, 'Prakticheskie zadachi iacheiki ODR v derevne', *Radio vsem*, no. 12 (1925): 1–2.

in a particular issue.[77] A few years later, there was even the proposal to set up 'radio halls' where listeners for a small entry fee could listen to music or theatre in better acoustic conditions than they could expect at home.[78]

The most propitious environment for organized listening, especially after the launch of high-tempo industrialization, was the factory. The first five-year plan saw the rapid spread of what we would call public address systems. Early in 1933, the Leningrad party organization reported that 220 enterprises in the city had radio networks, and 80 of them had their own local broadcasting. A report for Moscow oblast noted that the region could boast 350 networks, with 125,000 wired receiver points and 50,000 wireless; work had also started on installing radio in suburban trains.[79] In 1937, the transmission network for the automobile factory network in Gorky organized the collective listening of twenty different programmes in 830 different locations, with a total audience of 30,000.[80] Agitprop authorities gave some attention to the best ways of using factory networks. Much was said and written on the need to organize listening in workers' lunch breaks. Research was conducted on the value of radio in the labour process.[81] Above all, however, work-place radio was seen as a participatory medium that would erase the distinction between listeners and speakers. From the late 1920s onwards, one of its guiding missions was to turn workers into broadcasters. The automobile district network in Gorky reported that 158 more or less ordinary people had come to the micro-phone in 1937.[82]

This workforce participation took place in two main ways, neither of them at all spontaneous. The first was the individual worker statement (*vystuplenie*), which was normally an account of the speaker's work performance and good resolutions for the future. The second was the live link-up (*pereklichka*), either between dif-ferent workshops in the same factory or between different factories. The first inter-enterprise link-up, involving factories in Moscow and Leningrad, took place on 13 April 1929. This genre of broadcasting quickly established itself as a symbolic way of organizing 'socialist competition': a pledge made in public and orally was felt to be more of a commitment than one made in writing or before a small group of people.[83] To judge by the text of one such event that has survived in the archives, the *pereklichka* was a brutal forum where industrial managers and party-state func-tionaries were bombarded with questions about their activities.[84]

In theory, radio fit perfectly the kind of grass-roots mobilization that was required by the 'Great Break' of industrialization. On the ground, however, the situation

[77] TsGAMO, f. 180, op. 1, d. 1168, ll. 2–3 (June 1927).

[78] A. Borodin, V. Vinnikov, and K. Musin, 'Problema radioslushaniia: K postanovke opytov masso-vogo proslushivaniia khudozhestvennoi produktsii', *Govorit SSSR*, no. 2 (1933): 12.

[79] GARF, f. 5451, op. 17, d. 488, ll. 45–8.

[80] GOPANO, f. 3, op. 1, d. 860, l. 8 (report on broadcasting activities in Avtozavodskii district, 1937).

[81] I. Dukor, 'Opyt anketnogo obsledovaniia na zavodakh "Aviopribor", "Kr. Oktiabr'"' i v institute slepykh', *Govorit SSSR*, no. 23–4 (1932): 18–19.

[82] GOPANO, f. 3, op. 1, d. 860, l. 6ob. Sixty-two of these speakers were Stakhanovites.

[83] Dubrovin, *K istorii sovetskogo radioveshchaniia*, 33.

[84] GARF, f. 5451, op. 17, d. 521, ll. 18–69.

often looked very different. In the autumn of 1931, a representative of the Department of Local Broadcasting of the all-union radio was sent to one of the great construction sites of the first five-year plan, the automobile factory Avtogigant in Nizhnii Novgorod. She found that the radio network in the factory was extremely inadequate, and that it simply broadcast Moscow programmes all day long. No efforts were being made to broadcast local material, and no one was greatly concerned by this failure. Five issues of a broadcast radio bulletin had been produced for the factory network, but the editor then gave up because the radio centre was not paying him. As the guest from Moscow concluded, 'radio was regarded as a toy and an amusement'. The regional radio committee was constantly summoning workers to take part in radio link-ups, which were generally regarded as a time-wasting imposition.[85]

Plenty of further archival evidence could be supplied to indicate the difficulties that local broadcasters faced in squeezing resources out of party, trade union, and state organizations. They also had to cope with a constant shortage of technical personnel and educated cadres to organize the broadcasts. In 1932, only 47 out of 125 relay networks in Nizhnii Novgorod region had their own broadcasting, and in most cases this was sporadic or (worse still) 'politically illiterate'.[86] Similar problems could be found even in the environs of the Soviet Union's second city. In early 1935, reports on radiofication in Leningrad region showed that the network had actually shrunk in some places because villages could not afford the subscription fees for wired radio. Outside the urban centres, the figures were far from impressive: Novgorod district, with a population of 75,000, had only 1,634 receiver points. Perhaps most worrying to the authorities was the situation along the Estonian border. The collective farms in these districts—largely Estonian in ethnic composition—were finding the cost of installing wired radio prohibitive. A significant section of the population, however, had wireless sets—which it used largely to listen to Estonian-language broadcasts from over the border.[87]

At least in the major industrial centres, some organizational progress seems to have occurred. By 1937, the radio network of the Gorky automobile factory district had five full-time employees and offered quite a varied range of genres: news bulletins, lectures, live appearances, 'concerts' of gramophone recordings, broadcasts from local theatres and clubs, amateur performances, and paid advertisements. In the course of 1937 there were 290 evening broadcasts of the latest news and 284 morning broadcasts. A total of 158 different people were reported as having broadcast from the studio (62 of them Stakhanovites). By April 1938, Nizhnii Novgorod (by now renamed Gorky) region could boast 180 different relay networks and more than 100,000 reception points.[88] Even as far away as Vladivostok, radio had become an essential source of information for the population by the late 1930s, as war approached: the region had a total of 70 wired networks in 1940.[89]

---

[85] GOPANO, f. 2, op. 1, d. 1662, ll. 5–15.   [86] GOPANO, f. 2, op. 1, d. 2759, l. 31.

[87] TsGAIPD, f. 24, op. 8, d. 255, ll. 1–2, 11–12 (transcript of meeting of 16 February 1935).

[88] GOPANO, f. 3, op. 1, d. 860, ll. 6–9.

[89] N. Solov'eva, 'Radio slushali vse', in *Nemnogo o radio i o nas s vami: K 75-letiiu Primorskogo radio* (Vladivostok, 2001), 18–21.

By the mid-1930s, the *tochka* was a passport to enlightenment and *kul'turnost'*. Stakhanovites spoke of radio's role in introducing them to literature and classical music (even though even they complained of the difficulty of the latter).[90] Housewives appreciated broadcasts as an educational accompaniment to their household chores.[91] In Moscow, moreover, the *tochka* seems to have become a defining feature of urban life by the mid-1930s. As early as July 1932, the head of broadcasting Feliks Kon found time personally to respond to a letter of complaint from a Mossovet member and resident of 9, Bol'shaia Dmitrovka (in the very centre of the capital) who was outraged at the fact that the loudspeaker points in his block were out of action. Kon agreed that it was unacceptable for residents, who paid their subscriptions on time, to be 'cut off from the cultural life of our Union'.[92]

In the second half of the 1930s, moreover, came an increasing number of set-piece broadcasting events where the attempt was made to bring almost the entire population together in a communal real-time experience. May Day and Revolution Day programming became more elaborate. Most striking of all, given the leader's previous reluctance to be heard in public, was the broadcast of Stalin's speech to the Extraordinary Eighth Congress of Soviets in November 1936. Designed to promote the remarkable rights promised the Soviet people in the new constitution, the speech offered a propaganda opportunity not to be missed.[93] The wired radio network was fully mobilized. As early as July, broadcasting organizations were alerted to the need to be ready for the congress. In Leningrad region, more practical preparations for organizing collective listening began in late October: all district centres were to equip an auditorium for the purpose, and listening spaces were also set up in factories (the Kirov factory, for example, had thirty-four of these). The Leningrad radio committee provided tubes and earphones to improve radio access in collective farms in the region. Dress rehearsals in mid-November ensured that the listening network was functioning properly. Within an hour of the end of Stalin's speech at 7.48 p.m. on 25 November, the authorities started gathering telephone feedback from the region; by 11.30 that night, they had received reports from eighty-two different districts. On the basis of this information, Leningrad broadcasters were able to claim a total of 481,574 collective listeners in 5,229 public listening places. Together with the estimated 210,000 individual listeners (on the assumption that on average 3 people were gathered around each of the 70,000 *tochki*), this delivered a figure of almost 700,000 listeners in Leningrad region (not including the city of Leningrad, where there were reckoned to be more than 1 million listeners).[94]

[90] 'Stakhanovtsy o radioveshchanii' (1936), in *VKD*, 740–2.

[91] Domokhoziaika Iablonovskaia, 'Moi uchitel'', *Govorit SSSR*, no. 1 (1935): 9.

[92] *RGASPI*, f. 135, op. 1, d. 218, l. 13. Kon did add, however, that the complaint should be addressed not to the broadcasting agency but to the technical administration (Radioupravlenie).

[93] Karen Petrone describes how the speech was built up as a quasi-religious revelation by the propaganda authorities, though she also provides evidence that at least some listeners took a far less respectful view. Petrone, *Life Has Become More Joyous, Comrades: Celebrations in the Time of Stalin* (Bloomington, Ind., 2000), 181–2.

[94] TsGAIPD SPb, f. 24, op. 8, d. 367, ll. 8–10, 12–13. In the Gorky automobile district, 11,000 workers were reported as having heard Stalin's speech through organized collective listening: GOPANO, f. 3, op. 1, d. 860, l. 8.

LISTENER RESPONSE

For all these efforts to organize the listener's participation, the party-supervised All-Union Radio Committee, as well as its many regional agencies, remained largely ignorant of the mass response to broadcasts. The authorities were keen to find out what Soviet people were making of radio, but the audience was a mysterious phenomenon—as was bound to be the case in a society where the market had been throttled and open sociological research prohibited.

In 1928, a Soviet composer revealed his own straightforward way of gauging audience reaction. When he knew that one of his works was due to be broadcast, he went along in the guise of an 'ordinary mortal' to a square with a loudspeaker so as to observe the crowd's response.[95] This mass observation method was in fact often used by the party authorities, and Agitprop reports on audience response in public places—now scattered around regional party archives—are among our most intriguing sources on radio listening in the interwar period.

For the most part, however, radio committees, like their colleagues in the print media, relied on the feedback they received in letters from members of the public. In the early days, this did not amount to much. Over the first three months of its existence, the Nizhnii Novgorod station received about 300 letters. Only six of them were identifiably from workers; most authors were of unspecified social background. Only twenty-five gave any assessment of programme content. The station thus remained almost completely uninformed about audience response.[96] In 1927, even at the national level, listeners were reported as sending in very few letters: about 1,500 per month in the winter, but only 200 or so per month during the summer.[97]

Undoubtedly, access to broadcasts varied hugely across the USSR. Radio reception was concentrated in the major urban centres, especially those of strategic importance (that is, those located near borders with hostile states). The areas surrounding these cities benefited from a trickle-down of radio technology. One observer recalled finding a radio set in a peasant reading room (*izba-chital'nia*) in 1926 in the Vladivostok region: 'a massive oak case with a sloping front, four tubes on top, and next to them batteries and a loudspeaker with a bell'. This Marconi set had been bought in England, and although its batteries soon expired, *radioliubiteli* came along to revive them.[98] In 1928, in Serpukhov district, the most radiofied part of the Moscow region, an engineer came across touching scenes of local enthusiasm for the radio: an *izba* there was likely to contain 'a group of children of various ages, one of whom, mostly the owner of the radio set, was listening with a smile, while the others with eyes full of envy looked at their lucky friend and hung eagerly on his authoritative remarks'. Peasants and their children turned out to be

[95]	M. Koval', 'Zametki kompozitora', *Radioslushatel'*, no. 2 (1928): 6.

[96]	'Radioslushatel' i radiostantsiia: Kto pishet? O chem pishut? Kak nuzhno pisat'', *Nizhegorodskaia kommuna*, 4 March 1928, 5.

[97]	Al'nett, 'Radioslushatel' zagovoril', *Novosti radio*, no. 41 (1927): 2.

[98]	A. Kvach, 'K radio otnosilis' pochtitel'no', in *Nemnogo o radio i o nas s vami*, 9–10.

well acquainted with the radio schedule, and made sure they were free of household tasks when their favourite programmes were on.[99]

However, even in Serpukhov district, where the relatively urbanized peasants needed little convincing of the value of radio, radio sets were few and prohibitively expensive. It was not until the 1930s, when wired radiofication made headway in the major cities, that broadcasting achieved a serious breakthrough and came to take a fuller part in people's everyday lives. In Moscow at that time, the *tarelka* was later recalled as a constant presence in a *kommunalka* childhood.[100] The postbag of central broadcasting swelled accordingly. In 1934, the arts section alone was reported to have received 37,000 letters.[101]

Radio stood out from the other mass media of the 1930s (cinema and the press) for its capacity to serve up collective events that unfolded in real time. For a population that was almost permanently on a war footing, immensely sensitive to signals 'from above', yet also receptive to socialist sensation-making, this was an attribute of great value. In the spring of 1934, millions of Soviet citizens were glued to their *tochki* as they followed the rescue of the crew of the ill-fated Cheliuskin.[102] At the end of the same year came a Soviet 'JFK' moment, as the Radio Committee was inundated with letters from shocked citizens who had heard on the radio about the murder of Sergei Kirov. One railway technician on the Murmansk route found out the news on a work trip when he saw people in mourning; he then eagerly followed on the radio the campaign against the 'counterrevolutionary gang' held responsible for the killing.[103] Letters poured in from correspondents of all ages and educational levels, from small children to the following weakly literate 61-year-old woman: 'Inspite of the cold i sat 4 hours on the skwer with the radio listend to the funeral cried hard a woman came up to me and said dont cry granny but i cudnt help it.'[104]

A less raw sense of radio's emotional impact as a symbolic meeting place for the Soviet nation is given by the diary of Aleksandr Afinogenov. In 1937, Afinogenov was in deep depression, having apparently lost favour as a dramatist. His diary was a tortuous attempt to write himself out of this predicament. As he wrote on 25 December: 'Then I turned on the radio, for the latest news, and a strange thing happened: ordinary news about the life of our country, our people, their words and aspirations, lifted me up immediately, it was if I'd washed in cold water after a day

---

[99] GARF, f. 374, op. 28, d. 2131, l. 87 (engineer's report on radiofication in Serpukhov uezd, 14 May 1928).

[100] A. Ia. Gurevich, *Istoriia istorika* (Moscow, 2004), 76. Further evidence on the ubiquity of radio in the urban environment can be found in the Harvard Project, e.g. HP, vol. 2, no. 17, 64.

[101] V. Bekman, 'Rabota s pis'mami radioslushatelei', *Govorit SSSR*, no. 13 (1935): 11–13. A Radio Committee decree of July 1934 had enjoined radio personnel to respond more actively to listeners' letters: see 'O rabote s pis'mami i o massovoi rabote Upravleniia tsentral'nogo veshchaniia', extracted in *VKD*, 87–8.

[102] On the Cheliuskin affair, see John McCannon, *Red Arctic: Polar Exploration and the Myth of the North in the Soviet Union, 1932–1939* (New York, 1998), 61–8.

[103] GARF, f. 6903, op. 1, d. 8, l. 1.

[104] GARF, f. 6903, op. 1, d. 12, l. 2. The Russian reads as follows: 'Несмотря я намороз просидела 4 часа наплощади у радио слушала похороны горко плакала камне подходила иговорила неплачь бабушка ноя немогу отслез'.

of exhausting reflections.' He had been feeling isolated but, on hearing the news, he 'engaged with the life of the whole country, again felt the grandeur of this life and understood the insignificance of my own minor difficulties'.[105]

These highly strung sentiments (quite understandable, given that Afinogenov must have been expecting arrest at any moment) should not obscure the many ways in which radio clearly failed to unite the Soviet nation. For one thing, Afinogenov, as a member of the metropolitan literary intelligentsia, owned a radio set that permitted him to tune in to broadcasts from London as well as reports from the hot spots of the five-year plan.[106] Another radio addict was the doomed former émigré Nikolai Ustrialov, who listened attentively to Soviet coverage of the second major show trial in January 1937, but also to broadcasts from Spain, Berlin, and Paris.[107] Class stratification in radio ownership was clear. As one of the informants of the Harvard Interview Project noted, 'There are many radios in the shops. However, a kolkhoznik, even working a lifetime, would never be able to afford it. A laborer could afford, if there are at least 3–4 working members in the family, a radio for 500–1000 rubles, or a used one.' Another interviewee put it more bluntly: 'only the big Party people and military people could listen to the radio'.[108]

The emergence of a Soviet middle-class model of radio listening is evident on the pages of the radio journals in designs for radio sets, which by the end of the 1930s, had a secure place in the Stalinist version of domesticity (see Figures 2.4 and 2.5). Aesthetic impression was now a consideration. If once upon a time, back in the 1920s, it had even been a sign of prestige to have a set that showcased its technical function, by making levers, lamps, and wiring visible, now the Soviet urban consumer had very different requirements. The radio set was now an 'attractive piece of furniture' rather than a piece of cutting-edge technology. Radio listeners were now pressing buttons to tune in to preset stations rather than regulating the frequency themselves.[109] At the same time, inventors were developing a wider range of types of set—including, besides ordinary sets, 'console' sets that contained also a recording facility and even portable sets.[110]

Less privileged members of Soviet society were reliant on the functional *tochka* and had to take what they were given. And they could not have been entirely happy with what was on offer. Perhaps the most uncomfortable paradox of the radio was the mismatch between its stated mission (to spread irreligious enlightenment to those who needed it most, i.e. the peasantry) and its audience (which was

[105] A. Afinogenov, *Dnevniki i zapisnye knizhki* (Moscow, 1960), 481.

[106] Afinogenov, *Dnevniki*, 408. Radio is mentioned as an attribute of a well-appointed intelligentsia household in K. I. Chukovskii, *Dnevnik 1930–1969* (Moscow, 1997), 93 (apropos the Tynianovs' acquisition of a set in January 1934).

[107] Karl Schlögel, *Moscow, 1937* (Cambridge, 2012), 215, 224–5.

[108] HP, vol. 13, no. 121, 11; vol. 2, no. 17, 64.

[109] V. Legar, 'Komfort radiopriemnogo ustroistva', *Radiofront*, no. 17–18 (1940): 17–18. For an early sign of this aesthetic shift, see S. Ia. Mikhailichenko, 'Iashchik dlia radiopriemnika', *Radiofront*, no. 3 (1935): 25–6.

[110] A. V. Davidovich, 'Oformlenie priemnikov', *Radiofront*, no. 17–18 (1940): 19–21. Note, however, that these were designs by *radioliubiteli* rather than models available for ordinary consumers.

Figure 2.4. Image of 1930s middle-class listening.
Source: A. S. Popov Central Museum of Communications

Figure 2.5. The *tarelka* at the other venue for Soviet domesticity: the dacha, 1931.
Source: A. S. Popov Central Museum of Communications

mainly technologically savvy people—skilled workers and intelligentsia—in the cities).[111] The content of radio schedules in the 1920s seems to have made relatively few concessions to popular rural tastes. Critics kept up a robust defence of 'serious' music, despite evidence that *chastushki* were overwhelmingly the most popular form of music. Although by the late 1920s Moscow was putting out several types of broadcast designed for the rural listener, they were written, according to a meeting of June 1929, in an 'urban language' that was not getting through to the village. The problem was exacerbated by the style of radio announcers, whose pompous manner of 'declamation' was wholly alien to the peasant listener. From the late 1920s, moreover, the schedule started with morning gymnastics, which was hardly geared to the needs of people who spent their days in the fields. Analysis of more than 1,000 listeners' letters in 1929 delivered an unambiguous verdict on the class differentiation of the audience: levels of satisfaction declined from white-collar employees (85 per cent) to workers (72 per cent) to peasants (61 per cent).[112]

Music was always the main bugbear of the plebeian listener. As a radio representative observed in June 1929, anti-religious propaganda shot itself in the foot by broadcasting heavy classical repertoire. Peasants thought better of going to church while 'cheerful' music was on, but when they heard more forbidding pieces they said 'time to pay the priest a visit'.[113] Later that summer, a commission on village broadcasting debated how to engage the peasant listener. Broadcasters were advised to score music for the existing village ensembles (with their accordions, balalaikas, domras, and so on), to add suitably revolutionary texts to the catchy melodies of 'street song' (*ulichnaia pesnia*), and to schedule 'radio parties' (*vecherinki-gulianki*) that would offer young people a mixture of music, comedy, and quizzes and give them a good alternative to 'hooligan' behaviour.[114] At the same time, other cultural agencies were pondering how to accommodate the balalaika in the overall project of the 'musical education of the masses'. A directive of July 1929 by the Radio Council of the People's Commissariat of Post and Telegraph (the successor organization to Radioperedacha) mentioned that popular entertainment (*estrada*) still showed signs of vulgarity, eroticism, and *tsyganshchina*, but could not help noting that 77 per cent of the audience wanted more evenings of comedy and *estrada*.[115] Proletarian tastes in music, even as reflected in published letters, were brusque and unreceptive to the canon.[116] Yet a repertoire analysis of 1932 found that 57 per cent of Moscow music broadcasting, or 15,000–20,000 numbers per year, consisted of works from the 'heritage': first came Rimskii-Korsakov with

---

[111] For evidence of the efforts made by the broadcasting authorities to reach the rural audience in the late 1920s, see T. Goriaeva, ' "Velikaia kniga dnia": Radio i sotsiokul'turnaia sreda v SSSR v 1920–30-e gody', in H. Günther and S. Hänsgen (eds.), *Sovetskaia vlast' i media* (St Petersburg, 2006), 64–9.

[112] Information in this paragraph from the transcript of a Moscow Agitprop meeting from 1929, TsAOPIM, f. 3, op. 11, d. 808, ll. 6–7, 10–11, 54, 80.

[113] TsAOPIM, f. 3, op. 11, d. 808, l. 65.

[114] 'Protokol No. 6 Zasedaniia komissii po derevenskomu veshchaniiu', in *VKD*, 68–75.

[115] GARF, f. 5508, op. 1, d. 1597, l. 48.

[116] 'Nasha tribuna', *Novosti radio*, no. 9 (1928): 4.

1,300 numbers, then Chaikovskii and Schubert with 1,200 each, followed by Beethoven, Grieg, Mozart, Glinka, Musorgskii, Schumann, and so on.[117]

Although evidence on audience response is patchy, the available sources suggest that the disconnect between radio output and demotic tastes remained a feature of Soviet broadcasting throughout the 1930s. In 1933, a survey of listeners' letters recorded that in general listeners wanted fewer symphonies and more humour and satire, while *kolkhozniki* were asking for songs and *chastushki*.[118] In the spring of 1935, an agitator in Gorky reported workers at collective listening sessions making objections to the diet of canonical Western composers. *Chastushki*, popular songs, and kolkhoz concerts were their preference.[119] The Radio Committee's analysis of programming in 1940 revealed that *estrada* was still neglected.[120] A meeting with 'activist' listeners in September of the same year brought further evidence of the popular antipathy to opera. The audience wanted more variety, more songs, more foreign broadcasts, more interactive forms (such as radio debates), and more information on areas of everyday life (such as child-rearing). As one speaker put it bluntly, 'operas have driven us mad'.[121] A meeting of news broadcasters with eighty workers from a Moscow aviation factory revealed a degree of frustration with the unengaging delivery of radio bulletins: poor diction, broadcasters' apparent reluctance to change announcer from one broadcast to another, and the failure to alternate between women's and men's voices. It also revealed listeners' thirst for information—whether on international affairs, literature, foreign languages, or science and technology (see Figure 2.6).[122]

A survey of the postbag of central radio in 1940 suggested that listeners were still expressing their traditional grievances yet at the same time finding much to appreciate in the broadcasting schedule. About a third of the 70,000 letters went to the children's section and a further fifth to music. Quite a few listeners evidently valued radio for the instruction it provided. Most letters to the department of party propaganda contained requests for lectures to be read more slowly so as to enable note-taking. Programmes with information and advice on family life and medicine seemed to have an avid audience. Many listeners found news broadcasts dull and wished they would depart more frequently from the language of TASS. As for music, listeners wanted rousing tunes first thing in the morning to give them a good start to the day. Revolutionary and 'mass' songs were in much demand, and songs from the latest films were often mentioned specifically. Young listeners wanted *estrada*, gypsy romances, and operettas. They also wanted jazz, but as the music section wrote in its digest of listener feedback, 'good examples of jazz' (which meant Leonid Utesov rather than Aleksandr Varlamov or Aleksandr Tsfasman). 'Mystery concerts' were evidently popular, as were broadcasts of Red Army songs. Ol'ga Kovaleva and the Piatnitsky choir, notable exponents of folk music, were also

[117] T. Tsytovich, 'Rekonstruktsiia muzykal'nogo repertuara radioveshchaniia—neotlozhnaia zadacha', *Govorit SSSR*, no. 19 (1932): 10–11.

[118] Mikh. Angarskii and Viach. Knushev, 'Slovo slushatelei o peredachakh: Obzor pisem radioslushatelei', *Govorit SSSR*, no. 12–13 (1933): 33–4.

[119] GANO, f. 3630, op. 5, d. 54, ll. 15–16.   [120] GARF, f. 6903, op. 1, d. 52, l. 12.

[121] GARF, f. 6903, op. 1, d. 49, ll. 2, 4, 9.   [122] GARF, f. 6903, op. 1, d. 49, ll. 24–8.

Figure 2.6. Listeners take notes
from a radio lecture, 1930s.
Source: A. S. Popov Central Museum of
Communications

favourites.[123] A viable Soviet broadcasting repertoire—one that found an acceptable balance between listener tastes and ideological imperatives—seemed to be
taking shape.

CONCLUSION

In the 1930s, broadcasters, like their colleagues in other branches of Soviet culture,
subscribed to the necessary myth of the ever more 'cultured' audience. Chuvash
villagers, among others, were now far more discriminating listeners: accordions,
balalaikas, and *gusli* were no longer good enough for them.[124] So advanced were
Soviet mass listeners that they could now take to the microphone themselves. At
the All-Union Agricultural Exhibition, peasants were given the opportunity to
have themselves recorded at a pavilion entitled 'Spoken letters' (*govoriashchee
pis'mo*). Visitors first jotted down a text, then entered the studio to read it into

---

[123] GARF, f. 6903, op. 1, d. 54, ll. 2–5, 8–9, 16, 18, 20.
[124] P. Sokol'nikov, 'Samodeiatel'noe iskusstvo—k mikrofonu (Radiofestival' v Chuvashskoi ASSR)',
Rabotnik radio, no. 1 (1937): 29.

the microphone. In due course they were presented with a disk. About fifty such recording sessions were held each day. There was some idea that such 'sound recording ateliers' should be set up in cities around the country.[125]

Scepticism is the automatic, and reasonable, response to such cultural boosterism. Yet, while radio may not have turned Soviet people into epitomes of *kul'turnost'*, it did make its mark on the lives of millions of contemporaries. Recalling his childhood in a village in Tver' oblast, one informant (b. 1928) remembered decades later the arrival of wired radio in the second half of the 1930s: the flimsy-looking *tarelka* poured out 'all kinds of Soviet songs', while every New Year the family listened out, like millions of their compatriots, for the chiming of the Kremlin bells at midnight.[126] Letters found on the bodies of Soviet soldiers killed fighting the 'Winter War' against Finland, a sad but revealing source on Soviet society of the late 1930s, referred frequently to radio-listening, which had evidently spread far beyond the larger cities.[127] A young man of dekulakized peasant background could, on arriving in the big city in the 1930s, learn how to be a model Soviet person by listening to broadcasts; for such aspirational migrants, the latest models of radio sets on display in the shops of the capital were perhaps the ultimate objects of consumer desire.[128] Members of the cultural and intellectual elite, for their part, found in radio broadcasts a means of achieving communion with the Soviet people and its leadership: Nikolai Ustrialov, soon to fall victim to the Terror, was among those 'hypnotized' by Stalin's address on the Constitution in late 1936.[129] By the late 1930s, Soviet citizenship had an aural dimension that would only gain in significance over the following half-decade of crisis.

---

[125] T. Chakurs, 'Pavil'on zvukozapisi', *Radiofront*, no. 17–18 (1940): 15.

[126] Oxf/Lev V-04 PF 13 (B), p. 34.

[127] V. Zenzinov, *Vstrecha s Rossiei: Kak i chem zhivut v Sovetskom Soiuze: Pis'ma v Krasnuiu armiiu, 1939–1940* (New York, 1944), 113.

[128] For two interesting examples in this vein (Vladimir Edovin and Stepan Podlubnyi), see Natal'ia Kozlova, *Sovetskie liudi: Stseny iz istorii* (Moscow, 2005), 155–6 and 215.

[129] Schlögel, *Moscow, 1937*, 336–7.

3

How Russia Learned to Broadcast

As we have seen from the first two chapters, broadcasting was an enormous organizational task, especially in a country as large and poor as the USSR. For the whole interwar period, the Soviet authorities struggled to provide a critical mass of the urban population with regular access to functioning receiver points. No less complex a task, however, was establishing *what* should be broadcast—which, in turn, was inseparable from the question of *how* it should be broadcast. For the Soviet Union, as for the rest of the world in the 1920s, radio was entirely new rhetorical territory. Everyone could agree that this was a medium of huge potential; less clear was how that power was to be exploited.

THE EARLY DAYS: RADIO ESTABLISHES ITS INDEPENDENCE AS A MEDIUM

To begin with, as Lenin famously said, radio was a 'newspaper without paper and without distances'. He meant this less metaphorically than we might imagine. A year after the Bolshevik leader coined the analogy in his congratulatory message to M. A. Bonch-Bruevich, he repeated and elaborated on it in a letter to N. P. Gorbunov, the secretary of Sovnarkom: 'This is a *gigantically important* matter (a newspaper without paper and without wire), since with the loudspeaker and receiver that Bonch-Bruevich is developing...the whole of Russia will hear a newspaper read out in Moscow.'[1] For the Bolsheviks, long-term devotees of the printed word, the newspaper was without question the premier medium of political communication. In the early Soviet period, however, it experienced nothing short of a crisis. The distribution network came close to collapse during the civil war period and recovered with difficulty thereafter. Paper and newsprint were expensive for the revolutionary state, and the population was unwilling to part with its own money to buy what the socialist regime was offering it. Last but not least, the Bolsheviks had ambitions to spread their message to a population that was at best weakly literate; to this audience, the dense print and abstruse language of a Soviet newspaper were offputting to the point of impenetrability.[2]

---

[1] P. S. Gurevich and N. P. Kartsov (eds.), *Lenin o radio* (Moscow, 1973), 19 (letter of 26 January 1921).

[2] Jeffrey Brooks, 'Studies of the Reader in the 1920s', *Russian History*, 9/2–3 (1982): 187–202.

Radio, by contrast, was instantaneous and immediate. It allowed information from Moscow to be received in Khabarovsk or Baku without delay, and it promised to get through to even the most benighted listener. In its speed and directness, it could be regarded as a kind of oral telegraph, a technological extension of a punchy report or feuilleton from the Russian Telegraph Agency (ROSTA). In the archives of ROSTA we find various texts—evidently intended for transmission via loud-speakers or simply for public performance—that anticipate the imminent introduction of sound broadcasting. For example, pre-empting rap lyrics by half a century or so, a 'spoken newspaper' of August 1921 adopted the form of rhymed couplets to lash out at the enemies of the Revolution:

> Those foreign pundits, the White Guard bandits, are shrieking: the Soviets are creaking, the Bolshies are feeling sick, let's play our cunning tricks. Let's tighten the noose, cook the Soviet goose, make peasant and prole crawl back into their hole.

> Заграничная наша братия – белогвардейская шатия испускает вопли: стали, мол, советские дела плохи, износились большевики до ручки, значит, пора пускать нам в ход последние наши штучки. Надо усилить блокаду, чтобы все белогвардейцы были рады и чтобы мужик да рабочий очутились снова во мраке черной ночи.[3]

When regular broadcasts started in 1924, radio news—known as the *radiogazeta*—continued to be the bailiwick of the telegraph agency; its first head was V. G. Danskii (Komarovskii), who had previously taken important roles at *Pravda* as well as ROSTA.[4] The very first broadcast, of 23 November 1924, opened by stating modestly that this was 'the same kind of newspaper [*gazeta*] as any other'. It would include 'an editorial, a feuilleton, ROSTA telegrams from around the world, the day's events in Moscow, news from science and technology'. Yet, a few breaths later, it proclaimed that this would be 'the liveliest newspaper in the world'. Aiming to prove the point with its own syntax, it continued: 'The *radiogazeta* is written in a lively style. The *radiogazeta* consists of lively short articles. Lively short bulletins.' Short paragraphs, a chopped-up style, and a sprinkling of colloquialisms were indeed characteristic of the *radiogazeta* in its early years, as broadcasters tried hard to keep the attention of the still mysterious listener. International news, Soviet news, Moscow events, consumer information, science, books, theatre, sport, poems, and ditties followed each other in quick succession. At its punchiest, early Soviet radio had the semaphoric poetry of Vladimir Maiakovskii, whose 'Radio Agitator' was 'published' in the 100th broadcast of *radiogazeta* on 3 May 1925. The more discursive genres included the 'chat' (*beseda*) on a topic of public interest such as the cooperative movement, the more in-depth 'report' (*ocherk*), or the piece of 'correspondence' (such as an account in October 1925 of a group of Soviet sailors visiting Maxim Gorky in Sorrento). On 7 November 1925 came the first attempt by Soviet broadcasters to give the listener a 'real-time' experience, with an extended account of the

---

[3] Troianov, 'Kakov nash privoz iz-za granitsy: Radiofel'eton', in *VKD*, 202. My translation takes some liberties in order to preserve the rhythm of the original.
[4] *RR*, 60.

revolutionary anniversary festivities in Moscow that day. In due course, moreover, the *radiogazeta* was providing listeners with blow-by-blow accounts of the struggle against 'oppositionists' in the party.[5]

Although early broadcasters were not oblivious to the need to differentiate between speech and writing, their guiding model remained the print newspaper. They presented to listeners a long stream of unconnected items, which for the most part were delivered by a single speaker.[6] Before long, however, it became clear that such bulletins became unwieldy and indigestible if they attempted to cram into a 45-minute broadcast information for all groups in Soviet society.[7] In 1925, Soviet broadcasting began to diversify its output by creating different kinds of *radiogazeta*, while in the spring of 1926 came a fundamental bifurcation into worker and peasant varieties. By the start of 1930, there were as many as 300 different *radiogazety* in various languages of the USSR.[8] In the second half of the 1920s, under its proactive and combative head, A. Sadovskii, the workers' *radiogazeta* started to strive for more compelling forms of broadcasting. In a communication to the Central Committee in May 1927, Sadovskii insisted that radio should not simply be aping print newspapers, and that it deserved proper funding and a strong editorial team independent of Radioperedacha. In a long report he wrote later that year, Sadovskii contrasted the approach of *radiogazeta* with the War Communism method of attempting 'to bang into the heads of the masses long, tedious and boring lectures' without taking any interest in 'how the masses react to these speeches'. The correct, Leninist method was to draw those masses into political campaigning.[9]

No doubt there was plenty of points-scoring and political posturing in documents such as these—Sadovskii was, after all, in the middle of a bitter conflict with the leadership of Radioperedacha—but the commitment to mass participation by now appears to have been rather more than a slogan for broadcasters. It was already widely accepted that radio needed to do more than simply offer an expedited version of the newspaper. In the early days of the ROSTA *radiogazeta*, a sober, expressionless style of delivering radio news appears to have been the norm (with a strong preference for male voices).[10] At the First All-Union Congress of the Society of Radio Lovers in 1926, by contrast, broadcasters were urged to take radio out of the 'hothouse' of the studio and bring it to society.[11] If the great achievement of Soviet newspapers had been to transform the mass reader into a mass writer, broadcasting

[5] Texts of broadcasts mentioned in this paragraph in *VKD*, 207–8, 218, 221–8.

[6] This was the case, for example, in the broadcast of 7 November 1925: *VKD*, 223–6.

[7] Aleksandr Sherel', *Audiokul'tura XX veka. Istoriia, esteticheskie zakonomernosti, osobennosti vliianiia na auditoriiu: Ocherki* (Moscow, 2004), 18.

[8] *RR*, 62; V. N. Ruzhnikov, *Tak nachinalos': Istoriko-teoreticheskii ocherk sovetskogo radioveshchaniia 1917–1928* (Moscow, 1987), 135.

[9] RGASPI, f. 17, op. 85, d. 148, ll. 30–1, 38.

[10] According to Sherel', the head of the department of radio announcers (*diktorskaia gruppa*) was specifically instructed to take women readers off the *radiogazeta* (or at least only to use those women whose voices were 'like a man's'). Sherel', *Audiokul'tura XX veka*, 21.

[11] A. M. Liubovich, *Nuzhno li spetsial'noe radioiskusstvo: Materialy k I Vsesoiuznomu s" ezdu ODR* (Moscow, 1926).

now had to achieve something similar: to turn the mass listener into a mass speaker. Along the lines of the press, which had created the institution of the worker-peasant correspondent for this purpose, Sadovskii's *radiogazeta* had set about forming its own group of 'activists'. These *rabsel'kory* were tasked with delivering brusque exposés of malpractice in the workplace and management failures.[12] Contemporary accounts suggest that they were kept on a fairly tight leash. The main radio journal of the time bemoaned the timidity of the editors of such broadcasts—their reluctance to let worker-peasant correspondents have their say in case they let slip anything politically suspect.[13] Yet the factory *radiogazety* were reckoned to be popular with the workers themselves.[14]

Published guides give some indication as to how the balance between mass participation and political control was struck. Speakers could—should—be ordinary workers, but they should either write down their contribution and let it be edited or submit a summary (*tezisy*) in advance. In other words, close editorial control was obligatory. Yet the author of one such manual also insisted that a *radiogazeta* had to be 'made by the workers themselves' and that they were to speak at the microphone as straightforwardly as they did with their comrades. Contributions should be kept short (2–3 minutes) and concrete. Dialogue was recommended as a way of presenting information. Roving brigades should name and shame; 'microphone raids' could expose substandard practice anywhere from the factory workshops to the canteen.[15]

The best means of mobilizing such activists was by organizing 'radio meetings', where members of various 'collectives' around the country were brought together at their respective microphones to discuss a particular issue of common interest. As Sadovskii reported in late 1927, in the first five months of *radiomitingi* fifteen different subjects had been discussed in a total of ninety-two meetings, each with an average of four contributions, so about 370 people had aired their views.[16] Such virtual meetings had the advantage of making political issues—such as the significance of the Soviet constitution—concrete and immediate for workers. In six months of its existence, the workers' *radiogazeta* had received 2,500 letters, most of them from workers and peasants—a response that contrasted strikingly with the lack of listener feedback on other kinds of broadcast. The mass listener, Sadovskii argued, would never be capable of making a full and considered response to speeches by leading party figures such as Stalin or Lozovskii, but expressing views on practical questions in the company of class comrades was a different matter.[17] Two years later, Leningrad broadcasters were publicly praised for overcoming the

---

[12] See e.g. 'Golosa rabkorov' (22 October 1928), *VKD*, 237–8.
[13] 'Radiogazeta i ee rabsel'kory', *Radioslushatel'*, no. 3 (1928): 1.
[14] I. Malkin, 'Stengazeta bez bumagi', *Radioslushatel'*, no. 5–6 (1928): 4.
[15] V. Iurovskaia, *Radio-gazeta na predpriiatii* (Moscow, 1932), 16, 24–5, 35–6, 39. For another text on squeezing the maximum propaganda benefit out of factory broadcasting, see S. P. Chumakov, *Fabrichno-zavodskaia radiogazeta* (Moscow, 1932).
[16] Goriaeva gives what looks like a compatible figure of more than 600 such meetings in two years: *RR*, 69.
[17] RGASPI, f. 17, op. 85, d. 148, ll. 38–52.

habitual passivity of the audience and staging *mitingi* on how to carry out economy measures in industry.[18] As a manual for radio journalists reiterated, broadcast meetings were an opportunity for listeners to have their say. Editors were to avoid giving the impression of steering the discussion too firmly. They should draw up in advance the 'score' of a meeting that was to be broadcast, bearing in mind that workers were not professional announcers and making their text as simple as possible.[19]

In December 1927, Sadovskii's team held such a 'meeting' to mark the third anniversary of the *radiogazeta*. By now there were about fifty different *radiogazety* around the country, and some factories even had their own regular broadcasts, effectively 'wall newspapers on the radio'. Much of the text, as one might expect, was in celebratory vein. A 'worker correspondent' commented that he knew many workers who had stopped buying print newspapers, getting their information from the radio instead:

> It's convenient, they say. You get home from work, make yourself comfortable, have a bite to eat and a smoke, and, without straining your tired eyes, you listen to the radio newspaper. You find out all the news. You feel as one with the rest of the working people in a radio meeting. You have a laugh during the sketches. All in all, you get a load of enjoyment.

Yet, shortly afterwards, the views of a 'Kiev White Guardist' were also presented: 'As I have a radio set, I make sure to listen to your broadcasts every day, [to hear] how you make fools of people.' This sour intervention was presumably designed to set up a rousing editorial comment at the end: 'You White Guard bastard, you're trying to scare us that 1928 will be the end for us. But do you know how many years and how many times you dregs of the bourgeoisie have tried to scare us. No? Well, get this, you've been trying to scare us more than ten years.'[20]

As we see from this example, radio in the 1920s could have a crude and unruly edge to it. A broadcast of the workers' *radiogazeta* on New Year's Eve 1927 offered toasts from various 'living corpses'—stock figures of derision such as the bureaucrat, the spoiled materialistic young woman, the profiteer, the drunk, and the priest. The show was punctuated by musical interjections: an aria from Verdi's *Traviata*, popular songs, a military march, a set of rhyming ditties (*chastushki*).[21] In 1928, with the defeat of Radioperedacha, the *radiogazeta* appeared to be riding high and could afford to gloat about its triumph in an address to listeners. It admitted, however, that the question of how best to appeal to the worker and peasant audience was still open and enlisted listener feedback to that end.[22]

Over the next two or three years, Soviet broadcasting was able to serve up new kinds of 'live' experience to engage the listener. One of these was sporting events. The first stadium reports—gymnastics, athletics, football—took place in 1929;

---

[18] 'Leningradskii opyt', *Radioslushatel'*, no. 15 (1929), 3.
[19] I. Malkin, *Gazeta v efire: Soderzhanie i tekhnika radiogazety* (Moscow, 1930), 35–7, 45.
[20] RGASPI, f. 17, op. 85, d. 148, ll. 99–104.
[21] *VKD*, 229–32.   [22] *VKD*, 240–1 (broadcast of 24 October 1928).

Vadim Siniavskii (1906–72), later to become the most famous voice in Soviet sports broadcasting as well as a distinguished war correspondent, was there from the start.[23] A more politicized use of the *radioreportazh* was to whip up excitement as the country launched itself on the path of crash industrialization. The most spectacular achievement of radio during the first five-year plan was a broadcast of 2 December 1930 from one of the main engineering projects of the time, the Dneprostroi hydroelectric station. As listeners were informed in advance, the broadcast would 'from start to finish be a genuine reflection of nature'. Not a word would be scripted, not a single scene would be 'staged'. The broadcast required extensive preparatory work: two weeks taking the microphones around the site, and two 'rehearsals' where footage was sent over the wires to Moscow (1,100 kilometres away). The first such attempt was unsuccessful, but the installation of an American-made amplifier had fixed the problem. Moscow was now ready to receive these 'sound photographs' from Ukraine.[24] A few weeks later, the leading radio journal published mostly ecstatic feedback from listeners.[25]

Around the same time the most interactive genre of Soviet radio during the first five-year plan—the live link-up, or *radiopereklichka*—was gathering momentum. Not only did such occasions provide a powerful illustration of the capacity of radio to overcome distance, they also took immediacy and popular participation to a new level. These debates sounded more spontaneous than the *radiomitingi*: contributions could be short and punchy, and they were read out, as far as we can judge, by the workers themselves on site instead of being delivered by announcers in a studio in Moscow.[26] They could also become distinctly menacing occasions, as accusations flew back and forth against the backdrop of the first trials of 'wreckers' in industry.

The records of central broadcasting for this period are patchy in the extreme, but the files of the Nizhnii Novgorod radio committee reveal just how frequent *pereklichki* were in the period 1930–2. Here we find dozens, if not hundreds, of pages of texts of link-ups between different factories or districts. After a short introduction by the relevant party body, each collective participant would typically be given 5 or 6 minutes to make its case.[27] Radio was highly localized: the new automobile factory on the other side of the river from the old town had its own radio network, and this offered plenty of opportunity for targeting slackers among the workforce, fellow workers who were behind with their rent, or the

[23] G. Senkevich, *Vadim Siniavskii—pevets futbola* (Moscow, 2002), 23. For a contemporary account of one such broadcast, see 'Stadion v efire' (1929), *VKD*, 695–6.

[24] E. Stepnoi, 'Dneprostroi', *VKD*, 706–7.

[25] '100 minut na Dniprel'stane', *Govorit Moskva*, no. 36 (1930): 12–13. There was, however, one negative reaction which criticized the broadcast's over-reliance on sound effects and 'realism "on the American scale"'. On this broadcast, see also the unfootnoted account in Sherel', *Audiokul'tura XX veka*, 67–8.

[26] An early *pereklichka* from July 1928, on the upcoming grain harvest, brought together speakers from the Tula, Yaroslavl, and Middle Volga regions: *VKD*, 232–4. A livelier example from January 1933, with sharper dialogue and naming of names, was devoted to the campaign to liquidate illiteracy among railway workers: *VKD*, 261.

[27] For abundant examples, see GANO, f. 3630, op. 1, dd. 14, 20, 146.

providers of substandard food in the canteen.[28] The mass-participatory ethos of the *pereklichka* had support right from the top of the broadcasting organization. In 1932, the new head of radio, the Polish old revolutionary Feliks Kon, was commended by a group of worker inspectors for introducing the *brigadnyi metod*, which meant getting workers involved in radio on the factory floor, whether as listeners or as performers.[29]

Yet, on radio as in other places, the period 1928–32 was the high-water mark of plebeian brusqueness rather than a benchmark for the future. In the years to come, broadcasting would become considerably less demotic. This was largely, as in other areas of the Soviet arts, a matter of smoothing out the rough edges of proletarian militancy and working towards a stable and authoritative Soviet culture (which in due course would be given the name of socialist realism). *Pereklichki* were all very well, but they required very close editorial and technical supervision; in the early 1930s, the possibility that broadcasts could break down into chaos was never too far away.[30] On the radio as elsewhere, the *rabsel'kory* threatened to become the voice of a 'public opinion' that could not be steered by the party authorities.[31]

In April 1932, having previously held back from decisive intervention in the cultural sphere, the party issued an *ex cathedra* pronouncement that set the terms of cultural life for years to come. With its decree 'On Restructuring Literary-Artistic Organizations', the Central Committee liquidated the existing proletarian literary organizations and announced the imminent creation of a Union of Soviet Writers (with 'analogous' changes to follow for the other arts).[32] Two significant institutional developments in the field of broadcasting occurred soon afterwards: first, the replacement of *Radiogazeta* by 'Latest News' (*Poslednie izvestiia*) and, second, the creation in January 1933 of a new All-Union Radio Committee to take over from Narkompochtel.

These reshuffles were closely linked to changing norms of cultural expression. Having encouraged the development of class-specific *radiogazety* in the 1920s, the party now found it necessary to work towards a less rebarbative, supra-class culture that would convey Bolshevik success in building a united new society. The workers' *radiogazeta* had outlived its usefulness. Even during the first five-year plan, by no means everyone had been persuaded of the virtues of live outside broadcasts from major industrial sites. As one critic fulminated in 1931, speaking without text was

[28] For a sample of texts of broadcasts on the Avtozavodskaia radio network in November 1932, see GANO, f. 3630, op. 1, d. 101.

[29] RGASPI, f. 135, op. 1, d. 218, ll. 46, 50. The document is undated but seems to be from 1932. Kon headed the broadcasting organization from 1931 to 1933.

[30] See e.g. the discussion in the Nizhnii Novgorod radio committee of a regional *pereklichka* that had gone wrong because the material had run out; an emergency 'musical interlude' had had to be inserted. GANO, f. 3630, op. 1, d. 8, ll. 1–3.

[31] As argued by Goriaeva in *RR*, 73–4. For *rabsel'kory* in the newspapers, see Michael S. Gorham, 'Tongue-tied Writers: The Rabsel'kor Movement and the Voice of the "New Intelligentsia" in Early Soviet Russia', *Russian Review* 55 (1996): 412–29. Gorham similarly emphasizes the difficulty the Soviet authorities had in combining the demotic and the authoritative; soon enough, they largely abandoned the former in favour of the latter.

[32] For a good early study of party policy on the arts, including this decree, see C. Vaughan James, *Soviet Socialist Realism: Origins and Theory* (London, 1973).

an abdication of the broadcaster's responsibility, and broadcasters could do much better than the 'sound photographs' they took when away from the studio.[33] Although radio would continue to play its part in arousing enthusiasm for the great causes of socialist construction, it now had many other genres to work in: the interview, the 'radio composition', the sketch, the commentary, and the radio play. Many of these forms had emerged haphazardly in the 1920s, but in the 1930s, with the new quest for aesthetic stability, a sense grew among broadcasters and administrators alike that it was time for radio to come of age in formal terms: to establish clearly its methods and goals. By now it was now a truth universally acknowledged (and often repeated) that radio should not ape the print media, should exploit to the full its oral dimension for emotional and aesthetic effect, and should take into account the differentiated requirements of listeners. This was a large part of the rationale for the liquidation of *radiogazeta*, whose name alone suggested a parasitic relationship to print.[34]

BROADCASTING PRACTICE AND THE DEBATE ON 'RADIO ART'

In the early 1930s, Soviet broadcasters still had to settle a matter of principle: what exactly was the nature of radio as a medium? Could it lay claim to being an art in its own right? In the context of the recent furious polemics in various branches of the Soviet arts, these were far from idle questions. The status of radio depended not only on the performance of broadcasters. It also rose or fell according to the outcomes of a debate on the aesthetic functions of radio, and in particular its relationship to literature. In the 1920s, it was still possible to hold an open-ended discussion on the expressive possibilities of radio—to cite the sound effects, such as a sewing machine simulating a car engine, that were found on American radio, or to speculate that the broadcaster, who 'sent sounds out into invisible space', might be an 'artist of an entirely new kind'.[35] In the early 1930s, the debate was polarized in the same way as other areas of Soviet cultural production. At one undesirable extreme stood 'naturalism' (the unmediated reproduction of sounds from life); at the other stood 'formalism' (the excessive use of 'artificial' techniques such as sound effects and montage). Unlike the case, say, of literature or theatre, however, such polemics reflected fundamental uncertainty as to the nature of radio as a form of cultural expression.

The question of radio's status was all the more urgent in view of the fact that Soviet broadcasters had more airtime at their disposal than in the early days. Until

---

[33] Perel'man, Surkov, and Zaitsev, 'Radio—na sluzhbu bol'shevistskomu nastupleniiu', *Na literaturnom postu*, no. 25 (1931): 37–44.

[34] These points are made in two reports, possibly written by Kon himself, in the archive of Feliks Kon; one dates from 3 June 1930, the other from shortly before the fifteenth anniversary of the October Revolution in 1932: RGASPI, f. 135, op. 1, d. 218, ll. 29–33, 41–3.

[35] See respectively 'V mire radio (Zvukovye effekty)' (1928), *VKD*, 690–1, and P. S. Kogan 'Mysli o radio' (1928), *VKD*, 693–4.

the late 1920s, there was nothing approaching a full schedule even on Komintern: only on Sundays was there unbroken programming through the day. A new standard schedule, introduced in November 1928, provided a more elaborate range of programming for listeners of different class and age.[36] By 1929, Komintern was broadcasting from 6 a.m. to midnight every day with a break in the schedule only in the morning.[37] In 1932–3, radio schedules across the whole country were coordinated, and regional broadcasting centres were obliged to rebroadcast a set amount of programming from Moscow; in Turkmenistan in 1934, for example, Moscow radio accounted for about 20 per cent of the schedule.[38] Finally, after the introduction of another new schedule on 1 February 1937, the daily programming started at 5.35 a.m. and followed a rigid pattern, with fixed slots in the week for particular rubrics. This is not even to mention the multiplicity of regional stations and transmission networks, many of them with anywhere from a few minutes to a couple of hours of their own broadcasting each day in addition to rebroadcasts from Moscow.[39]

In the early 1930s, however, the question remained what the core radio rubrics should be and how best broadcasters should seek to fulfil their cultural mission. In the recent past, there had been extravagant efforts to create such extravagant hybrid genres as the 'artistic-documentary radio composition', but now it was time to settle on a stable genre system.[40] Such issues of self-definition were especially difficult for radio, which as the newest of the Soviet media had to struggle against the perception that it was a second-rate endeavour—a facilitator of theatre or print rather than anything in its own right. Still only weakly professionalized, radio was having trouble attracting the best talent—whether writers or musicians or actors. In the early days, broadcasters did not do much to reach out to performers: Radioperedacha tended to act on the principle that all Soviet theatres and concert halls were fair game—that it should not have to pay for the privilege of broadcasting whatever it chose.[41] For radio staff, salaries seem to have been respectable but not spectacular. In 1930, Osip Abdulov, one of the most high-profile broadcasters of his era, was paid 200 rubles a month—about twice the average worker's wage at the time.[42]

At the very least, radio had various formal tricks up its sleeve. By the early 1930s it was axiomatic that in order to get through to the audience—whether urban or

[36] Sherel', *Audiokul'tura XX veka*, 59.

[37] 'Programmnaia setka tsentral'nogo radioveshchaniia', *Radioslushatel'*, no. 44 (1929): 12–13.

[38] T. M. Novokreshchenova, *Sozdanie i razvitie radioveshchaniia v Turkmenistane* (Ashkhabad, 1991), 33.

[39] For the figures for Gorky in 1933, see GANO, f. 3630, op. 1, d. 173.

[40] For an example of such extravagance, see A. A. Tarkovskii's 'Povest' o sfagnume' (1931), in *VKD*, 248–54.

[41] In advance of a formal decree on the subject, Radioperedacha wrote to Narkompros in September 1926 to request, among other things, the right to 'broadcast without hindrance everything suitable for radio from all academic theatres'. *VKD*, 33–4.

[42] This in the post of assistant producer (*pomoshchnik rezhissera*): see extract from the relevant decree in *VKD*, 75. My estimate of an average worker's wage in 1930 is taken from A. A. Il'iukhov, *Kak platili bol'sheviki: Politika sovetskoi vlasti v sfere oplaty truda v 1917–1941 gg.* (Moscow, 2010), 408.

rural—broadcasters should not rely on existing techniques of face-to-face agitation or stage performance. The different *radiogazety* needed their own musical signatures.[43] Broadcasts for the village should not be heavy-handed theatrical illustrations of a particular political campaign (*radioinstsenirovki*) but instead needed to be fluid and varied, making use of different genres (from satire to oratory) and different kinds of music (not just the obligatory accordion).[44] Radio had comic potential that writers and producers were evidently beginning to tap. A standard satire on bureaucrats was livened up by musical motifs: an operatic aria signalled 'institutional bureaucratism', while a popular march signalled the protagonist's departure on a work trip where he experienced a conversion from pen-pusher to crusader for best practice.[45]

Yet some writers and critics continued to argue that radio must do more to differentiate itself from the printed word. The avant-garde poet Sergei Tret'iakov weighed in on this question in August 1932 (just a few months after the crucial Central Committee decree on cultural organizations, a time when 'Leftists' did not yet have to feel chastened). He complained that radio adopted the same heavy language used in newspaper articles, while the delivery did not do much to lighten it. Announcers could be divided into two types: the 'prayer-reader' (*psalomshchik*), who was concerned merely to 'mumble through the required quantity of papers' and the 'didact', who talked about even the simplest matters in the 'patronizing and edifying tone of a governess'. The quality of performance was crucial: announcers were nothing less than the 'printing press of the radio newspaper' (*tipografiia radiogazety*). When working for the radio, writers should take more account of its oral dimension. Certain sounds came over badly on air, so writers should avoid them and 'remember every second that every single word will be spoken out loud'. Radio speech needed to be 'conversational' in the literal sense of the word.[46]

Even more fundamental was the critique of the trenchant literary theorist and cultural commentator Viktor Shklovskii. In his view, literature had been 'poisoned by writing for hundreds of years'. The task of radio was 'to overcome written language'; the radio news should therefore be positively oratorical. It still had a long way to go to achieve this: Shklovskii mentioned the case of a radio performer who had let slip the phrase 'I will say something about this below', making clear that his frame of reference was typographic rather than oral.[47] Other writers of the time took news broadcasts to task for their failure to use dialogue, for their surfeit of newspaper clichés, for their excessively long sentences and factual (especially statistical) overload. Listeners were inherently less patient than readers: they 'craved

---

[43] G. A. Polianovskii, 'Radiogazeta i muzyka', *Radioslushatel'*, no. 36 (1929): 9; repr. in *VKD*, 699.
[44] 'Pokoinaia derevenskaia vecherinka: Vmesto nekrologa', *Govorit Moskva*, no. 2 (1931): 13; repr. in *VKD*, 709–11.
[45] A. Novogrudskii, 'Uzkoe mesto', *Govorit SSSR*, no. 1 (1933): 10–11. For more on the emergence of Soviet radio satire and comedy in the 1930s, see T. Marchenko, *Radioteatr: Stranitsy istorii i nekotorye problemy* (Moscow, 1970), 62–5.
[46] S. Tret'iakov, 'Pisatel' i radio', *LG*, 11 August 1932, 3.
[47] V. Shklovskii, 'Preodoleem pis'mennuiu rech'', *Miting millionov*, 1/5 (1931): 22–3.

variety' and could not be expected to listen to long texts on a single theme.[48] In October 1932, members of the radio committee in the major industrial city of Gorky bemoaned the persistence of dry 'newspaper language' in broadcasts. Script-writers had still not learned to write short sentences and avoid subordinate clauses, while announcers rushed over texts, leaving readers guessing as to their punctuation.[49] Such criticisms would be a regular refrain in radio committees around the country for at least another two decades.

In January 1934, one radio producer, V. Kantsel', went public with his frustration that radio had so far failed to achieve its potential to be a wholly new art form. Coining the term 'sound collector' (*zvukokollektor*), he observed that radio offered scope for a new 'sound art' that was 'not singing, not music, not reading, not the popular stage, not the theatre'. The problem, however, was that such an art did not yet have its listener. Radio was treated as a way of transmitting the 'real' art of theatre or music to those who were not able to attend concerts or plays in person. Kantsel' preferred to devote himself to 'real' theatre instead of marking time on the radio.[50]

Kantsel' seems to have exaggerated somewhat. There was a good deal of literary and theatrical talent on Soviet radio in the mid-1930s, and these practitioners were far from oblivious to the particular challenges of the aural medium. The genre of radio play—as opposed to stage broadcast—had long had its supporters. They notably included Lunacharskii, who in his unpublished 'Theses on Radio Art' (1926) backed the notion that radio should differentiate itself from other art forms. In December 1925, the Soviet radio audience heard the first ever home-grown radio play, Nikolai Volkonskii's 'Evening with Mariia Volkonskaia', written to mark the centenary of the Decembrist uprising. Even if there were as yet no sound effects (except music), this was already something radically different from a broadcast of a stage production.[51]

But precedent did not settle the issue of whether radio should serve merely as a convenient means of disseminating conventional staged theatre or should try to do something else entirely. A law 'On the Freedom of the Microphone' made it all too tempting to rely on existing staged theatre, since it gave broadcasters the right to place microphones in any venue they pleased without paying the performers. Theatres seem to have regarded this as little more than legalized piracy, and some tried to challenge the unlimited right to broadcast (though without success).[52] The question of whether broadcasting should nurture the distinct genre of 'radio play' became controversial in 1926, when prominent speakers at the First Congress of

---

[48] Quotation from 'Iazyk radiopressy (Iz doklada prof. A. Shneidera)', *Govorit SSSR*, 2 (1931). Other examples: ' "Krest'ianskaia radiogazeta"', *Govorit Moskva*, 29 (1930): 2–3; S. Bugoslavskii, 'Kakim dolzhen byt' radioiazyk? My prodolzhaem obsuzhdat' problemu zvuchashchego iazyka', *Govorit SSSR*: 5 (1931).

[49] GANO, f. 3630, op. 1, d. 74, ll. 4–4ob.

[50] V. Kantsel', 'Pochemu ia ushel iz radio?', *LG*, 17 January 1934, 5.

[51] The author was apparently a descendant of the heroine. On this production, and on Volkonskii's pioneering role in Soviet radio drama, see Sherel', *Audiokul'tura XX veka*, 324–32.

[52] Aleksandr Sherel', *Tam, na nevidimykh podmostkakh...: Radioiskusstvo: problemy istorii i teorii. 1922–1941* (Moscow, 1993), ch. 4.

the ODR took conflicting views on the subject. A compromise solution was to build 'radio theatres', which would offer studio conditions for broadcasting while at the same time allowing actors the experience of a 'live' audience. A Leningrad radio theatre was opened on the Moika in 1928 with space for 350 people; it was soon used as a venue for concerts and meetings as well as broadcasts. In 1929, it acquired a mobile, easily assembled stage so that it could equally well serve for ordinary theatre productions.[53]

In the late 1920s, then, it was becoming clear that traditional theatre had to take account of radio. At the very least, the microphone offered the opportunity to take a theatrical performance far beyond the walls of the theatre where it was taking place. Yet it was far from obvious how this opportunity was best to be exploited. Some highly successful stage productions were observed to be much less effective on air. A production of 3 or 4 hours was too long for the radio, but the severe cuts required to make it digestible to a radio audience ran the risk of oversimplifying the text. The compromise solution was often to insert a narrative voice.[54]

A more fundamental solution was to bring about a symbiosis of radio and theatre. Radio was introduced into the plot in a number of stage productions – Meierkhol'd's version of Maiakovskii's *Bedbug* (*Klop*), the Moscow Arts Theatre's production of Valentin Kataev's comedy *Squaring the Circle* (*Kvadratura kruga*), where in the final scene a loudspeaker announced the end of the show, and a production by the Workers' Youth Theatre (TRAM), where a hidden microphone allowed the voices of actors on stage to be 'broadcast' from loudspeakers in the auditorium. According to some 'patriots of radio', the time would soon come when theatre would turn entirely into a studio, while actors would be working primarily for the radio audience, and eventually also for 'radio viewers'.[55]

In the meantime, actors and directors were making their way to the studio to broadcast productions specially crafted for radio. Among the acknowledged achievements of radio theatre in the 1930s was the same Meierkhol'd's adaptation of Pushkin's version of the Don Juan story, *The Stone Guest*. This received high praise for its fluidity (*plastichnost*) and its power to make the listener forget the absence of the visual dimension. With judicious use of music and sound effects, and through shifts in the tempo of performance, Meierkhol'd gave the production momentum and emotional impact.[56] After its studio premiere on 17 April 1935, *The Stone Guest* was broadcast a further eight times up to June 1936. Each broadcast was a live performance; the production may have been recorded in summer 1936, but no copy has ever come to light.[57]

---

[53] Marchenko, *Radioteatr*, 26–7, 39. A Moscow equivalent was also built in 1928, but it seems to have been smaller and acoustically inferior to the Leningrad radio theatre. See Sherel', *Tam, na nevidimykh podmostkakh*, 82.

[54] On problems with broadcasting staged theatre, see Sherel', *Tam, na nevidimykh podmostkakh*, 88–9, 92–3. On the figure of the narrator in 1930s radio theatre, see Marchenko, *Radioteatr*, 53–4.

[55] N. G. Bazilevskii, 'Radio v teatre', *Radioslushatel'*, no. 31 (1929): 13; repr. in *VKD*, 697–9.

[56] A. Fevral'skii, '"Kamennyi gost"': Radiospektakl' Vs. Meierkhol'da', *LG*, 18 April 1935, 3.

[57] *RR*, 45–6.

As Meierkhol'd proved, the radio play was not just a simplified version of stage theatre. It also had aesthetic resources that the constraints of the physical stage did not allow. The actor and director V. D. Markov proposed in the early 1930s to create a 'studio-laboratory' to explore the expressive possibilities of radio. As he observed, just as cinema in its early days had been treated as 'theatre for the deaf', so radio was easy to dismiss as 'theatre for the blind'. But both cinema and radio were compelling forms of expression in their own right. A good theatrical actor was by no means guaranteed to succeed on the radio. The job of a radio producer, moreover, had rather little in common with that of a theatre director.[58]

The writer Aleksandr Afinogenov observed in 1930 that it would perhaps take a blind person to write the best possible radio play. When he set about composing a script for a radio broadcast on the Dniprel'stan construction project, he had to relearn his craft: visual images had to be turned into sound. In his opinion, what he produced was not in fact a 'radio play' but something more radical: he used the term 'radio film', given that time and action were dynamic and compressed in a way that conventional theatre did not permit (but cinematic montage did).[59] In other words, one of radio's main strengths was the capacity to combine psychological depth with the immediacy of reportage: facticity and fiction came together to mutual benefit. An early example of this symbiosis was a radio play broadcast in December 1928 about Roald Amundsen's recent transatlantic flight: the memory of this event was still so fresh that a small aural signal could trigger rich associations in listeners' minds.[60]

The concept of 'radio film' (traditionally dated to the broadcast 'Stepan Khalturin' of September 1928) underlines the extent to which radio, at this crucial stage in its development, was conceived by analogy with what Lenin had called the 'most important' of the Soviet arts.[61] The aesthetic lexicon of the 1920s had no other term for a form of aural performance that was not theatre (given the absence of live audience), not a literary or journalistic text (given the lack of single voice and authorial script), and not news report or commentary (given that it was a carefully formed aesthetic whole rather than a chunk of real-time news). This is not to say, however, that radio was a mere pale imitation of cinema. In some respects, it led the way.

Radio had its advocates among the leading lights of the 1920s avant-garde, who had made their main contribution in other fields but were fascinated by the possibilities of sound reproduction and editing. Among them was Sergei Tret'iakov, who argued that commentators on radio tended to overstate the significance of the 'artistic image' (*khudozhestvennyi obraz*) and to underestimate the power of juxtaposition and connection that could be achieved through montage.[62] But the most persuasive advocate of radio as entirely new mode of representation was Dziga

---

[58] 'Dokladnaia zapiska V. Markova o studii-laboratorii po khudozhestvennomu veshchaniiu pri MRTs', *VKD*, 78–80.

[59] A. N. Afinogenov, 'Kak ia pisal "Dniprel'stan"', *VKD*, 705–6.

[60] Marchenko, *Radioteatr*, 75–6.

[61] See Marchenko, *Radioteatr*, 69–73 for a general treatment of the *radiofil'm*.

[62] Tret'iakov, 'Pisatel' i radio'.

Vertov, who in the 1920s famously turned the movie camera into the protagonist of his documentary films. As early as the mid-1920s, Vertov also seized on the documentary potential of sound: as well as the *kinopravda* for which he is most renowned, there was also a *radiopravda*. In due course, he anticipated, new recording equipment would come along to supersede the gramophone: it would be capable of recording every last rustle and whisper. The business of radio was precisely the broadcasting of such sounds from life—not the transmission of *Carmen* or *Rigoletto*.[63] As the arrival of sound in Soviet cinema drew nearer, other film-makers expressed a similar view that sound should not be a mere appendage of the visual. If all sound did was allow previously 'silent' actors to speak, then cinema would just become a screen version of the theatre. As Vsevolod Pudovkin stated in 1929, 'the talking film has no future'. It would have an initial commercial success only, but theatre actors would 'crawl out with their theatrical voices and their theatrical diction'. Like several other prominent Soviet directors, Pudovkin worried that the advent of sound would have a corrupting effect on film, turning it into a mediocre mass-market version of the stage. In Pudovkin's view, sound had to be treated not as a replacement for intertitles but rather as a 'new raw material for composition'. His colleague Esfir Shub agreed: 'sound film must not be a mere acoustical illustration . . . it must be organic raw material just like the film footage, and . . . in this work a whole world of remarkable discoveries awaits us'.[64]

As ever, it was Vertov who set about demonstrating what this might mean in practice. In 1931, in his *Entuziazm* (subtitled 'Symphony of the Donbass') he turned the microphone into protagonist just as earlier he had made the camera his hero. Not only did he and his team conduct a successful experiment with a mobile microphone, they did not settle for simply synchronizing sound and image, instead taking 'the line of greatest resistance' by creating an eloquent counterpoint between the two. Vertov first recorded silent footage from the Donbass in autumn 1929 before then working on a sound score for each episode. For this score he likewise used documentary footage, which he subjected to creative montage in much the same way as he had worked with the visual image since the start of his career.[65]

None of this experimentation would have been possible without significant technological advances. Broadcasting sound quality was now a little better than in the very early days of Soviet radio, as were connections between Moscow and the regions. Most important of all, Soviet inventors had just developed usable recording equipment (commonly known as the shorinophone). All this meant that radio, rather than making its impact through unruly mass-participatory live events, could

---

[63] '"Kinopravda" i "radiopravda"' (1925), in Dziga Vertov, *Stat'i. Dnevniki. Zamysly* (Moscow, 1966), 84–6.

[64] Vsevolod Pudovkin, 'On the Principle of Sound in Film' and Esfir Shub, 'The Advent of Sound in Cinema', in Richard Taylor and Ian Christie (eds.), *The Film Factory: Russian and Soviet Cinema in Documents 1896–1939* (London, 1994), 264–7, 271.

[65] For Vertov's own account, see 'Obsuzhdaem pervuiu zvukovuiu fil'mu "Ukrainfil'm"—"Simfoniia Donbassa"', in his *Stat'i. Dnevniki. Zamysly*, 125–7. For an analysis of Vertov's working methods on the film, see Oksana Bulgakova, *Sovetskii slukhoglaz: Kino i ego organy chuvstv* (Moscow, 2010), 45–77.

aim for well-formed pronouncements on a given subject, which would draw on 'authentic' footage while sticking to a clear authorial design. In the early 1930s, recorded material for broadcast was called *radiofil'm*; it was not until a few years later that the now standard term *zvukozapis'* ('sound recording') began to take over. The analogy with film was all the more inviting because the tape used for recording was exactly the same as in the cinema.

The use of such recording technology on radio was such a novelty that *Govorit SSSR* felt it needed to explain to listeners a minor mystery of the Komintern schedule: how was it that the rendering of the Internationale that followed the Kremlin bells at midnight always kept to exactly the same tempo? The explanation was not that the orchestra played with miraculous mathematical precision, but rather that the real performer was the sound technician who loaded the bobbin of tape onto the player and turned on the motor. The traditional advantages of radio—its distance-transcending immediacy—could now be supplemented by reproducibility and precision.[66]

September 1933 saw the creation of a sound recording department within the VRK, whose task was to assemble the best specialists in this field so as 'to raise recording technology to a level fully corresponding to the great role that radio is to play in building socialism in the USSR'; supposedly, the inventors were also to be given the backing of industry to manufacture new equipment.[67] In this same year, Dziga Vertov was engaged in an 'almost fetishistic' quest to reconstruct Lenin's 'authentic' voice from the available archival footage, while the inventor Arsenii Avramov was attempting to find a method of electrical synthesis to generate Lenin's voice artificially.[68]

But the applications of sound recording were not limited to the aural heritage. Broadcasters of the mid-1930s were pondering how to use the microphone and the shorinophone for their own aesthetic ends. Among V. D. Markov's radio scripts was a 'radio film' of November 1933 named after Aleksandr Ostrovskii's play *It's a Family Affair (Svoi liudi—sochtemsia)* of November 1933. The leitmotif of the text was a text by the proletarian poet Dem'ian Bednyi exposing the 'Slavophile-chauvinist pomposity of "golden-domed Moscow"'. Ostrovskii's play was then raided for images of the dishonest Moscow merchantry and the hypocrisy of their Orthodoxy. The broadcast, as Markov explained in his proposal, offered a 'critical "appropriation and adaptation" of the classic literary heritage'. It also offered the listener numerous aural cues: a symphonic piece by V. Kriukov (later the composer of many well-known film tracks) imitating church bells, the voice of a consump-tive singer, the shouts of drunken wedding guests. Yet many of Markov's ideas were visual, and he offered his proposal as something that could equally well be made into a sound film, or as something best regarded as being 'on the way from radio

---

[66] 'Chto takoe radiofil'm?' (1932), *VKD*, 717–18.
[67] 'Polozhenie o sektore zvukozapisi i televideniia VRK pri SNK SSSR', *VKD*, 83.
[68] Lilya Kaganovsky, 'Elektrische Sprache: Dsiga Wertow und die Tontechnologie' and Andrej Smirnow, 'Frühe Versuche der Sprach- und Gesangssynthese im Sowjetrussland der 1920er und 30er Jahre', in Oksana Bulgakowa (ed.), *Resonanz-Räume: Die Stimme und die Medien* (Berlin, 2012), 41–54, 175–89.

to talking film'.[69] Evidently, he was disappointed when the work was only recorded for radio and not taken up by film-makers: for ambitious scriptwriters, there was no question that cinema was the place to work. But the fact remained that Markov was treating radio as fundamentally analogous to cinema in its expressive possibilities, not as a lower form of aesthetic life. Radio was no longer so ephemeral as in the early days, and it could aspire to the same wholeness and reproducibility as other arts such as literature and cinema. As another commentator observed in 1933, 'radio art'—a 'new synthesis of literature, music and theatre, a new quality'— 'was born simultaneously with sound film'.[70]

Adaptations of prose works could be similarly creative. Perhaps the fullest script of such a 'film' that we have from the 1930s is an adaptation of A. S. Serafimovich's Civil War novel *The Iron Flood* (*Zheleznyi potok*). After a short prelude and an introductory statement from the author himself, the broadcast plunged into fast-paced dialogue with snatches of music and supporting sound effects ranging from squealing pigs to artillery fire. All this went too far for one critic, who accused the broadcast of naturalism (in sound effects) and of slashing too much of the text.[71]

Among the leading exponents of broadcast adaptations of literary texts was Erast Pavlovich Garin, an actor who worked regularly in the studio and was a pioneer of the radio monodrama.[72] In 1932, N. O. Volkonskii, the author of the first ever Soviet radio play (in 1925), published an admiring and humorous review of Garin's performance of an adaptation of Henri Decoin's *Fifteen Rounds*. Posing as a secret boxing fan, Volkonskii described how he was metaphorically knocked out by Garin's rendering, which conveyed the sensations of the fighter as his blood started to flow and the crowd bayed.[73] Garin's 1934 adaptation of Aleksei Novikov-Priboi's *Tsusima*, a novel about a crucial battle in the Russo-Japanese War, drew much attention from critics: here was an attempt to create a new kind of radio narration that reflected the 'excitement and heightened passions' of the current era. Garin 'theatricalized' the figure of the naval commander Rozhdestvenskii, showing him to be a 'giant with feet of clay'. He also streamlined and accelerated the plot in an effort to convey the magnitude of this *ancien régime* military debacle. But the production was less convincing when it attempted to convey the revolutionary mood to which this defeat gave rise. Not just director but also sole actor, Garin adopted a high-flown style of delivery that worked better for Rozhdestvenskii than for the common sailor.[74]

Garin's own account of working on a slightly earlier production, a radio version of Grigorii Gauzner's *Journey through Japan* (*Puteshestvie po Iaponii*), reveals the extent to which he tried to make literary material fresh and engaging to the listener.

[69] Text of the proposal in *VKD*, 264–8.

[70] Ip. Sokolov, ''Est' li radioiskusstvo i v chem ego spetsifika?', *Govorit SSSR*, no. 4–5 (1933): 13.

[71] For the text and the review, see *VKD*, 268–88, 719.

[72] For a general account of Garin's radio career, see Sherel', *Audiokul'tura XX veka*, 334–48.

[73] N. O. Volkonskii, 'Iz dnevnika radioslushatelia', *Govorit SSSR*, no. 35–6 (1932): 9; repr. in *VKD*, 723–5.

[74] The points are taken from the discussion in Nemchenko, 'Tvorcheskaia rabota v litdramveshchanii', *Govorit SSSR*, no. 10 (1934): 7–8.

The narrator of these travel notes was not to be a lecturer, an announcer, or even an earnest tourist; he was an eager observer keen to share his sense of curiosity with the audience. He was sharply characterized by voice, and even textbook phrases on the geography of the Japanese archipelago were delivered 'with a touch of irony, which made listeners sit up and pay attention'. By dividing the material into short episodes instead of presenting it as a long monologue, and by carefully 'placing' the action through sound effects, the producer drew the audience in further. In 1931, however, radio of this kind was a fraught and highly labour-intensive affair. In the absence of recording technology that made montage possible, the broadcast, with all its different aural elements, went out 'live': the studio team had to perform their roles with maximal precision, to the extent of putting on gramophone records with background noise recorded in Japan.[75]

RADIO AND LITERATURE

For all the creative energies at work on Soviet radio in the first half of the 1930s, the Soviet Union in the 1930s was not a favourable environment for formal experimentation. The tide turned decisively in late 1933, when the Writers' Union called radio art a 'formalist theory', and before long the term 'radio play' was effectively banned from the discourse of the Radio Committee. It did not help that this genre was associated especially with the now-fascist Germany. Not until the end of the 1950s did it made a comeback in the Soviet Union.[76] In April 1934, an all-union 'creative consultation' applied the Central Committee decree of April 1932, 'On the Reconstruction of Literary and Artistic Organizations', to broadcasting. All those involved in radio were enjoined to avoid the leftist excesses of the now dis-credited Russian Association of Proletarian Musicians (RAPM) and Russian Association of Proletarian Writers (RAPP), while at the same time keeping up their vigilance with regard to 'bourgeois influences', nationalism, 'over-simplification', vulgarity, and assorted other ideological vices.[77] As the main radio journal editori-alized in 1935, a 'Bolshevik radio art' had no truck with the 'hostile formalist theory of "radio art"'. From now on, there was no question that the 'artistic word' had to play the leading role.[78]

What this all might mean in practice was elaborated in the extended discussion of 'artistic broadcasting' that took place during the consultation (and was published soon afterwards). The lead was taken by N. V. Nemchenko, who worked in the section of literature and drama on radio between 1933 and 1940 and was author of a radio adaptation of Romain Rolland's *Colas Breugnon*. Nemchenko branded the 'sound image' (*zvukovoi obraz*), which implied an unhealthy preoccupation with sound effects for their own sake, a formalist deviation. In his view, it was best not to distract the listener from the spoken word: the text was in fact even more

---

[75] *VKD*, 707–9. This is an extract from Garin's memoirs, which were published in 1974.
[76] Marchenko, *Radioteatr*, 28, 40–1, 74, 99–106.   [77] *VKD*, 85–6.
[78] 'Za bol'shevistskoe iskusstvo na radio', *Govorit SSSR*, no. 8 (1935): 2.

important on radio than in the theatre, since radio could not amplify it with visual effects.[79] As another contributor to the discussion put it, there was no such thing as a distinct 'radio genre', but radio did have potential to 'develop and enrich' existing literary and dramatic genres. Broadcasting lacked certain attributes of theatre, but had compensating advantages. Besides its mass audience, it offered a fuller acoustic range that made it possible to whisper and yet be heard; conversely, three or four actors at the microphone could create the illusion of a 'mass scene'. On no account, however, should radio neglect the text. Nor should it obscure the narrative or erase the authorial voice by presenting the listener with a melange of different extracts without attribution.[80]

In the 1930s, the radio press poked fun, or worse, at radio producers who took too many liberties with literary texts.[81] Critics commonly argued that adaptations of literary works for the radio were too fragmented and ended up baffling to the listener. Sound effects and montage were felt to go too far when they disrupted the narrative or broke up the integrity of the speaking subject. One reviewer of a 'radio composition' on the socialist village complained that the actor was given no more than 5 or 6 seconds at a time. The overall impression was artificial. As the reviewer concluded, 'there is no actor, he's not allowed to breathe, he's led on a string'. The new technique of sound recording held out the temptation for producers to abuse their power over the actor: 'tape recording is a very necessary thing, but do at least let the living person have a laugh and a cry'.[82] From 1933 onwards, 'naturalism' was a term of abuse in the radio press. Rather than giving their characters speech defects or stutters, actors and producers would be better advised to concentrate on conveying their 'social essence'.[83]

Conversely, the spoken word could be even more effective on radio than in a live stage performance, given the audience's total concentration on the voice of the performer. Although many dramatic works, even if written specially for radio, did not come across well on the radio, 'artistic reading' of literary works (*khudozhest-vennoe chtenie*) was another matter.[84] The importance of the unadorned spoken word meant that actors and producers should focus on clear diction and inton-ation and on providing the listener with a strong narrative. As one critic put it in 1934, a radio production 'needs the reader or presenter to take the role of a wise, creative composer'. Trying to achieve verisimilitude through cheap effects was a false move, as the Vakhtangov Theatre had proved recently in an unsuccessful adaptation of Gorky's *Egor Bulychev*, where at least one actor had tried too hard

[79] Nemchenko, 'Tvorcheskaia rabota v litdramveshchanii', *Govorit SSSR*, no. 10 (1934): 3–9.

[80] Z. Chalaia, 'Literaturnye zhanry na radio', *Govorit SSSR*, no. 10 (1934): 9–17.

[81] For a satire on this subject, see M. E. Levitin and V. S. Poliakov, 'Demoniada (Iz radiozhizni)', *Govorit SSSR*, no. 16 (1934): 41–2; repr. in *VKD*, 729–31.

[82] Evgenii Begak, 'Neravnyi boi: Radiokompozitsiia "Medvezhii rov"', *Govorit SSSR*, no. 2 (1933): 8–9.

[83] Viach. Emel'ianchenko, 'Bystro li my rastem?', *Govorit SSSR*, no. 4–5 (1933): 11–12. This art-icle was in fact a positive review of a radio production by N. O. Volkonskii, who was held to have kept well clear of 'naturalism'.

[84] Ip. Sokolov, 'Est' li radioiskusstvo i v chem ego spetsifika?', *Govorit SSSR*, no. 4–5 (1933), 13–14.

with her regional accent.[85] Equally, the two main schools of dramatic art—those associated with Stanislavskii and Meierkhol'd—were of dubious value on radio. Meierkhol'd's emphasis on movement did not translate well to the studio, given the lack of visual dimension, while Stanislavskii's 'realistic' acting and sound effects were confusing to the radio listener.[86]

As the literary text rather than the aural experience became the primary point of reference for radio performance, critics became less tolerant of anything 'excessive' in radio acting. A reading of Chekhov, for example, was found to have resorted to 'the old techniques—weighing down the words with aural depiction [*zvukovaia izobrazitel'nost'*]'. While this might sound like no bad thing for a radio broadcast, it was clear that the actor had committed offences against the puritanical norms of the mid-1930s: in describing a woman's appearance, he had given particular words, such as 'neck' and 'breast', a 'crudely emotive, physiological emphasis'.[87] Erast Garin was found to have erred in his adaptation of Novikov-Priboi's *Tsusima* by delivering the text 'in an excessively emphatic, pathos-laden tone that sometimes crossed the line into shouting'.[88]

Radio productions also needed to articulate a compelling authorial voice. The simplest way to achieve this was to let the actual author do the reading, as Konstantin Finin did in a 1933 production of his own 'radio story'. In a lyrical, intimate style that was not compromised by his 'somewhat monotonous and hoarse voice', he told the story of a station manager in Central Asia who has an affair on a trip to Samarkand before experiencing a standard Soviet Damascene moment as he returns home and notices the 'spiritual growth' of his signalman, a party member who can quote Pushkin. The musical interludes—extracts from Debussy, Chaikovskii, Rakhmaninov, and others—served a clear purpose in punctuating the narrative and did not become ends in themselves.[89] Even if the author was not available to read the text, the narrative voice could ensure that a broadcast was an integrated whole. Vasilii Kachalov, for example, received praise for his role as the authorial voice in a Moscow Art Theatre production of Tolstoi's *Resurrection*: he was not the 'usual narrator who just explains' but rather an 'active participant who was continually getting involved in the action'.[90] As another critic pointed out, anyone who thought that 'epic commentary' killed the drama of a radio production should remember the chorus in ancient Greece.[91]

After all the speculation on the nature and possibilities of 'radio art', it was now clear that the main paradigms for radio were to be drawn from literature. In high Stalinism, the written word (rather than theatre or cinema) was radio's aesthetic

---

[85] P. Novitskii, 'Teatr u mikrofona', *Govorit SSSR*, no. 10 (1934): 41–4.
[86] I.S., 'Problemy radioigry', *Govorit SSSR*, no. 7 (1933): 14–15.
[87] B. Velizheva, 'Chekhovskie dni na radio', *Govorit SSSR*, no. 4 (1935): 24–5.
[88] B. Alpers, '"Tsusima": Radiomontazh po romanu Novikova-Priboia', *Govorit SSSR*, no. 6 (1934): 7. Similar criticism of over-emphatic performance—this time in radio productions of Heine and Pushkin—can be found in A. Novitskii, 'Klassicheskaia poeziia i antireligioznaia propaganda', *Govorit SSSR*, no. 9 (1934): 34.
[89] I. Sokolov, 'Semeinaia istoriia', *Govorit SSSR*, no. 2 (1933): 10–11.
[90] M. Beer, '"Voskresenie"', *Govorit SSSR*, no. 6 (1935): 7–8.
[91] N. Bireng, 'Mysli vslukh o rabote pisatelia na radio', *Govorit SSSR*, no. 7 (1935): 7.

older brother (see Figure 3.1). At least in theory, this did not mean that writers and broadcasters had forgotten their earlier admonitions about the spokenness of radio and the need to avoid turgid formulas drawn from print. This was to be a symbiotic relationship where literature stood to gain as much as radio. By conquering distance and addressing themselves instantaneously to an audience of millions, writers could transcend the limitations of the printed page; paradoxically, this new mass medium allowed them to create an apparently unmediated relationship with the audience. Emblematic in this regard was the ailing Nikolai Ostrovskii, author of the instant socialist realist classic *How the Steel Was Tempered*, who broadcast direct from his Moscow apartment in the last months of his life. Not only that, he accorded radio an important part in the self-realization of his autobiographical hero, Pavel Korchagin, who, like the author, goes blind and uses the oral medium as compensation.[92]

The aesthetic alliance with literature did mean, however, that broadcasts were in general to be decluttered of background noise and to guarantee the purity and integrity of the spoken word. Something very similar happened in sound film. Vertov's acoustic experiments were brought to an end in the 1930s, and the soundtrack of Soviet cinema became accordingly 'clean': extraneous noises were not to distract the viewer from the all-important dialogue.[93] This primacy of the word in Stalin-era culture meant that the key question for the standing of broadcasting in the Soviet cultural firmament was the relationship between radio and writers. Roza Ioffe, later acknowledged as the finest producer on Soviet children's radio, complained in 1934 that the authority of the literary editor exceeded that of the producer. As their main criterion was that the text should be written in fine-sounding language, editors often proved resistant to formal experimentation and oblivious to the need to draw in the child audience through music and play.[94]

Literary readings steadily gained prestige in 1930s broadcasting. Dmitrii Orlov was among the pioneers who demonstrated the power of this mode of performance on the radio. In 1935, he read out an adaptation by A. I. Zavalishin of Nekrasov's 'Who Lives Well in Russia'. Although Zavalishin had simplified somewhat the original, at 1 hour 30 minutes the production was still unprecedentedly long for a broadcast with a single voice. Nor did Orlov resort to pronounced rhetorical effects. The listener's first impression was even of a slightly colourless, monotonous delivery. But in time one warmed up to this soft, pleasant voice, which made every word of the text audible and meaningful.[95] The broadcast evidently made a strong

[92] On Ostrovskii and the relationship between literature and radio in the era of socialist realism, see Iurii Murashov [Jurij Murašov], 'Elektrifitsirovannoe slovo: Radio v sovetskoi literature i kul'ture 1920–30-kh godov', in Hans Günther and Sabine Hänsgen (eds.), *Sovetskaia vlast' i media* (St Petersburg, 2006), 30–2.

[93] Oksana Bulgakova, *Sovetskii slukhoglaz: Kino i ego organy chuvstv* (Moscow, 2010), 99.

[94] R. M. Ioffe, 'Komu dolzhno prinadlezhat' khudozhestvennoe rukovodstvo?', *VKD*, 731–3. In the same year, Ioffe also complained—not for the last time—about poor working conditions on the radio: ibid., 733–5.

[95] N. Goncharova, '"Komu na Rusi zhit' khorosho"', *Govorit SSSR*, no. 10 (1935): 23–5.

impression: fan mail streamed in to Orlov from listeners of various occupations in places from Irkutsk to Rostov.[96]

Radio performers could now benefit from the sacred aura attached to those works of Russian literature that were selected for Soviet canonization. To mark the centenary of the death of Aleksandr Pushkin, the single greatest emblem of the new Soviet-Russian high culture, the Radio Committee provided an extensive cycle of programmes in all the languages of the USSR and for all social and age groups.[97] So holy were Pushkin's texts by the mid-1930s that not even the author could claim authority over them. As the main radio journal explained in 1936, although Pushkin made a great impression with his reading of *Boris Godunov* in 1826, his style of declamation could hardly be recommended for the present day: it was artificial and overblown, as the cultural norms of his era dictated.[98] To get Pushkin right, it took a Soviet Stakhanovite of the spoken word. In 1936, Iurii Levitan spent several months preparing himself meticulously for a broadcast of 'The Bronze Horseman'. He concluded that there was no need to overplay the tragedy of Evgenii's unequal struggle with the elements; resignation in the face of natural forces was not in fashion in the Soviet 1930s.[99]

The classics were all well and good, but the crucial litmus test of radio's cultural worth was the extent to which it could draw in the leading figures among living writers. In early 1934, it was still not clear that this was the case. Platon Kerzhentsev, head of the All-Union Radio Committee, was troubled that radio as yet had a low status among writers—although some big names (such as Vsevolod Ivanov, Bagritskii, and Novikov-Priboi) were starting to write for radio. Nemchenko argued that writers needed to take the microphone themselves: listeners wanted to get to know them better, and there was no better way than to hear their voice. These two keynote contributions were accompanied by letters from listeners in various parts of the USSR attesting to the cultural value radio had for them and by short contributions from writers proclaiming their readiness to work for the radio.[100]

Part of the reason writers were reluctant to work for the radio is that they could earn more money elsewhere. Film scripts, in particular, were much better paid.[101] In due course, however, writers started to overcome their reservations. Literature had its broadcasting breakthrough in the mid-1930s. The children's writer Kornei Chukovskii seems to have become a fairly regular broadcaster in 1933–4, though

[96] For a sample, see RGALI, f. 2216, op. 1, d. 243. Some listeners heard Orlov's 'Komu na Rusi' several times: like many successful radio productions, it was broadcast repeatedly during the 1930s.

[97] For the decree of December 1935 that set the Pushkin agenda for the radio, see *VKD*, 92–3. For a review of the broadcasts, see 'Pushkinskie radioperedachi', *LG*, 15 August 1936, 6.

[98] B. Rutkovskaia, 'Pushkin—chtets', *Govorit SSSR*, no. 6 (1936): 21–3. For more on this question, see P. Brang, *Zvuchashchee slovo: Zametki po teorii i istorii deklamatsionnogo iskusstva v Rossii* (Moscow, 2010).

[99] Iu. B. Levitan, 'Sila stikhii' (1936), in *VKD*, 742–3.

[100] P. Kerzhentsev, 'Nash balans' and N. Nemchenko, 'Literatura i radio', both in *LG*, 11 January 1934, 3.

[101] Al. Sipin, 'Avtorskoe pravo na radio', *Govorit SSSR*, no. 4–5 (1933): 12.

Figure 3.1. An early indication of the coming symbiosis of radio and literature: Gorky in headphones.
Source: Cover *of Radioslushatel'*, no. 8 (1928)

he had to conquer his nerves before a recording.[102] In January 1934, Ivanov, Leonov, Olesha, and Kataev all made appearances at the microphone; in that month alone, more writers spoke on radio than in any single quarter of 1933.[103] Olesha was prepared to weigh in on the virtues of the new medium: 'I get incensed by those snobs who say that radio is bad, that it's impossible to listen to music on radio, and so on.'[104] Even so unlikely figure as Osip Mandel'shtam, the poet in

---

[102] K. I. Chukovskii, *Dnevnik 1930–1969* (Moscow, 1997), 77, 99, 107.
[103] Nik. Sukhanchuk, 'Litdramveshchanie na perelome', *Govorit SSSR*, no. 6 (1934): 3–5.
[104] *Radiogazeta*, no. 2 (1934).

exile, made a contribution to broadcasting through his work as literary consultant on Voronezh radio in the mid-1930s.[105]

Later in 1934, at the First Congress of Soviet Writers, writers such as Serafimovich, Shaginian, and Chukovskii queued up to expound on the virtues of radio for the writer, both for expanding the audience of literature and for giving literature new means of expression.[106] In his response to the congress, the tireless Nemchenko argued even more robustly that the radio had much to offer writers. Repeating his argument about the importance of the integral literary text for radio, he added that literature was a fine way for writers to publicize their work to a huge audience in advance of its print publication. In short, there was every reason for writers to fight for first 'publication' of their work on air instead of looking askance at the new medium.[107]

The rise and fall of the Soviet radio play did not, therefore, prevent radio gaining prestige as a medium for more conventional literary works. Many works by well-known Soviet writers—Il'f and Petrov, Leonov, Afinogenov, Paustovskii, Serafimovich, Svetlov—did indeed first reach an audience over airwaves and wire. By the mid-1940s it could be plausibly claimed that there was 'no ordinarily well-known work of Soviet literature that has not been presented, at least in part, over the Soviet radio'.[108] On occasion, the authors themselves did the reading. As one article noted, 'we did not preserve Maiakovskii's voice, but the voices of Gorky, Serafimovich and many others should sound forever'. The author's own reading was 'the best possible commentary on the work'.[109] It also had an unrivalled authenticity and immediacy. As Marietta Shaginian observed in 1934: 'we writers must learn to communicate not only in writing but also orally'.[110] Not coincidentally, the genre of 'literary reading'—a spoken performance of the written word—took off around the same time. Irakli Andronikov, subsequently the Soviet Union's best-known raconteur, made his public debut at the Moscow Writers' Club in February 1935.[111]

BROADCASTING AND SOVIET SPEECH NORMS

All the broader debates on radio's aesthetic functions counted for little if Soviet broadcasting did not have performers capable of fulfilling the designs of authors

[105] M. I. Tsukanova, 'Stanovlenie i razvitie Voronezhskogo radioveshchaniia 1925–1991 godov (na primere VGTRK)', candidate's dissertation (Voronezh, 2007), 125.

[106] 'Pisateli u mikrofona', *VKD*, 727–9.

[107] N. Nemchenko, 'Pisatel' na radio', *LG*, 10 September 1934.

[108] Alex Inkeles, *Public Opinion in Soviet Russia: A Study in Mass Persuasion* (Cambridge, Mass., 1950), 261.

[109] Itlar, 'Grammofon—aktivnyi sotrudnik radioveshchaniia', *Govorit SSSR*, no. 2 (1931). On the idea of creating a sound archive of writers reading their work, first mooted in 1930 and put into effect in 1933–4, see L. Shilov, *Golosa, zazvuchavshie vnov': Zapiski zvukoarkhivista* (Moscow, 1977), 88.

[110] P. S. Gurevich and V. N. Ruzhnikov, *Sovetskoe radioveshchanie: Stranitsy istorii* (Moscow, 1976), 139–41.

[111] I. Andronikov, *Izbrannye proizvedeniia*, 2 vols. (Moscow, 1975), i. 13.

and producers. In the USSR as elsewhere, radio announcers and actors had to learn how best to use the new medium—how to talk on air.

Especially in the early days, they largely had to teach themselves. From 1924 until the introduction of preliminary censorship in early 1927, broadcasters were largely left to find their own ways of speaking. Much was determined by the available personnel. The Soviet broadcasting corps was for the time being made up not of proletarian orators but of moonlighting actors. Before the revolution, theatre had played a crucial role in setting speech standards. Sure enough, it was actors—especially from the Moscow Arts Theatre—who dominated on the radio in the early days of Soviet broadcasting. But these stage performers often reflected on the difficulty of adapting to the microphone and on the fact that broadcasters required specific microphone training that was lacking in the Soviet Union.[112] When first presented with a microphone, they were disorientated by the paradox of broadcasting: here was a medium that could reach an audience far greater than even the most powerful orator, yet it made possible an intimate and conversational style of delivery. Even the most talented performers would flop on radio if they took no account of the specifics of the studio. Many radio performers later mentioned the trepidation they had first felt at the sight of a microphone. Osip Abdulov, for example, recalled how he had had to keep shifting his position relative to the microphone to ensure sound quality. He also was thoroughly unnerved by the experience of sitting in an empty studio; he resorted to inviting in the on-duty fire officer to give himself the impression of at least some audience.[113] The microphone had a 'hypnotic' effect and was capable of turning even well-known musicians into nervous wrecks.[114] The syndrome was implicitly recognized by an Narkompochtel decree of 4 September 1929, according to which all performers working regularly on the radio had to receive special 'radiophonic' training.[115]

Broadcasting might have been an unnerving activity in the 1920s, but it was also an exciting one. Lev Kassil' remarked on the rarefied atmosphere of the studio—the sense of being enveloped in 'invisible cotton wool' as the sound was tamed by the draped walls and carpets, the commotion as final preparations were made, and then the silence and strange solitude of the broadcast itself.[116] Quite often, however, broadcasters had the company of colleagues and a 'live' audience. Nataliia Tolstova, later on the Soviet Union's second most famous newsreader, recalled being present at the broadcast to mark the first anniversary of the *radiogazeta*. Held in the Polytechnical Museum in central Moscow, it seems to have been the top attraction in the city that night: a crowd of mainly young people gathered outside

---

[112] A Western observer made the same point in the mid-1930s, noting a 'lack of "microgenic" feeling' as a failing of Soviet broadcasting. See Kurt London, *The Seven Soviet Arts* (London, 1937), 299.

[113] 'Akter i chtets u mikrofona', *Govorit SSSR*, no. 21 (1933): 25–6. Similar was the much later account of the actor Rostislav Pliatt, who made his radio debut as an announcer in 1931: Pliatt, 'O chtenii, golosovom grime i radio', *Sovradiotel*, no. 6 (1967): 27.

[114] M. Lokhvitskii, 'Radioboiazn", *Radioslushatel'*, no. 48 (1929): 8; repr. in *VKD*, 702–3.

[115] *VKD*, 75.

[116] L. A. Kassil', 'Nikol'skaia, 3', *Radioslushatel'*, no. 13 (1928): 5; repr. in *VKD*, 691–3.

the hall in the hope of obtaining a spare ticket. By 7 p.m., the time of the broadcast, the large audience maintained absolute silence as the three contrasting presenters—one soft-spoken and mellifluous, another sober and forceful, the third sharp-witted and able to do a turn on the balalaika—began their work.[117] These men were a fine advertisement for the broadcaster's art, and their performance that night accurately reflected the extent to which broadcasters in the 1920s were obliged to be jacks-of-all-trades. Due to the loss of most of the Radioperedacha archive, we have almost no programme transcripts for Moscow radio in the early days. But the archive of the Nizhnii Novgorod radio committee, one of the more ambitious regional radio stations, which already in the late 1920s had at least a couple of hours of its own programmes every day as well as rebroadcasts from Moscow, gives us some idea of the varied output of the time. Here we find jaunty ditties to encourage listeners to pay into the workers' cooperative; public information broadcasts on job opportunities, fire safety, or the postal service; broadcasts presenting new books; and lectures on current affairs.[118]

Children's broadcasting required a particularly wide stylistic register. Some of it took exhortatory form: programmes for Young Pioneers urged listeners to get involved in the great projects of the five-year plan—for example by searching out scrap metal—and to devote themselves to their studies.[119] Other types of broadcast, however, were more playful and sought to engage their young listeners' curiosity. Nizhnii Novgorod radio had riddles and quizzes (*viktoriny*) in programmes with titles like 'Evening of sensible entertainment' and 'Get your brain moving', which, to judge by their postbag, went down well.[120] On central radio, all the leading children's authors of the time (Marshak, Chukovskii, Kassil', Gaidar) wrote for the radio from the early 1930s onwards. Children's broadcasting seems to have been more creative and interactive than anything produced for adults.[121] Critics acknowledged that children's news needed to be engaging and make effective use of the dialogue format, not least because the Western capitalist countries were already making good use of the radio for patriotic education.[122]

Yet, the question of *how* exactly radio performers should deliver the material that came their way remained unresolved. As Soviet culture entered an ever more prescriptive phase, this normlessness could not be allowed to continue indefinitely. In 1928, the leading radio journal *Radioslushatel'* posed the question: 'What is a radio announcer? A reader? An orator? An actor?'[123] The implied answer was 'All

---

[117] N. A. Tolstova, 'U istokov radioperedach'; repr. from *Vnimanie, vkliuchaiu mikrofon!*, in *VKD*, 685–7.

[118] GANO, f. 3630, op. 1, d. 1, ll. 32–3, 49–51; d. 2.

[119] See e.g. the transcripts from December 1931 of 'Klich pionera', a programme put out by the Nizhnii Novgorod branch of the Komsomol, in GANO, f. 3630, op. 1, d. 47.

[120] GANO, f. 3630, op. 1, d. 91 (for letters) and d. 164 (for transcripts).

[121] Solomianskaia, 'Za kachestvo detskogo veshchaniia!', *Govorit SSSR*, no. 14–15 (1933): 49–52. For this reviewer, in fact, children's broadcasting seems to have been a little too creative: the emphasis on dialogue and interaction sometimes obscured the narrator figure.

[122] V. Tennov, 'Informatsii stali luchshe' and B. Levina, 'Radioveshchanie dlia detei za rubezhom', *Govorit SSSR*, no. 2 (1933): 3, 7.

[123] 'Naiti, sozdat' diktorov!', *Radioslushatel'* 2 (1928): 10.

of the above'. Yet these various identities were not straightforwardly compatible. It was hard for radio speakers to attain the charismatic spontaneity of oratory, given that they read out from a text composed by someone else. Soviet broadcasters professed disdain for 'bourgeois' rhetoric—but how was this to be differentiated from Soviet oratory, if the latter was artfully scripted? Early in 1929, Commissar of Enlightenment Anatolii Lunacharskii was asked whether radio journalists should always read from a written script, or whether they should improvise. His answer: 'the best form for political commentary is probably the unmediated oratorical declaration'. But Lunacharskii went on to say that much preparatory work was required if one were to improvise at the microphone.[124]

In due course the debate on appropriate styles of radio delivery became considerably more heated. A guide published in 1932 issued a clarion call for a proletarian style of speech that would have no place for 'rhetoric', which in the author's view was synonymous with 'bourgeois' oratory.[125] In January 1932, a reviewer took radio performers to task for a false style of declamation that was wholly inappropriate for a proletarian culture. She praised one actor's performance of Bulgarian revolutionary literature for its 'genuine fervour, stern passion, complete absence of tearful sentimentality'; in the same broadcast, however, she found another performer's delivery to be 'cold' and 'monotonous', although technically accomplished. As the reviewer concluded: '75 per cent of our broadcasts are based on words, but what proportion of them fails to achieve its aims because of poor and inexpressive delivery and form that kills content?'[126] The rhetorical question was picked up in a discussion later in the year. According to the wisdom of the time, a broadcaster should be 'at a high level of political consciousness' and capable of 'breaking off from the text at any moment and conveying the content in his own vivid fashion'; he was not only a reader but a 'co-author' of the broadcast text.[127]

In November 1933, Platon Kerzhentsev, the head of the All-Union Radio Committee, weighed in on the pages of the leading radio journal. He tried to chart his own course between the Scylla of 'theatricality' and the Charybdis of 'dreariness'. The radio announcer, in his view, should find a way of being 'emotional' without resorting to staginess. Even a 'note of humour' was permissible 'in small doses', as long as it did not become 'false' and 'theatrical'. Kerzhentsev went further in this vein than any of his comrades would have dared. 'Do we perhaps make too "serious" a matter of the presenter's performance?', he asked. If a radio presenter had a slip of the tongue, he or she could briefly apologize and no harm would be done.[128]

The debate rumbled on into the mid-1930s. In 1935, the actress N. N. Litovtseva made a high-profile plea for the 'creative' mission of the radio announcer. Any text—from the rescue of Otto Schmidt and his crew to the weather forecast—

---

[124] P. S. Gurevich and V. N. Ruzhnikov, *Sovetskoe radioveshchanie: Stranitsy istorii* (Moscow, 1976), 111.

[125] V. Gofman, *Slovo oratora (ritorika i politika)* (Leningrad, 1932).

[126] N. Goncharova, ' "Mademuazel' Zhorzh" i "Kniaz' Vasilii" ', *Govorit SSSR*, no. 1 (1932).

[127] N. Goncharova, 'Kakim dolzhen byt' diktor?', *Govorit SSSR*, no. 9 (1932): 13; 'Kakim dolzhen byt' diktor?', *Govorit SSSR*, no. 14 (1932): 5.

[128] 'Diktor—tvorcheskii rabotnik', *Govorit SSSR*, no. 22 (1933): 8–10.

could be read in such a way that it achieved an emotional effect on listeners. Announcers had to 'transform' themselves as they read, to be filled with enthusiasm
whatever the subject.[129] They had to establish a relationship with the audience: as
a later article observed, in the studio the announcer was 'talking with his family, his
audience, helping it, lovingly nurturing it, raising its general political and cultural
level by the most varied means'.[130] Yet Litovtseva's manifesto did not meet with
universal assent. As one colleague observed, announcers might try to deliver their
text as effectively as possible, but they could not afford to forget even for a moment
their role as 'administrator' in ensuring continuity on air. Another expressed scepticism that a reader could pour 'love' into delivering the weather forecast.[131]

The task of a radio presenter in the 1930s was unenviable. There were so many
pitfalls to avoid: 'bourgeois' rhetoric, 'aristocratic' declamation, staginess in all
its manifestations. It was not clear how the requirement for a 'proletarian' style of
delivery could be made compatible with the rigorous high-cultural standards that
obtained in public discourse. In 1935, the main radio journal of the USSR ran an
extended feature on how leading radio performers regarded their own field of activity. They were united in their conviction that radio was no less demanding than
stage work. Precisely because the visual aspect was absent, radio actors had to work
unusually hard on their voices: there was no greater test of one's 'speech culture'
(*kul'tura rechi*) than broadcasting, and work at the microphone required an unusual
degree of concentration. As Iurii Kalganov observed, 'radio is a test of an actor's
quality'; according to Ol'ga Knipper-Chekhova, radio, like cinema, did not permit
'any falseness or forcing'.[132] V. I. Kachalov, luminary of the Moscow Arts Theatre
and well-known radio actor (and, incidentally, Iurii Levitan's mentor), reflected on
the difficulty of performing to a 'live' audience with a microphone also present in
the theatre: it was hard to avoid feeling oneself split in two between the 'live' and
virtual audiences. Conversely, studio work with a group of other actors could be
especially rewarding, as one responded first and foremost to one's colleagues
without being distracted by an audience.[133]

SOVIET RADIO IN THE 1930S: VOICING
THE SOVIET EXPERIENCE

Yet radio in the 1930s had more to offer the listener than measured 'cultured
speech' from the studio. Although the plebeian excesses of 1920s *mitingi* and
pereklichki had been reined in, Soviet broadcasters in the 1930s played a full part
in an era of socialist sensation-making. The Soviet culture industry was keeping the
population in a near permanent state of nervous excitement, as death-defying feats

---

[129] N. Litovtseva, 'Za diktora-khudozhnika, za diktora-tvortsa', *Govorit SSSR*, no. 8 (1935): 42.
[130] G. Avlov, 'Kakim dolzhen byt' diktor', *Govorit SSSR*, no. 14 (1935): 28.
[131] O. Fridenson, 'Povyshat' kul'turnyi uroven'' and A. Neznamov, 'Za ku'turu slova', both in
Govorit SSSR, no. 18 (1935): 20–1.
[132] 'Mastera radio o rabote u mikrofona', *Govorit SSSR*, no. 7 (1935): 11–12.
[133] V. I. Kachalov, 'Uvlekatel'naia rabota', *Govorit SSSR*, no. 21 (1935): 37; repr. in *VKD*, 739–40.

of exploration alternated with war scares and gruesome accounts of 'wrecking' and 'terrorism' by enemies of the people. Radio's contribution to this project was uniquely powerful: in the 1930s, only sound broadcasting could provide 'live', real-time mass media experiences. By contrast, film footage of public events, such as party congresses, still had the quality of silent film. It employed narrative voice-overs rather than synchronized sound; speakers could be seen but not heard. This was useful for making 'oppositionists' look like ineffectual gesticulators or latter-day Kerenskys—and, conversely, for making Stalin look statesmanlike. As Oksana Bulgakova has observed, the norms of oratorical gesture turned static in the 1930s after all the charismatic public speaking of the revolutionary and early Soviet period.[134]

Radio was unrivalled in its capacity to convey 'reality', to construct a sense of the unfolding Soviet present. As an exclusively aural medium, it was not bound by the requirement for visual authenticity that hampered film. It could take listeners straight to the heart of events. An early example of this audio immediacy, from October 1931, offered a vivid account of a meeting of workers, managers, and technical personnel to mark the successful reconstruction of the AMO automobile works in Moscow that was now to be named after Stalin. After a scene-setting introduction, the correspondent announced excitedly: 'Attention! Listen to the recording of the celebratory meeting of 1 October 1931. Here is a broadcast from the canteen of the AMO factory in Moscow. Attention!' The start of the footage was signalled by a brass band playing the Internationale, and then followed a speech by the factory director Likhachev (punctuated by applause). Other speakers were then introduced to listeners by the correspondent, and the broadcast finished with cries of 'Hurrah!' and more from the brass band.[135]

A year later, an even more eloquent *radioreportazh* marked the launch of the Dnepr Hydroelectric Station (Dneproges). The correspondent opened with a bold gambit:

> Soviet Union, listen up! Our radio microphone is located between two capitals. Between the pale sun of the October sky and the socialist sun of Dneproges, born of the heroic Dneprostoi. We are talking to you from the roof of the new-born hydroelec-tric station. We are talking to you from the roof of an immense Bolshevik triumph![136]

There followed musical interjections, industrial noises, and speeches by Kalinin, Ordzhonikidze, and a 'technical consultant' (who spoke through an interpreter).

In 1934, the arresting qualities of Soviet radio were raised to a new pitch of intensity. This year was marked by two spectacular events that held the attention of the Soviet public like nothing had previously done: the Cheliuskin rescue and the Kirov murder. For the rest of the decade, the themes of adventure and heroism remained ever-present in Soviet culture, and radio continued to play a

---

[134] Oksana Bulgakova, *Fabrika zhestov* (Moscow, 2005), 226–47.

[135] 'V sherengu gigantov: Radioreportazh', in *VKD*, 243–8. Note that this document is not drawn from a *mikrofonnyi material* but transcribed from a shorinophone recording in RGAFD.

[136] 'Pusk Dneprogesa: Radioreportazh' (10 October 1932), in *VKD*, 256–7.

full part in promoting them. In May 1935 came a broadcast from on board an airship. In 1937, the polar explorer E. T. Krenkel' recounted how he and his team had maintained radio contact with Moscow even when drifting on an ice floe. In August 1937, a broadcast marked the return of the aviators who had made an unbroken flight from the USSR to the USA via the North Pole. The broadcast was evidently choreographed to the last detail, but it was designed to convey immediacy by placing correspondents at three different microphones: one in central Moscow, one by the railway track along which the express train carrying the heroes hurtled back to Moscow, and one at the station where the train came to a halt.[137]

Two years later, Soviet broadcasting went one better in marking the return of Vladimir Kokkinaki and Mikhail Gordienko, who had just made the first unbroken transatlantic flight from Moscow to America. This time the reporters lay in wait for the heroes at Negoreloe, the first radio station on the Soviet side of the border. Listeners were presented with snatched interviews on the platform followed by a full 'meeting', which featured a welcome address from a representative of the border guards (who were perhaps the only rivals of aviators as the main Soviet heroes of the age) followed by impeccably Stalinist speeches from Kokkinaki and Gordienko.[138]

This occasion was characteristic of 1930s broadcasting not only in its celebration of distance-conquering feats of daring exploration; it also conveyed speed and dynamism in its own structure—by breathlessly following the train as it approached Moscow, and by switching between journalists placed at different points. As well as its real-time immediacy, radio was uniquely equipped for the tasks of Stalinist myth-making in that it helped the Soviet listener to overcome space. The audience could be launched from one end of the country to another at will—from the tunnels of the Moscow metro to the summit of the planned Palace of Soviets, from construction sites in the Urals to the house in Gori where Stalin was born.[139] A broadcast on New Year's Eve 1938 celebrated the size of the Motherland by pointing out that greeting the New Year took a whole 9 hours in the USSR: from the Far East to Moscow. Then a 'roving microphone' was sent out to find 'the Muscovite as he gets ready to celebrate the new year, however he might hide from us and wherever he might be'. Listeners were offered a number of humorous scenes: between a driver and a policeman on Pushkin Square; between the driver and his passenger, who was rushing to the grocery shop to stock up for the evening; and between the passenger and the shop assistants.[140]

---

[137] Examples from *VKD*, 310, 736–9, 747–50.

[138] 'Vstrecha na pogranichnoi stantsii Negoreloe', *VKD*, 329–33.

[139] For some of these examples, see S. P. Zlobin, 'Skazka pro moskovskoe metro', *VKD*, 301–9; Vishnevskii's account of Gori, *VKD*, 317–21; Ia. F. Popov, 'Dvorets Sovetov stroit vsia strana: Beseda', 1940 (*VKD*, 339–43). For much more on Soviet culture's preoccupation with transcending distance, see Emma Widdis, *Visions of a New Land: Soviet Film from the Revolution to the Second World War* (New Haven, 2003).

[140] RGALI, f. 3061, op. 1, d. 94, ll. 1–7.

As this last example suggests, radio's task was not just to transmit political information and to mobilize enthusiasm for the great causes of socialism; it was also designed to communicate, or indeed to instil, Soviet everydayness. In June 1937 the Radio Committee set up a new section called 'Broadcasts for Housewives', which was instructed to provide fifteen broadcasts per month, each of 55 minutes. Soviet women were thereby encouraged to look after their homes and the common spaces of their apartment blocks, and generally to embrace *kul'turnost'*.[141] Radio was also expected to play a full part in advertising the consumer plenty proclaimed in the other media, although in practice it proved difficult to make adverts engaging to the listener without making them frivolous—and without in any way suggesting that goods in the Soviet Union might sometimes be hard to obtain. Short narratives—a shop director escorting a customer around the premises—or short dialogues, with suitably cultured musical accompaniment, were the only safe options.[142]

The younger audience was of particular interest to Soviet broadcasters, as to the Soviet propaganda industry as a whole. As early as the 1920s, children had been brought to the microphone to speak on the 'Young Pioneer *Radiogazeta*': Matvei Frolov (b. 1914), later a leading light of Leningrad radio journalism, recalled the radio theatre studio being full of young 'delegates' to such broadcasts.[143] A decree of May 1934 brought youth broadcasting under closer Komsomol supervision but it also recognized that the young audience required engaging material such as songs, sketches, *pereklichki*, and satire, all with a good dose of 'revolutionary romanticism'.[144] Children's programming had a firm place in the 1930s schedule, offering a mixture of patriotic education, music, and literary works from Pushkin's fairy tales to Soviet writers such as Marshak, Chukovskii, and Barto. The form of the 'mystery concert' (*kontsert-zagadka*), where children had to guess the pieces played, was especially popular.[145]

Music was critical for radio's appeal to all age groups. Although broadcasters were much exercised by the question of how to deliver the spoken word, their audience was very often paying attention to the soundtrack, not the text: the greater part of listener feedback in the 1930s consisted of musical requests. Nonetheless, the question of how Sovietness sounded was a fraught and controversial one in the 1930s. Criticism of 'vulgar' dance music, *tsyganshchina*, and *chastushki* was never absent in Soviet discourse of the 1930s.[146] But, after it

---

[141] For the decree, see *VKD*, 97–8. For something on the programme content, and for criticism of the decision to end these broadcasts in 1940, see the transcript of a meeting of listener-activists in September 1940 in GARF, f. 6903, op. 1, d. 49, l. 4.

[142] M. Artsybashev, 'Reklama v efire: Itogi Vsesoiuznogo konkursa na luchshuiu reklamu', *Rabotnik radio*, no. 3 (1937): 11–13. More criticisms—especially of long-winded or far-fetched adverts—can be found in G. Zhilin, 'Vnimanie radioreklame', *Rabotnik radio*, no. 5 (1937): 6–10.

[143] M. Frolov, *I snova k mikrofonu vykhozhu…* (Leningrad, 1979), 10.   [144] *VKD*, 84–5.

[145] See the survey of children's programmes for 1940 in GARF, f. 6903, op. 1, d. 52, ll. 46–54. The popularity of the programmes was confirmed by the large volume of letters from children, especially in response to broadcasts with Q&A formats. See GARF, f. 6903, op. 1, d. 54, ll. 27–33.

[146] For a representative example from Nizhnii Novgorod in 1932, see GANO, f. 3630, op. 1, d. 17, ll. 41–8.

reached a peak in the puritanical phase of the first five-year plan, it abated some-what; the spread of modern popular music in urban Russia amounted to a 'Red jazz age' in the mid-1930s.[147]

Evidently, it was not an easy task to balance the various priorities of musical programming. 'Serious music', in the form of operas and symphonies, had to have its place. The fresh output of Soviet composers needed promoting. Light entertain-ment (*estrada*) was important, not least because this was what listeners wanted, but it was a heterogeneous phenomenon that included Soviet 'mass song' and jazz of various strains from mainstream to risqué. And then there was folk music and amateur performances (*khudozhestvennaia samodeiatel'nost'*).[148]

The screws were never loosened too far, however. Critics were always vigilant with regard to any signs of 'vulgarity' in music programming.[149] With the mobil-ization of Soviet society rising to a new level in 1940, broadcasters reasserted the need for rousing Soviet mass song that avoided the extremes of quaint folksiness and meretricious jazz. At an in-house meeting of 'activist' listeners in the Radio Committee in September 1940, the 'stale' repertoire of Khenkin, Utesov, and other representatives of Soviet jazz came in for criticism; yet so did the over-reliance on symphonic music and the failure to provide rousing vocal music in the morn-ings. For their part, the broadcasters were resolutely high-minded. A representative of the music department reminded the activists that 'our task is not to lower our-selves to the level of appreciation of the masses but to raise the level of the masses. I therefore think that, if the comrades say that opera is boring and hard to under-stand, they should make an effort...so as to reach the heights of understanding musical art.'[150]

As well as producing an ambient Sovietness, radio's role in the 1930s was to pro-vide a stable voice of authority and instil in the population the rituals of public life. On the one hand, this meant denunciation and rhetorical violence, as in Mikhail Kol'tsov's vicious commentary on Bukharin in the wake of the latter's show trial in March 1938. On the other hand, it meant coverage of stage-managed rituals of participation and unity—quintessentially, the election campaign of late 1937. A characteristic report covered an election meeting where young Muscovites yelled their intention to cast their votes for 'the best person of our era, our beloved father and teacher, Comrade Stalin'. By 1937, even *pereklichki*—before they were banned in October of that year—were static and ponderous. On 1 May 1937, a father in Kuibyshev was put in touch with one of his two sons serving in a tank crew in the Far East. This was the occasion for paternal pride as well as exhortations to serve the Motherland well; the fact that a third son had already died in the line of duty received only a passing mention.[151]

[147] S. Frederick Starr, *Red and Hot: The Fate of Jazz in the Soviet Union, 1917–1980* (New York, 1983), ch. 6.
[148] See the report on music broadcasting in 1940 in GARF, f. 6903, op. 1, d. 52, ll. 10–17.
[149] A. Derman, 'Muzyka po radio', *LG*, 3 January 1940, 5.
[150] GARF, f. 6903, op. 1, d. 49, ll. 3, 7, 12.
[151] Examples in this paragraph from *VKD*, 309–10, 313–16, 321–3.

The rhetoric of Stalinism required regular contributions from 'ordinary' Soviet people. Even collective farm workers were put before the microphone on occasion. In one bucolic broadcast, a shepherd on a collective farm won over one reviewer with his fluency: 'The shepherd held the text in his hands but didn't use it—it was easier for him to speak than to read, and the editor didn't insist.'[152] Any such impression of spontaneity was, however, exceptional. By 1938, the genre of 'home broadcast' (*transliatsiia iz kvartiry*) was mentioned as a cliché. The pattern was described as follows: 'The announcer declares that the microphone has been set up in the home of a worker or collective farmer. He then says that comrades have come to see the resident of the apartment in order to share their experience. The resident is asked to speak. Forgetting about his guests, he delivers a speech to the radio listeners.' Broadcasters made only token efforts to liven up proceedings: 'halfway through the announcer suddenly tells us that there's a good spread on the table. The wife of the host invites the guests to have some tea, you hear spoons clinking against glasses...and then the speeches go on.'[153] Although the need to bring more ordinary people to the microphone was constantly emphasized, the penalties for allowing people to speak in the wrong way were severe. As a consequence, the gap between official and demotic speech became a chasm. In one grotesque instance, a peasant suddenly fell silent when recalling the famine of 1933 because, as an illiterate, he was unable to read the text that had been composed for him.[154]

More reliable contributors were Soviet notables from various spheres, whose 'statements' became a regular feature of set-piece broadcasts on public holidays. The chess champion Botvinnik spoke on May Day 1934, ending with the immortal words: 'Every worker in our Motherland should be able to play chess well'; on May Day 1935, the scientist Tsiolkovskii sent a 'warm paternal greeting' from Kaluga and stated that his dream of interplanetary travel was within reach; and on Revolution Day 1935 the champion coal-hewer Aleksei Stakhanov exhorted his comrades to similarly heroic feats.[155] In 1940, for example, 'Latest News' featured contributions from as many as 300 leading Soviet people (party functionaries, Stakhanovites, Heroes of the Soviet Union, scientists, writers, and so on).[156] In general, the set-piece broadcasts on Revolution Day became more elaborate in the second half of the 1930s, and writers more often made contributions.[157]

Speeches (*vystupleniia*) from prominent political figures became somewhat more frequent in the late 1920s, and the upper party elite contained some fiery orators who spoke on radio from time to time—Ordzhonikidze and Kirov, for example.[158] As a group, however, the Bolsheviks were not especially forthcoming on radio. It was not that the Soviet leadership failed to understand the power of the voice. In March 1924, for example, Narkompros resolved to make copies of existing recordings of

---

[152] Malov, 'Pastukhi u mikrofona', *Govorit SSSR*, no. 5 (1934): 51–2.
[153] V. Sysoev, 'Vnestudiinye peredachi', *Rabotnik radio*, no. 3 (1938): 30.   [154] *RR*, 158.
[155] Examples from *VKD*, 289, 299–301.   [156] GARF, f. 6903, op. 1, d. 55, l. 16.
[157] Gurevich and Ruzhnikov, *Sovetskoe radioveshchanie*, 158.
[158] A meeting of the Moscow broadcasters in June 1929 referred to a recent increase in radio appearances by leading comrades such as Kalinin and Bukharin (this in response to instructions from the Central Committee). See TsAOPIM, f. 3, op. 11, d. 808, l. 4.

Lenin and to ensure that other prominent revolutionaries were recorded.[159] In 1931, an editorial in *Govorit SSSR* lamented that the aural legacy of leading revolutionaries was still pitifully inadequate.[160] As late as 1940, when they had plenty else to occupy them, the recording technicians of the Radio Committee spent time restoring footage of the voices of Gorky, Tolstoi, Maiakovskii, Bagritskii, Briusov, Esenin, and others.[161] Broadcasters, for their part, were well aware that contributions from leading comrades would make good radio. Back in October 1926, Radioperedacha wrote to Molotov to say that listeners would like to hear from the leaders directly.[162] On the eve of the tenth anniversary of the Revolution in 1927, A. Berdnikov of Radiopere-dacha wrote to ask Stalin to address himself to the 'audience of millions' that the Komintern station could offer him. Ideally, Stalin would come himself to the studio on Nikol'skaia, 3; or a recording could be set up in his study; or he could send written texts to be delivered by the in-house announcers.[163]

If leading Bolsheviks did not always accept such invitations, this was probably because the technology for live radio broadcasts was still fragile and the potential for taboo-breaking error too great. In 1926, for example, a listener wrote in to complain that a broadcast of Lenin's 'What Is Soviet Power?' had mistakenly gone out at high speed and in a falsetto voice.[164] Although technology had improved slightly by the 1930s, the emphasis placed on solemnity and linguistic decorum was much greater. From the Seventeenth Party Congress onwards, the heavily accented Stalin increasingly ceded his place at the microphone to Iurii Levitan, who had pioneered a mellifluous but ponderous and heavyweight style of delivery that was eminently suitable as the Soviet voice of power. Stalin could still be heard from time to time on the radio—for example in the live broadcasts from the Eighth Congress of Soviets—but he was undeniably more reticent than his counterparts in Britain and America (let alone Hitler's Germany).[165]

It seems clear that linguistic purity was more important to broadcasters and many listeners that the authenticity of hearing an author's voice. Whether it was a writer or a political leader, there was no reason for someone to be allowed to the microphone if he could not make a good job of delivering his own text. As an 'activist' listener argued at a meeting with representatives of the Radio Committee in September 1940, 'often the speech of an important state figure...is wasted because they read this material themselves without having the vocal quality. It would be better to have announcers read their speeches.' Other speakers had little patience for contemporary poets, calling instead for a return to the classics.[166] The postbag of the Radio Committee that year showed that listeners were sometimes dissatisfied with authors' performances of their own works; by contrast, actors such as Dmitrii Orlov got rave reviews.[167]

[159] *VKD*, 30.   [160] *Govorit SSSR*, no. 3 (1931): 1.
[161] GARF, f. 6903, op. 1, d. 55, l. 26.   [162] RGASPI, f. 17, op. 60, d. 804, l. 149.
[163] RGASPI, f. 17, op. 85, d. 148, l. 32.   [164] RGASPI, f. 17, op. 60, d. 804, l. 146.
[165] For the contrasting—the one underwhelmed, the other rapturous—responses to Stalin's voice of Vladimir Vernadskii and Nikolai Ustrialov, see Schlögel, *Moscow, 1937*, 225–7.
[166] GARF, f. 6903, op. 1, d. 49, ll. 4–6.   [167] GARF, f. 6903, op. 1, d. 54, l. 25.

The linguistic conservatism of the Soviet public—which surely reflected the insecurities of a society that was just parting with mass illiteracy—was palpable. Radio set the terms of public decorum, so deviations from the linguistic standard were matters for reprimand. The theatres of the capital no longer set the standard, nor was there a single Moscow pronunciation. The population was now far too heterogeneous for that. What resulted, in the words of one commentator, was 'pronunciation chaos'. The education system was directing all its attention at inculcating written norms and neglecting the spoken word. In this light it was all the more important for radio to adopt a consistent standard.[168] In full agreement, evidently, were the listeners who showered the Radio Committee with letters complaining of faulty pronunciation and rushed delivery.[169] Whether in letters to Central Radio or in public meetings, listeners regularly expressed their indignation at poor diction and incorrect stress.[170] Slang, of course, was completely off limits.[171] Announcers were also to avoid 'provincialism', which meant in the first instance errors in stress: *ulitsa Vorovskógo* (Vorovskoi Street) was a very different place, in cultural terms, from the correct *ulitsa Voróvskogo* (Vorovskii Street); Gládkov was unrecognizable as the writer Gladkóv.[172] When Iurii Levitan, soon to be the most famous voice in Soviet history, auditioned for the Komintern radio station, he fell at the last hurdle: his Vladimir accent counted against him. He was offered an administrative job as a consolation, and in due course got his chance as an announcer after attending a course at the Shchukin theatre school to cure his speech of its regionalisms.[173]

TOWARDS WAR

Whether it was underwater in the Black Sea, at an aerodrome to record interviews with heroic aviators, or with the Red Army on Polish territory in September 1939, the roving microphone was by the early 1940s a crucial part of the representational arsenal of Soviet culture.[174] It connoted speed, modernity, immediacy, and the connectedness of all parts of the vast Soviet land to the centre in Moscow. If socialist realism was a sensibility as much as an aesthetic, then radio played a leading part in the project to make the mass audience of the 1930s feel Soviet.

[168] Sergei Bernshtein, 'Problema russkogo proiznosheniia', *Govorit SSSR*, no. 1 (1936): 23–7.
[169] GARF, f. 6903, op. 1, d. 54, ll. 33–5 (survey of listeners' letters for 1940).
[170] See the evidence from letters and meetings in 1940–1 in GARF, f. 6903, op. 1, d. 49, l. 25; d. 54, ll. 33–5; d. 58, l. 91.
[171] See the negative review of a recent programme on 'How our young people talk' in Nik. Sukhanchuk, 'Zametki mimokhodom', *Govorit SSSR*, no. 6 (1934): 17–18.
[172] Popov Museum, Burliand collection, d. 13, ll. 3, 6, 29ob (stenogram of meeting in Radio Committee, 20 September 1934). For a later, very similar criticism expressed at a meeting during the war, see GARF, f. 6903, op. 1, d. 89, ll. 9–10.
[173] D. Iablonosvskaia and M. Shul'man, '*Odessa—Tel'-Aviv' i 'Radio—liubov' moia'* (Tel Aviv, 1985), 130–1. For an only slightly different version of this often-told story, see B. P. Liashenko, 'Tak proletelo sorok let…', in *Iurii Levitan: 50 let u mikrofona* (Moscow, 1987), 16–18.
[174] V. A. Goncharov, 'S mikrofonom po strane' (1940), *VKD*, 751–3.

By 1940, the millions of wired listeners in the USSR were unlikely to be more than 1 hour 30 minutes away from their next injection of Soviet news. They could catch any of twelve broadcasts of 'Latest News' over the course of the day, and a further nine bulletins with summaries from newspapers. The network of news correspondents had expanded over the year from thirty-five to seventy people, and coverage of the more remote parts of the USSR (Khabarovsk, Iakutsk, Vladivostok, Cheliabinsk, and so on) was now much better. But the roving correspondents of Soviet radio had been used to most striking effect in the West: the main news of the year was the various military campaigns to 'liberate' new territory in the zone of Eastern Europe that Germany and the USSR had carved up between them. Broadcast journalists had been on the Finnish front, in Bessarabia, Northern Bukovina, and the Baltic republics. 'Radio films' had been made with titles like 'The Triumph of the Lithuanian People'. There had been a cycle of programmes on military training. Broadcasts had also been produced in fourteen different foreign languages, with special attention paid to life in the newly incorporated Soviet republics.[175] All told, the 'defence and sport' department had produced 673 hours of broadcasting over the year. In broadcasts of 'Red Army and Red Fleet News', the letters of 'military correspondents' (along the lines of the earlier worker-peasant correspondents) had been read out—as many as fifteen per week.[176]

In many ways, then, radio, like so many other aspects of Soviet life, was fully prepared for the very different kind of war that would arrive on Soviet territory on 22 June 1941. Yet the ensuing struggle for survival presented the broadcasting system with unprecedented challenges. For many people—broadcasters and listeners alike—the war years would prove to be the most memorable in the history of Soviet radio.

[175] 'Iz otcheta redaktsii "Poslednikh izvestii"', *VKD*, 105–6; GARF, f. 6903, op. 1, d. 55, ll. 15–16, 19, 27.
[176] GARF, f. 6903, op. 1, d. 52, ll. 18–19.

4

Mobilizing Radio
The War

The Great Patriotic War of 1941–5 can be hard to accommodate in long-range narratives of Soviet history, but for broadcasting its significance has always seemed enormous. That significance is best appreciated in comparative terms. Like the early days of Soviet power twenty years earlier, these were difficult times for the press. In conditions of extreme scarcity of all resources, even the print-orientated Soviet propaganda network found producing and distributing newspapers a Herculean task. Periodicity, circulation, and column inches were reduced drastically for all but the most essential central publications, and even those were affected by wartime privations. According to one historian's calculations, in 1942 there was only one copy of *Pravda* for every 100 Soviet people on the home front, while *Izvestiia* was harder still to come by.[1] Unlike the Civil War period, however, the Soviet Union also had at its disposal a medium of long-distance mass communication that did not require paper and ink. In the devastating first two years after the German invasion, radio finally became the most important channel by which the government transmitted information and ideas to the population. With the Soviet Union fighting for its very existence, one symptom of Russia's technological backwardness—its preference for wired over wireless transmission—became a strength. Relay networks were well suited to the needs of wartime national security, given that they allowed listeners no discretion to explore the airwaves.

To judge by many memoir accounts, this was also a moment when the gap between broadcasters and audience narrowed as far as it would ever do in the Stalin era. In time of war, given the critically high stakes of current events, Soviet people were eager for any information they could obtain about the world beyond their factory, city, village, or army unit. Thanks to radio, many of them had a connection to that world even at the bleakest moments. During the Siege, Radio Leningrad famously broadcast the tick of a metronome to reassure listeners that life was continuing—not, of course, 'as normal', but at least in some form. A daily 'radio

---

[1] Karel C. Berkhoff, *Motherland in Danger: Soviet Propaganda during World War II* (Cambridge, Mass., 2012), 16–18; on measures to reduce the periodicity of newspapers, see also a letter from the head of Agitprop on 26 June 1941, in A. Ia. Livshin and I. B. Orlov (eds.), *Sovetskaia propaganda v gody Velikoi Otechestvennoi Voiny: 'Kommunikatsionnye ubezhdeniia' i mobilizatsionnye mekhanizmy* (Moscow, 2007), 101.

chronicle' started in Leningrad on 1 July 1941 and continued almost uninter-
rupted for nearly 500 days.[2] Other beleaguered sections of the population were
also provided for: from May 1942, Soviet radio had a separate department for
broadcasting to partisans and the other population of occupied territories.[3] The
closer relationship between radio and society was also a matter of style and content. During the war, a greater range of ordinary people had the opportunity to
speak on air, and stilted 1930s speech norms loosened slightly. The exigencies of
wartime forced the Soviet broadcasting administration to put aside some of the
ambivalence it felt about popular participation on the radio and recognition of
popular tastes.[4] As the renowned actor-orator Vladimir Iakhontov put it, 'Radio
was somehow especially fine, you could hear a new, wartime style of programming,
new not only in content but in the way it blended feelings and intonations.'[5]

Yet a few words of interpretative caution are also in order. The period 1941–5
is sometimes considered to be an interlude of liberation for Soviet broadcasting
(and for Soviet society as a whole) between the bacchanalia of the Terror and the
renewed repression of late Stalinism, but that is surely an overstatement. The war is
now the primary point of reference for just about everything in twentieth-century
Russian history: it is the only collective experience that people can look back on
with undiminished pride. In the case of radio, this basic historiographical orientation is greatly strengthened by a mismatch in sources. For the first two decades of
Soviet broadcasting we have very little documentation: perhaps a few hundred
pages of transcripts of broadcasts scattered thinly across several different reposi-
tories, and mere fragments of once voluminous internal correspondence between
broadcasting, state, and party agencies. For the war years the archival record is
fuller (although here too there were politically motivated purges of wartime documents, notably at the time of the Leningrad Affair in the late 1940s). Moreover,
historians have been far more active in soliciting testimony on the war experience,
while witnesses, for obvious reasons, have been much more willing to volunteer
their memories of heroic national struggle than those of the brutal internal war
fought with 'enemies of the people' in the 1930s. Radio history has benefited especially from the recent surge of publications on the Siege of Leningrad.

If we bear in mind that the war years have been so much more thickly and admiringly described than the interwar period, there are several good reasons to doubt
that they constituted such a new departure. One is that the war itself was not quite
as much of a break for Soviet people as it was for the USSR's Western allies. The
Bolsheviks had been on a war footing for practically the whole of the interwar
period: feeling themselves to be encircled by hostile powers, they expected further
large-scale conflict to erupt at any time. Radio had played a full part in the militarization of Soviet society. In the early twentieth century, the new technology of

    [2] A. Rubashkin, *Golos Leningrada* (rev. and expanded edn., St Petersburg, 2005), 18–19.
    [3] For the relevant decree of the Radio Committee, see *VKD*, 108.
    [4] James von Geldern, 'Radio Moscow: The Voice from the Center', in Richard Stites (ed.), *Culture and Entertainment in Wartime Russia* (Bloomington, Ind., 1995).
    [5] *VKD*, 768.

wireless transmission was adopted in Russia in large part for reasons of national security, and during the 1920s and (especially) the 1930s the association between radio and defence of the realm only strengthened. In early September 1939, a full Politburo resolution ordered the Ministry of Communications (Narkomsviaz') to produce within two weeks an updated plan for combating hostile foreign broadcasts; in the previous two years, new stations in Siberia and the Far East had been built with the primary purpose of jamming foreign radio.[6] In the second half of the 1930s, the formerly freewheeling *radioliubiteli* had to knuckle down and devote their skills to military preparation. Towards the end of the decade, moreover, the Soviet authorities took specific measures to improve the radio network's readiness for the coming conflict. During the Soviet–Finnish war of 1939–40, for example, steps were taken to extend the wired network of Leningrad, a city that was then, and soon would again be, critically close to the front. Broadcasting content was also subject to militarization, especially after the campaigns of conquest in the Western borderlands in 1939–40. On 22 June 1941, after the announcement that war had broken out, Leningrad radio broadcast a poem by the Baltic poet Iurii Inge, 'Our Cannons Have Begun to Speak Again'. Although it sounded as if the poem had been composed specially for the occasion, it had in fact been written several weeks earlier on the request of Leningrad radio; the author was by this time not even in the city.[7]

Not only were Soviet broadcasters already well accustomed to militaristic rhetoric, they also quickly came under the sway of the most centralized wartime propaganda apparatus anywhere in the world. The Soviet Information Bureau (Sovinformburo) was set up on 24 June 1941 with a strict monopoly on news. Headed by Aleksandr Shcherbakov, the country's premier propaganda chief, and supervised very closely by Stalin, it generated or vetted all reports, which were then channelled to the media by TASS. At the same time, a formidable censorship apparatus remained in place: in the middle of the war, Glavlit had at its disposal 700 full-time and 2,250 part-time staff members.[8]

Yet centralization on its own would not have been sufficient. The Soviet media network also required extensive resources and personnel, and these were still lacking in June 1941. For all that it had made the leap into industrial modernity, the USSR remained a poor, exhausted, and demoralized country. As meetings in the Radio Committee in the early months of 1941 made clear, these problems applied in full measure to the country's broadcasting organizations.[9] There were also profound failures of leadership and management. On 31 May, just three weeks before the German invasion, no less a figure than the head of the Radio Committee wrote to the Central Committee to express his concern that Soviet radio was likely to come off worse in any battle for hearts and minds with the fast-moving

---

[6] V. N. Khaustov, V. P. Naumov, and N. S. Plotnikova (eds.), *Lubianka. Stalin i NKVD–NKGB–GUKP 'Smersh'. 1939–mart 1946* (Moscow, 2006), 125.

[7] Rubashkin, *Golos Leningrada*, 9–10, 14.

[8] Berkhoff, *Motherland in Danger*, 13–14, 31–2.

[9] See GARF, f. 6903, op. 1, d. 58. On the technical inadequacy of the Soviet radio network in 1941, see ibid., d. 56 (correspondence between the Radio Committee and Sovnarkom).

and streamlined Nazi media system. Broadcasting officials were hampered especially by the apparent unwillingness of the higher political authorities to provide a clear direction for propaganda and by the failure of the news apparatus (primarily TASS) to serve up information fast enough for the purposes of radio.[10] Whether we speak of basic infrastructure, of professional know-how, or of management structures, we should not exaggerate the extent of Soviet broadcasters' readiness for mobilization on a different scale from anything they had prepared for in the 1930s. This war would demand of them strong nerves, inventiveness, and phenomenally hard work.

RADIO AND WAR: THE FIRST PHASE OF MOBILIZATION

The outbreak of war was a radio memory for many Soviet people. In Leningrad, the first inexplicit signal came early in the morning of 22 June 1941, just a few hours after the German invasion, when an announcement on rules of conduct during air raids went out unheralded at 6 a.m. In due course, the Leningrad station switched to Moscow radio, which broadcast 2 hours of continuous music; then, as later in the Soviet period, this was a sure sign that something was wrong. At midday, finally, Leningraders heard a short statement from Foreign Minister Viacheslav Molotov on the outbreak of war.[11] In Tver' oblast, a village lad (b. 1928) visiting his sister in the town of Vyshnii Volochok was sent straight back home to his mother. Molotov's broadcast, remembered by the man sixty years later as 'nineteen forty-one, ten o'clock in the morning', announced a time of troubles that for this informant would end only when he entered the army in the late 1940s and ate his fill for the first time in years.[12]

Molotov's contribution was followed by a less terse statement from Stalin two weeks later. Whereas Molotov had used 'citizens' as his term of address, Stalin spoke not only of 'citizens' and 'comrades', but also, in a remarkable shift from his previous rhetoric, of 'brothers and sisters' and 'my friends'. After admitting that the USSR had already lost Lithuania and significant parts of Latvia, Belorussia, and Ukraine, he permitted himself a historical excursus back to 1812 and 1918 in order to show that 'there are not and never have been unbeatable armies'. After raising only to dismiss the suggestion that the Molotov–Ribbentrop pact had been a mistake, he called for 'our people, Soviet people' to throw all their efforts into the cause.[13]

These two broadcasting events, especially Stalin's address, are important *lieux de mémoire* of twentieth-century Russia. Scenes of Soviet citizens huddling around a loudspeaker to listen to the voice from Moscow would become emblematic of

---

[10] Document published in Livshin and Orlov (eds.), *Sovetskaia propaganda v gody Velikoi Otechestvennoi voiny*, 92–5.
[11] Rubashkin, *Golos Leningrada*, 13–14; the text of Molotov's broadcast can be found in *VKD*, 345–6.
[12] Oxf/Lev V-04 PF14 (A), p. 48.   [13] Text in *VKD*, 347–52.

wartime mobilization. The writer Grigorii Baklanov, then a young man in Voronezh, recalled his excitement on hearing Molotov's 'stumbling speech'.[14] Further afield, when interviewed in her early seventies, one woman (b. 1932) recalled the start of the war as the first real event she could remember in her childhood in a village in Mordovia. The local population was brought together in the village soviet and heard the information on the radio. The solemnity of the occasion was obvious from the presence of local officialdom: 'there were all kinds of party communists as well'.[15]

As this last example suggests, Molotov's address, and many of the broadcasts that followed in the first weeks of the war, were greeted not only with patriotic resolve but also with apprehension and—from some more educated listeners—distrust. Viktor Kravchenko found himself at the time in a factory in the Western Siberian city of Kemerovo, where the broadcasts from Moscow immediately put the audience on edge: 'Work at our plant was already in full blast when it was announced that we would pause to hear an important radio address by Commissar Molotov. This procedure was unusual and sent a tremor of apprehension through the plant.'[16] In the very different social milieu of the Moscow intelligentsia, Evgeniia Gutnova, daughter of a prominent Menshevik, was caught at the dacha by the outbreak of war. She had little time for Molotov's dry and bureaucratic style.[17] Vladimir Vernadskii, world-renowned geochemist and an exceptionally outspoken observer, had no patience for Soviet propaganda in the first days after the German attack.[18] The accounts of Soviet victories on the Western front were obviously at odds with the reality that bombing raids by August were getting ever closer and more intense. As Kravchenko later wrote, 'The war communiqués in the first weeks proved so misleading, that few Russians believed them at any time thereafter.'[19]

Stalin's speech, however, was a rather different matter: this was a rhetorical gesture that broke with all previous Soviet practice. Even a sceptical and independent-minded observer could appreciate that fact. Vernadskii called Stalin's radio address 'very good and intelligent'. Kravchenko recalls the speech making a

---

[14] Grigorii Baklanov, *Zhizn', podarennaia dvazhdy* (Moscow, 1999), 32.

[15] Oxf/Lev V-04 PF1 (A), p. 10. The original reads: 'Там же были и коммунисты всякие партейные'. Evidently, this woman (who had only three years of formal schooling) did not otherwise have much to do with the Soviet Union's leading organization. For a similar example from a sovkhoz in Pskov region, see Oxf/Lev V-04 PF 25 (A), pp. 20–1 (informant b. 1926).

[16] Victor Kravchenko, *I Chose Freedom: The Personal and Political Life of a Soviet Official* (London, 1947), 353.

[17] E. V. Gutnova, *Perezhitoe* (Moscow, 2001), 192. Later on, when evacuated to Siberia, she continued to find broadcasts on the course of the war depressing—until the first convincing evidence of Soviet resistance to the invasion came with the defence of Moscow in December 1941. Ibid., 202, 213.

[18] *VKD*, 765.

[19] Kravchenko, *I Chose Freedom*, 358; Lidiia Osipova, 'Dnevnik kollaborantki', in O. V. Budnitskii (ed.), *'Svershilos'. Prishli nemtsy!': Ideinyi kollaboratsionizm v SSSR v period Velikoi Otechestvennoi voiny* (Moscow, 2012), 73. Both these observers are consistently hostile to the Soviet regime, but on this point there seems no reason not to trust their accounts. Von Geldern makes a similar point about radio coverage in the first months of the war.

stunning, if not straightforwardly positive, impression on the Kemerovo workers. As one worker quipped, 'The Boss must be in a hell of a pickle to call us brothers and sisters'. The fact remained, however, that Stalin had decisively asserted himself at this moment of vulnerability. As Alexander Werth noted in his eyewitness account of Russia in 1941, 'There could be no doubt about Stalin's authority, especially since that July 3 broadcast. He was the *khoziain*, the boss, who it was hoped knew what he was doing. Even so, people felt that things had gone badly wrong, and many were greatly surprised that Russia should have been invaded at all.'[20]

Stalin's two broadcasts to mark Revolution Day later that year were possibly an even more resonant gesture. First, on the evening of 6 November, from the safety of Maiakovskaia metro station in central Moscow, the Soviet leader delivered a speech to a meeting of the Moscow Soviet and leading government representatives. This was a trademark piece of methodical Stalinist argumentation: a partial account of Soviet losses in the first four months of war was followed by a list of reasons why blitzkrieg had failed on Soviet soil and the defeat of Germany was already inevitable.[21] It made a strong impression on the future dissident Lev Kopelev, then a soldier on the North-Western front. In recalling his tears on Stalin's death in 1953, Kopelev said he 'was crying for the Stalin I began to love on 6 November 1941'.[22] The following day, in an undoubted coup for Soviet political communication, Stalin delivered a punchier address to the soldiers ceremonially gathered on Red Square. With the Germans drawing dangerously near, it had not even been clear that the parade on 7 November would go ahead.[23] In fact, the event surpassed all expectations. For the radio audience the voice of the commentator introduced proceedings with a rousing account of the situation at the front. The Soviet armed forces then processed through Red Square: first the infantry, then the artillery, then 200 tanks. In a counterpoint to events on the ground, 300 aeroplanes flew by. The atmosphere of the occasion was intensified by drumming, march commands, hurrahs, and music. Most significant of all, and in a departure from 1930s convention, Stalin himself delivered an address that was broadcast in its entirety. According to Vadim Siniavskii, the sports reporter turned war correspondent who was presenting the event, this was a surprise even to the radio team perched in the GUM department store opposite Lenin's Mausoleum. Siniavskii had been expecting Budennyi, who greeted the parade, to come to the microphone, but in fact the speaker was a different Marshal of the Soviet Union: Stalin himself.[24] While admitting that the

---

[20] *VKD*, 766; Kravchenko, *I Chose Freedom*, 359; Alexander Werth, *Russia at War, 1941–1945* (New York, 1964), 184. On the impact of Stalin's July address, which Werth calls 'an extraordinary performance' and compares to Churchill's speech after Dunkirk, see *Russia at War*, 162–6.

[21] The text of the speech of 6 November can be found in I. V. Stalin, *Sochineniia*, ed. Robert H. McNeal, ii/15 (Stanford, Calif., 1967), 11–31.

[22] R. Orlova and L. Kopelev, *My zhili v Moskve, 1956–1980* (Ann Arbor, 1988), 16.

[23] It seems the broadcasting team had assumed the report would be pre-recorded, but they were informed at the last minute that it was going out live. See Mikhail Platov, 'Zimoi 1941-go…', in Gleizer and Potapov (eds.), *Radio v dni voiny*, 14–15, and Aleksandr Sherel', *Audiokul'tura XX veka: Istoriia, esteticheskie zakonomernosti, osobennosti vliianiia na auditoriiu: Ocherki* (Moscow, 2004), 72.

[24] Vadim Siniavskii, 'O samom pamiatnom', in Gleizer and Potapov (eds.), *Radio v dni voiny*, 54–5.

situation at the front was critical, the Soviet leader assured listeners that 'the enemy is not as strong as some scared intellectuals make out. The devil is not as terrifying as he is painted.'[25] With the life-or-death battle for Moscow imminent, the mere fact of this broadcast was a powerful statement. Now the Boss was broadcasting not from the comfort of a studio but from Red Square—at a moment when there was speculation that the entire government would turn and run east. In December 1944, with victory certain, Lev Kassil' wrote of the speech as a crucial morale-booster, thus helping to canonize it as a defining moment of harmony between ruler and ruled.[26] A few years later, the broadcast of 7 November moved to tears a fictional audience in Vasilii Azhaev's prizewinning novel *Far from Moscow*.[27] Socialist realist embellishment aside, the speech does seem to have served its purpose: back in late 1941, Vernadskii again found it to be 'intelligent'.[28]

The impact of wartime broadcasting was not limited to such set-piece occasions. The war turned the *tarelka* into the mode of listening for all Soviet people, not just most. Unlike other states, the USSR confiscated the population's wireless radio sets for the duration of the war. In Voronezh oblast, for example, implementation of this measure began within days of the outbreak of war, while the regional party organization stipulated on 11 October 1941 that wireless radio sets could only be used for collective listening in the presence of 'responsible' comrades.[29]

Now that the authorities had the radio audience's undivided attention, they set about using the medium to achieve their immediate goals. In the first instance, radio was a means of disseminating important practical information. Soon after the launch of radio for the occupied territories, partisans were instructed how to cut telephone wire and sabotage electricity cables; on the home front, listeners were advised how to extract the maximum quantity of potatoes from their allotments.[30] Interviews and memoirs support the notion that radio permeated daily life during the war. One woman, only a small child at the time, recalled even decades later the disturbing sound of sirens broadcast over the *reproduktor*.[31] With events moving so fast, current information, whatever its limitations due to censorship, was crucial, and radio was the main way to obtain it. Living without the *tarelka* meant being cut off and seems to have been perceived

[25] For the text of the broadcast, which was put together by a team from 'Poslednie izvestiia', see *VKD*, 352–60 and note on 660.

[26] Lev Kassil', 'Vsesvetnoe slovo', *LG*, 16 December 1944, p. 2.

[27] Thomas Lahusen, *How Life Writes the Book: Real Socialism and Socialist Realism in Stalin's Russia* (Ithaca, NY, 1997), 138–41. The scene was heavily rewritten after the first drafts to make it more emotive.

[28] *VKD*, 766. On the impact of the speeches of 6 and 7 November, especially the latter, see also Werth, *Russia at War*, 244–9.

[29] Kravchenko, *I Chose Freedom*, 358; Werth, *Russia at War*, 181; E. I. Golovchenko, 'Funktsionirovanie sredstv massovoi informatsii voronezhskoi oblasti v gody Velikoi Otechestvennoi Voiny', candidate's dissertation (Tambov, 2002), 15.

[30] *VKD*, 374–5; 'Sovety ogorodnikam' (16 June 1943), *VKD*, 388–9.

[31] Informant b. 1936, Oxf/Lev P-05 PF 3 (A), p. 3.

at the time as exceptional and unsatisfactory.[32] As the actor Vladimir Iakhontov noted of the war, 'You couldn't live without listening to radio. Radio informed, signaled, directed us, connected families and close friends.'[33] For the future actor Aleksei Batalov, then an adolescent, radio was a constant accompaniment to life in the spartan conditions of evacuation. It provided an emotional connection to his pre-war childhood in central Moscow, where on a quiet evening the family could hear the famous Kremlin bells that ended the daily broadcasting schedule. For Batalov's generation, the radio had an almost mystical authority: it was 'a prophet, an omnipotent master who determined and announced our fate'.[34] Nowhere was radio's role in supporting morale more significant than in starving Leningrad. As one survivor of the Siege recalled, 'the radio really was the only thread of life that connected the freezing and starving city with the outside world'. If radio fell silent in a particular district due to bomb damage, it was quickly restored. Broadcasters had reserve batteries in case of power failure so that they could continue working. According to another observer, 'Leningrad was completely gripped by radio broadcasts'. Not only did radio deliver potentially life-saving information on the direction of the next air raid, it also offered uplifting literary and musical programmes. More important than any specific content, however, was the mere fact of broadcasting: here, in Lisa Kirschenbaum's words, was a crucial reminder to Leningraders that they 'remained part of a larger human community'.[35]

Yet, although radio was allotted a leading part in the huge propaganda effort of the first months of the war, it was far from clear that it was up to the task. As before the war, the most fundamental concern was the weakness of broadcasting infrastructure. In Gorky region it was soon discovered that, of 174 relay networks run by government institutions (*vedomstva*), only 133 were actually working. Expansion and improvement of infrastructure was accompanied by restrictions on private listening. More than 7,000 new reception points were set up around the region in the second half of 1941, while more than 18,000 privately owned radio sets were taken in by the authorities. Some over-zealous local committees had reportedly confiscated radio sets that were designed for collective listening. At the same time, vigilance was heightened with regard to programme content: three

---

[32] See the recollections of a woman (b. 1937) who spent the war in an orphanage that did not have radio (until a protest drove the administration to fix matters). See Oxf/Lev SPb-02 PF 4 (A) LZV, p. 95. No doubt, further from the cities this situation was more common. The director of a children's home in Sverdlovsk oblast similarly recalled that her institution had no radio during the war. See Oxf/Lev SPb-02 PF 11 (B) BAV, p. 47.

[33] *VKD*, 768.

[34] A. V. Batalov, 'Moi vstrechi s radio', *VKD*, 787–8. It was only later, when confined to hospital for a period with nothing but radio for company, that Batalov began to perceive the creative possibilities of the medium (ibid., 788–9).

[35] Irina Lapechenkova, 'Vladimir Osinskii: "V kholode i temnote radio osveshchalo zhizn' vsemu gorodu"', 104–5, and Aleksandr Berezhnoi, 'Radio zvuchalo dlia goroda', both in T. V. Vasil'eva, V. G. Kovtun, and V. G. Osinskii (eds.), *Radio. Blokada. Leningrad: Sbornik statei i vospominanii* (St Petersburg, 2005), 104–5, 118–19; Lisa A. Kirschenbaum, *The Legacy of the Siege of Leningrad, 1941–1945: Myth, Memories, and Monuments* (Cambridge, 2006), 64.

local networks were said to have put out 'enemy programmes', and those responsible were punished 'severely'.[36]

In the major cities, conditions for broadcasters and listeners alike were becoming
perilous. Already in late summer 1941, the air raids began. Some broadcasts came
from underground, as a makeshift studio could be set up on the platform of a
metro station.[37] In Leningrad, bombing sometimes knocked out radio in certain
districts. Between September and December 1941, the city's cable network, which
extended for a total of 12,000 kilometres, was reported to have been damaged
in 1,177 separate places. The long-wave station RV-53 was put out of action
by German bombs in early September 1941. The weaker station RV-70 was
re-equipped for short-wave transmission, quickly becoming Leningrad's most reliable channel of communication to the rest of the country.[38]

The risk to the informational nerve centres of the Soviet Union was so great that
evacuation east was the only solution.[39] By November 1941, the three major
broadcasting centres in the wartime USSR—Moscow, Kuibyshev, and Sverdlovsk—were dividing responsibilities between them. The staff of youth radio, for
example, comprised five people in Kuibyshev, four in Moscow, and two in Sverdlovsk. In mid-December, regional Komsomol organizations were informed that
the Central Committee had decided on daily broadcasts in view of problems with
delivering newspapers; local Komsomol leaders were given the task of organizing
listening around *tochki* at the relevant times. No efforts were to be spared to mobilize young people for the cause: *radiomitingi* and even a *pereklichka* were planned,
and broadcasters were even instructed to make use of Red Army soldiers being
treated in Sverdlovsk hospitals.[40] Later on the Komsomol continued to rely heavily
on radio as a channel of propaganda. On 28 June 1942 its Central Committee
decreed that oblast and republican Komsomol newspapers should be liquidated
and replaced by broadcasts three times a week; in addition, youth broadcasts were
put out on city and district transmission networks.[41]

Such was the commitment to radio as a means of wartime communication
that by 1943 Soviet broadcasting capacity had even increased relative to the pre-
war era. That year saw the completion of a new, enormously powerful station in

[36] GOPANO, f. 3, op. 1, d. 2372, ll. 69–70. For a later account in a heroic vein of wartime broadcasting in the city, see V. E. Batakov and V. A. Ukhin, *Govorit gorod Gorky* (Gorky, 1978), ch. 11. For
more on the strictness of wartime controls over listeners and broadcasters alike, see V. A. Somov,
'Radio kak kommunikativnoe sredstvo formirovaniia trudovoi motivatsii v gody Velikoi Otechestvennoi voiny 1941–1945 gg. (na primere Volgo-Viatskogo regiona)', *Noveishaia istoriia Rossii*, no. 1
(2012): 133–5.

[37] For an account of one such occasion in Moscow in autumn 1941, see V. N. Iakhontov, 'Teatr
odnogo aktera', in *VKD*, 767.

[38] Rubashkin, *Golos Leningrada*, 32–3, 65–6.

[39] For a memoir of the evacuation of radio personnel to Kuibyshev in October 1941, see Dina
Iablonovskaia and Mikhail Shul'man, *Odessa—Tel'-Aviv i Radio—liubov' moia* (Tel Aviv, 1985),
152–4.

[40] RGASPI-M, f. 1, op. 32, d. 6, ll. 87–9, 95–6. As always, however, one must be wary of assuming
that all these recommendations were implemented: other documents in the file indicate how difficult
the situation was on the ground in Sverdlovsk in late 1941: see ibid., ll. 98–100.

[41] RGASPI-M, f. 1, op. 32, d. 44, ll. 4–6.

Kuibyshev (1,200 kilowatts).[42] Soviet radio's most valuable asset was also moved east. Iurii Levitan spent the first half of the war in monastic seclusion in the Urals city of Sverdlovsk, practically living above the studio where he delivered hundreds of Sovinformbiuro decrees. Careful measures were taken for his security—he had by now been declared public enemy number one by Hitler—and even his appearance was a strictly guarded secret. One listener who encountered Levitan at close quarters was surprised to see that the possessor of this mighty voice was in fact 'a small, skinny four-eyes [*ochkarik*], whose high forehead was topped by a fine head of curly dark hair'.[43]

BROADCASTING IN WARTIME CONDITIONS

The start of the war placed radio personnel under colossal strain. In Leningrad, from the very first days of the war, broadcasters queued up at meetings of their party organization to declare the importance of discipline and vigilance and the need to concentrate absolutely on the task of patriotic mobilization. As one speaker warned, there might be attempts to hijack the radio for unsanctioned purposes: local broadcasting networks, for example those based in factories, had to make sure microphones were securely guarded. As for Leningrad radio's own activities, a radical change of gear was required. In the words of artistic director Iakov Babushkin, '95 per cent of the reportoire we had before is no good any more'.[44]

After 22 June 1941 Soviet broadcasters had to react to events faster than they were accustomed. They scrambled to establish a version of events at the front that could be broadcast to the population. They brought in writers, military men, and ordinary citizens to speak on air. They broadcast accounts of public meetings to mobilize patriotic sentiment. They also undertook to provide authentic footage: within two or three days of the German invasion, the first radio correspondents set off for the front line.[45] Broadcasters also had to do more with fewer resources. As one of several rationalization measures, the department of children's broadcasting was liquidated in late July 1941; for the next three years or so, children would be treated above all as patriotic subjects.[46]

At the same time, broadcasters had to bear in mind more than ever the requirements of ideology and state security. No doubt many of them needed little

---

[42] Sherel', *Audiokul'tura XX veka*, 71.

[43] Alla Zubova, *Znamenitosti v domashnem inter'ere* (Moscow, 2001), 12. For a somewhat over-wrought account of Levitan's wartime working conditions, see Ella Taranova, *Levitan: Golos Stalina* (St Petersburg, 2010), 8.

[44] TsGAIPD SPb, f. 755, op. 1, d. 1, l. 2 (transcript of party meeting on 28 June 1941). One of the earliest victims of anti-Semitic purging, Babushkin was fired from his job in April 1943 and died at the front later that year. See Rubashkin, *Golos Leningrada*, 195.

[45] N. M. Potapov, 'V pervyi den'', in Gleizer and Potapov (eds.), *Radio v dni voiny*, 9–13. Vadim Siniavskii happened to be in Kiev on Saturday 21 June to report on the opening of a new stadium. Soon after, he was converted from sports correspondent to war correspondent: Siniavskii, 'O samom pamiatnom', 53–4.

[46] Decree in *VKD*, 107. For a sample of the edifying material directed at children and young people during the war, see A. A. Ignat'ev's talks on military history (delivered in Kuibyshev from 1941 onwards), in RGALI, f. 1403, op. 1, d. 125.

encouragement to engage in patriotic self-censorship. Vasilii Ardamatskii, a reporter on Latvian radio, was caught in Riga at the outbreak of war. Consumed by journalistic curiosity, he made an attempt to drive west to get closer to the front line, but was soon forced by the mayhem on the road to return to Riga. In July 1941 he arrived in Moscow to work in news broadcasting. Overwhelmed by the magnitude of the Soviet retreat, Ardamatskii made some effort to convey this to a senior colleague but was firmly rebuffed. The subject of chaotic evacuation, he was given to understand, was of no interest. His boss on Leningrad radio, where he was transferred in August, made the same point at their first meeting: Soviet radio needed fresh first-hand material, but not on depressing subjects like the forced retreat. Ardamatskii soon got the idea and became a distinguished wartime correspondent.[47]

Yet, of course, the wartime regime was never likely to trust the instincts of broadcasting personnel. Political supervision of broadcasting remained stifling, and at least some observers resented the rigid patriotism demanded of them in all their radio work.[48] Even a luminary such as the writer A. N. Tolstoi was forced to stick rigidly to the text authorized for broadcast.[49] The authorities kept a very watchful eye over programme content. In August 1941, the wartime head of the Radio Committee, D. A. Polikarpov, decreed that he would personally sign off on all texts of news broadcasts.[50] The department of radio censorship monitored Soviet broadcasts in more than twenty different languages. Its routine tasks were to correct translation errors and to ensure that broadcasts did not betray military secrets such as the location of evacuated factories. But it also made more discretionary political interventions to remove from the schedule literary broadcasts that were 'sloppy', 'vulgar', or simply 'written at a low level'.[51] Radio did not stop misinforming the population when the war started. Internal Leningrad broadcasting was if anything the exception: in a starving city, it was impossible even for the Soviet propaganda machine to pretend that all was well. As the Leningrad poet and broadcaster Ol'ga Berggol'ts discovered on a visit to the Soviet capital in March–April 1942, things were very different in the information hub of Moscow. Quite simply she found it 'impossible to tell the truth about Leningrad'. The main block was Polikarpov, who stuck to the fiction that the stricken city did not need emergency supplies. The Soviet authorities were continuing to lie, and Berggol'ts saw no prospect of this changing even after the war.[52]

Broadcasters knew all the while that they ran the risk of undermining morale or state security if they erred in content or delivery. If anything, the war added to the

[47] Vasilii Ardamatskii, 'Zametki o rabote na voine', in Gleizer and Potapov (eds.), *Radio v dni voiny*, 31–5.

[48] See the unpublished poem by Nikolai Aseev, 'Radiosvodki "Na fronte—bez peremen"', and the editor's extended note on scepticism among the literary intelligentsia, in *VKD*, 779–80, 961–2.

[49] Evstigneev, 'Pozyvnye muzhestva', 25–6. This story relates to February 1943: Tolstoi was irate to discover in the studio that his final paragraph had been rewritten and had to be talked round into going through with the broadcast.

[50] Decree in *VKD*, 107.

[51] See reports on the department's activities in 1941 and 1942 in Livshin and Orlov (eds.), *Sovetskaia propaganda v gody Velikoi Otechestvennoi voiny*, 176–9, 182–5, quotations at 183.

[52] Ol'ga Berggol'ts, 'Iz dnevnikov 1939-1942 godov', in *Olia: Zapretnyi dnevnik* (St Petersburg, 2010), 83, 89, 92–3.

pressure on radio announcers: any slips were likely to be considered treasonous, while the volume of work only increased. One Komi announcer, who had trained as an actor before the war and started work on the radio in the summer of 1941, recalls having to think on her feet and correct errors in printed texts as she read them out. There was, moreover, a good deal of material to get through: quite often the local papers were read out on air from cover to cover. Studio conditions were woeful. Music was broadcast by placing a gramophone next to the microphone; the broadcaster had to announce the piece and then run round to put the record on.[53] Even in Gorky, the available wax records only played for 2–3 minutes, so studio technicians had to transfer swiftly between left- and right-hand player on the turntable so as to provide a continuous flow. Studio temperatures went as high as 40 degrees, and air raids were routine. In these conditions broadcasters had to make sure they got things right: their sense of responsibility when handling Sovinformbiuro material was immense.[54]

Besides the simple avoidance of error, broadcasters also had a more positive mission to inform and inspire. The importance of radio in conveying real-time information was only heightened by the dramatic and shocking events of summer and autumn 1941. The debates of the 1930s on whether radio constituted an 'art' were put to one side. Given the need for immediacy and rapid response to events, not to mention the strain on the printing industry and the distribution network, radio offered the best chance of getting through to a mass audience. Writers were in high demand on radio, and set aside any indifference they might previously have felt towards the medium. In the first half of 1942 more than 500 works by Soviet authors were performed in more than 1,000 separate broadcasts. The hundreds of letters received daily were eloquent testimony to their impact.[55] As even the author admitted, Aleksandr Tvardovskii's *Vasilii Terkin* would never have become quite so popular if it had relied purely on instalment publication in *Krasnoarmeiskaia pravda*: it was Dmitrii Orlov's radio performance that turned this poem into the best-loved piece of Soviet wartime literature.[56]

In fact writers were even more closely involved in the day-to-day operations of radio than the bare figures suggest. During the war years some of them would spend as much of their time talking as they did writing. In the process, they acquired a literal as well as a metaphorical 'voice' for the Soviet listener. The two rhetorical extremes were represented by the two Leningraders Ol'ga Berggol'ts and Vsevolod Vishnevskii. Vishnevskii was a writer, front-line correspondent, and Civil War veteran. He was also the archetypal fiery orator, with long experience of military broadcasting, who was recalled as possessing a hypnotic power over radio listeners,

[53] Kira Moiseeva, 'Eto bylo nedavno—eto bylo davno', in *Radio: Vremia i liudi*, 27, 29.

[54] Interview with Iraida Fedorovna Sukhonina, Nizhnii Novgorod, 19 April 2006. Sukhonina started working on the radio as a technician at the age of 19 in March 1942.

[55] 'O literaturnykh peredachakh', *Literatura i iskusstvo*, 1 August 1942, 4. On the close involvement of Leningrad writers in the city's broadcasting, see Rubashkin, *Golos Leningrada*, 17–19.

[56] A. T. Tvardovskii, ' "Vasilii Terkin" Dmitriia Orlova', *VKD*, 769–71. This is reprinted from Iu. S. Kalashnikova, *Dmitrii Nikolaevich Orlov* (Moscow, 1962), which contains much further information on the actor.

a 'Baltic elan and selfless commitment'.[57] The galvanizing directness of his wartime addresses—which seem to have contained a large element of improvisation—is preserved in a few recordings.[58] Berggol'ts started her wartime career on Leningrad radio with satirical feuilletons but soon moved on to poetry. It might be a stretch to speak of a Bolshevik 'fireside' style of delivery, but Berggol'ts's style certainly became more intimate and conversational after the first few months of the war. As Berggol'ts herself wrote, 'art rose to the position of an unprecedented tribune for the whole city, and not just to hold meetings, conduct agitation, rouse people to action—in addition it was simply talking to its fellow citizens—talking quietly, in a real sense "heart to heart"'.[59]

The need for rapid response combined with the mobilization of the Soviet literary intelligentsia meant that broadcasters quickly became more fluid and inventive in their approach to genre. A strong authorial voice was now legitimate, and some radio performers had new licence to editorialize. The outstanding exponent of the Soviet version of the commentary genre (*ocherk*) was Il'ia Ehrenburg, who produced a long series of biting texts for broadcast (many of which he read out himself). With their short sentences, rhythmical repetition, and blend of passion and sarcasm, these pieces struck a new rhetorical note for Soviet radio. For Ehrenburg, writing in December 1941, the Germans were 'the Bosh', and he spared no scorn in addressing his former adopted home of France:

> The surrender-mongers handed the Bosh Alsace and Lotharingia. They said they wanted this way to save Champagne and Burgundy, but Reims and Dijon have become German garrisons. You can't save your leg by cutting off your arm, and you can't save your arm by handing over your leg.[60]

Another radio genre in which writers operated during the war was quasi-reportage. Viktor Shklovskii, who back in 1930 had written about the distinctive language required for radio, now had the chance to put his ideas into practice. In his 'Front-line notebook', he offered short, punchy vignettes of everyday heroism or German atrocity.[61] Other broadcasts were less reports than carefully formed short

---

[57] O. Berggol'ts, *'Govorit Leningrad'* (Leningrad, 1946), 8–9.

[58] For example a speech to Leningrad youth at a meeting on 14 September 1941, RGAFD, call number 2355, where powerful evocation of the threat from Nazi Germany was combined with moral pressure: until now, Soviet youth had had it easy, enjoying all the fruits of the Revolution; now it was time for them to repay their debt to Soviet society. Unusually for the time, this speech was released as a gramophone record after being recorded on tape: Rubashkin, *Golos Leningrada*, 132. On Vishnevskii's predilection for departing from the text, see ibid., 127, and Platov, 'Zimoi 1941-go...', 21. Vishnevskii was also the author of a strikingly personal and expressive voice-over for a 1942 documentary on the Blockade (though this was later overwritten by Moscow's plenipotentiary, Roman Karmen). See Jeremy Hicks, 'Challenging the Voice of God in World War II-Era Soviet Documentaries', in Lilya Kaganovsky and Masha Salazkina (eds.), *Sound, Speech, Music in Soviet and Post-Soviet Cinema* (Bloomington, Ind., 2014), 131–8.

[59] Berggol'ts, *'Govorit Leningrad'*, 8. For more on Berggol'ts's career, including the war, see Katharine Hodgson, *Voicing the Soviet Experience: The Poetry of Ol'ga Berggol'ts* (Oxford, 2003). On her wartime broadcasting exploits, see Rubashkin, *Golos Leningrada*, 114–26.

[60] 'Slushai, Parizh!' (7 December 1941), *VKD*, 364. This broadcast was read out by Erenburg himself. Example from 1942: *VKD*, 382–4.

[61] Shklovskii, 'Iz frontovogo bloknota' (19 April 1943), *VKD*, 386–8.

stories, and on occasion they might be intimate and even whimsical. Lev Kassil', a regular performer on radio since the 1930s, constructed a touching short narrative around an encounter outside the studio building with a woman wanting to hand over a letter to the front on behalf of a friend.[62] By 1944 writers were extremely well established on radio. A new format, 'From the notebook of a Soviet writer', offered first-person responses to current events, fuller and more thoughtful than the normal newspaper *ocherk*. Listeners could now look back on a long list of successful radio productions, and literary broadcasting had its proven masters of the microphone (Abdulov, Zuravlev, Shvarts, Iakhontov, Orlov, Kachalov, and so on).[63]

Radio was tugging harder on listeners' heartstrings than before. One radio play on a soldier's escape from German capitivity was introduced by the sound of a lullaby and his mother's sobbing, then replaced by rapture as she received a long-awaited letter from her son with an account of his experiences.[64] Although resolute patriotism remained the dominant tone of Soviet broadcasting, the regime was trusting the population with bad news to an unprecedented degree, and broadcasters accordingly had new opportunities to acknowledge the suffering of Soviet people.[65] As the future broadcaster Lev Markhasev (b. 1929) recalled of wartime Leningrad, it was now even acceptable to cry on air.[66] Gender may also have played a part in making emotional delivery legitimate. If the ideal speaker of the 1930s had been the stern Bolshevik male, during the war 'women's' speech could also be authentically patriotic—for example in the 'letters to the front' that fused the domestic with the public. Thus, the feminization of national symbolism—notably through the figure of *Rodina-mat'*—may have had an aural corollary. The newsreader Ol'ga Vysotskaia confirmed the point in a later memoir: 'there were broadcasts where we women found it particularly difficult to maintain our poise and avoid impermissible weakness. I often had to pause to swallow a lump in my throat or hold back the tears.' It is hard to imagine a similar admission from Iurii Levitan.[67]

Wartime radio could also offer the immediacy of genuine front-line reporting. After the successful defence of Moscow in the winter of 1941–2, the Radio Committee dispatched several mobile groups of correspondents and sound technicians to locations on the front line. Especially when they made the transition from the cumbersome *shorinofon* to the more reliable Presto machine, radio correspondents set about creating an aural documentary record of the war.[68] Broadcasts from the Western front in the first year of the war were sometimes able to convey the experience of battle with the sound of artillery fire and shouted commands; there were

---

[62] L. A. Kassil', 'Deviat' minut: Radiorasskaz' (15 March 1942), in *VKD*, 366–9.

[63] V. Ardamatskii, 'Literatura po radio', *LG*, 16 December 1944, 2.

[64] A. Glebov, 'Russkoe serdtse: Radiop'esa' (1944), *VKD*, 399–404.

[65] This is also the general thrust of von Geldern, 'Radio Moscow'.

[66] Lev Markhasev, *Belki v kolese: Zapiski iz Doma radio* (St Petersburg, 2004), 50.

[67] Ol'ga Vysotskaia, 'Nezabyvaemoe', in Gleizer and Potapov (eds.), *Radio v dni voiny*, 186. For Levitan's parallel account, which is couched in the terms of Bolshevik resoluteness, see ibid. 177–85.

[68] For the account of a wartime sound technician, see Aleksei Spasskii, 'Po dorogam voiny: Zapisi frontovogo zvukooperatora', in Gleizer and Potapov (eds.), *Radio v dni voiny*, 165–73.

also snatched interviews with commanders. The linking narrative was provided by the correspondent.[69] The Leningrad Radio Committee received its first German tape recorder as early as August 1941, though the equipment could not be put to use until 1942 because of a lack of magnetic tape. Whether with shorinophone or with *magnitofon*, reporters would venture out to the front line around the city, sometimes quite literally dodging bullets on their way to collect footage.[70] Elsewhere the work of a war correspondent could be just as dangerous. In March 1942, Vadim Siniavskii was seriously wounded while recording a report from Sevastopol under siege, while his sound technician was killed. Later on, Siniavskii would return to the fray in Stalingrad, where every 3 hours he sent Moscow the latest news on the fighting from a mobile transmitter. On 31 January 1943 he witnessed the capitulation of General Paulus, then transmitting the news to Moscow and the wider world. Even then, Siniavskii's war was far from over: he would go on to report from the Battle of Kursk and the Ukrainian front.[71]

Yet, for all the feats of Soviet front-line reporting, it was the incessant stream of Sovinformbiuro bulletins that provided most people's guide to the course of the war. These texts were read out on air in their hundreds by the Radio Committee's team of announcers. By now, this occupation was a good deal more professionalized than in the uncertain early days of the 1930s. Early in 1941, for example, a commission was assembled to assess the performance of radio announcers. Ratings were to be given for several different categories: news broadcasts, lectures, newspaper articles, continuity announcements for concerts and literary programmes, and musical programmes. E. A. Iuzvitskaia was employed through the war as a coach for radio performers.[72] The well-known actor Vladimir Iakhontov became an 'unofficial mentor' to the group of announcers as well as bearing a heavy workload himself at the microphone; on 24 June 1945, he would be among those entrusted with the report on the victory parade from Red Square.[73]

It was Levitan, of course, who became the voice of the Soviet war. His slow, momentous style of delivery proved admirably well suited to the crucial government announcements that were entrusted to him. Yet Levitan's vocal authority did not necessarily provide a winning formula for others. Some newsreaders, in fact, were thought to strive too hard for a solemn tone. When they tried to imitate their famous colleague, the results were more often pompous than inspiring. A declamatory, theatrical style of delivery was hardly the most effective way of reading out telegrams. One wartime announcer was accused of 'literally screaming' his broadcasts to the front line.[74] By now, broadcasters and listeners alike were well aware of

---

[69] 'Govorit Zapadnyi front' (25 March 1942), *VKD*, 369–74. This particular report was the work of Iurii Ardi, one of the Soviet Union's most renowned war correspondents.

[70] Rubashkin, *Golos Leningrada*, 91–8.

[71] V. S. Siniavskii, 'O samom pamiatnom', *VKD*, 761–4.

[72] RGALI, f. 1958, op. 1, d. 133, ll. 18, 25, 28, 30.

[73] N. A. Krymova, *Vladimir Iakhontov* (Moscow, 1978), 297, 313. Less than a month later, Iakhontov would be dead: having suffered from depression for years, he threw himself out of a window on 16 July 1945.

[74] GARF, f. 6903, op. 1, d. 90, l. 36 (meeting of August 1944); d. 89, l. 16 is similar.

the radio's most powerful distinguishing feature: this medium could at one and the same time be both a 'mass orator' and 'the most intimate of companions'. As one observer noted, 'no theatre can to that extent be both for everyone and at the same time just for a single person'.[75] Wartime radio's quest for a collectivist form of intimacy forms the main subject of the next section.

WARTIME RADIO AND THE POPULAR VOICE

Wartime editorial meetings in the Radio Committee contained many of the same complaints about bureaucratic language that we find in the 1930s. In combination with zealous criticism of any lapses in *kul'tura rechi* on air, these suggest that turgid political correctness remained the order of the day.[76] Yet something did change in broadcasting culture during the war. Never before had the question of popular participation in the Soviet media been so acute. Partly, no doubt, this was a matter of reviving 1930s forms of criticism, self-criticism, and exclusion from the collective. In 1943, two-thirds of the 3,223 people who had quit work at the Stalin Aircraft Factory in Kuibyshev faced criminal prosecution as 'deserters', and their show trials were broadcast to the whole factory.[77] The familiar mobilizatory genre of *radiomiting* was much in evidence, and the *pereklichka* made a comeback.[78] There was also no shortage of the familiar ritual promises by workers to fulfil and overfulfil production norms.[79]

But broadcasters were nonetheless striving to make radio sound more human: *of* the people as well as *for* the people. The war placed a renewed premium on broadcasting a plausibly popular voice. In the archives we find interviews that are more direct and engaging than the staged *vystupleniia* of the 1930s. In August 1942, for example, a Red Army cook was recorded describing—in language with traces of non-standard speech—how he killed several Germans in hand-to-hand combat.[80] Fictional speakers might also show a folksy turn of phrase. One of the more popular characters in Red Army broadcasts was Foma Smyslov, a Russian everyman who peppered his speech with popular sayings and colloquialisms, while remaining impeccably vigilant and patriotic.[81]

---

[75] V. Ermilov, 'Radio i literatura', *Literatura i iskusstvo*, 23 February 1943, 3.

[76] See e.g. GARF, f. 6903, op. 1, d. 89, ll. 8–10 (meeting of 27 July 1944).

[77] A. V. Zakharchenko, 'Sotsial'no-bytovoi aspekt zhizni rabochikh aviatsionnykh zavodov povolzh'ia v gody Velikoi Otechestvennoi Voiny', *Otechestvennaia istoriia*, no. 2 (2005): 83.

[78] For example 'Antifashistskii miting rabotnikov iskusstva i literatury' (29 November 1942), which was chaired by A. N. Tolstoi and included speeches by Dmitrii Shostakovich and the actor Nikolai Cherkasov: *VKD*, 378–82. On *mitingi* in Leningrad, see Rubashkin, *Golos Leningrada*, 60–2. For references to *pereklichki* in Komsomol broadcasting, see RGASPI-M, f. 1, op. 32, d. 6, ll. 92, 96; d. 129, l. 1.

[79] 'Stakhanovtsy—frontu' (25 August 1943), *VKD*, 389; D. M. Garmash, 'Chem i kak ia pomogaiu frontu' (13 March 1945), *VKD*, 431–2.

[80] *VKD*, 376.

[81] S. I. Kirsanov, 'Zavetnoe slovo Fomy Smyslova: Radiofel'eton' (13 January 1943), *VKD*, 384–6. This particular text was on the need for Soviet soldiers to keep up their guard in the face of German propaganda. The broadcasts went out once a month, and the role of Smyslov was taken by A. S. Kiselev, a well-known performer of folk tales. See Georgii Evstigneev, 'Pozyvnye muzhestva', in Gleizer and Potapov (eds.), *Radio v dni voiny*, 26.

Non-fiction, however, provided the most compelling broadcasting experiences of the war years. The Nazi invasion immediately induced mobilization on the radio, as ordinary Leningraders were brought to the microphone in Leningrad to express their outrage at Hitler's aggression and their determination to help the war effort in whatever way they could. Many walks of life were represented: workers, women, students, academics, old and young.[82] The first 'statements' from ordinary Leningraders went out on air within hours of the announcement of the war. One of the speakers was a certain Nadezhda Bespalova, who was instructed by the party committee to say her piece in such a way that 'people won't cry when seeing off their fathers, husbands and brothers to the front'. As early as 23 June, Lazar' Magrachev, Leningrad's most enterprising radio correspondent, had a microphone turned on at a recruiting station. A little later, he gathered people together to answer the question 'What is each one of you doing for the front in these terrible days?' Magrachev kept up his output through the Siege and beyond. In one sample broadcast, of 26 December 1943, he reported on the award of medals to a group of children for their role in the defence of the city, he visited Vera Inber and got her to read out her poetry, and he recorded the balalaika player Boris Troianovskii.[83]

Nor were all speakers as self-controlled as Nadezhda Bespalova. Ol'ga Berggol'ts recalled how on 19 September 1941 a woman stormed into the studio to tell how her two children had been killed an hour before in a bombing raid: 'the whole of Leningrad ... listened to a mother's account of how her son and daughter perished on Stremiannaia Street, they listened to her breathing, the breathing of pure grief, pure courage, and they remembered all this'.[84] Whether they were bloodthirsty and vengeful or family-centred and intimate, individual contributions of this kind brought to wartime radio a more authentic and less doctrinaire popular voice than had been possible in the 1930s. For the first time ever, ordinary Soviet people were permitted to go on air to let their husbands and sons know that their children were safe at the dacha or the Young Pioneers camp, or simply that all was well at home.[85] On Leningrad radio, 20,000 letters to and from the front had been broadcast by the end of 1942. In May 1943 it was reported that more than 3,000 soldiers from the Leningrad front had spoken on radio over the twenty months of the war to that point.[86] At the All-Union level, the Radio Committee started receiving thousands of letters from early July 1941, mainly from the families of men at the front. As well as their boost to morale, these broadcast brought practical results: by the spring of 1944, 'Letters to and from the Front' was reckoned to have helped more than 23,000 families to find each other again after wartime displacement.[87]

[82] TsGALI SPb, f. 293, op. 2, d. 99 (the texts of broadcasts in the very first days of the war, 22–5 June 1941).

[83] Lev Magrachev, *Golosa zhizni: Iz zapisnoi knizhki radiozhurnalista* (Leningrad, 1962), 5, 15; Magrachev, *Siuzhety, sochinennye zhizn'iu* (Moscow, 1972), 9; 'Leningrad v dekabre: Dokumental'naia radiokompozitsiia', *VKD*, 389–92.

[84] Berggol'ts, '*Govorit Leningrad*', 8.

[85] For a sample from mid-July 1941, see TsGALI SPb, f. 293, op. 2, d. 147.

[86] Valentin Kovtun, ' "Govorit Leningrad! Govorit gorod Lenina!" ', in Vasil'eva et al. (eds.), *Radio. Blokada. Leningrad*, 6; TsGALI SPb, f. 293, op. 2, d. 346, l. 2.

[87] GARF, f. 6903, op. 1, d. 87, l. 10.

Yet it took Soviet broadcasters some time to decide how best to make use of this material. To begin with, the military section was in charge of organizing the resulting broadcasts, but it did so in an unimaginative way: by simply reading out long lists of names. In August 1941, by order of the Central Committee, a separate department for 'Letters to and from the Front' was set up with the mission of making more of this genre of broadcast correspondence.[88] A report of July–August 1942 found that the letters format was proving successful in many ways. On average, the Radio Committee received 30,000 letters per month, and in some months the figure went as high as 60,000–70,000. This was enough to sustain ten daily broadcasts (six 'to the front' and four 'from the front') amounting to 2 hours 30 minutes, which evidently had a large and appreciative audience. But editors often managed to spoil these eminently individual documents, peppering them with 'newspaper formulations' and political clichés or not taking enough trouble over style and expression.[89]

As so often, there was a tension between these two criticisms: on the one hand, broadcasts were to transmit the authentic voice of the people, on the other hand this voice was not allowed to violate Stalinist norms of cultural and political propriety. To judge by the transcript of a later meeting, by January 1943 Soviet broadcasters were no closer to a resolution. As one speaker noted, most letters were alike in their personal preoccupations: 'What can we do, if every husband writing to his wife absolutely must give her a kiss?' The editors in the letters department were very clumsy in the ways they found to inject politics into these documents: 'People are telling their family news, but the editor has to shove a political slogan right in the middle.' The main task of the department was to make letters for broadcast more varied and authentic-sounding, and to increase the number of letters that were read out by their authors, whether at home or on the front line.[90]

As the director of the department, Kabluchko, later admitted, the 'epistolary genre' was a difficult one for her and her staff, given that their experience was primarily with newspapers. Two questions were especially challenging. First, to what extent should editors be bound by the original texts of the letters, or what degree of rewriting was legitimate? Second, how to balance the need to present an authentic 'popular' voice with the political demands of the moment? Enemy propaganda, of course, alleged that these letters were rewritten wholesale to make them more 'political'. Defending herself against such suspicions, Kabluchko argued that the reverse was true. In the first few months of the department's activities, it had broadcast letters without significant rewriting. But the problem was that the letters were themselves written in the idiom of crude agitation. At this point, towards the end of 1941, the editors started removing 'commonplaces' from the letters, and

---

[88] See the account by the head of the department in May 1944 in GARF, f. 6903, op. 1, d. 87, ll. 1–2.

[89] GARF, f. 6903, op. 1, d. 70, ll. 5–7. The conclusions of the commission, which called for improvements in editorial work so as to preserve the 'individuality' of the letters, can be found in *VKD*, 108–9.

[90] GARF, f. 6903, op. 1, d. 62, ll. 80ob–81.

they also brought in a group of writers to 'make the letters literary'. This phase, which lasted until the middle of 1942, also brought undesirable results: after the writers had done their work, it was very difficult to make the letters sound 'straight-forward, human and convincing'. The basic problem, however, lay in the letters themselves: 'There is the view that we homogenize them. That's not true. The letters come to us homogenized. People all write about the same thing: they all want victory over the enemy.' There was a well-established genre of wives' letter that the editors dubbed 'Vadik has started at kindergarten' (*Vadik khodit v detskii sadik*). Letters from the front all contained accounts of military encounters along with requests for family news and greetings. In order to ensure some degree of variety, editors had to sift through the postbag and extract the 10 per cent that could make good radio; typically, they would read 200–300 letters in order to make one 10-minute broadcast. Even then, a good deal of stylistic editing might be required: broadcasters could not allow Red Army commanders to sound 'uneducated', and all kinds of writers sprinkled their letters with clichés from the newspapers or phrase-mongering. Sometimes, soldiers were inclined to exaggerate their own military exploits. The editors tried to leave in some 'rough edges' in letters, but they sometimes received criticism for doing so. Yet another problem, noted by Kab-luchko's deputy M. S. Gleizer, was that many letters were terse and inexpressive, because listeners imagined that shorter letters had a better chance of being read out on air. As another colleague observed, editors' efforts to 'beautify' letters were often appreciated by the authors, many of whom wrote in afterwards to thank the editors for their literary 'reworking'.[91]

A perusal of material in the archive of the Radio Committee suggests that these observations were not entirely without foundation. Letters from 1941–2 seem largely to be couched in the same resolute and heroic terms. Evidently, many authors considered these to be public at least as much as personal statements. In August 1941, two parents addressed their three sons as follows: 'Despite our advanced years we are completing two or three [work] norms. Our parental directive to you is selflessly, not sparing your strength or your blood, to strike the enemy until victory is complete.' Another father permitted himself a historical excursus as he wrote to his two sons: 'Fascism wants to restore the old regime, but that is not going to happen. I have myself have felt the full burden and shouldered the revolutions of 1905 and 1917. I fought to bring about freedom and will now defend it.' In the bleak winter of 1941–2, letters seem to have been largely short and factual, with a sprinkling of clichés about crushing the 'fascist scum'.[92]

In May 1944, however, Kabluchko's account was not accepted by broadcasting colleagues who had been surveying the output of the letters department. These internal reviewers were appalled by the liberties that editors had been taking with the original texts. This was a matter partly of simply inventing details, partly of

[91] GARF, f. 6903, op. 1, d. 87, ll. 1–12, 37, 55.
[92] GARF, f. 6903, op. 9, d. 3, ll. 6–7; d. 83.

adding rhetorical flourishes. The phrase 'Dad's dead, he was shot by the fascist monsters in the chalk quarry in January 1942' was changed to the following:

> Do you remember, Styopa, the old chalk quarry on the northern edge of town? The Germans dragged father there, beaten and bloodied, hardly alive, put him on the edge of the pit, and basely shot him in the back of the head. They threw his body into the pit onto a heap of other bloodied corpses.

A woman who simply mentioned that she had been tortured by the Germans was credited with the following passage: 'What agonies I went through with the German monsters. They beat me with whips, drove me out naked into the freezing cold.' The reviewers piled up examples of outright fabrication as well as garbled names and addresses. They also alleged that certain details were systematically suppressed—for example, if the author of the letter mentioned that he had joined the party, this was often left out of the broadcast (in order to avert the suspicion that one had to be a party member to get a letter aired). But the main objection was more fundamental. Puzin, the future head of the Radio Committee, had no time for the editors' excuses that the raw material of the letters was unusable. The editors, he alleged in a rhetorical *coup de grâce*, were 'slandering our people' by stating that what they wrote was monotonous and unworthy of broadcast. 'I think you do not like the language of the people', he concluded. As other colleagues observed, the editors of the letters department were getting ideas above their station and thus threatening to undermine the trust of the Soviet listener.[93]

SOVIET BROADCASTERS LOOK TO THE FUTURE: 1944–1945

Another weakness of 'Letters to and from the Front' could not be laid at the editors' door. For all that these broadcasts were supposed to project the voice of the people, it was still uncommon for the authors themselves to have the opportunity to read out their letters. The Soviet authorities, during the war as before, were intolerant of error or ideological lapses. The department of agitation, when preparing interviews, was told to instruct the subject carefully on what to say and how to say it, and then carefully to check the text in advance.[94] In practice, this meant that interviews had to be pre-recorded on to film or tape. But the still inadequate state of recording technology did not allow broadcasters to do this as often as they might have liked. As Kabluchko recalled: 'We were recording four Heroes of the Soviet Union. We recorded them the first time—didn't work, we had to record again. We played it back—again useless, the disk was no good. In short, we had to record them five times...And remember these weren't public speakers, and we'd had to rehearse them in advance.' The difficulties of dealing with the recording department were by now almost legendary in the Radio Committee. 'It's not only

93 GARF, f. 6903, op. 1, d. 87, ll. 17, 26, 32–3, 36, 38, 42, 49–50.
94 GARF, f. 6903, op. 1, d. 70, ll. 55.

with staff at the Radio Committee that the young girls in our equipment rooms can be quite rude. We were recording a divisional commander. The girl actually shouted at him. He walked out of the studio, went into the equipment room and said that he would like to teach our staff how to behave to people.'[95]

Rude staff, we may safely assume, were no novelty in Soviet institutions of the early 1940s. What is perhaps more worthy of note is the wartime demand for the services of the recording department and the craving of broadcasters for 'authentic' documentary footage. The conditions of wartime served up non-stop events. The opportunities for front-line reporting and vivid first-hand footage were enormous, as was the propaganda potential of such material. In principle, the static, stage-managed character of many 1930s broadcasts could be traded for freshness and immediacy. Yet, even leaving aside the question of ideological supervision, there were severe practical limitations on the ability of journalists to bring 'authentic' war reporting to the Soviet listener. Even 3 minutes of footage required heroic efforts. In bad-tempered exchanges in the Radio Committee in January 1943, well-known war correspondents such as Iurii Ardi and Vadim Siniavskii were chided for their failure to provide a steady flow of up-to-date material. The targets of the criticism retorted that they constantly had to contend with the shortage of equipment and the obstructive attitude of the shorinophone department. As one colleague complained, 'every time you need to produce a tape or wax recording for broadcast, you have to waste half a day on it and resort to a thousand tricks, you even find yourself telling the girl in the recording department that you've never in your life seen such a beauty!' The famous Dneprostroi broadcast of 1930 had lasted only 1 hour, but had taken 2 or 3 weeks of preparation by a whole team of reporters and technicians. War correspondents had nothing like that amount of time or technical backup.[96]

In May 1944, Soviet war reporters were still gnashing their teeth in frustration. At a meeting in the Radio Committee, Siniavskii complained that Moscow's report on the liberation of Sevastopol had not done justice to the event. All it offered was 'three interviews recorded by chance' and the sound of cannon fire. As usual, shortage of equipment (cars, petrol, mobile recording equipment) was a large part of the problem. Understaffing was another issue. Reporters had to take everything upon themselves: not just delivering the text, but also lobbying for equipment, composing and editing the text, recording it, and making sure it was safely dispatched to Moscow. According to another speaker, Soviet radio news had only ten war correspondents on all the fronts of the war combined; of these, six had cars that were badly damaged, while four had no transport of their own. They did not have the mobile transmitters enjoyed by their English counterparts, so had to find the nearest radio station in order to send their material back to Moscow. The situation had been better in the early months of the war, when there had been several broadcasts each day from the Western front, or even during the Battle of Stalingrad, when information went on air 2–4 hours after it was dispatched from the

[95] GARF, f. 6903, op. 1, d. 87, l. 12.
[96] GARF, f. 6903, op. 1, d. 62, ll. 21, 23–23ob, 26ob.

front. Now there was commonly a delay of 24 hours or longer. For his part, Ardi weighed in to ask why sound technician was not considered a 'creative' profession.[97]

But the problem was not just poor equipment. Siniavskii also drew attention to Soviet broadcasters' ingrained suspicion of live broadcasts that did not go out in controlled conditions. Quite simply, they were 'cowardly'. To illustrate his point, Siniavskii mentioned the recent start of the football season, which had merited a report of all of 3 minutes: 'For some reason we've suddenly started worrying about going out live, maybe people think that someone might shout something out into the microphone. People who say that ought to spend a bit of time at the stadium and see the conditions I have worked in…To reach me, you need to get past at least 50 checkpoints. And the second microphone is on the roof, which only pigeons can get to.' Even Siniavskii had been made tame. As a colleague observed, although he remained one of Soviet radio's best speakers, his recent contributions had not made much of an impression. 'When he used to talk about football, hundreds of thousands of people knew him, he was a very popular comrade. Now he talks about other things, more important, but, although his mouth may not be shut, it's open just a crack, and he now talks in such a way that people have forgotten about him.'[98]

These were the Soviet Union's celebrity reporters. As concerned routine news bulletins, we find in 1944–5 a familiar litany of complaints. Broadcasts were indigestible, composed in leaden language, and overloaded with information. They still tended to follow the norms of written texts without making allowances for the listener. There were also simple errors in texts, which announcers had to be vigilant to catch. Soviet radio as a whole was monotonous, containing little in the way of musical interludes or interviews.[99] Announcers often did not help matters by reading in an expressionless style and giving no indication that they had taken in the content.[100] Familiar criticisms of the *diktor* resumed. In September 1944, no less an authority than Iurii Levitan observed that radio announcers were working 'amateurishly' (*kustarno*) and relying too heavily on their own initiative. His eminent colleague, Nataliia Tolstova, noted cases where broadcasters had kept their sangfroid under pressure—even in the midst of bombing—and observed that writers too often served up heavy material that was unsuitable for broadcast delivery. But she observed that announcers were often unable to simulate—let alone inspire in the audience—interest in technical and agricultural topics. It was crucial to vary rhythm and intonation if listeners were to pay attention throughout the broadcast.[101] Yet, as always, there were compelling reasons for broadcasters to err on the side of caution: the Orgburo of the Central Committee had instructed

[97] GARF, f. 6903, op. 1, d. 100, ll. 7–8, 33, 82–4, 92.

[98] GARF, f. 6903, op. 1, d. 100, ll. 8–9, 50–1.

[99] GARF, f. 6903, op. 1, d. 90 (15 August 1944); d. 95 (19 October 1944); d. 105 (6 February 1945).

[100] GARF, f. 6903, op. 1, d. 102 (meeting of announcers on *Poslednie izvestiia*, 16 September 1944; participants included Iurii Levitan and Nataliia Tolstova).

[101] GARF, f. 6903, op. 1, d. 102, ll. 2, 4–6, 12, 16.

that texts should be given to an announcer to read if there was any doubt about a person's ability to read them well.[102]

Working conditions continued to be desperately poor in all areas of broadcasting. In September 1944, *Pionerskaia zor'ka* was produced by a staff of only two people.[103] Regional stations and district transmission networks struggled with the limited resources—human and technical—at their disposal. On Gorky radio, only four out of fifty-eight members of staff had higher education. As of January 1944, the station was putting out each day two news broadcasts of 30 minutes each, two agitational programmes of 35 minutes, a survey of the regional newspaper for 15 minutes, as well as a number of musical and literary programmes three times a week or less frequently. District networks were at best reading out from the local newspaper twice a day and broadcasting the odd *vystuplenie* by an important person.[104]

Admittedly, the authorities were making some efforts to improve the situation. Restoring broadcasting infrastructure was a high priority for the Soviet government as it re-established its authority in territory clawed back from the Germans. Starting in the second half of 1943, the authorities set about restoring wired networks in former occupied regions (Khar'kov, Kiev, Leningrad, Rostov, Stavropol, Krasnodar, and others). As of December 1943, local broadcasting had resumed in 17 out of 24 regional centres in liberated territories, though in only 24 out of 200 districts (*raiony*).[105] As of November 1943, the Ministry of Communications (Narkomsviaz') controlled the larger transmission networks, of which there were more than 2,700 in the USSR with a total of 3,000 receiver points. In addition, there were as many as 5,000 small networks, largely in rural areas, which were under the jurisdiction of trade unions, ministries, and many other organizations. According to the latest information, however, these were not functioning well at all: perhaps as many as one-third were out of action.[106] In the first half of 1944, a total of 136 transmission networks were built or reconstructed—in oil and gas plants, heavy industry, collective farms, hospitals, and forestry regions. As of early autumn 1944, there were still only about 5 million wired receiver points in the country, but progress was being made.[107]

Yet, in 1944–5, discussions in the Radio Committee suggested that broadcasters were thinking about rather more than a return to the status quo ante. The consensus

[102] GARF, f. 6903, op. 1, d. 105, l. 85.
[103] GARF, f. 6903, op. 1, d. 91, l. 53. In February 1945 another representative of the children's section, Roza Ioffe, also complained of poor working conditions (lack of rehearsal space and recordings, shortage of musicians and actors). Ibid., d. 107, ll. 29–30. However, a colleague noted that the pay for writers was not bad: programmes like *Murzilka* or *Druzhnye rebiata* paid 1,500 rubles for 3–4 printer's sheets of text (l. 46).
[104] GANO, f. 3630, op. 2, d. 70, ll. 127–31.
[105] Polikarpov to Shcherbakov, December 1943, RGASPI, f. 17, op. 125, d. 215, l. 66.
[106] GARF, f. 6903, op. 1, d. 78, ll. 2–5 (Radio Committee to Agitprop, 11 November 1943).
[107] GARF, f. 6903, op. 1, d. 92, ll. 3, 7, 35 (meeting of 5 October 1944). In heavily damaged Voronezh region, for example, the number of *tochki* by the end of the war had been restored to about two-thirds of the figure in August 1941. Golovchenko, 'Funktsionirovanie sredstv massovoi informatsii', 15–16.

was that radio had stuck with the limited stylistic repertoire of wartime for a little too long. It was now time for more regular, but shorter and punchier, news bulletins through the day;[108] for more satire and humour; for a greater range of light music; and for a revival of children's broadcasting after the wartime hiatus. One speaker at a meeting in the Radio Committee of February 1945 chose a memorable metaphor: 'Radio is like arsenic—in small doses it increases your haemoglobin levels, but in large doses it can kill a horse.'[109] In its international broadcasts, moreover, Soviet radio had to stop 'copying the newspapers' and make use of 'forms that are extremely popular abroad' so as to 'fight for the listener'.[110] The radio newsreader, as a mere 'speaking machine', was not able to establish an intimate relationship with the listener. As a contributor to the discussion of news broadcasting in May 1944 noted, Soviet radio should supplement its offerings with the commentary genre found on foreign radio.[111]

As we shall see in Chapter 7, there were indeed formal innovations in Soviet broadcasting at the very end of the war, especially in children's programming. But the single clearest sign of new intent was to increase the number of channels and expand their geographical reach. In November 1944, the Radio Committee discussed plans for constructing a new broadcasting house (*radiodom*), which would provide a single centre for radio and TV and be highly cost-effective. But, as the participants in the discussion noted, improved studio facilities were no substitute for simple transmission capacity. Before the war, Soviet radio had four channels, but of these only one was all-union in its reach. In order to meet the target of five channels, the USSR would need five times as many stations as at present, including short-wave transmitters to reach the Far East.[112]

For the time being, Soviet broadcasters had to make do with the launch of a second channel in March 1945.[113] This was to run from late afternoon to late evening and to offer mainly music, but also children's programmes, literature, and science. As the head of the Radio Committee recognized, this would mainly be a channel for 'our intelligentsia', which was the section of society most likely to own the wireless radio sets necessary to pick up anything other than Channel One.[114] Such sets were now being returned to the population after wartime confiscation.[115] The expectation—and, in due course, the reality—of a large 'wireless' component in the Soviet radio audience was the single most important change in post-war broadcasting culture.

---

[108] On the rationale for short news broadcasts in the morning, see Skleznev in meeting of 21 February 1945, GARF, f. 6903, op. 1, d. 110, l. 50.

[109] GARF, f. 6903, op. 1, d. 106, l. 59.   [110] GARF, f. 6903, op. 1, d. 94, ll. 25, 39.

[111] GARF, f. 6903, op. 1, d. 100, ll. 12–13.   [112] GARF, f. 6903, op. 1, d. 97, ll. 6–7.

[113] This strained Soviet transmission capacity at the time to the limit. The launch had to be postponed because the existing transmitters were already fully occupied with broadcasting the first channel. GARF, f. 6903, op. 1, d. 111. There were also separate schedules (a few hours per day) for the Far East, Siberia, and Central Asia: ibid,, d. 104 (Puzin to Aleksandrov, 13 March 1945).

[114] GARF, f. 6903, op. 1, d. 106, l. 7.

[115] On the return of radio sets to the population, and measures to revive *radioliubitel'stvo*, see Puzin's letter to Agitprop of 24 March 1945: GARF, f. 6903, op. 1, d. 104, l. 5.

CONCLUSION: RADIO AND THE LEGACY OF THE WAR

By the spring of 1945, it appears, the prestige of radio had reached a new peak in the Soviet Union. On 17 March, broadcasting enjoyed the privilege of a front-page editorial in *Literaturnaia gazeta*, which noted the unique capacity of the medium to address a 'multi-million audience' and its ability to attract top literary talent such as Aleksei Tolstoi, who offered the latest chapters of his historical novel *Peter I* to be read on the radio even before they were published.[116] On 7 May, moreover, the authorities inaugurated an annual 'Radio Day' to mark the fiftieth anniversary of Alexander Popov's epoch-making invention. Soviet broadcasters continued to record the war in the West to its final moments. On 2 May 1945, General Weidling was put before the microphone to read out the decree on the capitulation of Berlin. The first time he delivered the text, it sounded too plaintive to be a military command; he had to be asked to repeat it. Only when the recording was played back to Weidling did he take in the full enormity of what he had done.[117]

In 1945, radio still had a monopoly on this kind of documentary immediacy. Around the same time as Weidling made his statement, the reporters P. I. Manuilov and Arkadii Fram were driving about Berlin with a microphone running. Against the background noise of machine gun fire and exploding shells, their account juxtaposed the blooming of spring with the scene of a city in near-ruins before offering listeners short interviews with a young officer, a nurse who had taken a German soldier prisoner, and the commander of a tank division.[118]

The biggest broadcasting set-piece to mark the victory was the report on the Victory Parade of 24 June, which involved such luminaries as Levitan, Kassil', and Vishnevskii. Soviet broadcasters, of course, already had substantial experience of such showcase events. In purely formal terms, however, there was a clear difference between this and the main broadcasting occasion of the first months of the war—the November 1941 parade on Red Square. There was more rapid interchange between the voices of the different presenters and more of an emphasis on vivid observed detail than on the framing narrative. This alone suggested that the ponderous style of 1930s broadcasting was starting to become something more fluid, even if the content would remain Stalinist for a few years longer.[119]

The broadcast of 24 June 1945 raises a question that cannot fail to interest anyone who studies Soviet culture in the 'long 1940s' from 1939 to 1953: what exactly was the contribution of the war to the representational system we know as 'socialist realism'? To what extent did it give Soviet society new tools for imagining itself? Was 'normal' Stalinist service resumed in 1945, or was this new terrain for the Soviet media?

---

[116] 'Literatura po radio', *LG*, 17 March 1945, 1. This article also contained much criticism of the failings of certain regional radio committees.

[117] Spasskii, 'Po dorogam voiny', *VKD*, 786.

[118] 'V Berline: Radioreportazh', *VKD*, 436–8. For Fram's own account of his wartime exploits, see his 'S mikrofonom i bloknotom', in Gleizer and Potapov (eds.), *Radio v dni voiny*, 70–8.

[119] *VKD*, 440–4.

Anyone who has struggled through the oppressive texts of political broadcasts in the late Stalin era is likely to be sceptical about the extent of change. Nonetheless, the war does seem to have turned radio into a medium of national life to an unprecedented extent. It was as if the real-time intensity of the Cheliuskin rescue or the show trials was sustained day after day for a whole four years. Radio was drawing on the best literary and journalistic talent that the Soviet culture industry had to offer. Perhaps most significant of all, its rhetorical arsenal was greatly expanded: a listener in the early 1940s could hear the voices not only of 'leading' comrades but also of 'ordinary' Soviet people. Party-mindedness took a back seat to patriotism. Although public discourse was still strictly policed, this was a new, demotic turn in Soviet culture. Radio played a large part in a process of cultural rapprochement that many historians and memoirists have observed as taking place during the war: profound differences of class and culture were transcended by a new patriotic culture to which both villager and *intelligent* could subscribe. This culture is evident in listeners' letters and requests from the immediate post-war period, where listeners might complain about the use of 'foreign' instruments in Russian folk ensembles and expressed an enduring preference for *Vasilii Terkin*.[120]

The war may also be seen as a pivotal phase in Soviet broadcasting for technological reasons. It was in 1941–2, as they headed off to the front lines, that Soviet war correspondents first felt acutely the lack of user-friendly recording equipment. They did the best they could with Presto machines and shorinophones, but by the end of the war they started to have the benefit of the superior magnetic tape recorders (*magnitofony*) that were among the trophies of victory over Nazi Germany. As I suggest in Chapter 6, this was a development of some consequence for the post-Stalinist future of Soviet broadcasting.

The Great Patriotic War was also, of course, the first major war that the Soviet Union had fought in the broadcasting era. Back in 1914–17, the Russian Empire had only been able to communicate wirelessly with its allies by Morse code. By 1941, sound broadcasting was already a highly sophisticated weapon of propaganda into which the main rivals of the USSR had been pouring vast resources. The Soviet authorities were acutely aware of the need to fight back—not just for the immediate period of armed conflict, but also for the foreseeable future of competitive coexistence with the non-socialist world. During the Russian Civil War, Bonch-Bruevich had worked away in Nizhnii Novgorod on developing a technology for wireless transmission of the human voice. In November 1942, another 'radio laboratory' was set up by decree of the wartime regime, but its primary task was destructive rather than constructive: to develop methods of jamming hostile broadcasts in locations from Finland to Bulgaria. Currently, long- and medium-wave stations in Kazan, Moscow, Arkhangel'sk, and Tbilisi were engaged in interference of this kind.

---

[120] TsGALI SPb, f. 293, op. 2, d. 4198. The performer of *Terkin* was Dmitrii Nikolaevich Orlov, whose other well-known credits included *Komu na Rusi zhit' khorosho* and *Tikhii Don*. Orlov's archive contains abundant fan mail for all of these roles: RGALI, f. 2216, op. 1, dd. 243–5.

The plan now was to use a more powerful station in Kuibyshev for the same purpose and to develop short-wave techniques of jamming.[121]

The Soviet Union not only had to defend itself against enemy propaganda; it also needed to project its own propaganda more effectively beyond the borders of the USSR. In May 1944, Puzin wrote to the Central Committee to point out that current transmission capacity was not adequate to guarantee that Moscow's foreign broadcasts reached their addressee. In general, only about half of broadcasts could be heard 'well' in their target territories. To remedy the situation, Puzin recommended that a powerful short-wave station in Petropavlovsk-Kamchatka be dismantled and moved to Moscow.[122]

Even more fundamentally, however, the Soviet Union needed to ensure that its broadcasts could be heard by its own population. As we have seen, from 1943 onwards the authorities struggled to restore as much as possible of the pre-war wired network and even to expand it. Maximum 'radiofication' of the Soviet territory was one of the main cultural campaigns of the next decade and a half. Yet, crucially, this goal could not be achieved so expeditiously without supplementing wired networks with wireless receivers. This broad transition 'from wire to *efir*' set many of the parameters for Soviet radio in the second half of its existence, and it forms the main subject of Chapter 5.

[121] RGASPI, f. 17, op. 125, d. 215, ll. 3–4 (Agitprop memo to Stalin, November 1942).
[122] RGASPI, f. 17, op. 125, d. 296, ll. 20–2 (Puzin to Shcherbakov, 31 May 1944) and ll. 24–51 (report by Puzin on state of broadcasting to enemy and occupied countries).

5

From Wire to *Efir*
Radiofication and Beyond

In April 1946, a citizen from Ul'ianovsk describing himself as an 'ordinary radio lover' wrote directly to Stalin to complain of the deficiencies of Soviet broadcasting. At present, he observed, radio was at the bottom of the hierarchy of media—below the press, oral propaganda, and cinema—but it could so easily be in second place. It was held back in the first instance by the still woeful state of technology. Only 25 per cent of the population was within reach of radio, and given the condition of much equipment, that figure was probably an overstatement (in the author's view, one-seventh would have been closer to the mark). Villages and worker settlements were especially poorly served. The content of broadcasts was no better. This correspondent could not understand the Radio Committee's 'enthusiasm for "serious" music', which was 'a kind of higher mathematics' even for musically literate listeners. What people needed as they left for work in the morning was lively marches, polkas, waltzes, and plenty of popular music with accordion and brass bands. The spoken word also failed to be suitably upbeat, and broadcasters' attempts at humour were consistently disappointing. It would be no bad idea for Soviet radio to learn some lessons from Britain and America and even from the music broadcasting of Bulgaria, Romania, Italy, Estonia, and Latvia. After all, Radio Moscow had to be capable of attracting listeners from around the world.[1]

The responsible editor wrote back with a partial rebuttal, and the main effect of letters like this was probably to hasten the onset of jamming. This document captures a pre-Cold War moment when it was possible to cite foreign radio with approval; it also faithfully reflects the antipathy of many listeners to the highbrow musical repertoire of Soviet radio. But most fundamental was the problem of technology. What hope did Soviet radio have of fulfilling its cultural and political mission if it was only reaching one-seventh of the population? Here the authorities and the radio hams were as one.

At a Radio Committee meeting of July 1946, broadcasting administrators were invited to reflect on a sobering statistical comparison. At the start of the war the USSR had had about 1 million wireless radio sets of all types and about 5.8 million

---

[1] GARF, f. 6903, op. 1, d. 136, ll. 6–9.

receiver points (*tochki*); in 1946, the wired network had held up through the travails of the previous five years (5.5 million receiver points), but the number of sets
had halved relative to 1941. The United States in 1946 had an astonishing 100
times more radio sets than the USSR—56 million. The implication was clear: the
most pressing task for the Soviet radio industry was to design a 'cheap, small, compact set which would require for its manufacture a minimal quantity of shortage
materials and would be a true people's radio set, at a cost of 200–250 rubles'. Price
was indeed a key consideration. The latest tube radios in the West were remarkably
neat and portable, but they were also prohibitively expensive to make: a Leningrad
factory that had just adopted the Marshall model was producing only eight sets per
day. The low-cost alternative was the crystal receiver, which would have the advantage of permitting rapid radiofication of the much-neglected village. But this was
technologically a step backwards: Soviet people might not need a radio that could
fit into their cigarette case but they did not want to be 'tied to the table'. The time
had passed, one speaker observed, when 'people listened just so as to listen, as a
technical novelty'. V. A. Burliand, leading light of *radioliubitel'stvo*, made the revolutionary suggestion, unpopular with his colleagues, that the industry might ask
consumers what kind of radio they wanted: was short-wave reception a priority for
them, or were they content with a combination of the main Moscow stations and
one local station? Whichever way, something had to be done. Many Soviet people
had to travel as far as 20 kilometres to find the nearest radio. As Aleksei Puzin, the
head of the Radio Committee, observed, it would take decades for the USSR to
attain the level of electrification enjoyed by Germany on the eve of the recent war.
The *tochki* on which Soviet broadcasting had hitherto relied so heavily were not a
practical or an economical option. They offered very poor sound quality, and they
cost 96 rubles per year to run. The search was on for a wireless radio set that would
be more attractive in terms of both price and quality.[2]

In practice, of course, *apparatchiki* had priority when it came to allocating the
scarce resource of wireless sets. In December 1946, the head of Agitprop Georgii
Aleksandrov recommended that 30,000 radios be made available for secretaries of
district Komsomol organizations, party committees, and executive committees.[3]
But the campaign for mass wireless radiofication was nonetheless meant seriously.
In the post-war period, as previously, radio offered the best (or in some cases the
only) chance of getting through to large swathes of the population. The sheer size
of the country made arguments for funding broadcasting infrastructure irrefut-
able. When the party secretary of Khabarovsk region wrote to Moscow in March
1946, his pleas for investment in broadcasting in the Far East met a sympathetic
response. Although the region had many radio stations, its northern reaches were
almost inaccessible to short-wave broadcasting in the winter months. What was
required was a powerful new long-wave transmitter. Another problem was the
shortage of tape (*tonfil'm*) and gramophone records, given the need to fill 10 hours
of regional broadcasting each day and the shortage of local performing talent.

---

[2] The transcript of the discussion is in GARF, f. 6903, op. 1, d. 152.
[3] RGASPI, f. 17, op. 125, d. 470, l. 10.

The Ministry of Communications supported the project for a new transmitter; the Council of Ministers provided the region with 1,000 radio sets and 15,000 loudspeakers in 1946; and the Committee for the Arts even promised to send conservatory graduates east to Khabarovsk to make good the shortage of local talent.[4]

Radio coverage in the Far East was an enduring problem. Almost ten years later, in 1955, this region was still heavily dependent on Khabarovsk radio stations, which lagged far behind Moscow in their quality. Even in Western Siberia (serviced primarily by the Novosibirsk station) it was hard to pick up central radio, and the substantial time difference in any case made the schedule unfriendly to listeners east of the Urals.[5] In Tiumen' region in Western Siberia, only about 10 per cent of the population had access to radio in 1946. Although the number of relay networks tripled between 1947 and 1952, in June 1954 only a little more than 10 per cent of settlements in the region were 'radiofied'.[6] It almost goes without saying that the situation to the south-east was even worse. In Tadzhikistan in the late 1940s, considerably less than 10 per cent of collective farms had radio receivers.[7]

The main proposed solution to such problems was to increase distance-conquering short-wave transmission capacity. The figures from the immediate post-war period are striking: at the start of 1941 the USSR had had 109 medium- and long-wave transmitters (with a combined power of 3,210 kilowatts) and six short-wave transmitters; on 1 January 1948 there were fewer (though more powerful) long-wave transmitters, but more than five times as many short-wave transmitters. Even so, as a briefing to Stalin in April 1948 made clear, the USSR was failing to keep up with the competition from the USA and England: the country needed to build 34 medium- and short-wave transmitters, with a combined power of 5,110 kilowatts, over the next three years.[8] A year later, similarly, an account of Soviet achievements was undermined by a nagging sense of their inadequacy in international perspective. In May 1949, the Central Committee was informed that the USSR now had 133 broadcasting stations, 13,525 wired networks, about 8 million receiver points, and more than 1 million wireless sets. But, at a moment when the BBC and Voice of America 'could be heard in any point of the USSR', Soviet broadcasting was unable to reach many parts of the Americas, India, and Australia, and was not even getting through reliably to all parts of Europe. Powerful medium-wave stations had been built in Kishinev, Odessa, and Simferopol with the aim of broadcasting to Turkey and the Balkans, but these stations had no wired connection to Moscow, so they were not yet being used. The statistics on listening technology continued to make uncomfortable reading: the USA had one wireless radio set for every 2 people, the USSR one for every 25–8 people.[9]

[4] RGASPI, f. 17, op. 125, d. 470, ll. 14–17, 19, 21.

[5] GARF, f. 6903, op. 1, d. 474, ll. 14–16, 22–4.

[6] O. I. Gaiduchok, 'Istoriia razvitiia radio i televideniia Tiumenskoi oblasti (1946–1991 gg.)', candidate's dissertation (Tiumen', 2006), 36, 107–8.

[7] Teresa Rakowska-Harmstone, *Russia and Nationalism in Central Asia: The Case of Tadzhikistan* (Baltimore, 1970), 219.

[8] RGASPI, f. 17, op. 125, d. 640, ll. 158–61.

[9] RGASPI, f. 17, op. 132, d. 254, ll. 119–25.

In April 1948, even such a major part of European Russia as Leningrad relied overwhelmingly on wired networks, of which there were almost 17,000 in the region (only 10 per cent of them in collective farms).[10] Yet industry was not adequately supporting these networks. In 1951 a simple loudspeaker for domestic use was reported by Agitprop as a shortage item: production had halved in 1951 to 485,000.[11] A plenum of the Gorky oblast party committee in February 1949 found that the number of receiver points in the villages had grown at 'the tempo of a tortoise': by only about 500 per year since the war. In the better connected rural areas, 15–25 per cent of kolkhoz households had radio, but overall the Gorky region had recently been overtaken by Sverdlovsk. Even where radio equipment existed in the villages, it was often neglected or damaged.[12] As of 1 January 1953, Gorky oblast had just under 50,000 radio sets and almost 250,000 *tochki* (of which a little more than 50,000 were in rural areas). Despite investment in radio infrastructure, there were continuing problems with energy supply, which meant that certain transmission networks had fallen silent for large portions of the year.[13] As for wireless radio sets, these remained in acute shortage in the early 1950s. A report from the automobile factory district in Gorky showed that people were interested in acquiring such listening equipment, but it was not available in sufficient quantities. When a number of Neva radios went on sale in a department store, a long queue quickly formed, and many sets were sold under the counter. All told, in April 1953 there were little more than 5,000 radio sets in a district of 180,000 people.[14] In the Soviet Union's second city, Leningrad, with its population of 2.7 million and high concentration of industrial enterprises, 20,000 radio sets were sold in 1950—by no means an enormous figure.[15]

THE BROADCASTING MILIEU IN THE LATE STALIN PERIOD

The period 1945–53 has a dismal reputation as the apogee of Stalinist xenophobia, conformism, and obscurantism. As later chapters will suggest, these years in fact brought interesting developments in both the form and the content of broadcasting. Nonetheless, it would be perverse to deny that they were profoundly marked by the ideological rigidity and repression of the time.

Broadcasting was also affected by the sheer hardship of the immediate post-war years. In July 1945, Puzin informed Mikoian that the staff of the Radio Committee were too poorly clothed to do their jobs properly. Their duties often brought them into contact with artists, academicians, writers, and generals, but they did not look the part. Similarly, musicians on the staff of the Radio Committee sometimes had

---

[10] RGASPI, f. 17, op. 125, d. 640, ll. 51–3. [11] RGASPI, f, 17, op. 132, d. 490, l. 37.
[12] GOPANO, f. 3, op. 1, d. 7006, ll. 107–8. [13] GOPANO, f. 3, op. 1, d. 9570, ll. 78–9.
[14] GOPANO, f. 3, op. 1, d. 9572, ll. 118–20.
[15] A. Z. Vakser, *Leningrad poslevoennyi. 1945–1982 gody* (St Petersburg, 2005), 101. According to Vakser, radio sets were still at this time a prerogative of the *nomenklatura*, Stakhanovite workers, and members of the intelligentsia elite.

to decline invitations to perform at open concerts because they had nothing suitable to wear.[16] This was the view from central broadcasting; at the regional and district level, radio looked in even worse shape. Some regional broadcasters were operating in extraordinarily difficult conditions. The Kostroma radio committee complained to Moscow in 1948 that it had no furniture, let alone acoustic curtains, while the studio was unheated.[17] The Kabardinian *obkom* reported to Malenkov in September 1951 that its radio committee was broadcasting out of a temporary hut on the outskirts of Nalchik. It broadcast for 2 hours 30 minutes each day; the staff of thirty-five was accommodated in five small rooms amounting to 68 square metres.[18] Even in published accounts, official encouragement for local broadcasting was tempered by recognition of the wretched working conditions that many regional radio committees faced.[19]

Yet local wired networks were the bedrock of the Soviet broadcasting system as it had taken shape in the 1930s. At the grass-roots level, there were hundreds of small district (*raion*) networks, each with their own responsible editor, which produced anything from a few minutes to a couple of hours of broadcasting each day. These networks were almost always underfunded and staffed by poorly qualified personnel. During the Terror they had elicited much criticism and denunciation. In the immediate pre-war period, radio administrators could agree in principle that rationalization of these networks was desirable—it was hardly worth continuing to service tiny networks with only a few dozen receiver points—but the practicalities were harder. To set a minimum size of 350 *tochki*, as one proposal ran, would effectively be to abolish broadcasting in 'national' districts in places such as Saratov region, Kirgizia, Kazakhstan, and Uzbekistan.[20]

During the war, with effective channels of propaganda at a premium, the district networks were far too useful to be discontinued. In practice, much radio seems to have reverted to its early 1920s function of oral adjunct to the press. According to a Central Committee decree of 3 June 1943, wired broadcasting at the district level was to take the form of reading out newspapers and Sovinformbiuro bulletins. Editing was the job of the editors of the district newspapers, while overall supervision was entrusted to the second secretaries of the *raion* party committee. Yet, while this was a practical solution for the wartime moment, in due course district broadcasting would arouse the same misgivings in the Radio Committee as in the late 1930s. An audit showed that newspaper editors neglected their radio responsibilities. Given the lack of qualified cadres, in 1947 the Central Committee dispensed with independent radio editors at the *raion* level. As Agitprop glossed the decision in February 1947, *raion* broadcasting had had an important function

[16] GARF, f. 6903, op. 1, d. 104, l. 39 (Puzin to Mikoian, 23 July 1945).

[17] GARF, f. 6903, op. 1, d. 204, l. 179 (letter to Suslov from Bystrov, head of Kostroma radio committee, May 1948).

[18] RGASPI, f. 17, op. 132, d. 492, ll. 78–9.

[19] D. Polianovskii, 'Raion slushaet…', *LG*, 3 February 1951, 2. This article mentions Molotov region specifically.

[20] GARF, f. 6903, op. 1, d. 58, ll. 59–60 (stenogram of meeting in Radio Committee of 28 January 1941).

during the war, when newspapers were unavailable, but it had now overgrown this purpose: there were no fewer than 2,700 district broadcasters, each needing to provide 30–60 minutes of programming per day. On the whole, they just read out old newspaper articles. Furthermore, as the party's ideology chief Andrei Zhdanov was informed on 21 March 1947, an investigation had shown that many small broadcasters managed only 10–12 minutes per day instead of their allotted 30.[21] In the spring of 1948 came a proposal to rationalize the provision of district broadcasting: to liquidate local *redaktsii* that served fewer than 1,000 reception points and transfer their responsibilities to the local newspaper. Some thinly populated regions (such as Molotov, formerly Perm') expressed concern that this would lead to the neglect of remoter districts, but better connected regions such as Tambov and Belorussia approved the measures.[22]

Outside Moscow and Leningrad, it was hard to speak of an established broadcasting 'profession'. Especially after the upheaval of the war, many members of staff on radio had minimal training and experience. In the Gorky radio committee in August 1945, almost half the staff had worked on radio for less than a year; only eight out of fifty-eight people had more than two years' experience.[23] By 1946, Gorky radio was at least organizing courses for announcers from district broadcasting; thirty-four people attended, each of them being recorded and then having their performance discussed. But the salary for such a job was a miserable 100 rubles, so it was essential to combine work on the radio with some other employment.[24] No wonder that internal reports from the late Stalin era found that district radio was too often parroting central broadcasting without producing any locally specific material.[25] The records for 1953 were littered with similar complaints of 'contrived and schematic depiction of Soviet people'.[26] Given the extremely close supervision by the regional party committee, however, it was not altogether clear how these failings were to be eliminated.

In Moscow and Leningrad, broadcasting was certainly on a firmer footing. By the late 1940s, for example, there was an elaborate system for training and assessing radio announcers. In 1948, no fewer than 3,200 people, most of them already with relevant educational qualifications, auditioned for central broadcasting. Of these, a mere seven people were selected for the three-month course for radio announcers, and only five were ultimately taken on as trainee announcers.[27]

Yet, even for the lucky few who found themselves a niche on Moscow radio, the late Stalin era was a testing time. The notorious Zhdanov decree of summer 1946 had predictable repercussions for broadcasters: radio was to conform to the same

---

[21] Documents on *raion* broadcasting at RGASPI, f. 17, op. 125, d. 470, ll. 91–100.

[22] RGASPI, f. 17, op. 125, d. 640, ll. 62–78.

[23] 'Spravka o sostoianii kadrov-upolnomochennykh po radioveshchaniiu Gor'kovskogo Oblastnogo Radiokomiteta na 10 avgusta 1945', GANO, f. 3630, op. 2, d. 70, l. 83.

[24] GOPANO, f. 3, op. 1, d. 5580, l. 2.

[25] Examples for 1951 in GOPANO, f. 3, op. 1, d. 8292.

[26] GOPANO, f. 3, op. 1, d. 9570, l. 2.

[27] Puzin to Malenkov, 15 February 1949, GARF, f. 6903, op. 1, d. 248, ll. 11–12.

rigid party-minded patriotism as other branches of the Soviet culture industry.[28] Even more damaging to the morale of the broadcasting organization was the personnel purge, at least partly anti-Semitic in motivation, that forced many outstanding staff members into temporary or permanent retirement in the late 1940s. The damage was perhaps most obvious in Leningrad, where such luminaries as Lazar' Magrachev, Liubov' Spektor, and Iakov Bliumberg were driven out of their jobs.[29] The transcript of a meeting of party members in Leningrad radio reveals the full ugliness of the atmosphere in late 1949. Colleagues queued up to cast aspersions on Magrachev, the now dethroned 'king of reportage', evidently a strong character who had only galvanized his adversaries by launching a campaign for his reinstatement. Bliumberg, for his part, was forced into the invidious position of defending himself against the charge that he had protected Magrachev.[30]

Harassment of radio workers was motivated not only by ideological vigilance. It also had to do with the inherent suspicion of the Soviet authorities towards any autonomous professional group. A recurring theme in documents of the late Stalin era is hostile scrutiny of payments made to broadcasting personnel. If Iurii Levitan could simply draw a large salary, some of his colleagues were not so lucky.[31] The children's producer Roza Ioffe fought a running battle to be granted the additional freelance payments she felt were her due for work on specific commissions that went beyond her formal duties.[32] The authorities were hardly sympathetic to such arguments. In May 1946, the Ministry of State Control had reported to the Central Committee 'gross violations of personnel and financial discipline' in the Radio Committee, alleging that unauthorized posts had been created and that salaried

---

[28] For a Radio Committee decree on music broadcasting that followed hot on the heels of the Zhdanov decree, see *VKD*, 114–16.

[29] According to one account, Magrachev was accused after the war of falsifying his reports by passing off studio broadcasts as reportage. See M. G. Zeger, 'My eti dni uzhe zavoevali', in P. A. Palladin, M. G. Zeger, and A. A. V'iunik (eds.), *Leningradskoe radio: Ot blokady do 'ottepeli'* (Moscow, 1991), 127. More accurate seems the version of Lev Markhasev, who emphasizes anti-Semitism along with the fact that during the war Magrachev had recorded interviews with many people who later (during the Leningrad Affair) were exposed as 'criminals'. See Markhasev, *Belki v kolese: Zapiski iz Doma radio* (St Petersburg, 2004), 152–3.

[30] TsGAIPD SPb, f. 755, op. 2, d. 12 (stenogram of meeting of 12 November 1949). The 'king of reportage' jibe is on l. 37.

[31] Levitan's salary in 1946 appears to have been a healthy 2,500 rubles per month: see a decree awarding him a month's salary as reward for his fifteen years of service on the radio, in *VKD*, 119. The average per capita income in worker households across the USSR at this time seems to have been just below 450 rubles: see RGAE, f. 1562, op. 15, d. 2129, ll. 80, 89, 100. For further comparison, the head of Gorky radio in 1952 (by which time average earnings had risen by 20 per cent or so) was paid 1,300 rubles per month, and an announcer on Gorky radio earned 700: GOPANO, f. 3, op. 1, d. 8968, ll. 63, 66. At this time, average per capita income in the household of a skilled worker was in the region of 520 rubles; for low-skilled workers it was around 480 rubles. See RGAE, f. 1562, op. 26, d. 25, ll. 116–116ob. RGAE references and calculations in this footnote are courtesy of Donald Filtzer, to whom many thanks.

[32] See Ioffe's letter of complaint to the deputy head of the Radio Committee, 29 November 1947, and the letter of support written by the head of the children's section the following month, in *VKD*, 121–4.

employees had been paid inflated fees for freelance work.[33] The party authorities also disliked the fact that broadcasters did not conform to the prevailing norms of work discipline. As Agitprop reported to the Central Committee in August 1948, work rotas were not drawn up a month, or even a week, in advance, but rather from one day to the next. Lunch breaks were not fixed, and staff indulged in idle conversation and private telephone calls. As the report concluded, the staff of the Radio Committee had formed a 'false opinion of the supposed special nature of their work, which they say can't be confined to a timetable, because "this isn't a factory or a ministry, where you work from 9 to 5"'.[34] Even in January 1953, a report to the Central Committee claimed that 6,000 of the almost 15,500 people employed by the Radio Committee were paid outside any established salary scale; the differences in pay for members of staff doing approximately the same job were hard to justify.[35] Broadcasters also had ample opportunity to exploit work facilities for private ends. In February 1953, a correspondent on Leningrad radio was dismissed for running up a phone bill of 1,300 rubles on calls that were not work-related.[36]

The combination of close ideological supervision and aggressive scrutiny of broadcasters' work practices must have poisoned the atmosphere in many radio committees of the late 1940s.[37] Given the poor working conditions and low quality of staff outside the major city, it was not hard to find evidence of malpractice. Although it is hard to judge the facts of any single case from the records deposited in the Central Committee archive, inspections found some of the remoter radio committees to be hair-raising work environments. A report of April 1953 found that Irkutsk broadcasting was headed by 'random people'; almost everyone seemed to be drunken or violent or to have a dubious past. Even the orchestra was 'strewn with people of anti-Soviet disposition who have been exiled from the central regions of the country'.[38]

FROM RADIOFICATION TO *RADIOKHULIGANSTVO*

Yet, if we take a slightly longer view, it becomes clear that 'radiofication', along with the housing programme and other areas of post-war reconstruction, was one of the success stories of the age.[39] Official accounts proclaimed that the process was

---

[33] Mekhlis to Zhdanov, 7 May 1946, RGASPI, f. 17, op. 125, d. 470, ll. 37–40. During the late Stalin period there was also some unease at the large royalties some performers were drawing for radio broadcasts: see Kirill Tomoff, *Creative Union: The Professional Organization of Soviet Composers, 1939–1953* (Ithaca, NY, 2006), 232–3.

[34] Il'ichev to Malenkov, 22 August 1948, RGASPI, f. 17, op. 132, l. 93, ll. 41–2.

[35] RGANI, f. 5, op. 16, d. 643, ll. 1–4.   [36] ERA.R, f. 1590, op. 4, d. 44, l. 2.

[37] A sample of the accusations and counter-accusations of the time can be found in the files of the Central Committee, for example RGASPI, f. 17, op. 132, dd. 436, 490, 562.

[38] RGANI, f. 5, op. 16, d. 644, ll. 97–100.

[39] The successes, at least in quantitative terms, are also emphasized in Kristin Roth-Ey, *Moscow Prime Time: How the Soviet Union Built the Media Empire That Lost the Cultural Cold War* (Ithaca, NY, 2011), 137–8.

completed, and the country fully radiofied, by 1960. In 1959, the Central Committee was informed that no fewer than 3,683,000 radio sets and radiolas had been put on the market in 1958 (as compared with a total of 912,000 TV sets); the equivalent figure for 1951 had been just over 1 million. By the end of 1958, the USSR had more than 9.5 million registered radio sets (as opposed to just under 2.4 million at the end of 1951).[40]

The public narrative of success is supported by interview material. At the end of the war, and for several years afterwards, many Soviet people found themselves out of broadcasting range. Just a few dozen kilometres north of Leningrad, in Vyborg region, news of the end of the war spread from leaflets dropped by plane; there was no radio in the vicinity.[41] In rural Pskov oblast it was perfectly possible to be without radio until the 1950s; the same went for at least one Leningrad orphanage.[42] In Lugansk oblast in the same era, the electricity supply was too unreliable to allow regular listening. One family only gained access to radio when the father improvised a way of charging batteries for the radio in the late 1950s; it was not until 1961 that a normal electricity supply was established.[43] When people did have access to radio in the 1950s, very often they were the same collective listeners as in the 1930s. Much like Kirov's murder in 1934, the death of Stalin in 1953 was recalled by many people outside the main cities as an occasion for organized listening. In an orphanage in Perm' oblast, children cried around the *tarelka* (even though Stalin had deprived some of them of parents).[44] In a village in Taganrog region, everyone assembled in the club to listen to coverage of the funeral.[45]

Over the course of the 1950s, however, radio made fresh headway. By the early 1960s, even boarding schools, traditionally under-resourced, were taking receiver points for granted.[46] The same was true also of many rural areas, as the post-war radiofication campaign pursued the familiar mission of spreading culture and enlightenment to those who needed it most.[47] In the village of Viriatino, subject of one of the very few ethnographic studies of the contemporary Soviet rural world, radio was playing its part in the new leisure patterns of the 1950s; folk songs and lectures on agriculture and childrearing were of particular interest to these collective farm listeners.[48] An interview informant born in Briansk oblast in 1941 recalled vividly the role radio—especially theatre broadcasts—played in her childhood after her home was wired up in the late 1940s: she could 'sit for half a day' under the *tarelka*.[49]

---

[40] GARF, f. 6903, op. 1, d. 578, ll. 19–20.

[41] Oxf/Lev V-04 PF24 (A), p. 29. Informant b. 1935.

[42] Oxf/Lev V-04 PF 22 (A), p. 63; Oxf/Lev SPb-02, PF4 (A), p. 95.

[43] Oxf/Lev T-05 PF12 (B), p. 12.   [44] Oxf/Lev P-05 PF29 (A), p. 8 (informant born 1938).

[45] Oxf/Lev T-04 PF 6 (A), p. 6.

[46] See the following two Leningrad examples from Oxf/Lev SPb-04: PF49 (A), p. 9 (woman b. 1935 who worked in school from 1962); PF64 (B), p. 20 (informant b. 1932 who worked in school for Chinese from 1960).

[47] For example, *Radio—v kazhdyi kolkhoznyi dom* (Krasnoiarsk, 1954).

[48] P. I. Kushner (ed.), *Selo Viriatino v proshlom i nastoiashchem: Opyt etnograficheskogo izucheniia russkoi kolkhoznoi derevni* (Moscow, 1958), 221.

[49] Oxf/Lev T-05 PF 21 (A), p. 7.

Figure 5.1. A listener in Leningrad region enjoys the new Rodina model, 1947–1948.
Source: A. S. Popov Central Museum of Communications

Soviet industry was now giving individual listeners a helping hand. Immediately after the war came the launch of a range of mass-market radio sets that offered coverage of long-, medium-, and short-wave broadcasts. First came the five-tube Rekord, released in 1945 and in improved models thereafter. With its simple design and three buttons at the bottom, it was perhaps the most recognizable radio set of the age. Its battery-powered equivalent was the Rodina (see Figure 5.1). The VEF M-557 and the Vostok offered more powerful sound suitable for larger spaces. The Soviet consumer industry was incorporating what it had learned from 'trophy' sets and sweating to establish mass production of such luxuries as plastic cases and multicoloured dials. The plan for 1946 was 300,000 sets.[50]

Admittedly, the quality of the electronics in these sets left much to be desired, and their sound quality tended to deteriorate rapidly as the elements wore out. In Moscow, the one workshop that offered repair of radio sets covered by guarantee was fixing about 250 sets per month already in summer 1946.[51] In 1946–7 more than 160,000 Rodina sets were sold to the village but without the necessary spare tubes and reserve power.[52] Both Rekord and Rodina would be subject to constant refinements over the following years.[53]

In the post-war period such problems were alleviated by the fact that Soviet broadcasting could count on the large and growing technophile section of the listening public. In the late 1940s, especially given the return of sets confiscated during the

[50] B. N. Mozhzhevelov, 'Chto dast nasha radiopromyshlennost' v 1946 g.', *Radio*, no. 1 (1946): 20–2. For further information and photographs I draw on the invaluable 'virtual museum' *Otechestvennaia Radiotekhnika XX Veka*.

[51] L. V. Kubarkin, 'Nedostatki fabrichnykh priemnikov', *Radio*, no. 1 (1947): 10–11.

[52] G. Komissarova, 'Radiopriemniki ili…polirovannye iashchiki', *LG*, 7 January 1948, 4.

[53] See e.g. S. N. Afendikov, 'Novye radiopriemniki', *Radio*, no. 11 (1947): 43–6.

war, *radioliubitel'stvo* was emphatically back in fashion. As a relaunched specialist periodical declared in advance of Radio Day (7 May) in 1946, 'in all areas of radio communications—the army, the fleet, and the partisan movement—radio enthusiasts have showed themselves to be skilful fighters'.[54] World War II had been a far cry from 1904–5, when the Russian army had suffered against the Japanese because it lacked radio stations.[55] A few years later, even *Literaturnaia gazeta*, a periodical of far broader profile, published an article celebrating the achievements of Soviet radio hams in the great tradition established by Popov on 7 May 1895.[56] In the late Stalin era, radio expertise was nothing less than a matter of national prestige, and Popov's reputation was jealously guarded. When a radio technology congress in Rome in 1947 declared the priority of Italy in inventing the radio, the Soviet authorities launched a counter-propaganda effort to show that their man was first.[57]

In February 1947, Puzin wrote to the Central Committee for an increase in the print run of the journal *Radio*. The circulation of 20,000 it had been granted on its post-war resumption had proved completely inadequate: the publisher was 'literally under siege' by radio enthusiasts requesting subscriptions. Many readers were copying articles by hand and redrawing or photographing technical diagrams.[58] Given the rapidly growing level of radio use, moreover, the Radio Committee was by early 1947 expressing serious doubts that the system of collecting registration payments for radio sets was worth continuing. Even in Moscow a few months before the war, only about half of the radio sets in use were properly registered, and with the numbers of radio sets projected to rise to 3 million and beyond, the system threatened to become completely unworkable.[59]

As in the 1920s, radio hams had a large role to play in the grass-roots spread of radio technology. In one exemplary narrative, a *radioliubitel'* arrived as a village schoolteacher in a heavily damaged part of Ukraine at the end of 1944. On arrival, he found there was not a single radio set in the village. The only solution was to put together crystal receivers. When he had built himself one, the teacher started receiving a constant stream of visitors to listen to Khar'kov radio (and, via Khar'kov, Moscow). With a bit of help from the district party committee, he then obtained a radio set with four loudspeakers for one of the classrooms. He found that there was no difference in quality of reception between home-made and factory-produced sets. Obtaining the necessary parts was, however, a struggle: not everything could be made at home. To begin with, the teacher had to ask his pupils to bring along material they might have scavenged from trophy sets as well as wire for coils and antennas.[60]

---

[54] '7 maia—Den' radio', *Radio*, no. 1 (1946): 2.
[55] I. T. Peresypkin, 'Radio v Otechestvennoi voine', *Radio*, no. 1 (1946): 10–13.
[56] A. Berg, 'Uspekhi sovetskikh radioliubitelei', *LG*, 6 May 1952, 2.
[57] GARF, f. 6903, op. 1, d. 177, ll. 28–9 (Lapin to Suslov, 2 October 1947). For an Agitprop memo a few days later on the need to organize a 'collective statement' on the subject in *Izvestiia*, see D. G. Nadzhafov and Z. S. Belousova (eds.), *Stalin i kosmopolitizm: Dokumenty Agitpropa TsK KPSS 1945–1953* (Moscow, 2005), 145–7.
[58] GARF, f. 6903, op. 1, d. 177, l. 2.   [59] GARF, f. 6903, op. 1, d. 180, ll. 6, 9.
[60] I. V. Kolpashchikov, 'Kak my nachinali', *Radio*, no. 7 (1947): 5–7.

Amateur inventors were also directing their energies at tasks of a higher order. At the Sixth Amateur Radio Exhibition, an occasion that showcased the expertise and ingenuity of *radioliubiteli* around the country, there was a new emphasis on simple, user-friendly design. Inventors were less interested in constructing ever more complex circuits and ever more powerful sets; rather, they were increasingly striving for compact, streamlined design.[61] One Leningrad inventor was given third prize at the exhibition for a diminutive design called *Malysh* (Baby).[62] Second prize went to a set that was a mere 18 × 16 × 14 centimetres in dimension.[63] Radio enthusiasts were also pouring their energies into building short-wave receivers.[64]

Post-war *radioliubitel'stvo* draws our attention to a fundamental, and rather significant, fact about Soviet society: its technical proficiency. This was a culture where the prestige of science, technology, and engineering was high—and would only rise further in the era of space exploration. Thanks to Lewis Siegelbaum, we know how much the last generation of Soviet men enjoyed looking after their cars.[65] For two or three generations before car ownership acquired significant dimensions, Soviet people (primarily male) had enjoyed tinkering with their radio sets. The extent of radiophilia in post-war Russia is reflected most obviously in discussion communities in today's Internet forums (such as Live Journal). It is also confirmed by interview material. One informant born in 1956 recalled enjoying his activities in the *radiokruzhok* (radio club) in a children's summer camp in the 1960s. One game was called 'fox hunting' (it involved searching for a transmitter hidden in the woods).[66] The fondest desire of post-war radio enthusiasts remained to build a radio set that was as small and portable as possible. In 1962, one pair of technically adept youths planned to mitigate the tedium of a summer in the village by assembling 'pocket sets' (presumably transistor radios), which required careful planning to collect in advance the necessary parts.[67] This kind of expertise could be put to profitable uses in late Soviet society. One man (b. 1960) who later qualified as a radio repair technician recalls enjoying tinkering with radios from his mid-teens. In due course he started picking up spare parts from discarded sets, repairing them, and selling them at the Avtovo market for a profit that sufficed to buy jeans (the gold standard consumer item of the era).[68] A man (b. 1949) brought up in Perm' recalls repairing his first radio at the age of 13 or 14 and refitting it to

[61] L. V. Kubarkin, 'Priemniki 6-i zaochnoi vystavki', *Radio*, no. 8 (1947): 20–2.

[62] 'Priemnik "Malysh"', *Radio*, no. 8 (1947): 26–7.

[63] 'Prostoi "knopochnyi"', *Radio*, no. 9 (1947): 46.

[64] See e.g. A. Kamaliagin, 'Korotkovolnovye peredatchiki na 10-i Vsesoiuznoi vystavke tvorchestva radioliubitelei-konstruktorov', *Radio*, no. 7 (1952): 37–9.

[65] Lewis H. Siegelbaum, *Cars for Comrades: The Life of the Soviet Automobile* (Ithaca, NY, 2011), 247–51.

[66] Oxf/Lev M-04, PF 43 (A), p. 20. For another man (b. 1950, Taganrog) who tinkered with radios in his younger years, see Oxf/Lev T-05 PF17 (B), p. 10.

[67] This evident from a letter to Vladimir Samsonov of 19 June 1962. I am grateful to Marina Samsonova for permission to cite this document from her family archive and to Catriona Kelly for alerting me to its existence.

[68] Oxf/Lev SPb-03 PF 25 (A), pp. 29–30.

listen to short-wave broadcasts by Voice of America and Radio Liberty; this way he was able to evade the oppressive jamming of the late Khrushchev era.[69]

To judge by this informant and other accounts of the period, by the early 1960s it was not actually considered illegal to listen to foreign radio—it was just made as difficult as possible by the authorities. A more deviant application of radio expertise in the later Soviet period was to broadcast home-made programming. Evidently this was a well-known phenomenon even in the Khrushchev era. In 1960, an outraged citizen from Krasnodar region wrote to the journal *Partiinaia zhizn'* (*Party Life*) to complain of rampant 'radio hooliganism': respectable listeners turned on their sets expecting a decent programme but instead had to put up with pop concerts recorded on tape or X-ray plates, much of it performed by 'the hoarse voice of a drunk to the accompaniment of a guitar'. As the listener concluded plaintively: 'We have established order on earth, but we have handed the airwaves over entirely to radio hooligans, who are corrupting our youth.'[70] Such complaints were not just the product of moral panic. In 1963, the Komsomol estimated a figure of 11,000 such unofficial broadcasters, and they were spread quite widely across the Russian Republic (RSFSR) and Ukraine.[71] One proud radio hooligan was active in the late 1960s in the town of Eisk on the Sea of Azov. His first broadcast was music played on a gramophone (*patefon*) with an earphone as improvised microphone. Thereafter he played his part in making known the music of the guitar poets Vladimir Vysotskii and Evgenii Kliachkin. With his friends in the Eisk broadcasting underground he also put out live performances, as tape recorders were still in short supply.[72] A similar story comes from Tver', where in the early 1980s a community of young enthusiasts used the local wired network to 'broadcast' their music during the night.[73] Thus, while the authorities could certainly notch up post-war radiofication as a success story, it had among its unintended consequences the metamorphosis of patriotic *radioliubitel'* into BBC devotee or outright *khuligan*.

PROGRAMMING

However resourceful Soviet radio owners might be, they could not be expected to organize their own programming all the time: they needed something to listen to. The war had brought the apotheosis of totalitarian broadcasting, as broadcasting was reduced to a single authoritative channel (disseminated to the vast majority of listeners by wire). But this was a response to a national emergency, not a blueprint

[69] Oxf/Lev P-05 PF 7 (A), p. 21.   [70] RGANI, f. 5, op. 33, d. 148, ll. 48–9.

[71] Roth-Ey, *Moscow Prime Time*, 146–7 n. 61.

[72] I am grateful to Catriona Kelly for passing on this document, 'Iz vospominanii "radiokhuligana" 1960-kh', which was posted on Facebook by Andrei Blinushov. The original document is located in the collection of Riazan' Memorial.

[73] Oleg Mamonov, personal communication, June 2013. Mamonov was a schoolboy (aged 14 or 15) at the time; he used a tube radio as his amplifier, connecting this to the family's *tochka*. I am grateful to Aleksandr Mamonov for soliciting this account of *radiokhuliganstvo*.

for the future. As thoughts began to turn to the post-war order, broadcasters began to plan an expansion of broadcasting output. They were still hampered by the lack of transmission capacity. As the Radio Committee reflected in November 1944, the number of broadcasting stations was not sufficient to fulfil the ambition to broadcast more than one channel to the whole country. (Before the war there had been four channels, but in reality only one had been national in its reach.) Given this severe limitation, to build a new state-of-the-art Broadcasting House (such was the project that had come up for discussion) was to put the cart before the horse.[74]

Broadcasters' room for manoeuvre began to expand in March 1945 with the (re-)launch of a second channel. It ran from 5.00 p.m. to 11.30 p.m., while Channel One broadcast for 20 hours daily, from 6.00 a.m. to 2.00 a.m. the following day.[75] Channel Two was to consist mainly of music, but would also offer children's programmes, literature, and science and education. As for the audience, on the eve of the launch Puzin was clear that this would primarily be an intelligentsia channel, as the more educated strata were as yet the only section of society that owned the radio sets necessary to receive the channel. For the time being there was no means of transmitting the two channels simultaneously by wire (*po setke*).[76]

In the late 1940s, a third channel was added to the schedule. Listeners in European Russia could tune in to Channel One on long or medium wave (or short wave for remote northern regions) for up to 20 hours per day, to Channel Two for up to 16 hours per day, and to Channel Three for up to 12 hours per day. Individual regions also offered their own programming for up to 2 hours per day on long or medium wave. Non-Russian republics in the Western part of the USSR received 20 hours of Moscow broadcasts, 14–16 hours of their own republican programming (which might include some rebroadcasts from the second Moscow channel), and the third Moscow channel on short wave. In the other two broadcasting zones of the RSFSR, listeners received a mixture of 'live' broadcasts from Moscow and Moscow programming rebroadcast at more convenient times, as well as a relatively small amount of local programming (2–4 hours). In addition, several of the major cities of the USSR (Leningrad, Kiev, Novosibirsk, Khabarovsk, Vladivostok, Riga, Tbilisi, Baku, Sverdlovsk, L'vov, Minsk, Tallinn, Vil'nius, Petrozavodsk, Alma-Ata, and Tashkent) had their own programming.[77]

In the post-Stalin era, the scale and complexity of the Soviet media industry steadily increased. The most obvious evidence of its increasing institutional clout

[74] GARF, f. 6903, op. 1, d. 97, ll. 6–7.

[75] There were separate timetables for the Far East, Siberia, and Central Asia, which amounted to 5 hours 40 minutes daily: GARF, f. 6903, op. 1, d. 104, l. 1. The decree on the introduction of the second channel, dated 7 March 1945, is reproduced in *VKD*, 112.

[76] GARF, f. 6903, op. 1, d. 106, ll. 6–7. For more on just how overstretched the Soviet broadcasting network was at this moment, see the meeting of 24 February 1945 on final preparations for the launch of Channel Two: ibid., d. 111.

[77] RGASPI, f. 17, op. 132, d. 93, ll. 1–4 (memo from Puzin to Shepilov, probably late 1948, on a new template for the broadcasting schedule).

was the reshuffle that in summer 1957 brought into being a separate State Committee for Radio and Television. The first head of this institution, Chesnokov, wasted no time in trying to raise the status of media professionals. As he pointed out in an early memo, the salaries of staff in radio and TV were clearly inadequate compared to those paid in the press, theatre, and cinema. Chesnokov followed through on his promises, writing to the Central Committee early in 1958 to argue for the need to raise payment rates for radio authors.[78] Later that year, a decree of Gosteleradio simplified the system for paying authors and performers for programmes made in one radio committee but supplied to another in the increasingly common practice of exchange of material between different radio committees.[79]

In general, it seems that the post-Stalin era made more money available to broadcasting organizations. Estonian broadcasting, for example, was given an extra 100,000 rubles to pay authors, 3,000 rubles for travel expenses, salary costs for three new correspondents, one sound technician and one announcer, and a car.[80] All the while, training of media personnel became more elaborate and more professionalized. In 1960, Leningrad and Kiev universities joined Moscow in offering courses for radio and TV journalists. Even party schools introduced radio and television onto their curriculum in this era.[81] When N. N. Mesiatsev took over as head of broadcasting in 1964, he discovered that the Radio and Television Committee had more than 30,000 employees in Moscow alone.[82]

The radio professionals of the post-Stalin era also quite simply had more to do. Until the mid-1950s, only Channel One broadcast through the day. Channel Two started only in mid-afternoon (apart from Sundays), while Channel Three broadcast only in the evenings.[83] In July 1956, Channel Two was given significantly more airtime: 15 hours per day instead of 10.[84] Qualitative changes followed in April 1958, when a new schedule doubled the number of news broadcasts and introduced regular evening commentaries ('Themes of the Day') at 9 p.m. It also increased the amount of satire and humour, science and technology, and drama (including both radio plays and relays from the theatre). The amount of broadcasting time on the Moscow city wired network was to increase by a factor of two or three to 4.5–5 hours per day, while a number of measures were taken to coordinate better the central and local radio schedules.[85]

On 1 July 1960 came another expansion of the schedule: the daily airtime of the central channels rose to an impressive 69 hours 40 minutes. There was a small increase for Channel Two and Moscow city radio and a larger one for short-wave

---

[78] Memo of 2 August 1957, in *VKD*, 140–2; letter to Central Committee in RGANI, f. 5, op. 33, d. 72, ll. 19–22.

[79] Decree of 30 October 1958, which I read in the archive of Estonian radio at ERA.R, f. 1590, op. 4, d. 109, l. 42.

[80] Decree of 18 July 1953, at ERA.R, 1590.4.44.4.

[81] *Problemy televideniia i radio* (Moscow, 1971), 5.

[82] N. N. Mesiatsev, *Gorizonty i labirinty moei zhizni* (Moscow, 2005), 463.

[83] In the 1950s, radio listings were given in full in the newspaper *Radioprogrammy*.

[84] According to P. S. Gurevich and V. N. Ruzhnikov, *Sovetskoe radioveshchanie: Stranitsy istorii* (Moscow, 1976), ch. 8.

[85] Chesnokov to Agiprop, 21 February 1958, GARF, f. 6903, op. 1, d. 542, ll. 22–5.

broadcasting. A news broadcast was installed at 9.00 p.m. (previously there had been a gap in news coverage between 7.00 p.m. and 10.30 p.m.); surveys of international issues were inserted, due to popular demand, at 7.20 p.m. Satire and humour gained an increased presence, becoming a regular element of the Saturday evening schedule as well as featuring two to three times on weekdays; on Sundays, moreover, the existing 'Cheery Companion' (*Veselyi sputnik*) was joined by 'Good Morning' (*S dobrym utrom*). There was now even a monthly equivalent for children, 'Have a Giggle' (*Smeshinka*). The children's schedule also expanded in other areas to cater better to listening patterns. *Pionerskaia zor'ka*, the bedrock of programming for the younger audience, was now broadcast not only at 7.35 a.m. but also at 2.35 p.m. (three times per week) so that children could listen after school as well. More generally, children's programmes were being moved to the second half of the day, given that one-shift schooling was increasingly the norm. The new programme also took more account of listeners east of Moscow. Radio plays, operas, and operettas went out between 4 p.m. and 7 p.m., which made them convenient for the Urals and Western Siberia.[86]

There was still obvious room for improvement. For example, many listeners wanted more music in the morning, but this was impossible while only Channel One was available between 6.00 a.m. and 8.45 a.m. In the early 1960s, additional channels were introduced for Soviet citizens living abroad and for those regions of the country mainly accessible by short wave; from October 1960 All-Union Radio could boast 24-hour broadcasting.[87] By the late 1970s, central broadcasting was responsible for almost 160 hours of airtime per day on its five channels.[88] But by far the most significant change to the schedule was the launch in August 1964 of Radio Maiak on the basis of the existing Channel Two. Maiak was an obvious riposte (or homage) to engaging Western radio stations: it offered a winning blend of short half-hourly news bulletins and abundant light music, all of this delivered round the clock.

Maiak was without question the outstanding success story of Soviet radio in its last two decades. But this coup for Soviet broadcasting policy, as well as the accompanying general expansion of the schedule, was undermined by continuing failures in technology and infrastructure. It was perhaps not surprising that in 1954, still less than ten years after the end of the war, listeners in provincial Russia were having difficulty picking up the second and third channels.[89] Even at the very end of the 1950s, however, the Radio Committee was informing the Central Committee that only Channel One could be received all over the USSR, but that in the Baltic republics, Karelia, Western Ukraine, Belorussia, southern Central Asia, the South Caucasus, and the North, even this was not guaranteed. Channel Two was mainly limited to central European Russia. More than fifty regions did not have

---

[86] M. Kiperman, 'Chto novogo v novoi setke?', *Sovradiotel*, no. 4 (1960): 17–18.

[87] A. A. Sherel', *Audiokul'tura XX veka. Istoriia, esteticheskie zakonomernosti, osobennosti vliianiia na auditoriiu: Ocherki* (Moscow, 2004), 88.

[88] *Televidenie i radioveshchanie SSSR* (Moscow, 1979), 155.

[89] GARF, f. 6903, op. 10, d. 8, l. 17 (letter from Rostov, 1954).

their own radio station and were dependent on their neighbours (which might not broadcast at a convenient time). Although the plan was to increase the network of short-wave stations, it was not clear how many people would have short-wave sets; it should still be a priority to increase the reach of the second and third channels on medium and long wave.[90] Even in 1963, the main journal for media professionals frankly acknowledged that only one channel could reach the whole of the country.[91] As of the mid-1960s, there were still tens of millions of wired transmission points in the country: listeners reliant on the *tochka* could only hear the first programme.[92] It was not until 1967 that the Soviet radio network started to introduce three-channel broadcasting over wire.[93] For many wired listeners, it seems, the early 1970s were the moment they finally got a choice of channel. Maiak, now the second 'button' on a wired receiver point, could finally claim to have entered the fabric of Soviet life.[94]

Yet, as of the 1960s, the disturbing fact was that foreign broadcasts were sometimes easier to tune into than Soviet. In 1963, one Moscow radio professional tried to catch what he could on short wave between 7 p.m. and 9 p.m. on his six-tube Czech set. He was able to get the first Soviet channel, the second less clearly, and the third not at all. This was in the context of intensive 'enemy' broadcasting into the USSR: between 6 p.m. and midnight it was possible to catch 'not less than nine and sometimes 12 news broadcasts in Russian directed at the Soviet Union'.[95]

BROADCASTING TO AND FROM THE WEST

One defining feature of post-war Soviet broadcasting was the shift from wired to wireless listener as the imagined (and, in large measure, actual) addressee of Soviet radio. Another was that Soviet broadcasters were operating in an unprecedentedly international media world: they were locked in a defining relationship of rivalry and grudging imitation with their counterparts on the other side of the Iron Curtain.

In theory, this was an opportunity as much as a threat. After all, head of broadcasting Puzin had pointed out to his colleagues as early as May 1945 the need to shift from hostile wartime propaganda to more subtle forms of appeal to the Western listener.[96] In May 1946, Agitprop reflected on the immense opportunity represented by the more than 60 million radio sets in the USA. It was essential for Soviet broadcasts to find the right arguments to appeal to this audience—for example by emphasizing to this God-fearing nation that the USSR guaranteed

---

[90] GARF, f. 6903, op. 1, d. 578, ll. 61–2 (Chesnokov to Kirichenko, 8 June 1959).

[91] M. Kiperman, 'Vazhnaia mera', *Sovradiotel*, no. 11 (1963): 23–4.

[92] A. Akhtyrskii, 'Neskol'ko voprosov dlia obsuzhdeniia', *Sovradiotel*, no. 9 (1965): 4.

[93] Sherel', *Audiokul'tura XX veka*, 94.

[94] It is hard to say exactly how fast three-channel wired broadcasting spread, but anecdotal evidence suggests that many families did not acquire such sets until the 1970s.

[95] TsAOPIM, f. 2930, op. 1, d. 42, ll. 131–2.   [96] GARF, f. 6903, op. 1, d. 115.

religious freedom.[97] A few weeks earlier, the head of Agitprop Georgii Aleksandrov had informed Molotov of plans to increase the power of Soviet radio stations broadcasting to foreign countries. Short-wave transmitters would be provided with better antennas, while medium- and long-wave station would be established in the Baltic republics, Belorussia, Ukraine, and the South Caucasus.[98] In 1950, Agitprop was able to report that powerful medium-wave stations had been built in Riga, L'vov, and Tallinn with a view to reaching the foreign listener.[99] By now, foreign broadcasting was an extensive undertaking: there were three broadcasts per day to the USA (total 3 hours 35 minutes), four to China (2 hours), almost 3 hours to France, and so on.[100]

In addition to their domestic tasks, post-war Soviet broadcasters were charged with spreading the word of socialism to the rest of the world, including its decolonizing parts, as well as firing informational broadsides at the Cold War adversary. The importance of this mission meant that Soviet foreign broadcasting—Radio Moscow, as it was known—in due course became the most glamorous and prestigious workplace for aspiring media professionals. Radio Moscow was also more generously resourced than domestic broadcasting, whether in terms of foreign correspondents, transmission capacity, or linguistic expertise. The number of languages spoken on Radio Moscow more than tripled from twenty-one at the end of the war to sixty-five or more in the late 1960s. At a time when central radio remained firmly Russocentric and even republican stations were doing little to recognize the linguistic diversity of the Soviet population, the sad fact was that 'most of the USSR's Korean and German speakers would have had a better chance of hearing their languages on Radio Moscow than on the domestic network'.[101]

The significance of Radio Moscow in the early Cold War era was reflected in a bifurcation of the administrative apparatus in 1949: foreign broadcasting acquired a separate organizational identity as the 'Broadcasting Committee' (*Komitet radioveshchaniia*) as opposed to the 'Radiofication Committee' (*Komitet radiofikatsii*) that was responsible for radio within the USSR. Yet foreign broadcast personnel were subject to the same pressures as their domestic counterparts. On the one hand, they had to maintain ideological rectitude at all times. Certain radio commentators were felt to indulge in 'empty joking' instead of delivering a 'worthy rebuttal to the Anglo-American slanderers'. One excessively flippant passage that raised the hackles of the ideological watchdogs was the following: 'Just try to buy the same thing at the same price in Paris or London that you can

---

[97] 'O sovetskikh radioperedachakh na SShA' (13 May 1946), RGASPI, f. 17, op. 125, d. 470, l. 126.

[98] RGASPI, f. 17, op. 125, d. 470, ll. 192–5.

[99] RGASPI, f. 17, op. 132, d. 434, l. 44 (Agitprop to Suslov, 1 April 1950). Previously Soviet broadcasts had been going out on short wave, while most listeners in Western Europe had medium-wave sets.

[100] RGASPI, f. 17, op. 132, d. 435.

[101] Roth-Ey, *Moscow Prime Time*, 150; and note the useful discussion of the overall performance of Radio Moscow, ibid. 150–6.

buy today in Moscow. If you can't do it, blame your economic system. And try, in so far as your intellectual capacities allow, to grasp our socialist system.'[102] On the other hand, the foreign radio service was urged to take more account of the specific profile of its target audiences abroad and to respond more promptly to the latest developments. As Agitprop confessed to Malenkov in a memo of 5 May 1950, Soviet broadcasting was still much too slow to react. Soviet radio news came out 12 to 18 hours after the publication of the central newspapers and was heard by listeners well after the BBC and VOA had delivered their verdicts.[103]

Naturally, the requirement of rapid response was in tension, if not in contradiction, with the imperative to maintain ideological standards. As the deputy head of the Broadcasting Committee made clear in a memo to Malenkov of 7 September 1950, a large part of the rationale for the creation of this committee in place of the old Administration for Foreign Broadcasting (*Upravlenie inoveshchaniia*) had been the need to purge foreign broadcasting of undesirable elements. As part of the transition, just over 200 members of staff were dismissed and more than 400 new people appointed, mainly young graduates of places like the Institute of Foreign Relations, the Higher Diplomatic School, and the Institute of Foreign Languages. Now, well over half of staff members had higher or incomplete higher education. The proportion of party and Komsomol members had increased. Even more pertinently, the Soviet Union's leading nationality was now better represented: after the reorganization, the proportion of Russian staff members had risen from 46 per cent to 67 per cent, while the Jewish contingent had fallen from 30 per cent to 10 per cent. Although foreign broadcasting still had to use the services of foreigners, given the need for translators and announcers, most foreigners in the employ of the Radio Committee had now taken Soviet citizenship, and the aim in future was to train up Soviet people to take these roles.[104] Unsurprisingly, a report presented to the Central Committee in December 1952 found that the 174 foreigners and Soviet citizens of foreign origin working in the Radio Committee were isolated and largely ignorant of Soviet life.[105]

No wonder the broadcasting authorities were taking such an interest in cadre questions. Viewed from the Central Committee, foreign broadcasting contained a worrying number of moving parts. A great deal of it was being produced in centres other than Moscow. In early 1950, for example, foreign broadcasting from Tallinn comprised 30 minutes in Finnish and 20 minutes in Estonian; Riga broadcast 40 minutes to Latvians abroad; Vilnius for 20 minutes to Lithuanians; Kiev for

---

[102] RGASPI, f. 17, op. 125, d. 640, ll. 19–21 (internal report of 13 March 1948 delivered to Suslov).

[103] RGASPI, f. 17, op. 132, d. 435, l. 47.

[104] RGASPI, f. 17, op. 132, d. 434, ll. 97–9. For more on practical measures taken to train up translators, see ibid., ll. 21–7 (memo from head of Komitet radioveshchaniia S. Vinogradov to Malenkov, 31 January 1950).

[105] RGASPI, f. 17, op. 132, d. 563, ll. 110–14. For a later letter to Khrushchev on the poor living conditions of foreigners working on the radio, see RGANI, f. 5, op. 16, d. 659, ll. 72–4 (1 February 1954).

more than 1 hour to the Ukrainian diaspora; Baku for 100 minutes in Turkish and 100 minutes in Farsi; and so on, all the way to Khabarovsk (Chinese, Japanese, and Korean) and Tashkent (Farsi and Uigur). There was always the possibility that these far-flung radio committees might be overstepping their authority: an investigation had shown, for example, that the Kazakh radio committee, in its broadcasts to the Kazakh population over the border in China and Mongolia, had allowed local authors to pronounce on international themes that were off limits to them.[106] There was also the perennial Soviet anxiety about slips of the tongue. The only fail-safe way to avoid such accidents was to ensure that all material was pre-recorded. But, as of late 1950, only ten of thirty-two committees responsible for foreign broadcasts were taping their programmes even in part. Broadcasts to China, Germany, France, Korea, Japan, the Near and Far East, almost all the people's democracies, and the Scandinavian countries went out live.[107] The nervousness about coverage of international affairs also extended to broadcasts for the domestic audience. In 1951 Puzin asked for permission to hire permanent commentators on international affairs to strengthen international coverage. His request was turned down by Agitprop on the grounds that the Radio Committee had been insufficiently vigilant in its recent broadcasting on international affairs.[108]

All the while, Soviet broadcasters clutched at any evidence that they were getting through to their target audiences. In April 1951 the Radio Committee discovered that American soldiers in Korea were listening to Soviet broadcasts intended for the USA. Since then extra broadcasts in English had been sent in the direction of Korea; in the preceding two months, the Radio Committee had received more than twenty letters from American soldiers (including some collective letters).[109] Rather more typical, however, were complaints that broadcasts were failing in their propaganda mission: not only was there often a time lag in Soviet coverage of news, broadcasts were delivered in stilted and abstract language and gave an implausibly cloudless account of life in the USSR.[110] The Soviet authorities could not even agree on a slogan for their foreign broadcasts: in June 1950, the head of the Broadcasting Committee wrote to Suslov to propose that foreign broadcasts begin with the phrase 'Defending Peace Is the Cause of All the World's Nations' (before the war, predictably enough, the mantra had been 'Proletarians of All Countries, Unite!'). But Agitprop soon rejected the idea on the grounds that 'Propaganda for the achievements of the supporters of the peace camp and attacks on the plans of the Anglo-American warmongers for a new imperialist war comprise one of the most important, but not the only task of our broadcasting to foreign countries'.[111] Concerns that Soviet foreign broadcasting was failing to hit its target only intensified

---

[106] RGASPI, f. 17, op. 132, d. 434, ll. 18–19 (Agitprop to Suslov, 18 April 1950), ll. 39–41 (Agitprop to Suslov, 1 March 1950).

[107] RGASPI, f. 17, op. 132, d. 434, ll. 103–5 (secretary of party bureau on radio to Malenkov, December 1950).

[108] RGASPI, f. 17, op. 132, d. 491, l. 8.

[109] RGASPI, f. 17, op. 132, d. 491, ll. 130–1.

[110] RGASPI, f. 17, op. 132, d. 563, ll. 9–15 (Agitprop memo to Malenkov, 28 January 1952).

[111] RGASPI, f. 17, op. 132, d. 434, ll. 56–7.

in the Khrushchev era, as culture became more of a focus for Cold War competition. In August 1954, Khrushchev was informed by the Finland correspondent of *Trud* that Soviet broadcasts to the country were not working. The announcers sounded as if they had spent too long abroad, interviews were stilted, and Finns were not much impressed by talk of outstanding milkmaids (theirs were better).[112] The authorities anxiously gathered feedback such as the following opinion of an Italian communist in early 1956: 'Your information is hopelessly old, often the whole profile of broadcasts has a Russian character, it's not "Italianized".'[113]

None of this would have mattered so much if the other side had not mobilized its broadcasting resources so effectively. As Aleksandrov reported to Zhdanov as early as March 1946, the British were already broadcasting in Russian to the USSR for more than an hour each day, focusing mainly on the awkward issue of Soviet reluctance to withdraw troops from Iran.[114] Voice of America launched its broadcasts to the USSR in February 1947. Although the Soviet authorities commenced jamming the following year, and in the late Stalin era Soviet citizens were sometimes prosecuted under the notorious article 58-10 for listening to foreign radio, by 1950 the Americans already claimed that they had regular listeners as far away as the Urals.[115] In April 1948, to give one striking example of ideological illiteracy, an elderly Leningrader wrote to his diocese to complain of the absence of functioning churches in his district and to request that services be broadcast, mentioning that 'you often find yourself hearing from abroad, from Finland and England and others, but you can't hear your very own church services'.[116] By the early 1950s, many border regions were appearing helpless in the face of the propaganda barrage from the West. The Lithuanian first secretary reported that anti-Soviet broadcasts had started on the BBC and VOA from February 1951. The only jamming was taking place in Vilnius; the regional centres of Klaipeda, Siauliai, and Kaunas were entirely defenceless.[117] In September 1951 the Kirgiz first secretary reported that his capital Frunze had recently been targeted by anti-Soviet programmes from the USA and England; all the resources of the city were being devoted to jamming these broadcasts, but five or six programmes were still getting through.[118]

In the Khrushchev period, likewise, Soviet broadcasters were forever in reactive and defensive mode. It is almost poignant to read documents such as the letter the

---

[112] RGANI, f. 5, op. 16, d. 677, l. 49.

[113] RGANI, f. 5, op. 33, d. 10, l. 4. Nor was the problem restricted to the Western Cold War audience. Tashkent International Radio was criticized by Soviet officials in the 1950s for not broadcasting in languages other than Russian and for failing to engage the listener. As a result, it was failing in its mission to spread the Soviet word to India, Afghanistan, and beyond. See Paul Stronski, *Tashkent: Forging a Soviet City, 1930–1966* (Pittsburgh, 2010), 240–1.

[114] RGASPI, f. 17, op. 125, d. 470, ll. 113–14.

[115] Rósa Magnúsdóttir, 'Keeping Up Appearances: How the Soviet State Failed to Control Popular Attitudes to the United States of America, 1945–1959', PhD dissertation (Chapel Hill, NC, 2006), 117–21.

[116] Arkhiv Sankt-Peterburgskoi Eparkhii, f. 1, op. 11, d. 13, ll. 6–6ob. My thanks to Catriona Kelly for this reference.

[117] RGASPI, f. 17, op. 132, d. 491, l. 1.   [118] RGASPI, f. 17, op. 132, d. 491, l. 15.

Sakhalin *obkom* sent to Khrushchev in January 1954. In the face of hostile propaganda from the USA, England, and Japan, this remote border region had set up no fewer than thirty-eight jamming stations in three different centres on the island. But even this had proved insufficient: the BBC and VOA could be heard freely, especially on a wavelength of 16–19 metres.[119] By the second half of the 1950s, the Soviet authorities were well aware that jamming was not working; maybe, a report of June 1958 suggested, it was time to rationalize by abandoning jamming of broadcasts in little-known languages such as Farsi.[120] A couple of months later, another memo to the Central Committee reported that, although the power of jamming stations was three times that of the hostile stations broadcasting to the USSR, jamming was ineffective except for the centre of Moscow, Leningrad, Kiev, and Riga. The sobering conclusion was that 'in essence the whole country is open to enemy radio'.[121] In the 1960s, if you were at a sanatorium (i.e. out of range of jamming), it was possible to surf the airwaves and hear foreign speech even with an old radiola, once you had fixed it with a good antenna.[122]

By the turn of the 1950s it was widely accepted that, given finite resources, jamming should be used selectively. Radio committees in border regions also suggested a more subtle way of combating hostile foreign broadcasts: they would schedule the most appealing parts of their programming for the times of day that enemy propaganda was at its most intense.[123] They also had to make sure that listeners had reliable access to Soviet broadcasts. As Puzin observed in 1956, the failings of Soviet broadcasting infrastructure were practically driving listeners into the clutches of Western broadcasters. For a large part of the day, Soviet radio effectively had only one channel to offer the population. During the Twentieth Party Congress, programming from Moscow had to be transmitted over wired networks in fifty cities of the USSR; the wireless transmission network still offered no guarantee of reaching the bulk of the population. Jamming of Western broadcasts into the Soviet Union was interfering with the Soviets' own programming and threatened to 'paralyse' Soviet short-wave broadcasting.[124] The following year, Puzin's successor Chesnokov stated bluntly in a report to the Central Committee that the long-standing emphasis on building powerful broadcasting stations to reach foreign countries meant that broadcasting capacity in many regions of the RSFSR had been badly neglected.[125]

Yet Cold War imperatives did not become any less urgent in the 1960s. In April 1963, a fifth channel was launched for Soviet citizens living abroad and for

---

[119] RGANI, f. 5, op. 16, d. 659, ll. 102–3.

[120] 'Spravka ob effektivnosti zabivki antisovetskikh radioperedach po sostoianiiu na 10 iiunia 1958 g.', RGANI, f. 5, op. 33, d. 75, ll. 146–8.

[121] RGANI, f. 5, op. 33, d. 75, l. 164.   [122] Oxf/Lev M-04, PF 43 (A), p. 18.

[123] For examples of this argument in March 1959 from Latvia and the Far Eastern (Primorskii) region, see RGANI, f. 5, op. 33, d. 106, ll. 8–11.

[124] Plan for speech entitled 'O sostoianii material'no-tekhnicheskikh sredstv radioveshchaniia', *VKD*, 137–8.

[125] Report of 2 August 1957; repr. in *VKD*, 140–2.

foreigners who knew Russian.[126] Broadcasters continued to worry about delivering effective rebuttals and counter-attacks to 'slanderous' treatments of the Soviet Union by American radio.[127] And broadcasting committees in border regions were constantly urged to stay on their mettle. At a gathering of editors from foreign broadcasting in June 1965, staff were reminded of the need to take account of, and counteract, hostile propaganda. The Uzbek, Armenian, and Belorussian sections were deemed especially remiss in this regard. The recommendation was to reduce the reliance on material from central radio and to prepare, two or three times per week, commentaries on international affairs crafted specifically for the target audience. Yet the central authorities were not willing to withdraw entirely: it was desirable for all such commentaries to be sent to Moscow for approval. If a republican radio committee did not have suitably qualified personnel, then they could pay Moscow radio journalists to do the job for them.[128]

As ever, the politics of broadcasting depended not only on transmission capacity but also on reception. The Cold War could only be waged with such intensity over the airwaves because of the Soviet Union's post-war turn to production of wireless radio sets, many of them with short-wave capacity.[129] Puzin stated the point with exemplary clarity in 1956: by making available millions of short-wave radio sets to Soviet consumers, the Soviet authorities were playing into the hands of Western radio stations. At the time he wrote there were about 5 million such sets; according to the projections, that figure would rise to 20–30 million by the end of the current five-year plan. Maybe, Puzin suggested, it was time to change course.[130] The same point was made even more bluntly in a report to the Central Committee of August 1958: the mass production of short-wave radios, it concluded, had not been a necessity and had been driven 'merely by commercial considerations'. As a result of this wrong-headed policy, about 85 per cent of short-wave sets in the USSR were held in the European part of the country, where there were no domestic short-wave broadcasts and only enemy radio could be heard.[131]

At the start of the 1950s there were perhaps 3 million wireless radio sets in the USSR. By the end of the decade, there were more than 20 million, and listeners no longer needed to fear prosecution for tuning in to foreign broadcasts. Towards the end of the Khrushchev period, the authorities gave up jamming as a game not worth the candle, while also trying to curtail production of the short-wave sets that

---

[126] Sherel', *Audiokul'tura XX veka*, 88.

[127] See e.g. a memo by the head of the Propaganda Department of Gosteleradio in 1967, *VKD*, 169–72.

[128] ERA.R. 1590.4.429.12–18 (minutes of meeting of 10–12 June 1965). On the basis of letters received from listeners, Riga and Tallinn were deemed the most effective stations in foreign broadcasting.

[129] On this point, see Kristin Roth-Ey's excellent account of the 'ironies of *radiofikatsiia*': *Moscow Prime Time*, 135–46.

[130] *VKD*, 138.   [131] RGANI, f. 5, op. 33, d. 75, l. 165.

gave the population access to foreign radio.[132] This measure, however, came much too late to bring about any change in Soviet citizens' listening patterns. Almost every account of Soviet society in the 1960s–70s contains nuggets of information on the audience of foreign radio in the USSR. In 1968, for example, a young correspondent from Odessa informed the KGB of the undisguised preference for Western radio stations among students in the city.[133] A survey conducted by the Moscow city party organization in 1975 found that four out of five students in the city, and well over half of the working population, were listening to Western radio.[134] In 1977, the authorities in Gorky found that, despite a fanfare on the subject from the Soviet media, some citizens were getting their information on the new Soviet constitution from foreign radio.[135]

CONCLUSION

The Soviet population of the post-Khrushchev era was without question more media-savvy than hitherto. We should not rush, however, to infer from its listening habits disaffection or disloyalty. As Donald Raleigh observes in the introduction to his collection of interviews with Soviet 'baby boomers', foreign radio did not necessarily change people's views, and did not necessarily turn them into anything other than Soviet patriots. Largely congruent are the conclusions of Victor Zaslavsky, who finds that the spread of short-wave radio sets and the abandonment of jamming did not affect the mainstream view of the events in Czechoslovakia in 1968, which very much followed the official line.[136]

Certainly, the constant background presence of Western radio acted as a spur to the Soviet media industry. The most significant innovations in Soviet broadcasting practice of the 1960s were directly imitative of foreign models.[137] But that should not lead us to underestimate the distance travelled by Soviet broadcasting in the first three post-war decades. In the late 1940s, radio in most parts of the Soviet Union was a shoestring operation and appeared to have regressed to the 1920s in

---

[132] As the minutes of a Presidium meeting of 25 April 1963 recorded, the task was to produce radio sets 'so that they only pick up our programmes'. See A. A. Fursenko (ed.), *Prezidium TsK KPSS. 1954–1964. Chernovye protokol'nye zapisi zasedanii. Stenogrammy. Postanovleniia*, i (Moscow, 2003), 702.

[133] Nikolai Mitrokhin, *Russkaia partiia: Dvizhenie russkikh natsionalistov v SSSR. 1953–1985 gody* (Moscow, 2003), 361.

[134] Timothy J. Colton, *Moscow: Governing the Socialist Metropolis* (Cambridge, Mass., 1995), 422. For more on radio in the student milieu, see Benjamin K. Tromly, 'Re-Imagining the Soviet Intelligentsia: Student Politics and University Life, 1948–1964', PhD dissertation (Harvard University, 2007), 279; Donald J. Raleigh, *Russia's Sputnik Generation: Soviet Baby Boomers Talk about Their Lives* (Bloomington, Ind., 2006), 40–1.

[135] *Obshchestvo i vlast'. Rossiiskaia provintsiia 1917–1980-e gody*, v. *1965–1985* (Moscow and Nizhnii Novgorod, 2008), 484.

[136] Raleigh, *Russia's Sputnik Generation*, 19; Victor Zaslavsky, *The Neo-Stalinist State: Class, Ethnicity, and Consensus in Soviet Society* (Armonk, 1982), 28. Poland in 1980 may have been a rather different matter, however: see Michael Binyon, *Life in Russia* (London, 1983), 127–8.

[137] See Roth-Ey, *Moscow Prime Time*, 156–74 and my own discussion in Chapter 7.

its parasitical relationship to the print media. By the 1970s, although concerns were still periodically expressed about the low educational level of personnel in local broadcasting,[138] Soviet radio was a vastly more elaborate and sophisticated branch of cultural production. To judge by the slew of celebratory works published in recent years, radio presenters in the provinces could acquire the status of local celebrities. This is not even to mention the Soviet Union's greatest media treasure, Iurii Levitan, who kept up a strenuous public speaking schedule until his death in 1983.[139] By the late 1960s, moreover, Soviet radio had achieved an unprecedented degree of integration and coordination. The exchange of programmes between different studios took on a new significance in the 1960s and ensured that the various regional radio committees combined harmoniously to project a stable Sovietness. The Estonian radio committee, for example, was asked to prepare eight to ten broadcasts for use by other radio committees over the course of 1962; overall, central broadcasting was hoping to elicit twenty-five to thirty 'exchange' broadcasts per month. From time to time, the Estonians received specific requests such as a request from Far Eastern radio to send greetings from Estonian fishermen to their counterparts in the Pacific region.[140] A few years further on, in 1967 (the fiftieth anniversary of the Revolution) and 1970 (the centenary of Lenin's birth), radio committees were drawn into a massive effort of cultural coordination. In Chapters 6 and 7, then, I seek to explain how—with a little help from its 'enemies' abroad—Soviet radio came of age.

---

[138] In Gorky region in 1974, less than half of editors on *raion* radio had higher education, while the level of party membership on factory radio was considered low. But even this set the bar much higher than anyone would have thought to do in the 1940s or early 1950s. See *Obshchestvo i vlast'*, 42.

[139] Alla Zubova, *Znamenitosti v domashnem inter'ere* (Moscow, 2001), 13; on Levitan's long career, see also Binyon, *Life in Russia*, 123–5.

[140] ERA.R, 1590.4.247.8 and 1590.4.250.61.

6

The *Magnitofon* and the Art of Soviet Broadcasting

In the autumn of 1945, the scriptwriter Mark Tseitlin and the journalist Boris Iagling proposed a 'new form of radio report'. Their idea was to introduce a new comic hero. Like a well-known American counterpart, he would be hyperactive, speak in a squeaky voice, and have gigantic ears. He would go out and about, interviewing Soviet people on trains, in worker clubs, at home, in maternity wards, and simply on the street. His name would be Microphone.[1]

No doubt this new concept owed much to the high spirits of the immediate post-war moment and to the brief cordial relationship between the Soviet Union and the United States. Eight months earlier the head of the Radio Committee had squashed the idea for a series entitled 'Taking a Microphone around Moscow';[2] six months later it would be hard to imagine Soviet scriptwriters citing Mickey Mouse as their inspiration. But Tseitlin and Iagling's proposal, and their script for a New Year's broadcast, reflected the exciting power of a new technology. The roving microphone could reach parts of Soviet life inaccessible to sound cinema. With compelling immediacy it brought listeners into contact with Soviet people in all walks of life. Scornful of the presenter's efforts to keep him cooped up in the studio, Microphone set out on his mission to roam. On New Year's Eve, he observed writers sipping champagne in the Central House for Workers in the Arts; met the first child born in 1946; heard Dmitrii Shostakovich play the piano on a home visit to the composer; and spoke to a demobilized soldier on the train from Vladivostok as it neared the capital.[3]

Existing accounts of post-war Soviet radio have a teleological character: with dismal inevitability, they show Soviet broadcasting facing and failing the challenge of mass-cultural competition from the Cold War adversary. The example of 'Mickey Microphone', however, suggests that at least some Soviet broadcasters in 1945 were more cutting edge than blunt instrument. Not only had they gained crucial know-how over the previous decade, they also benefited from the newly acquired status of their medium. At war's end the prestige of radio had never been

---

[1] RGALI, f. 2965, op. 1, d. 34, ll. 1–2. According to Tat'iana Goriaeva, the script was designed for the Anglo-American department of the Radio Committee: Goriaeva, ' "Velikaia kniga dnia": Radio i sotsiokul'turnaia sreda v SSSR v 1920–30-e gody', in Hans Günther and Sabine Hänsgen (eds.), *Sovetskaia vlast' i media* (St Petersburg, 2006), 71.

[2] A. Puzin, at a meeting of 21 February 1945: GARF, f. 6903, op. 1, d. 110, l. 56.

[3] For the script of the New Year's broadcast, see RGALI, f. 2965, op. 1, d. 34, ll. 3–19.

higher. If anything, it rose further over the following two decades. In the late 1940s, the government launched a campaign to make radio accessible to the entire Soviet population; by 1960 it would claim that full 'radiofication' had been achieved. The period 1945–65—from the end of the war to the displacement of radio by television as the primary medium of Soviet mass culture—has a strong claim to be considered radio's golden age.

During the war broadcasters' stylistic repertoire had still been limited by the imperative to mobilize listeners and to maintain military discipline—and by the desperate shortage of time and resources. Many insiders were clear-sighted about the inadequacies of Soviet radio. As so often in the past, a regular source of complaint and (self-)criticism was the practice of taking material wholesale from the newspapers.[4] When broadcasters tried to compensate for the dryness of their texts, they sometimes rushed to the opposite extreme: they did not read out the material but 'declaimed' it with 'incredible pomposity and pathos'.[5] Wartime broadcasters also faced the by now traditional problem of producing a Soviet vox pop that was both authentic and ideologically impeccable. In practice, they often compromised on the former goal. Even the popular 'Letters to and from the Front', which accounted for ten daily broadcasts amounting to 2 hours 30 minutes and drew an average of 30,000 letters per month to the Radio Committee, did not always succeed in preserving the 'individuality' of letter writers in the process of 'literary reworking' of texts for broadcasting. 'Newspaper formulas', 'political slogans', and 'clichéd phrases' were the order of the day.[6]

Early in 1945, however, radio professionals could turn their thoughts to how the medium might be revitalized for the coming new era: by diversifying broadcasting formats and increasing the quality of performance both of music and of the spoken word.[7] That summer, they received an early post-war test when Stalin personally instructed that the parade of 24 June should be made a major broadcasting event. The radio staff who gathered to discuss this commission a little more than a week in advance were already under pressure: the text of the broadcast had to be submitted ahead of time for editing and authorization, and that meant a deadline of the evening of 19 June. Time pressure alone was nothing new for wartime broadcasters. A more unfamiliar challenge was the need to find a fresh and compelling way of narrating the occasion. Previous set-piece public events—May Day, Revolution Day—had been carefully staged and choreographed. Radio commentators always had plenty of detail to give listeners and faced little risk of discrepancy between script and event. This time, however, the production values of the parade would be more modest. At the same time, it was important to find an alternative to the high-flown account that radio had given of the recent May Day parade.

---

[4] For examples of this complaint from meetings of October 1944 and June 1946, see GARF, f. 6903, op. 1, d. 94, ll. 7–8, 25; d. 157, ll. 4–6.

[5] The quotation is from a meeting of 1 August 1944: GARF, f. 6903, op. 1, d. 89, l. 16.

[6] GARF, f. 6903, op. 1, d. 70, ll. 5–6 (report on 'Pis'ma na front i s fronta, 15 July–15 August 1942).

[7] These points were raised at a meeting in the Radio Committee of 7 February 1945: GARF, f. 6903, op. 1, d. 106.

Broadcasters needed to break up political commentary into shorter sections of text, with regular changes of voice and of scene. Telephone points would be set up in central Moscow for reporters to give ground-level accounts; as they did so, moreover, they should ensure the listener imagined they were not reading a prepared text.[8]

Whether this last ambition was achieved is, however, quite another matter. One of the speakers at the June meeting raised a heartfelt objection: 'I have been improvising at the microphone for six or seven years, but you don't produce much natural conversation [*zhivoi razgovor*] that way, because you get so tense at the thought of millions of people listening to you that you feel horribly constrained.'[9] Here, in a nutshell, was the perennial dilemma of Soviet broadcasters: radio was meant to be a charismatic force for mobilization but it was also strictly controlled, and the penalties for even minor errors were severe.[10]

ADOPTING THE *MAGNITOFON*

In the post-war era, however, a new technology arrived to ease the plight of Soviet broadcasters: mobile and reasonably user-friendly recording equipment (the magnetic tape recorder, or *magnitofon*). Before the war, the vast majority of non-musical programmes (and a fairly large majority even of music broadcasts) had gone out live: technology was not advanced enough to permit much recording or careful editing. The situation began to change with the arrival of the first 'trophy' recorders, which as well as being easier to work with offered vastly better sound quality.[11] The tape recorder held the potential to transform Soviet broadcasting practice: in theory at least, the more adventurous journalists could now depart from the leaden Stalinist formula of scripted 'declarations' (*vystupleniia*) and strive for a more natural broadcasting style.

A technology for sound recording on to tape had existed in the USSR since the late 1920s. Named the 'shorinophone' (after the inventor A. F. Shorin), it used cinema film to record sound.[12] A mobile version of this equipment took some time to develop, though during the war it was used to record some important footage. The drawback of the shorinophone was that editing was time-consuming and

---

[8] GARF, f. 6903, op. 1, d. 118 (meeting of 15 June 1945).

[9] GARF, f. 6903, op. 1, d. 118, l. 20.

[10] One file from the Gorky party archive in 1949 neatly illustrates the dilemma. It contains both an exposé of vulgar *chastushki* and general sloppiness by broadcasters *and* criticism of clichés such as the parroting of material from Moscow and an implausibly elaborate *vystuplenie* by a Stakhanovite. GOPANO, f. 3, op. 1, d. 7302, ll. 1–3, 159–63. For similar material from 1952, see ibid., d. 8968, ll. 23–37.

[11] As noted especially by music broadcasters: see GARF, f. 6903, op. 1, d. 161, ll. 4–5 (meeting of music department, 24 January 1946). For a later account, see M. Shalashnikov, 'V dni, kogda ne bylo magnitofonov...', *Sovradiotel*, no. 5 (1961): 35–6.

[12] In fact, the Leningrad-based Shorin developed his machine at the same time (and independently of) the Moscow-based Pavel Tager. As usual with such inventions, there is some dispute as to who has the strongest claim to primacy. See Dmitri Zakharine, 'Tonfil'ma kak zvukovoe oruzhie. Rannii opyt sovetskogo zvukovogo kino', *Die Welt der Slaven* 54 (2009): 244–5.

cumbersome: producing broadcasts this way might be possible for a few high-profile events, but it could hardly become routine. An alternative recording technology that appeared during the war was the American 'Presto' machine, which recorded straight on to disk; this was how the Soviet broadcasting team made their report on the German act of capitulation late in the evening of 8–9 May 1945.[13]

In January 1943, a discussion among editors and journalists in the Radio Committee made abundantly clear that existing recording equipment (the shorinophone) was not sufficient—whether in quantity or in sound quality—to provide a supply of fresh footage for wartime news broadcasts. The luminaries of the Soviet broadcasting profession—prominent among them Vadim Siniavskii—were already straining at the leash, wanting to serve up material to the listener without the usual time delays and contrivances of Soviet radio.[14] Right through to the end of the war, the scale of recording was severely limited by material scarcity. In February 1945, A. Puzin, the head of the Radio Committee, noted that good-quality imported disks had almost run out and should only be used for special occasions such as speeches by political leaders or selected musical performances.[15] Already convinced of the long-term advantages of magnetic tape over Presto disks, he wrote to Georgii Malenkov in July 1945 to point out that supplies of magnetic tape brought back from Germany were almost exhausted. As a temporary solution, Puzin requested permission to move back to Moscow a stockpile of 50,000 music recordings on magnetic tape that had been discovered in Prague; he would need five train carriages for the purpose.[16]

In the immediate post-war years, radio officials would regularly complain of the shortage of necessary equipment. In July 1946, Puzin wrote again to Malenkov to lobby for the increased production of *magnitofony*, which in his view offered a quality of reproduction indistinguishable from live performance. At this point the Radio Committee had at its disposal thirty-six studio tape recorders and eight mobile sets.[17] Evidently, this did not stretch very far: early in 1950, with broadcasters needing to play their part in the latest ritual of Stalinist democracy, there was not enough equipment to record statements from Soviet citizens in more than three electoral districts.[18] On Moscow radio, the first mobile *magnitofony* appeared just after the war and were reserved for especially important expeditions. Nor were they especially mobile: together with the batteries and auxiliary equipment, they weighed 100 kilograms.[19] Technical support was inadequate, and broadcasters did not always make best use of their new tool. One of the speakers at a meeting to discuss music in early 1946 adopted topical hyperbole in his assessment of the use

---

[13] Mikhail Shalashnikov, 'Poslednii reportazh', in M. S. Gleizer and N. M. Potapov (eds.), *Radio v dni voiny* (Moscow, 1982), 224–32.

[14] GARF, f. 6903, op. 1, d. 62, ll. 27–8 (for Siniavskii's contribution to the discussion).

[15] GARF, f. 6903, op. 1, d. 105, l. 84.   [16] GARF, f. 6903, op. 1, d. 104, l. 51.

[17] RGASPI, f. 17, op. 125, d. 470, ll. 52–6.

[18] RGASPI, f. 17, op. 132, d. 432, l. 141 (party meeting in Radio Committee, 1 February 1950).

[19] Iu. Letunov, *Vremia. Liudi. Mikrofon* (Moscow, 1974), 92. On the similarly bulky recording equipment owned by Vladivostok radio in 1948, see Georgii Gromov, 'Kak nabivat' matrasy morskoi vodoi', in *Nemnogo o radio i o nas s vami* (Vladivostok, 2001), 22–5.

made of the new recording technology: 'fate has delivered into our hands an atomic bomb, but we treat it like barbarians'.[20]

Perhaps the most striking illustration of the limited technological capacity of Soviet broadcasting in the immediate post-war period is an account by Mikhail Gus of his work as a correspondent at the Nuremberg Trials. According to Gus, the Soviet team were the envy of their Western colleagues as the only delegation to have separate office space and studio. They had recording equipment, two lines from the courtroom providing the speeches in the original language and in Russian translation, and—best of all—a direct telephone line to Moscow. Yet tape was in such short supply that the Soviets were not able to record proceedings in their entirety but had to limit themselves to the speeches and cross-examinations by the Soviet prosecutors; unlike the British or the Americans, moreover, the Soviets were not able to broadcast direct from Nuremberg but had to send everything back to Moscow.[21]

Yet, although technology might often lag behind broadcasters' ambitions, pre-recording was fast becoming the new standard practice on post-war Soviet radio. At the start of March 1946, a conference in the Radio Committee debated thoroughly the question of sound recording technology. This was already an urgent matter given the goal of increasing the proportion of recordings in the radio schedule to a hefty 80 per cent of broadcasting time by the end of the first post-war five-year plan: from now on, 5,000 hours of new material would have to be recorded each year. The clear majority of speakers agreed that magnetic tape (primarily a German technology, as the Americans had hitherto invested mainly in vinyl) was the preferable method of sound recording. It offered reliable quality, allowed for rapid editing, and (unlike sound film) did not present a fire risk; nor was it affected by damp or by temperature changes. Even if, given the absence of alternatives, sound film (*tonfil'm*) would have to be retained in regional broadcasting centres for some while longer, in the long term the *magnitofon* was the preferred option. Technicians were already '85 per cent' of the way to designing a Soviet tape recorder that would match its German equivalents, and production plans for 1946 would be adjusted in favour of magnetic tape.[22] A few days later, a speaker at another meeting in the Radio Committee commented quite simply that 'the tape recorder has now become our main means of recording'.[23] By the early 1950s, moreover, the *magnitofon* had joined the radio set as a focus for the energies of Soviet amateur inventors (which, admittedly, suggests that state production left something to be desired).[24]

---

[20] GARF, f. 6903, op. 1, d. 161, l. 18.

[21] 'Otchet Ia. Gusa o rabote korrespondentskogo punkta radiokomiteta na Niurnbergskom protsesse' (1946), in *VKD*, 119–21. Although the author of this internal report is given as 'Ia. Gus' in *VKD*, almost certainly this is a misprint. Mikhail Gus was a prominent member of the counter-propaganda section of Soviet broadcasting during the war. For his later published account of his experiences in Nuremberg, which contains none of the qualifications of the 1946 report but otherwise covers much of the same ground, see Mikhail Gus, 'Spetsial'nyi korrespondent radio', in Gleizer and Potapov (eds.), *Radio v dni voiny*, 237–42.

[22] GARF, f. 6903, op. 1, d. 159.   [23] GARF, f. 6903, op. 1, d. 143, l. 37.

[24] A. Volkov, 'Zvukozapis' na 10-i Vsesoiuznoi radiovystavke', *Radio*, no. 12 (1952): 42–4.

With the advent of the tape recorder, sound became storable and controllable as never before. In November 1945, the Radio Committee issued a decree on procedure: particularly valuable gramophone records were to be transferred to tape, and sound interference in the original recordings was to be eliminated in the process; important concert and theatre performances were to be recorded; and at least two copies were to be made. At the same time, resources remained scarce: in the interests of saving precious tape, speech was to be recorded only after the text had received prior approval, and such recordings were to be wiped after a week unless there were instructions to the contrary.[25]

For the first time, Soviet broadcasters had to think systematically about creating and maintaining a sound archive. The music department set about establishing a core repertoire of the Russian classics that could be stored securely on tape. A similar task faced talk radio. As the children's producer Roza Ioffe noted in November 1948, after two years' experience of working with the new recording technology, it was high time to start identifying programmes of special significance: these should be recorded to the highest possible standard and carefully stored.[26] There were, admittedly, two practical complications. The first was that, in the early post-war era, no one was quite sure how long magnetic tape could be expected to keep. The Germans, who led the world in this new technology, tended to re-record material every two to three years. The Soviets, however, were concerned to save resources. They were still making some use of the cheaper *tonfil'm*, even though it offered inferior recording quality. Magnetic tape was still to be strictly rationed: in January 1947, Puzin firmly reminded his colleagues of the stipulation that speech recordings be erased after seven days unless earmarked for archiving.[27] Even in the post-Stalin era, the aural past would be subject to the same purging as the written archive. In a decree of 7 August 1963, the heads of all republican and regional radio committees were sternly instructed to remove from tape collections all material that was 'out of date in its content'.[28]

In the late Stalin era, the authorities quickly sought to exploit the potential of sound recording for controlling content and eliminating even the remotest possibility of error. As the secretary of the Radio Committee's party bureau wrote to Malenkov in December 1950, 'state interests demand that the Radio Committee should immediately start broadcasting all material in pre-recorded form'. It was unacceptable, for example, that ten of the thirty-two Soviet studios broadcasting to the outside world lacked facilities to tape programmes in advance. Broadcasts to such crucial countries as China, Germany, and France were going out live—with the consequent possibility of embarrassing slips.[29] Even so, it was clear that pre-recording had already made serious inroads into the Soviet schedule. The plan for 1949, for example, projected that 65 per cent

[25] Text of decree in *VKD*, 113–14.   [26] Text of Ioffe's memo in *VKD*, 799–800.
[27] GARF, f. 6903, op. 1, d. 180, ll. 31, 47–8.
[28] Text in *VKD*, 158–9. This decree followed up on an earlier one of 15 November 1961.
[29] RGASPI, f. 17, op. 132, d. 434, ll. 103–4.

of music programming would consist of recordings (as compared to around 25 per cent just before the war).[30]

The *magnitofon* continued to make progress in the 1950s. In early 1953 none other than Nikita Khrushchev wrote to the Presidium of the Council of Ministers to recommend launching production of tape recorders in a Moscow factory in view of the 'growing demand for sound recording equipment for the propaganda of political and scientific-technical knowledge and the extensive organizing of cultural enlightenment events among the population'.[31] In January 1954 Puzin reported to Khrushchev, now First Secretary, the latest invention in the field of sound recording: a portable tape recorder, weighing a mere 5 kilograms, which would cost 500–600 rubles if authorized for mass production. The proposal again met a sympathetic ear: on 9 February 1954, the Council of Ministers duly passed a decree on organizing production of tape recorders for the general public.[32]

To judge by a further discussion in the Radio Committee early the following year, progress in this area remained halting. It was taking a very long time for the Ministry for the Electrical Industry to develop a viable model of tape recorder. Soviet broadcasters were still relying on the magnetic tape they received from Germany—which was of much lower quality than American tape.[33] At a conference in April 1957, news reporters delivered a now familiar litany of complaints about the quality of Soviet tape recorders and the shortage of equipment. As one participant recalled, he had been ready to 'jump for joy' when he received a 'Dnepr-8' tape recorder the previous year. But after only two recordings he realized that it was unusable. Reporters from other regions had no mobile recording equipment at all. Under such conditions, and given the continuing taboo on non-standard speech, the only viable solution was to script material and hand it over to the announcers. The number of news reporters (a mere seventy) was inadequate to cover the vast expanses of the country, and money for trips was short. At times in the meeting, the frustrations of reporters boiled over into resentment towards producers and administrators: 'you have an arrogant attitude to us…Reporters run around, spend all night writing a piece, and then they just get a pat on the shoulder…We want to get on with you, and you couldn't care less.'[34]

By the early 1960s, Soviet industry seems to have catered rather better to the needs of its front-line broadcasters. The authorities could be more generous in their allocation of magnetic tape to regional and republican radio committees. In June 1963, for example, the head of the Estonian radio committee was informed that his annual allocation would increase by more than 25 per cent (even though the amount of broadcasting time had not increased).[35] Recording technology had improved further. In 1961, the Institute of Sound Recording reflected on the progress it had made since 1954. Its first model of reporter's tape recorder was spring-mounted and had to be wound up; this was not a great success. Then came the

[30] RGASPI, f. 17, op. 132, d. 93, l. 10.   [31] GARF, f. 6903, op. 1, d. 425, l. 33.
[32] RGANI, f. 5, op. 16, d. 663, ll. 48–9.
[33] GARF, f. 6903, op. 1, d. 475, ll. 6, 9 (meeting of 14 January 1955).
[34] GARF, f. 6903, op. 1, d. 537, ll. 9, 12, 21.   [35] ERA.R, 1590.4.329.10.

model 'Reporter-2' with an electric motor. Now there was a third generation of tape recorder that used semiconductors and weighed 2 kilograms less than its immediate predecessor. All the same, at a conference of radio journalists, a representative of the institute had to face plenty of scepticism regarding the convenience of the new technology. His reply betrayed the mild exasperation of Q introducing the latest lethal gadget to an unappreciative James Bond: 'You would like to have a matchbox, very high quality... for it to record for an hour or two. You are right, we know this perfectly well, this is the ideal we're also striving for.'[36]

In the post-war era tape recorders spread even to the remoter regional centres. During the war announcers in Syktyvkar, capital of the Komi Republic, had operated under trying conditions: in a freezing cold studio they would read out newspaper articles and the latest announcements from Sovinformburo, often without having the chance to peruse them in advance and check for errors in the printed text. Music was broadcast by placing a gramophone next to the microphone: the announcer would read out the title of the piece and then run over to put on the disk. In 1944, however, the first tape recorder appeared in the Komi studio. The first models were all 'trophy', but they were followed in due course by a home-produced Dnepr (which weighed 100 kilograms, and sometimes had literally to be dragged around rural parts of the region). In 1951 came a minor milestone, with the acquisition of high-quality MEZ-2 recording equipment for use in the studio.[37] The chronology was not much different in the Far East, where the Khabarovsk radio committee received its first tape recorder in 1948: all told, the equipment weighed 75 kilograms. In the early 1950s Khabarovsk broadcasters acquired a Dnepr recorder that could actually be carried by one person (it weighed a mere 25 kilograms); a little later came the Dnepr-2, which was only 5 kilograms but had to be wound up like an old-fashioned gramophone and had a habit of breaking down in the process.[38] Improved models would continue to appear right up to the 'Reporter-7', a lighter model of recorder that became available in Vladivostok after the 1980 Olympics.[39]

BROADCASTING PRACTICE IN THE POST-STALIN ERA: HOW SOVIET RADIO THAWED

Yet the question remained of what exactly the new technology would mean for the way broadcasters did their job. The spread of pre-recording was good news for the authorities, who could now ensure that broadcasters did not misspeak or otherwise step out of line. Now there would be fewer sabotage scares. But the mere avoidance of error was not enough. A perennial complaint of broadcasters

[36] GARF, f. 6903, op. 1, d. 713, ll. 174–8.
[37] See the various short memoirs in *Radio: Vremia i liudi* (Syktyvkar, 2001), 27–30, 41–3, 51.
[38] V. V. Pogartsev, 'Stanovlenie i razvitie sistemy radioveshchaniia na Dal'nem vostoke Rossii (1901–1956 gg.)' (candidate's dissertation, Khabarovsk, 2006), 146–7.
[39] N. Solov'eva, 'Ne byt' podstavkoi k mikrofonu', in *Nemnogo o radio*, 68–71.

and officials alike was that Soviet radio was dreary: the language was heavy and bureaucratic, sentences were long and complex, listeners were bombarded with facts and statistics.

How were broadcasters to remain word-perfect and politically impeccable while at the same time to sound engaging and authentic? In the post-war era a number of radio journalists drew on both their wartime experience and new recording technology to find their own answers to this age-old conundrum of Soviet cultural production. One of the pioneers was Lazar' Magrachev, who started his radio career in 1937 having made an impression by a report he had written on the Leningrad factory where he worked as a lathe-operator. In those days, he later recalled, broadcasters took enormous trouble preparing programmes, and only trained announcers were allowed to perform on air. Speaking into the microphone was a real art: if you spoke too quietly, you risked disappearing in the ether; if you spoke too loudly, you risked damaging the equipment.[40]

Magrachev's work habits were transformed by the outbreak of war. He threw himself into the cause, proving himself an intrepid reporter and gathering a substantial archive of sounds and voices from besieged Leningrad. His opportunities for gathering material increased greatly when he gained access to Leningrad's 'trophy' tape recorder just after the war. He experimented with background sound as a counterpoint to the human voice. One of his reports was interrupted by an explosion as the last barricade set up in the city was blown up; on another occasion he broke the atmospheric silence of the reading room to mark the 125th anniversary of Leningrad's Public Library. But Magrachev was interested less in adventurous sound effects than in achieving a new quality of interview: instead of the stilted, scripted Stalin-era *vystuplenie*, he wanted his subjects to sound spontaneous. As he later confessed of his early career on radio, 'sometimes I simply tormented my interviewees by rehearsing them to make their intonation natural'. Given that broadcasts were no longer going out live, he could now experiment with unscripted interviews. His first attempt came on 17 May 1946, and was by his own account not a success. He often found it difficult to persuade interviewees to depart from their prepared text. A report on the award of the first post-war 'gold medals' for Leningrad schoolchildren, for example, was fully scripted and choreographed and featured the Stalinist equivalent of Oscar acceptance speeches from the high-achieving youngsters.[41] In the 1950s, however, on returning to the radio after an enforced absence due to the anti-Semitic purges of the late Stalin era, Magrachev became an acknowledged master of Soviet 'human interest' radio. He crashed the fiftieth wedding anniversary of a sailor who had written to him with a song request; he attended a geography exam in a Leningrad school; he interviewed a former pickpocket and camp inmate who had become a model worker; he tracked down an exemplary milkmaid, the subject of an earlier radio feature, who had mysteriously left the collective farm for the city (it turned out that her heart had been

[40] L. Magrachev, *Siuzhety, sochinennye zhizn'iu* (Moscow, 1972), 5–6.
[41] TsGALI SPb, f. 293, op. 2, d. 2287, ll. 1–5 (5 January 1946).

broken by a man back in the village, but that she was now pining for home).[42] By the late 1950s, Magrachev had withdrawn from day-to-day reporting and concentrated instead on more elaborate feature broadcasts. A younger colleague later remembered him for his perfectionism (mixed with vanity). He still rehearsed his interviewees exhaustively, on one occasion becoming so exasperated with an inarticulate subject that he ran out of the studio and burst into tears. In the cutting room he was absolutely meticulous. He also enjoyed dramatic pauses, had a weakness for happy endings, and was no stranger to artistic licence.[43]

Even after his reinstatement and return to prominence in the 1950s, Magrachev was always a maverick figure. The relative freshness of his material is placed in sharp relief by the far more anodyne reports of Matvei Frolov, another well-known journalist working in the same genre.[44] Well into the 'Thaw' period, many staple items in the schedule were recognizable in generic terms from the Stalin era. The decree sent out by the All-Union Radio Committee on coverage of the elections to the Supreme Soviet in 1958 allotted to the media their familiar role in projecting Soviet 'democracy': broadcasters were to prepare reports from the electoral meetings where candidates were selected and then to bring the candidates themselves to the microphone, while also profiling them and reporting on their meetings with voters.[45] As in other fields of endeavour, the Khrushchev era represented not a straightforward rejection of Stalinist culture, but an attempt to make popular mobilization meaningful. The number of statements (*vystupleniia*) by ordinary people continued to be an important index of radio's success in performing its mission. In Tula in 1960, for example, 1,663 people spoke on the radio, of whom a good half were impeccably 'ordinary' workers from factory or farm. Radio 'worker-peasant correspondents' (*rabsel'kory*) were making a comeback, as were 'radio debates' on subjects such as 'Are you ready to live under Communism?'.[46] On the Gorky radio committee in 1959, similarly, broadcasters were telling themselves that they should increase the number of *vystupleniia* while somehow making them less formulaic. A tally was kept of the number of radio appearances by 'leading workers' (*rukovodiashchie rabotniki*) such as chairmen of regional and district executive committees.[47]

Soviet broadcasters in the 1950s were an understandably risk-averse group. They had long been taught that the main criterion for a successful *vystuplenie* was that

[42] Examples in this paragraph drawn from three books by Magrachev: *Vstrechi u mikrofona* (Moscow, 1959), 4–5, 12, 16, 18–25, 86–8; *Golosa zhizni: Iz zapisnoi knizhki radiozhurnalista* (Leningrad, 1962), 5; and *Siuzhety, sochinennye zhizn'iu*, 61–5, 181.

[43] L. S. Markhasev, *Belki v kolese: Zapiski iz Doma radio* (St Petersburg, 2004), 149, 154–7.

[44] M. Frolov, *Reporter u mikrofona* (Leningrad, 1966). On Frolov as the epitome of Soviet 'good news' journalism, see Markhasev, *Belki v kolese*, 171. See also the collection of short memoirs on Frolov, *Vol'nyi syn efira: Reportazh-vospominanie* (St Petersburg, 1997).

[45] 'Ob osveshchenii po radio i televideniiu izbiratel'noi kampanii po vyboram v Verkhovnyi sovet SSSR' (15 January 1958), ERA.R, 1590.4.109.2–9. I came across this in the archive of the Estonian radio committee, but presumably it was filed away in every other republican committee as well.

[46] A. Grigor'ev, *Nash drug—radio* (Tula, 1966), 86–8.

[47] GANO, f. 3630, op. 2, dd. 455, 621.

they select an 'advanced' (*peredovoi*) member of Soviet society.[48] Radio journalists did not necessarily relish their own broadcasting style—to judge by editorial discussions in the early 1950s, they constantly berated each other for colourless news broadcasts, cliché-ridden reports, and over-abundant statements from Stakhanovite workers who had overfulfilled their norms—yet it was hard to imagine how things might be otherwise. This was still a time when the phrase 'enemy of the people' was being hurled around staff meetings. Nor did the death of Stalin make things more straightforward, at least in the short term. How should the meetings in the city to mourn the dictator be reported? How solemn a tone should be struck when discussing Stalin? In Leningrad, M. N. Melaned, the 'Leningrad Levitan', had been fired for coughing while broadcasting the news of Stalin's death, and was lucky to avoid more severe punishment.[49] The whole culture and propaganda industry was on edge at this time. A bulletin of 4 March 1953 on Stalin's fading health had reportedly been disrupted by a few foreign words, probably in English, that ended with the word 'America'. In early August 1953, the propaganda department of the Central Committee received a report that a pronunciation error had been made in one of the most prominent moments in the radio schedule: the second word of the Soviet national anthem had been heard as *nerulimyi* (unsteerable) rather than the correct *nerushimyi* (unbreakable). The initial instruction was to re-record the anthem, but further investigation revealed that existing recordings were all correct—it was just that the sibilant *sh* had a tendency to be distorted in transmission.[50] Later on in the 1950s, although the penalties for erring on air were no longer so severe, broadcasters quickly became nervy when the question arose of who might have to take responsibility for glitches. A perennial complaint from announcers was that they received the text for broadcast too late to prepare themselves adequately. In October 1957, for example, a meeting of the party organization on Moscow radio threatened to dissolve into mutual recrimination as a studio worker fought back fiercely against the suggestion that she and her colleagues put announcers on the spot.[51]

Yet, for all the accumulated fear and inertia, not to mention the constraints of preliminary censorship, the life of a reporter in the 1950s could be invigorating. With the end of the worst forms of Stalinist exploitation, radio correspondents were no longer obliged to perpetrate acts of outrageous dishonesty such as ignoring the fact that the labour force on the Volga-Don canal project of the early 1950s consisted mainly of prisoners. After Stalin's death, broadcasting could become more open and engaging. Leningrad radio pioneered a weekly half-hour survey of

[48] Late Stalinist attempts to render the vox pop are discussed in A. Il'ina, 'Ob opyte raboty redaktsii "Poslednikh izvestii" nakanune i v dni XIX s"ezda partii', *V pomoshch' mestnomu radioveshchaniiu*, no. 5 (1952): 16–19 and A. Krylov, 'Nerushimoe slovo tovarishchu Stalinu (o radiokompozitsiiakh, podgotovlennykh mestnymi komitetami radioinformatsii)', *V pomoshch' mestnomu radioveshchaniiu*, no. 6 (1952): 6–11.

[49] According to one colleague, the head of the Leningrad radio committee had Melaned put in a psychiatric unit for a month, presumably as a way of protecting him from worse sanctions. A. A. V'iunik, 'V "Poslednikh izvestiiakh": 50-e gody', in P. A. Palladin, M. G. Zeger, and A. A. V'iunik (eds.), *Leningradskoe radio: Ot blokady do 'ottepeli'* (Moscow 1991), 141.

[50] RGANI, f. 5, op. 16, d. 643, ll. 44–5, 82–4.   [51] TsAOPIM, f. 2930, op. 1, d. 1, l. 14.

news in the city, which was found to be an engaging format and soon adopted by central radio. Live reports from stations, metro tunnels, construction sites, and the like might seem tame in retrospect, but they were evidently exciting experiences for Soviet reporters, who had to think on their feet and adapt to circumstances. All in all, the 1950s would later be remembered by broadcasters as an optimistic time: their audience was huge, the schedule was filling up with broadcasts by well-loved writers, performers, and sports commentators, and the possibilities of radio seemed to be growing by the year.[52] Like their colleagues in print journalism, and in sharp distinction to their counterparts in the West, broadcasters saw their *raison d'être* in instruction and improvement, not in surfing the 'breaking wave of the present instant'; but their notion of edification now comprised less state ideology than the values of 'humanity' and 'the person'. The socialist media were acquiring a human face.[53]

Transcripts of party meetings of Leningrad radio staff in 1956 reveal just how far the atmosphere had changed. In the spring and summer of that year, broadcasters, like party members in other fields, wrestled with the question of how exactly to interpret Khrushchev's denunciation of the 'cult of personality' at the Twentieth Party Congress. They also discussed the new forms and styles that might best correspond to the mood in the country. As one Leningrad broadcaster observed at the end of April, the key question was 'how to speak to radio listeners'. Too often, in her view, 'programmes where everything is as it should be get the green light, but if you try to find a key to the listener's heart, you run into difficulties'. She cited specifically a recent case where a programme by Magrachev on teenage relationships had been suppressed by the supervising editor.[54] In the late Stalin period, Magrachev had struggled in vain to keep his job. In 1956, however, he could be entirely forthright in defending his way of doing things: 'We have no right', he told his party comrades at the end of March 1956, 'to carry on working today the way we did yesterday'. As he elaborated: 'We utter the necessary words, we inform the people about the right things, but we need to find something that will make the subject interesting.' His particular grievance was a programme he had made on domestic 'hooliganism' which had been declined (on the grounds, it emerged, that material of this kind could not be broadcast in the period directly preceding a public holiday). As a colleague complained, a text for broadcast often passed through the hands of three different editors, who sometimes contradicted each other. Corrections on grounds of 'taste' often robbed a text of its freshness: 'We often say: "That sounds badly written". Yes, a live [i.e. unscripted] interview may sometimes not conform to the rules of grammar, but this is live speech, not a polished text.'[55]

---

[52] V'iunik, 'V "Poslednikh izvestiiakh"', 133, 136–7, 139, 142–4. V'iunik joined Leningrad radio news in April 1950, so was well placed to comment on the transition from Stalinist to post-Stalinist journalism.

[53] On print journalism, see Thomas C. Wolfe, *Governing Soviet Journalism: The Press and the Socialist Person after Stalin* (Bloomington, Ind., 2005), quotation 7.

[54] TsGAIPD SPb, f. 755, op. 6, d. 1, l. 22.   [55] TsGAIPD SPb, f. 755, op. 6, d. 2, ll. 26–8.

For the post-war generation of broadcasters, the importance of departing from the 'crib-sheet' of the Stalin era was close to axiomatic. Complaints about the clichés of Soviet broadcasting, fairly routine even during the Stalin era, now reached a new level of intensity. As one radio journalist from Ukraine noted in 1957, 'Why should we have to listen all the time about the same old collective farms and the same old people? [Fedor] Dubkovetskii and [Pasha] Angelina have already had so much written about them! It's like in the theatre, when an old prima donna doesn't allow others to develop.'[56] Dissatisfaction with the tight-lipped platitudes of the Stalin era was not limited to professional broadcasting circles. It was also expressed in the most high profile of all media in the 1950s: cinema. Thaw films such as *Bol'shaia sem'ia*, *Karnaval'naia noch'*, and *Delo bylo v Pen'kove* all included ironic treatments of the worker-peasant *vystuplenie*, while the internationally award-winning *Letiat zhuravli* even allowed one of its characters to express frustration with Iurii Levitan's falsely upbeat Sovinformbiuro performances. In the Soviet Union, as elsewhere in the post-war world, the oratorical and theatrical style of rhetoric so prevalent in the 1930s and 1940s was replaced by more modest verbal norms. Now speech might be soft, slow, even indistinct and halting—not least because recording technology was now far more acoustically sensitive.[57]

As early as August 1953, the All-Union Radio Committee took the initiative on the question of the new speech norms by organizing a week-long conference for broadcast journalists from all around the USSR. Towards the end of proceedings, Iurii Gal'perin was given the floor to present a short masterclass on interviewing. Gal'perin was already something of a celebrity reporter. He had taken up radio journalism after leaving the air force at the end of the war on health grounds. After serving his broadcasting apprenticeship, he soon moved to the vanguard of the transition to unscripted interviews.[58] In February 1953, at an editorial meeting in the Radio Committee, he was cited admiringly by a colleague as someone who did not allow his interviewees to 'talk themselves out' by rehearsing them in advance; instead, he started recording them immediately.[59] In his presentation to colleagues at the August conference, Gal'perin emphasized that journalists should do everything to put interviewees at their ease. They should not interrupt their subjects; if the interviewee was having difficulty pronouncing a particular word, then it was best to replace it with another word; and, above all, broadcasters should not present interviewees with a text to learn in advance. Although a written text would usually still be the basis for a recorded interview, it should be the result of more collaborative work between the two parties—and the interviewee should feel free

[56] GARF, f. 6903, op. 1, d. 537, l. 21 (conference of radio news correspondents on 12–13 April 1957).

[57] An argument put forward in Oksana Bulgakowa, 'StimmBrüche: Marlon Brando, Innokenti Smoktunowski und der Klang der 1950-er Jahre', in Bulgakowa (ed.), *Resonanz-Räume: Die Stimme und die Medien* (Berlin, 2012), 81–98.

[58] See the admiring profile in Evgenii Riabchikov, 'Zhizn' v efire', *Sovradiotel*, no. 7 (1967): 22–5. According to this article, Gal'perin's first fully unscripted broadcast came in 1948. For Gal'perin's own account of himself, see his *Vnimanie, mikrofon vkliuchen!* (Moscow, 1960).

[59] Extract from the transcript in *VKD*, 131.

to insert the odd phrase here and there as he or she spoke. If the journalist had decided to record someone without a text, then it was important not to discuss the matter in advance: 'No one is going to say the same thing well twice.' Even non-standard speech—for example by Ukrainians or other non-Russians—could be left intact in a recording, since it added authenticity.[60] By all appearances, the recommendations of this conference soon percolated down to regional radio committees. Later the same month, a staff meeting on Gorky radio was referring to instructions from Moscow to record 'live speech' more often, though opinions differed on how interventionist broadcasters should be in 'correcting' the words of ordinary people.[61]

The message was emphasized in the main journal for broadcasting professionals, which over the following decade published approving reports on the ability of Gal'perin and others to ask good questions of their subjects and make effective use of unscripted interviews.[62] Novice reporters were advised to try their hand at unscripted broadcasts, while also taking care over editing.[63] Preparing a *vystuplenie u mikrofona* was still one of the most important tasks of a radio journalist, but it was less and less acceptable to allow subjects to read out a prepared text.[64] The practice of unscripted broadcasts was also spreading to regional radio committees. In Vladivostok, as one radio worker later reflected, the late 1950s were a time when 'radio was slowly and painfully moving from scripted to free speech'.[65] When Gennadii Tur'ev returned from military service to Syktyvkar as a young radio journalist in the early 1960s, he found Komi radio lagging behind the capitals: broadcasters were still foisting pre-prepared texts on their interview subjects. The light dawned when Tur'ev attended a seminar in Moscow and was able to learn from Magrachev, Konstantin Retinskii, Iurii Letunov, and other leading lights. On his first expedition after his return to Komi he recorded 90 minutes of material for a 20-minute broadcast. It still took a long time to convince people to depart from Soviet clichés when they approached the microphone. Yet, while the battle for unscripted speech on Komi radio was not conclusively won in the 1960s, it had at least been joined.[66]

So pronounced was the trend towards unscripted recording that it was placing significant strain on the system of censorship. In March 1959, representatives of the Radio Committee met with the deputy head of the main censorship bureaucracy, Glavlit. The censor, Avetisian, sharply drew the broadcasters' attention to the fact that they had been failing to provide texts of interviews for advance scrutiny

[60] GARF, f. 6903, op. 1, d. 450, ll. 255–72.

[61] GANO, f. 3630, op. 2, d. 134, ll. 4, 30, 50, 53, 159.

[62] G. Manevich, 'Reportazh odnogo dnia', *Sovradiotel*, no. 1 (1957): 3–5; 'O reportazhakh K. Retinskogo i Iu. Letunova', *Sovradiotel*, no. 5 (1959): 23–5.

[63] D. Protopopov, 'Golosui "za"!', *Sovradiotel*, no. 1 (1961): 30–1. The importance of montage is also emphasized in S. Chupikov, 'Eksprompt ili montazh?', *Sovradiotel*, no. 5 (1960): 36, and A. Revenko, 'Prodolzhaem razgovor o nashem remesle', *Sovradiotel*, no. 3 (1963): 30–2.

[64] T. Bogoslovskii, 'Iskusstvo agitatsii faktami', *Sovradiotel*, no. 2 (1965): 5–8; N. Eremeev, 'Nachalo bol'shogo razgovora', *Sovradiotel*, no. 2 (1967): 5–7.

[65] Nina Khrul'kova, 'Mne povezlo na uchitelei', in *Nemnogo o radio*, 36. See also the report from Novosibirsk in M. Ginden, 'Glavnoe—kachestvo', *Sovradiotel*, no. 1 (1960): 13–14.

[66] G. Tur'ev, 'Troe sutok shagat'...', in *Radio: Vremia i liudi*, 70–1.

by Glavlit. The radio representatives, however, were not prepared to concede the point. Given the quantity of unscripted material, it was unreasonable of Glavlit to expect to see written texts in advance: censors should be prepared to listen to the tapes instead. Moreover, if Glavlit wished to exercise such close control over radio broadcasts, it needed to provide round-the-clock staffing. At present, censors started work at 10 a.m., by which time three news broadcasts had already gone out. Even in the Soviet Union, this was an era that required more rapid media response to events, and there was a clear tension between the requirement for immediacy and timeliness and the demands of censorship. Although Avetisian stuck to his principle that 'without the censor it's not allowed to broadcast anything', the meeting did not seem to have removed all the grey areas. When asked about the policy regarding live outside broadcasts, Avetisian answered that 'from collective farms you can broadcast what you like'; as for factories, however, it depended on 'which factory, which workshop'.[67]

The unscripted interview was by no means the only field of innovation in 1950s broadcasting. With the move to more sophisticated recording technology, discussion in the Radio Committee also turned to various kinds of formal experimentation. In a meeting of January 1953, for example, the focus of attention was the genre of 'radio composition', which allowed broadcasters to combine heterogeneous elements: commentary on current affairs, literary material, music, and other sound effects. This gave radio a better chance of acting on listeners' emotions as well as raising their ideological level. Sometimes these techniques could be taken to excess—when transitions between different formal effects were clunky, where the quality was uneven, or where producers got carried away with music and sound effects at the expense of text—while the practice of dividing text up between two voices was described as a 'cliché' and an 'uneconomical use of human voices'. Although judgements such as these no doubt still attested to Stalin-era aesthetic conservatism, the discussion did at least put formal innovation on the agenda.[68]

One key question—the use of sound effects—was taken up again in the conference of August 1953. As one speaker observed, too many radio reports were taking the form of 'bare' microphone speech; it was time to exploit the full potential of tape recording and make more imaginative use of montage and juxtaposition.[69] It remained difficult, however, to strike the right balance between formal innovation and ease of listening. In a meeting with sound technicians in January 1954 Puzin weighed in with a note of caution: 'we have a lot of enthusiasts for all kinds of documentary recordings that are often unsuitable for broadcasting, such as cows mooing or the noise of machinery in the factory'. It was important not to go too far in the search for documentary quality: on radio everything should 'caress the ear'.[70]

[67] 'Iz stenogrammy zasedaniia Gosudarstvennogo komiteta po radioveshchaniiu i televideniiu pri Sovete Ministrov SSSR "O faktakh narusheniia poriadka tsenzorskogo kontrolia materialov radioveshchaniia i televideniia"' (23 March 1959), in *VKD*, 144–9.

[68] GARF, f. 6903, op. 1, d. 451, ll. 14–15.   [69] GARF, f. 6903, op. 1, d. 450, ll. 242–3.
[70] GARF, f. 6903, op. 1, d. 460, l. 56.

In general, however, the second half of the 1950s saw a definite loosening of the norms and genres of Stalin-era broadcasting. In an effort to make broadcast speech less stilted, broadcasters made more use of more informal genres such as the 'story at the microphone' (*rasskaz u mikrofona*) and the 'conversation' (*beseda*). By 1960, forty to fifty items per day went out under the latter designation. As the name suggested, the *beseda* was to have characteristics of 'oral, conversational speech', while at the same time remaining a 'literary' genre. Here it was legitimate to take inspiration from Western broadcasting: studios abroad had shown that it was possible to 'conduct a conversation in a completely relaxed environment that approximates to that of ordinary rooms in the home'.[71]

Broadcast journalism, meanwhile, continued to thaw. In March 1961 came another huge conference on recording technology, interview technique, and other matters of pressing concern to radio practitioners. Once again it was emphasized that recording allowed for more engaging storylines (*siuzhetnost*). Of course, it required broadcasters to overcome their inhibitions. As one speaker admitted, 'we're not used to taking the microphone, standing in the middle of a square and starting to speak. I can honestly say that when I was forced to do that for the first time, I felt as if I'd been stripped naked on that square.' Estonian broadcasters were in the vanguard of this new, more engaging style of reporting. In his contribution to the conference, their representative made the obligatory qualification that the legacy of the 'bourgeois' period had held back Estonian radio. In formal terms, however, there were some techniques that Soviet-era broadcasters had been able to borrow from the preceding era. One distinctive feature of Estonian radio was that it made the reporter (rather than the announcer) the central figure. The flagship Estonian news broadcast was the daily half-hour 'Echo of the Day' (*Ekho dnia*), which started with a very brief statement of content (a mere thirty-five words) before proceeding directly to the material. What made reporters the best vehicle for the narrative was the impression they created of immediacy: 'to feed the reporter's microphone with paper [i.e. a written text] is the same as quenching the reporter's thirst with distilled water. It's pure but unappealing, even harmful.' The Estonian spokesman went on to recommend that reporters should take complete ownership of their broadcasts: they should be the producer, the editor, even the sound technician. At present reporters were still restricted by the need to send their reports down the wires to their broadcasting station, but the future lay with short wave, which would greatly expand the potential for live outside broadcasts.[72]

Soviet broadcasters were making more sophisticated demands on their craft. As Letunov observed, the novelty of sound effects had now worn off: almost twenty years into the era of the *magnitofon* it was no longer possible to amaze listeners with the sound of waves or of aircraft; it was time for a more discerning use of

---

[71] GARF, f. 6903, op. 1. d. 663, ll. 3, 11 (transcript of editorial meeting on forms and genres of broadcasting, 14 November 1960). On the introduction of the *rasskaz u mikrofona* in the mid-1950s, see Aleksandr Sherel', *Audiokul'tura XX veka. Istoriia, esteticheskie zakonomernosti, osobennosti vliianiia na auditoriiu: Ocherki* (Moscow, 2004), 85.

[72] GARF, f. 6903, op. 1, d. 713, ll. 129, 158–61, 164–5.

montage.[73] By now well acquainted with sound editing, broadcasters were able to depart from the naturalistic conventions of earlier Soviet radio. Instead of striving to create the impression of a live broadcast, broadcasters could use sound effects and depart from strict chronology in the material they presented. The guiding principle should be the journalist's own compositional design rather than 'real time'.[74] Yet some commentators felt that the boundary between 'documentary' and 'artistic' broadcasting still needed to be maintained: it was one thing to super-impose the noise of the factory floor on a worker interview recorded in a quieter place, quite another to play fast and loose with facts.[75] Perhaps, moreover, the advent of recording technology had made journalists sloppy in their work habits: they now eschewed rehearsals, assuming that an acceptable product could be manufactured out of whatever they managed to record.[76]

Consequently, there was a modest backlash against the hegemony of recording on the radio. Live broadcasts, which had been the norm in the first two decades of Soviet broadcasting, had much greater impact and immediacy, but now they were rarely found except in sports reports.[77] At least in Moscow, there were plenty of tape recorders, and it was relatively easy to produce footage (even if facilities to transfer this raw footage to the studio were still inadequate).[78] Yet, by 1965, with the launch of Yunost and Maiak and the greater rhetorical emphasis on rapid response, the downside of recording technology was becoming apparent: it slowed down the passage of the material to the listener. The quality of sound in recordings delivered over the wires (*po kanalu*) by reporters in various parts of the USSR left much to be desired; sometimes a tape sent back from Tokyo would sound better than a recording wired from Tula.[79]

Of course, the main reason that radio reports took a long time to reach the lis-tener was that they were subject to the scrutiny of the censorship apparatus. Even in this era of 24-hour broadcasting, the authorities were ever vigilant lest broad-casters take liberties. In July 1964, staff on Yunost were severely reprimanded by the Radio Committee for broadcasts that did not correspond to the written texts submitted in advance.[80] In August 1965, the latest rules on compiling the written 'file' for each broadcast must have made exhausting reading for Soviet radio produc-ers: the text required three different signatures, and the editor responsible for the programme had to sign every single page as well as initialling all corrections. All files required a stamp from Glavlit (or the signature of the head of the relevant department confirming that Glavlit approval was not required). Texts for broadcast

[73] Iu. Letunov, 'Razgovor o reportazhe', *Sovradiotel*, no. 2 (1961): 7–9.

[74] N. Taube, 'Vnimanie: v efire rastrachena minuta!', *Sovradiotel*, no. 8 (1964): 12–14. Estonia had always been the aesthetic vanguard: see I. Trikkel', 'Spetsifika radiokommunikatsii, ee vyrazitel'nye sredstva i zhanry' (candidate's dissertation, Tartu, 1967).

[75] M. Polonskii, 'Pravo na uslovnost'', *Sovradiotel*, no. 3 (1967): 10–13.

[76] P. Palladin, 'Magnitofon i…bukhgalteriia', *Sovradiotel*, no. 8 (1967): 22–3.

[77] L. Khataevich, 'Efir trebuet "efira"', *Sovradiotel*, no. 4 (1965): 8–9.

[78] TsAOPIM, f. 2930, op. 1, d. 8, l. 25 (party meeting of Moscow broadcasters, 4 March 1959).

[79] TsAOPIM, f. 2930, op. 1, d. 277, ll. 41, 45 (party meeting of Moscow broadcasters, 7 January 1965).

[80] Text of decree in *VKD*, 160–1.

needed to be submitted at least three full days in advance (not including Sundays and holidays).[81] There was also close in-house monitoring of performance. Broadcasters in the 1960s apparently lived in fear of the monitors (*kontrolery efira*) whose job was to maintain linguistic standards. These authorities had at their elbows dictionaries of Russian stress, and no less a figure than Nikita Khrushchev would be made to re-record a speech if it offended against linguistic norms.[82] Truly 'live' broadcasting remained an exceptional occurrence on Soviet radio. Even on Maiak, there was only a very short list of people allowed to speak live, and such occasions still had to be meticulously prepared. A 2-minute injection of live speech from a concert hall, stadium, or street required elaborate technical backup and absolutely precise timing. In the 1970s, preparations for the two biggest broadcasting events of the year—1 May and 7 November—started a full two months in advance, and the head of Gosteleradio, Sergei Lapin, personally edited the text for Revolution Day.[83] Lapin had never disguised his intentions on this score. When he took over as broadcasting boss in the spring of 1970, he wasted little time in reminding his subordinates of the need to avoid programmes that were 'not prepared, not listened to in advance, not checked'. As he went on: 'we have the opportunity, starting on 3 May, to include in the schedule only things where we're absolutely sure that they are right, that they are needed, and not end up spending a week to establish whether they're accepted or not'.[84] The debate rumbled on into the later Soviet period. Even at the end of the 1970s broadcasters were being enjoined to eschew scripted broadcasts and show the individual person 'without simplifying or glossing over'.[85] But linguistic standards had to be maintained. As a Vladivostok journalist observed of the 1970s: 'We didn't hesitate to stop even top bosses if they violated linguistic norms during a recording'.[86] On Leningrad radio, one senior editor meticulously rehearsed with party bosses to make sure they got their stresses and diction right, evidently drawing some gratification from these brief moments in the studio when power was in thrall to culture.[87]

CONCLUSION

Perhaps the apotheosis of sound recording on Soviet radio was the campaign to mark the two major celebrations of the early Brezhnev era: the 50th anniversary of the Revolution (1967) and the 100th of Lenin's birth (1970). These events brought an immense mobilization of the Soviet culture industry in all its branches. Thanks

[81] Text in *VKD*, 163–4.

[82] Georgii Zubkov, 'Razmyshleniia bez mikrofona', in G. Sheveleva (ed.), *Pozyvnye trevog i nadezhd. K 40-letiiu radiostantsii 'Maiak'* (Moscow, 2004), 33–4.

[83] Mikhail Leshchinskii, 'Vospominaniia slishkom daviat plechi…', *Pozyvnye trevog i nadezhd*, 112, 114–15.

[84] Text of Lapin's speech (of 27 April 1970) in *VKD*, 175–7.

[85] O. Kudenko, 'Radiopublitsistika segodnia: Problemy masterstva', in V. M. Vozchikov (ed.), *Zvuchashchii mir: Kniga o zvukovoi dokumentalistike* (Moscow, 1979), 20.

[86] Pavel Marchenko, 'Odinnadtsat' let sredi druzei i tovarishchei', in *Nemnogo o radio*, 40.

[87] Markhasev, *Belki v kolese*, 191–2.

to the legacy of several decades of recording technology, the celebrations could strive for aural authenticity. The sound archive could now be mined to help to tell an authoritative story of the Soviet past. After the war, the leader cults of the Soviet Union acquired an aural dimension to go along with their established iconography. In early 1951 the decision was taken to produce 150,000 gramophone records with the speeches of Lenin and a colossal 1.8 million with recordings of Stalin (including the twenty-one-disk set of his speech to the Extraordinary Eighth Congress of Soviets in November 1936).[88] While Stalin's cult was extinguished in the 1960s, Lenin's continued to blaze. In January 1964, members of the team that had restored recordings of Lenin's speeches were formally thanked and awarded prizes by the head of the Radio Committee.[89]

The aural document gained further prominence as 1967 and 1970 drew closer. The task, as an editor from the 'Leniniana' department of Leningrad radio noted, was to search out 'a Fact that can speak for itself in the literal sense of that word'.[90] In September 1965 broadcasting organizations around the USSR were asked to send in any documentary material (sound or film) that could be used in programmes to mark the upcoming anniversaries.[91] In May 1966, a special group was set up in the literature and drama section of the Radio Committee to assemble a 'sound chronicle of our Motherland'. Its task was to arrange the recording of the reminiscences of 'outstanding people of our age', and in particular 'active participants in the proletarian revolution and Civil War', as well as to expand the collection of documentary material by gathering material from other archives, private collections, and even abroad.[92]

Yet, while the celebrations of the late 1960s demonstrated the enduring capacity of the Soviet system of cultural production to throw itself into campaign mode, as well as the now substantial resources of the Soviet sound archive, they were misleading as a guide to prevailing practice. Broadcasting in the USSR was now a complex and diverse industry, and the combination of new technology and cultural de-Stalinization (however attenuated) had changed for good the forms and norms of Soviet radio. Chapter 7 will explore the varied output of Soviet broadcasting as it developed from the mid-1940s to the late 1960s.

---

[88] GARF, f. 6903, op. 1, d. 333, ll. 1–3 (Puzin to Suslov, 3 February 1951).

[89] Text in *VKD*, 160.   [90] L. Markhasev, 'Moia revoliutsiia', *Sovradiotel*, no. 6 (1967): 2.

[91] ERA.R, 1590.4.429.23.

[92] Text of relevant decree in *VKD*, 165. The rules for selecting and archiving sound documents for this chronicle were drawn up in late 1968: see *VKD*, 173–4.

7

Radio Genres and Their Audiences in the Post-War Era

The reputation of Soviet radio as mind-numbing propaganda instrument is often belied by the recollections of people who lived through parts of the post-war Soviet era. Most Russians born before the mid-1970s can name several programmes and rubrics they remember fondly. At least some of these programmes date from the dark years of the late Stalin period; several more were launched in the Thaw era. Between the 1940s and 1970s, the infrastructure of Soviet broadcasting was strengthened enormously, and media professionals developed a more secure sense of their own worth. The present chapter investigates how exactly they went about communicating with a far larger and more sophisticated audience than that of the pre-war era.

PLAYING WITH THE MEDIUM: CHILDREN'S BROADCASTING IN THE LATE STALIN ERA AND BEYOND

In a 1947 poem by Agniia Barto (1906–81), a young boy calls his friends over for a special occasion: his own mother is due to speak on the radio. He sits impatiently through the other items, but eventually gets his reward: he hears a very familiar voice 'speaking with the whole country' and indeed 'being heard all over the world'.[1] This fusion of the domestic and the public encapsulated the Soviet broadcasting dream of mediated national community. But perhaps a fact more worthy of note at this post-war moment is the underage protagonist of the poem. In the late 1940s, the child addressee was firmly back in the sights of broadcasting professionals, while children's radio had some claim to be the vanguard of a new, more imaginative, more differentiated Soviet broadcasting culture.

To judge by interview material, young listeners were an appreciative section of the post-war audience. Radio is mentioned by informants as a memorable aspect of growing up in the 1940s—a time not over-endowed with comforts and recreations. In Leningrad, one especially well-loved voice was that of Mariia Petrova, an actress who had appeared frequently on radio since the mid-1930s, played a leading

---

[1] Agniia Barto, 'My slushaem radio' (1947), in ead., *Sobranie sochinenii v trekh tomakh* (Moscow, 1969–71), i. 180–2.

role on radio during the Siege, and was best known for her performances of folk tales (*skazki*).[2] Further afield, especially in rural areas, radio sets might be few—only two or three in a whole village. But this rarity value made *Pionerskaia zor'ka*, the main children's news broadcast, all the more memorable for one girl (b. 1936) from Perm' oblast: she would retell the content of the programme—the pioneer flag and other insignia and rituals, the songs, the tales of exemplary revolutionaries—to the other small children in the village.[3]

An axiom of the Stalin era was that culture could have a single addressee: there was decreed to be a single Soviet reader, viewer, listener, and so on.[4] But this presumption was less binding with respect to children's culture. Here, if nowhere else, a degree of whimsicality could be tolerated; talented children's writers and editors had better chances than their colleagues of flying under the radar of the authorities. Children's broadcasting in the 1930s could already boast an impressive line-up of talent: Samuil Marshak, Kornei Chukovskii, Lev Kassil', Barto, Arkadii Gaidar, and others. Writers were involved in children's radio to an extent that was not true of those who wrote for an adult audience.[5] That said, the patriotic exigencies of wartime, as well as the sheer shortage of personnel and resources, had meant that children's broadcasting in the early 1940s resembled radio for miniature adults rather than something qualitatively different. With the rise in Soviet fortunes in the war, however, children's radio not only re-established itself but became a vanguard of formal innovation. The children's section of the Radio Committee was liquidated at the start of the war but re-formed as an independent unit in January 1943. In due course, writers such as Kassil', Barto, Marshak, and E. A. Blaginina fully resumed their participation.

By the last year of the war, administrators were granting children's writers and editors more leeway. A meeting in the Radio Committee of August 1944 acknowledged that broadcasting needed to become more engaging and interactive, with children themselves being handed the microphone more often.[6] The same idea was stated more imposingly in a Radio Committee decree signed by Aleksei Puzin in August 1945, which called for special care with the 'literary editing' of children's programmes; the aim was to present material in a way that was 'lively, straightforward and accessible to children' as well as, of course, linguistically flawless. Children's broadcasters were enjoined to show 'inventiveness in searching for new forms'.[7]

---

[2] These are mentioned, for example, by a Leningrad brother and sister born in 1940 and 1946 respectively, Oxf/Lev SPb-03 PF 36 (B), p. 24. On Petrova's career, see Lev Markhasev, *Belki v kolese: Zapiski iz Doma radio* (St Petersburg, 2004), 41–55, and the profile at http://www.radioportal.ru/articles/2012/golos-blokadnogo-leningrada-mariya-petrova (checked 30 April 2013).

[3] Oxf/Lev P-05 PF-19 (B), p. 28.

[4] On the Soviet reader, see Evgenii Dobrenko, *Formovka sovetskogo chitatelia: Sotsial'nye i esteticheskie predposylki retseptsii sovetskoi literatury* (St Petersburg, 1997).

[5] See the survey in N. Sukhova, 'Radioveshchanie dlia detei', article posted at http://www.tvmuseum.ru (checked 27 June 2014).

[6] GARF, f. 6903, op. 1, d. 90, l. 23 (meeting of 15 August 1944).

[7] 'O rabote otdela radioveshchaniia dlia detei', *VKD*, 113.

Radio professionals were only too happy to respond to these signals from above. M. Kalakutskaia, the head of children's broadcasting, was able to report that the amount of children's programming on central radio had risen in March 1945 from 2 hours 5 minutes to 3 hours 20 minutes daily. Quantitative changes had been accompanied by qualitative: more use was now made of literature and music, while programming had become more varied to reflect the interests of different age groups—from nursery to the later years of school. There had been readings and adaptations of works by major writers such as Kassil', Marshak, Sergei Mikhalkov, Barto, Chukovskii, Veniamin Kaverin, and Andrei Platonov.[8] In August 1945 Kalakutskaia was able to report further improvements in musical performance as well as noting the swelling postbag of letters from appreciative young listeners. Priorities for the near future included increasing the quantity of folk tales and adventure stories and striking a 'warmer' tone when addressing children. Her colleagues chipped in to say that *Pionerskaia zor'ka*, the main fixed point in the children's schedule, was also its weak point: this children's news digest could be every bit as dreary as its counterpart for adults. Puzin agreed: 'we do better with artistic programmes, but very badly with political programmes'. High-quality concerts or the successful recent adaptation of *Don Quixote* would count for nothing if broadcasters could not get *Pionerskaia zor'ka* right.[9]

It seems safe to assume, however, that many contemporary listeners felt differently. Some of the best-loved children's programmes on Soviet radio date precisely from this immediate post-war phase. *Kolobok*, a series aimed at preschool children and derived from a well-known folk tale, had as its hero a round creature, a kind of *perpetuum mobile* bread loaf, which rolled its way into various adventures. Other programmes offered more interactive formats. 'Meeting at the Round Table' presented ethical issues to children in the form of a conversation as well as giving them inspiring examples of wartime heroism. The series 'Guess If You Can' (*Ugadai-ka*) communicated important knowledge (some of it military) to children by setting them riddles to solve.[10] This was not the first time that children had been set puzzles on Soviet radio, but never before had the activity been woven into a long-running narrative with an established set of characters.[11] The creator of the series, Sergei Bogomazov, had found a winning new form.

To be sure, it was sometimes difficult to stimulate and entertain children while at the same time communicating the gravity of current affairs. *Pionerskaia zor'ka* was felt to be 'between Scylla and Charybdis' in its uneasy combination of 'saccharine' style and 'dry, newspaper-like' content. It was not always clear how

[8] GARF, f. 6903, op. 1, d. 104, ll. 7–21.
[9] GARF, f. 6903, op. 1, d. 123, ll. 7, 10, 26, 41 (meeting of 9 August 1945).
[10] The text of the first broadcast on 22 February 1944 is in *VKD*, 392–5. The programme continued to go strong into the post-war and post-Stalin periods. In October 1958 it went out for the 150th time and was regularly receiving 10,000–12,000 letters per broadcast. See A. Men'shikova, '"Ugadai-ka"', *Sovradiotel*, no. 1 (1959): 13–14. See also the article by Vera Vartanova, producer of *Ugadai-ka* from 1952 to 1982, at http://www.tvmuseum.ru: this gives a total of 2 million letters received over the whole run.
[11] The novelty of *Ugadai-ka* on its appearance in 1944, and the failure of an earlier programme of the same name, are mentioned in T. Volobaeva, 'Sekret dolgoletiia', *Sovradiotel*, no. 3 (1967): 14–15.

children's programming should tread the line between fantasy and reality. One episode of *Kolobok*, which described the protagonist rolling into a newly liberated part of the Soviet Union and finding there sparkling new schools in place of war devastation, was taken off air on the grounds that it would raise children's expectations too high.[12] *Pionerskaia zor'ka*, at least, appears not to have pulled its punches. The broadcast of 17 April 1945 contained harrowing accounts of children's experiences of 'German slavery' in the Majdanek camp. The report contained interview footage of three former inmates, now safe in an orphanage in Moscow region.[13]

But, although they were produced on a shoestring, there was no question that by 1945 children's programmes had earned the right to a regular and significant place in the schedule.[14] Perhaps the greatest triumph of post-war children's broadcasting was the series 'The Club of the Famous Captains' (*Klub znameni-tykh kapitanov*), which first went out on New Year's Eve 1945. Set in a school library, it showed characters from well-loved adventure fiction coming to life after dark. Gulliver, Captain Nemo, and Robinson Crusoe, once released from the books they inhabited, sang songs, asked interesting questions, and swapped stories about their past adventures. The series managed like few others to be both playful and impeccably enlightening; it also satisfied the immense yearning of Soviet people—both children and adults—to travel the world (however vicariously). This was a remarkable combination of storytelling, exoticism, rousing music, and sheer *romantika*. Both writers and geographers were involved in preparing the programmes, while the performers represented an impressive roster of acting talent: Osip Abdulov, Rostislav Pliatt, Valentina Sperantova, and Mikhail Nazvanov.[15]

Many other children's programmes in the post-war era exploited radio's capacity to transcend distance and to combine adventure and play with geographical and scientific knowledge. In 1947 two more programmes in an exploratory vein were launched: 'Around Our Native Land' (*Po rodnoi strane*), which was directed at older children, and 'The Radio Club of Young Geographers' (*Radioklub iunykh geografov*), which brought geographers, geologists, zoologists, and botanists to the studio to enlighten young listeners and answer their questions.[16] New programmes in the same scientific-geographical vein continued to appear in the 1950s: 'The World We Live in' (*Mir, v kotorom my zhivem*, from March 1954) and 'Travels

[12] Details drawn from Radio Committee discussion of children's broadcasting, GARF, f. 6903, op. 1, d. 91 (September 1944). On *Kolobok* specifically, see Blaginina's archive at RGALI. Her postbag reveals that some listeners—especially boys—wanted more, not less, direct reference to the war: what if, for example, Kolobok delivered the Germans into the hands of the partisans? RGALI, f. 1448, op. 1, d. 272.

[13] Text in *VKD*, 432–6.

[14] On the material predicament of children's broadcasting, see GARF, f. 6903, op. 1, d. 107: as of February 1945, the section had no rehearsal space, no orchestra, and only four actors (all of them women).

[15] For an enthusiastic account of the programme's virtues, see Volobaeva, 'Sekret dolgoletiia', 16–17. An archive of listeners' letters makes it clear that the programme's appeal was not by any means limited to children. See RGALI, f. 2889 (Vladimir Mikhailovich Kreps), op. 1, d. 232.

[16] A. A. Sherel', *Audiokul'tura XX veka. Istoriia, esteticheskie zakonomernosti, osobennosti vliianiia na auditoriiu: Ocherki* (Moscow, 2004), 86.

around Our Beloved Motherland' (*Puteshestvie po liubimoi Rodine*, April 1958). 'The Club of the Famous Captains' was discontinued in 1953, apparently on the grounds that it was 'out of date'; selective repeats were broadcast in 1966, and there were calls for the series to be continued with fresh material.[17] A cult programme for the technophile 1960s was *KOAPP* (an acronym for 'Club for Protecting Nature's Copyright'), a series launched in July 1964 that was devoted to the science of bionics, or what human beings could learn from nature. The programme offered a winning blend of whimsicality—meetings of the 'club' were opened and closed by squawks from a bird acting as 'secretary'—and carefully prepared scientific topics.[18]

To a greater extent than any other branch of Soviet broadcasting, children's radio had a strong and stable team of authors, producers, and performers. The leading creative force of the post-war era seems to have been Roza Ioffe (1907–66), who had a long and distinguished career despite a sometimes strained relationship with her employers. Among Ioffe's achievements was the most instantly recognizable voice in Soviet broadcasting history: that of Buratino, the Russian Pinocchio. In a 1949 adaptation of the work by Ioffe, all the roles were performed by a single actor, Nikolai Litvinov, although when he played Buratino his voice rose to an eerily high pitch. At a meeting with factory workers in November 1953, Litvinov explained (presumably at popular request) how this had been achieved: his normal speaking voice had been recorded on tape at a low rate of revolutions and then made squeaky by playing it back at normal speed.[19]

For several decades, until the mid-1980s, the head of Soviet children's broadcasting remained Anna Aleksandrovna Men'shikova, who managed to assemble and maintain a similarly long-serving team of colleagues. Nina Anatol'evna German, for example, was the producer of 'Guess If You Can' for more than twenty years. In public Men'shikova paid her due to the pedagogical function of children's radio: 'very often', she noted, 'children first find out what is good and what is bad from radio programmes'. Yet, besides obviously educational offerings such as 'A New Book Is Coming to Us' (*K nam novaia kniga idet*), where a librarian named Pal Palych introduced children each month to a newly published book, there was plenty of room for game-playing: 'Guess If You Can', for one, was still going strong after almost twenty years. Above all, however, Men'shikova was concerned to convey the value of storytelling for children—and in particular to mount a defence of the *skazka*, a form that had had its travails in the Stalin era. A key item in the weekly schedule was 'One Story after Another' (*Skazka za skazkoi*), where the celebrated Litvinov was the narrator. In 1963, moreover, children's broadcasting launched a daily evening story at 7.50 p.m. on Channel Two, which was intended

---

[17] Volobaeva, 'Sekret dolgoletiia', 16–17.

[18] See the interview with the author of the series, Mailen Aronovich Konstantinovskii, at http://www.tvmuseum.ru (checked 27 June 2014).

[19] GARF, f. 6903, op. 3, d. 90, l. 9. On the significance of the high-pitched voice in an earlier form of Russian popular entertainment, see Catriona Kelly, *Petrushka: The Russian Carnival Puppet Theatre* (Cambridge, 1990), 106.

to provide a fixed point in the bedtime ritual of Soviet children (as 'Good Night, Little Ones' (*Spokoinoi nochi, malyshi*) later would do on TV).[20]

In the 1970s, children's broadcasting once again demonstrated its powers of invention by launching the programme that provided the signature tune for the childhood of what turned out to be the last Soviet generation: 'Radio Nanny' (*Radioniania*). Devised as a children's equivalent of 'There We Go Again' (*Opiat' 25*, a high-spirited 25-minute morning broadcast that had been launched in 1968), it brought together Nikolai Litvinov, twenty years on from Buratino the best-known voice in children's broadcasting, with two younger and jauntier performers, Aleksandr Livshits and Aleksandr Levenbuk. Although there was some concern that the title sounded old-fashioned, the doubts were soon dispelled by the evident appeal of the programme's playful format to an audience that extended far beyond children. As Litvinov apparently remarked, the age range of listeners was 8–80.[21] Although this was already the era of TV, interview material suggests that radio remained a constant presence in the childhood of Soviet people raised in the 1970s.[22]

RADIO AS ART FORM: THE REHABILITATION OF RADIO THEATRE

When Soviet people of the post-war generation are asked about their strongest radio memories, more often than not they mention 'Theatre at the Microphone'—live broadcasts of stage productions. Theatre broadcasts of the 1950s are remembered fondly by those otherwise far removed from sources of cultural stimulation—a man who grew up in Perm' oblast, or a Taganrog woman of working-class background who especially valued the radio because the lighting at home was too dim to read by in the evenings.[23]

This popularity was achieved despite the fact that radio theatre faced ugly political pressures in the late Stalin era. As part of the general Zhdanov-led crackdown on the arts, broadcasters were given a stern reprimand for their poor choice of literature and drama.[24] More than a decade after the conclusive defeat of 'formalism' in the Soviet cultural establishment, aesthetic norms on Soviet broadcasting remained highly restrictive. For two decades the ruling orthodoxy of Soviet broadcasting was, as one participant in a Radio Committee discussion of February 1945 put it, that 'on the radio, art is reproductive, i.e. it reproduces rather than

---

[20] A. Men'shikova, ' "Poseesh' kharakter—pozhnesh' sud'bu" (O nekotorykh voprosakh radioveshchaniia dlia samykh malen'kikh)', *Sovradiotel*, no. 11 (1963): 18–20. For a useful survey of Men'shikova's career and children's broadcasting in general, see Sukhova, 'Radioveshchanie dlia detei'.

[21] See the article by the programme's creator, Elena Lebedeva, 'Radioniania—byla takai peredacha...', at http://www.tvmuseum.ru (checked 27 June 2014).

[22] See e.g. Oxf/Lev SPb-02 PF 14 (B) ONN, p. 31 (Leningrad woman b. 1969).

[23] See respectively Oxf/Lev P-07 PF37 CHMA, p. 20 and Oxf/Lev T-05 PF 9 (A), p. 3. Both informants were born in 1946.

[24] 'O nedostatkakh literaturno-dramaticheskogo veshchaniia i merakh po ego uluchsheniiu' (19 September 1946), in *VKD*, 117–19.

producing'.[25] Yet radio's aesthetic demotion did not prevent it from being an un-rivalled conduit for literature and theatre. In 1951 alone, more than 200 broad-casts went out under the 'Theatre at the Microphone' rubric, and they included performances by many of the capital's leading troupes. It may even be that the radio enjoyed more latitude than other media: in the summer of 1951, an adapta-tion of Maiakovskii's satirical play *The Bathhouse* was broadcast—this at a time when the work was effectively proscribed for the stage. In the words of one his-torian, this was nothing less than 'a signal to many of the educated elite that a change of policy might be in the air'.[26] Whichever way, two-thirds or more of the hundreds of letters received each month by the department of literature and drama were devoted to 'Theatre at the Microphone'.[27]

In due course, moreover, the Stalin-era insistence that the microphone was a facilitator of literature and drama rather than an artistic medium in its own right began to weaken. Radio drama was one of the many beneficiaries of the cultural thaw of the 1950s. At a conference of radio producers in February 1958, one of the speakers stated bluntly: 'we are obliged to discover new forms, otherwise our radio will stagnate'. No meaningful progress had been made since the early days of radio drama; scripts written specifically for broadcast were vanishingly few, and mere adaptations of scripts intended for reading were not sufficient, as they did not make use of the expressive possibilities of radio. At the same time, as other partici-pants in the discussion noted, Soviet listeners were craving fresh material on con-temporary themes. It was still hard to overcome the assumption that the province of radio was mere current affairs (*publitsistika*) and to raise the prestige and the material rewards for writing radio scripts. As one speaker noted plaintively, 'why is it considered art when someone reads something out on the stage, but when an actor performs on the radio, after rehearsing with a producer and with an audience of tens of millions of people around the whole country, that is not considered art?'[28]

Although similar complaints could be heard at meetings in the following years,[29] the tide of under-appreciation of radio art had turned. True enough, theatre people had needed more than a little convincing that radio drama might be an art form in its own right, but they now had to recognize the achievements of a whole string of distinguished artists who had combined careers in theatre and cinema with work on the radio: Osip Abdulov, Nikolai Litvinov, Mariia Babanova, Aleksei Konsovs-kii (to name but four). By the early 1960s, it was possible to revisit the aesthetic debates of the 1930s and—implicitly or even explicitly—express sympathy for the losing side. 'Theatre at the Microphone', the dominant form of radio theatre since

---

[25] GARF, f. 6903, op. 1, d. 106, l. 64.
[26] Karl E. Loewenstein, 'The Thaw: Writers and the Public Sphere in the Soviet Union 1951–1957', PhD dissertation (Duke University, 1999), 57; more generally on post-war 'theatre at the microphone', see Sherel', *Audiokul'tura XX veka*, 84–5.
[27] For a digest of the postbag in July–October 1952, see GARF, f. 6903, op. 10, d. 2.
[28] GARF, f. 6903, op. 1, d. 577, quotations on ll. 6, 59.
[29] For an example from 1962, see an excerpt from a Radio Committee discussion of the work of the 'Theatre at the Microphone' department, *VKD*, 153–4.

the mid-1930s, had brought aesthetic stagnation, as a limited number of productions were endlessly recycled. Now, in the 1960s, the Soviet Union could learn from successful precedents in the socialist bloc and commit itself to the radio play without succumbing to earlier formalist excesses. In the main professional journal for broadcasters, a colleague from Bratislava radio offered a robust defence of the aesthetic value of radio drama.[30] Another contributor pointed out a pragmatic consideration: now that radio authors were paid at the same rate as scriptwriters for the cinema, there was no reason whatsoever for them to stay away from radio drama.[31] Nor would their pride need to suffer: authors could now expect a far more respectful response if they wrote for radio. New productions were reviewed at length and, on the whole, sympathetically, while sound effects were now recognized as fully legitimate.[32]

SOVIET RADIO NEWS IN THE MASS MEDIA AGE

Radio news was ostensibly a much less promising field for experimentation. Here even the slightest deviations from authoritative discourse were unlikely to be tolerated. As before the war, there was a general sense that the stultifying content that resulted was not a good thing: the broadcasting administration continued to field and issue ritual complaints about the dreariness of Soviet broadcasting. Yet, as radio made the transition from war to peace, there were also more practical suggestions as to how the failings might be remedied. As early as August 1944, a speaker at a Radio Committee meeting argued that it was important to present the news not in 45-minute streams of text but in punchier bulletins of 10 or 15 minutes. In addition, more thought needed to be given to scheduling: high-impact news bulletins should go out at the peak time of 7.45 a.m.[33] The international situation at the end of the war made the task of broadcasting all the more urgent. Soviet propaganda during the war had been straightforwardly anti-German, but now it needed to be 'more subtle, more clever, and more flexible'. Soviet radio news and current affairs would need to do more to differentiate itself—in style if not in content—from official propaganda. Soviet broadcasters could learn something from the free-style 'commentary' genre that was adopted by the Americans and the British.[34]

The onset of the Cold War and the *zhdanovshchina* ensured that these ambitions would remain largely unrealized for the following decade. The rhetoric and the rhythms of Soviet broadcasting remained recognizably Stalinist until the old dictator's death, and indeed for some time beyond. Radio was still used as the oracle of dictatorship for major real-time events in the late Stalin era such as the lifting of the Berlin blockade.[35] In early March 1953, radio coverage of Stalin's lying-in-state

[30] I. Teren, 'Iskusstvo, rozhdennoe nashim vekom', *Sovradiotel*, no. 9 (1963): 32–3.
[31] Mistislav Mikriunov, 'Radioteatr—iskusstvo', *Teatr*, no. 12 (1964): 42–56.
[32] P. Bondarev, 'Zvuchashchie kraski', *Sovradiotel*, no. 6 (1967): 30–2.
[33] GARF, f. 6903, op. 1, d. 90, ll. 7–8 (meeting of 15 August 1944).
[34] GARF, f. 6903, op. 1, d. 115, ll. 2, 75 (meeting of 15 May 1945).
[35] See Harrison Salisbury, *Moscow Journal: The End of Stalin* (Chicago, 1961), 27.

and funeral was meticulously choreographed to include a succession of eulogies. When Beria was executed in December 1953, he was subject to much the same kind of radio character assassination that had been perpetrated on Bukharin fifteen years earlier. A broadcast on New Year's Eve 1955 was a thoroughly earnest account of the year's achievements in socialist construction rather than remotely playful. In 1963, an account of the trial of the Western spy Oleg Pen'kovskii contained all too familiar language of 'unmasking' and 'vigilance', even if the tone was less shrill than in the 1930s.[36] Soviet broadcasters were always hampered by the need to obtain prior approval for any information they broadcast. No less a figure that Nikolai Mesiatsev, head of State Radio and Television from 1964 to 1970, later recalled his vain attempts to secure for himself authority for broadcasting basic 'facts' without having to run everything by the Central Committee.[37]

Yet, over the course of the first post-Stalin decade, the style and rhetoric of Soviet broadcasting underwent significant changes. At the end of March 1952, the half-hour weekly news bulletin included items on the recent session of the Supreme Soviet of the RSFSR; on the most powerful steam turbine in the world; on the construction of the Volga-Don canal; on the 125th anniversary of Beethoven's death; on the writer Semen Babaevskii; and on the start of the school spring break. Although there were short snatches of dialogue and music, for the most part the broadcast consisted of set-piece statements. For example, the main item on the Supreme Soviet was a three-page prepared text by one of the delegates.[38] Four years on, while the themes were similar, the style of presentation was slightly more interactive, and greater use was made of sound recorded at the scene of events. A report from the Mytishchi machine-building factory, for example, plunged listeners into the aural environment of the factory floor; only after a few seconds did the voice of the presenter begin to explain what was happening. In the Stalin era, by contrast, the voice-over had always been a more insistent and directive presence. In March 1956, listeners could even hear a snatch of English-language dialogue, as the broadcast reported on the visit of a delegation from Manchester to a Leningrad family.[39] The liberation of the microphone was a notable feature of the Thaw era, which in 1957 saw the launch of an influential programme that took listeners on an aural virtual tour of the USSR. Entitled 'Taking a Microphone around Our Native Land' (*S mikrofonom po rodnoi strane*), it was soon inundated with requests from listeners to make their own city or region the subject of a broadcast.[40] In due course, moreover, Soviet radio could transport its listeners into space, receiving radio bulletins from astronauts almost in real time. At 10.02 a.m. on 12 April 1961, with the Vostok mission still in progress, the Soviet public was given the sensational news of Gagarin's flight. At 9.22 a.m., listeners were told, Gagarin had transmitted the following message from his location above South America: 'The flight is going fine, I feel good.' At 10.15 a.m.—in

---

[36] Examples in this paragraph from *VKD*, 505–17, 526, 573–4.
[37] N. N. Mesiatsev, *Gorizonty i labirinty moei zhizni* (Moscow, 2005), 487.
[38] GARF, f. 6903, op. 11, d. 674.   [39] GARF, f. 6903, op. 11, d. 758.
[40] GARF, f. 6903, op. 11, d. 788, ll. 1–14.

other words, while the broadcast was still in progress—he had sent an update while flying over Africa: 'The flight is passing fine, I am coping well with the condition of weightlessness.'[41]

It was in the mid-1950s that Soviet broadcasters seem finally to have grasped the need to make news broadcasts more punchy and immediate.[42] The importance of effective broadcasting was demonstrated to the Soviet authorities in dismaying fashion in Hungary in 1956, which was undoubtedly a radio-assisted revolution. In Radio Free Europe (RFE), urban Hungarians had a near-constant and valued source of information from abroad. As the Soviet leadership struggled to reach a decision on how to calm the situation, it countered by broadcasting a moderate declaration on the 'further strengthening of friendship and cooperation' on 30 October. But much more influential on the popular mood were RFE broadcasts, which backed the rebel cause during a critical phase and almost certainly made the uprising more violent than it would otherwise have been.[43] Even if the stakes of political communication were not quite so high in the Soviet Union, a return to the ponderous forms of Stalinist broadcasting was widely recognized as undesirable. The Soviet Union moved towards 24-hour broadcasting as it sought to compete for the listener with foreign radio stations.

A trailblazer among Soviet broadcasting organizations was Estonian radio, whose main news broadcast, 'Echo of the Day', placed a premium on live footage and insisted that reports last no longer than 3 minutes 30 seconds. How, though, to guarantee the impression of freshness? One Estonian journalist recommended that each radio committee set up its own 'office of preliminary information', which would communicate in advance to front-line journalists where the main events in the USSR were going to occur.[44] A Leningrad radio news journalist bristled at this lesson in good practice. All radio committees shared the aspirations of the Estonians, but resources did not permit them always to have reporters on the ground. A 'service of preliminary information' would just add another layer of bureaucratic complexity. In any case, since the start of 1960 Leningrad radio had almost completely ceased broadcasting pre-scripted interviews.[45]

In 1963, 'Latest News' celebrated its thirtieth anniversary, having taken over from the *radiogazeta* in 1933. By now it went out about fifty times per day, with a

---

[41] *VKD*, 560–1. It seems that the broadcast of 10.02 a.m. went out half an hour later than planned, perhaps because the communiqué had to be rewritten to take account of a last-minute promotion for Gagarin: see Andrew L. Jenks, *The Cosmonaut Who Couldn't Stop Smiling: The Life and Legend of Yuri Gagarin* (DeKalb, Ill., 2012), 134. On the significance of space reports for broadcasting culture at the turn of the 1950s, see also Sherel', *Audiokul'tura XX veka*, 88–9.

[42] M. Frolov, 'Reportazh—glavnaia forma informatsii', *Sovradiotel*, no. 2 (1957): 20–2.

[43] Johanna Granville, *The First Domino: International Decision Making during the Hungarian Crisis of 1956* (College Station, Tex., 2004), 68, 171–81; Charles Gati, *Failed Illusions: Moscow, Washington, Budapest, and the 1956 Hungarian Revolt* (Washington, 2006), 96, 183–5.

[44] A. Slutsk, ' "Ekho dnia" i ego problemy', *Sovradiotel*, no. 4 (1960): 2–4.

[45] T. Bogoslovskii, 'Proshu slova!', *Sovradiotel*, no. 6 (1960): 33–5. For a contribution from Central Radio that similarly accuses Slutsk of setting up a straw man, see L. Giune, ' "Za" i "protiv" ', *Sovteleradio*, no. 2 (1961): 5–6. This last article suggests that listeners had limited patience with news reports that carried useful 'information' but were not linked to the day's events.

total airtime of 17 hours.[46] Later in the 1960s, the average length of news items continued to come down, and the text delivered by the newsreader was more regularly interrupted by recorded footage from the scene of events. Experience had shown that effective reports could be delivered in 4 or 5 minutes—and sometimes in as little as 1 minute.[47] Even items on such a well-established subject as the Putilov factory in Leningrad were expected to provide listeners with stylistic variety and human interest (by placing individual stories at the heart of the broadcast).[48] One of the more ambitious projects of the time was a project by the newly formed 'mobile broadcasting unit' (*vyezdnaia redaktsiia*) which took a group of radio journalists from Vladivostok to Moscow over a period of seventy days. Here, as in the more established 'Taking a Microphone around Our Native Land', the prized virtues were freshness and directness. As two of the participants enjoined their colleagues: 'Let's speak more calmly, straightforwardly and emotionally on the radio.'[49]

The corollary was that the reporter became a leading actor in events rather than a vessel for information. In 1962, Estonian radio launched a programme called 'With a Microphone and a Notebook'. As the title suggests, this programme was designed to be pared down and immediate. The programme opened to the sound of the approaching steps of a reporter followed by a knock on the door, while it ended to the sound of receding steps (with light musical accompaniment in both cases).[50] The *radioocherk*—a more elaborate form of report with a stronger authorial voice—gave broadcasters scope to use the full expressive possibilities of the medium: first-hand recordings, music, sound effects. If reporters were capable of blending these elements into a seamless whole, the result would be powerful and convincing—for, in the words of one practitioner, 'the microphone is not capable of lying'.[51] For some reporters, however, it remained unclear how much artifice was permissible before the 'documentary' status of a broadcast was compromised.[52]

It almost goes without saying that Soviet criteria of newsworthiness were very different from those employed in the contemporary Western media. An important function of radio, as of other branches of Soviet culture, was to provide positive examples for emulation. Overachieving milkmaids were given their share of airtime, as were exemplary proletarians.[53] Gorky radio even had a programme entitled 'We Live among Good People'. Its heroes included a woman whose husband had died in the war but who had then taken over his role as medical assistant on the collective farm; a stonemason who had taken a turn for the good after spending

[46] I. Rabin, L. Giune, 'Tridtsat' let zvuchit v efire: "Peredaem 'Poslednie izvestiia'"', *Sovradiotel*, no. 9 (1963): 2–3.

[47] N. Taube, 'Volshebnaia lenta', *Sovradiotel*, no. 3 (1966): 22–4.

[48] D. Sitnikov, 'Itak, nachalo sdelano …', *Sovradiotel*, no. 3 (1960): 13–14.

[49] Iu. Letunov and K. Retinskii, '70 dnei v puti', *Sovradiotel*, no. 3 (1960): 15–18, quotation at 18.

[50] K. Iaagura, 'S mikrofonom i bloknotom', *Sovradiotel*, no. 9 (1963): 8–9.

[51] B. Khessin, 'Po zakonam efira', *Sovradiotel*, no. 10 (1963): 28–30, quotation 28.

[52] M. Polonskii, 'Pravo na uslovnost'', *Sovradiotel*, no. 3 (1967): 10–13.

[53] See GANO, f. 3630, op. 2, d. 139, ll. 8–9 (example from 1954) and f. 6204, op. 1, d. 12 (transcripts of factory district news in Gorky in 1958).

half his life in colonies for adolescent criminals; and a hard-working war invalid who never made any excuses or asked for concessions. As the announcer concluded: 'Take a look around you, dear friends, and you will see many splendid deeds by your comrades that you can talk about on our programme.'[54] Yet, although the references to the war and the emphasis on self-improvement fit a long-established tradition, the tone of broadcasts such as this was in marked contrast to the Stalin era or even the early post-Stalin period. The announcer's manner was engaging, even ingratiating. Even the preferred term of address was new: instead of the formal 'comrades', it was becoming habitual to call radio listeners 'friends'.[55]

The new broadcasting rhetoric of the post-Stalin era also implied a more prominent role for the ordinary citizen; at least some of those friendly listeners were to become speakers. By the early 1960s, as we have seen in Chapter 6, the unscripted interview was clearly established as 'best practice' on Soviet radio (although not always the actual practice). As one correspondent wrote in the leading professional journal: 'in my view, long and painful pauses while the interviewee tries to finish a phrase he has already started, stumbling corrections by the speaker as he goes along, and other such rough edges in a recording are far more valuable than even the smoothest and most elegant speeches that have been scrupulously written out beforehand'.[56] Conversational spontaneity even had its place in news broadcasts. 'Conversation partner' (*Sobesednik*), a Sunday supplement to 'Latest News' in the 1960s, contained rapid-fire dialogue between correspondent and interviewee.[57]

The vanguard of immediacy and interactivity in Soviet news was the new channel Maiak, which started broadcasting in August 1964. In the words of one journalist, it was responsible for 'the first breach in that wall of information that for decades had separated the Soviet people from the rest of the world'. With its regular snappy bulletins throughout the day and night, and its vital, upbeat style of delivery, Maiak was the Soviet riposte to the siren call of Western broadcasting. As one participant recalled, 'we were told that a new channel was starting along the lines of Voice of America. It would be called "Maiak". There would be a special editorial team. The announcers would need not to "read" but to "tell".'[58] Judging by the Radio Committee's digest of listeners' letters, Maiak did much to perform this mission. Not the least sign of its success was the regular handful of letters complaining of the 'glut of jazz music, of songs without melodies, without thoughts'.[59]

---

[54] GANO, f. 3630, op. 2, d. 685, quotation on l. 74. Note also the programme 'Vashi pis'ma, tovarishchi radioslushateli!', ibid., dd. 850 and 1092, and 'Radioslushateli rasskazyvaiut', ibid., d. 988 (1962). For information on a very similar programme put out by Novosibirsk radio, see Iu. Mostkov, 'Obraz sovremennika', *Sovradiotel*, no. 2 (1961): 2–3.

[55] By 1963, at least in human-interest radio, this form of address seemed to be standard: see GANO, f. 3630, op. 2, d. 1092.

[56] N. Taube, 'Korrespondent i ego sobesednik', *Sovradiotel*, no. 10 (1963): 25–6.

[57] See an example from June 1964 in *VKD*, 582–4.

[58] Quotations from G. A. Sheveleva (ed.), *Pozyvnye trevog i nadezhd: K 40-letiiu radiostantsii 'Maiak'* (Moscow, 2004), 23, 41.

[59] GARF, f. 6903, op. 10, d. 71, l. 342ob (digest for December 1967).

Form was one thing, content quite another. Maiak announcers might sound more welcoming and engaging, but how were they to get hold of 'news' worthy of the name, given the stranglehold of Soviet censorship? As one Maiak journalist recalled, the station paid the ultra-conservative TASS news agency to obtain the 'offcuts' from official bulletins. Along with the contributions of a network of reporters in the republics and regions of the USSR, this allowed Maiak to present listeners with 'something resembling information'. Even Western news agencies could be mined for suitable material.[60] The quest for immediacy on Maiak led as far as a programme called 'The Country and the World This Minute' (*Strana, mir v etu minutu*), which provided live link-ups between correspondents in different cities around the world where interesting events were occurring. According to listeners' letters, the result was so vivid that radio could be considered the equal of television in its capacity to make the audience 'see' events. Indeed, the term 'radio-vision' (*radiovidenie*) had come into use among some reporters. Not for the first time, radio was finding itself an identity by analogy with a visual medium.[61]

SPONTANEITY SOVIET-STYLE: SPORT, HUMOUR, AND YOUTH

Despite all the censorship constraints, news reports had certainly became more vivid by the mid-1960s. Yet the more engaging style of the post-Stalin era came more naturally to certain other genres of radio output. Perhaps the most obvious example was sports broadcasting, which had long been the exception to the Soviet rule of strict preliminary control. Here there was inherently a 'live' element, and chance and spontaneity could never be ruled out. On one legendary occasion, Viktor Nabutov, the former goalkeeper who became a sports commentator on Leningrad radio, kept the audience entertained by ad-libbing for 40 minutes when the goalposts collapsed at a Zenit game.[62] The dominant figure in sports broadcasting was Vadim Siniavskii, whose radio career extended back to the late 1920s. After spending the war broadcasting from various theatres of combat (the failed defence of Smolensk in 1941, the successful defence of Moscow, Sevastopol in February 1942, later on the Briansk front), he returned to his vocation—notably with his commentary on the matches Dinamo played with British teams in November 1945. Few broadcasters could match the trust that Siniavskii enjoyed with listeners.[63] In a decree of January 1963, sports reports were among the few genres of broadcasting—others included official reports on government delegations

---

[60] Sheveleva, *Pozyvnye trevog i nadezhd*, 43–4, 57.
[61] K. Retinskii and V. Novikov, 'Pokazyvaet radioprogramma "Maiak"', *Sovradiotel*, no. 5 (1968): 8–10. Even the 1930s term *radiopereklichka* made a comeback in the late 1960s. See L. Khataevich, 'Vozrozhdenie zhanra', *Sovradiotel*, no. 10 (1970): 11–12.
[62] A. A. V'iunik, 'V "Poslednikh izvestiiakh": 50-e gody', in P. A. Palladin, M. G. Zeger, and A. A. V'iunik (eds.), *Leningradskoe radio: Ot blokady do 'ottepeli'* (Moscow, 1991), 153.
[63] G. Senkevich, *Vadim Siniavskii—pevets futbola* (Moscow, 2002), 121 and *passim*.

and broadcasts direct from theatres and concert halls—that were explicitly exempted from preliminary censorship.[64]

Radio comedy had shallower roots in the USSR than football reports. In the era of *The Goon Show*, Soviet broadcasters were doing very little to make listeners laugh. To improve the situation, a 'department of satire and humour' was set up on central radio by decree of 27 February 1958 and charged with preparing a number of regular programmes.[65] Both in Moscow and in the regions, radio satire seems to have enjoyed a corresponding boost in the late 1950s.[66] A sample of the programming suggests, however, that humour barely disguised the edifying content. Listeners could hear lurid items about blackmail and murder in the USA or former Nazis flourishing in West Germany. Closer to home, the writer Viktor Ardov read out a story about a babushka who goes out for bread one morning without realizing that the queue outside the bakery is the set for a film about February 1917. She then takes part vigorously in beating up the director of the shop when he announces that there will be no bread. After her starring role, she serves as historical consultant for the director. In conclusion she notes sententiously to her husband: 'As the two of us lived under Tsarism, we absolutely must help young people to find out how hard life was back then.' The staple diet of Soviet radio humour was low-key social satire: the fat canteen cook who had to try all the ingredients before letting his customers taste any of them, or the worker correspondent (*rabkor*) who suggested that couches or ping-pong tables should be set up in bureaucrats' waiting rooms. Yet, although the content was standard fare, the medium of radio provided a more engaging and interactive way of serving it up. As early as 1958, we find what might be called a Soviet stand-up routine—complete with scheduled laughter.[67]

The programme that formed the vehicle for much Soviet radio humour was the weekly 'Cheery Companion' (*Veselyi sputnik*, launched 1957), which offered a mixture of sketches, stories, and jolly musical interludes, all of this delivered at a tempo higher than the Soviet norm. At feedback meetings with ordinary Soviet listeners, it drew mainly favourable responses, though the occasional negative assessment revealed just how deep the puritanical streak ran in the Soviet audience: the charge of 'vulgarity' (*poshliatina*) was still hard to avoid for any broadcaster who aimed to make Soviet people laugh.[68] The authors, V. A. Dykhovichnyi and M. R. Slobodskoi, received a considerable postbag in the early days of the programme in January and February 1958. These letters showed that many Soviet listeners regarded satire not as a source of open-ended laughter but as a spur to practical improvement.

---

[64] 'O poriadke predstavleniia radioperedach na kontrol' tsenzoram Glavlita' (12 January 1963), *VKD*, 155.

[65] The decree, signed by the head of the Radio Committee D. Chesnokov, is in *VKD*, 144.

[66] For the example of Tiumen', which had more radio satire from 1959 onwards, see O. I. Gaiduchok, 'Istoriia razvitiia radio i televideniia Tiumenskoi oblasti (1946–1991 gg.)', candidate's dissertation (Tiumen', 2006), 180.

[67] Examples from programme transcripts in GARF, f. 6903, op. 12, d. 386 (1958) and d. 475 (1961).

[68] The charge was levelled at *Veselyi sputnik* by a listener in Perm' at a meeting of January 1959: see GARF, f. 6903, op. 1, d. 130, ll. 41–2.

This was after all an era of revived 'people's control' in which radio was expected to play a full part in identifying problems, exposing culprits, and proposing solutions.[69] One worker from Ufa wrote in to complain that the real names of the managers criticized in the programme were withheld: how would they be made to reform, he asked, if they did not have to face public responsibility for their actions? Another listener wanted the programme to criticize a specific indolent club manager. Still another was exercised by the problem of antisocial behaviour on the Moscow–Petushki route (which a few years later would provide the inspiration for Venedikt Erofeev's literary rhapsody on alcoholism). Many responses fit the pattern of 'guild' readings: the programme's makers were asked to provide more on school, on demobilized soldiers, on collective farm workers. Several younger listeners wanted the programme to provide general advice or specific assistance with their love life.[70]

Soviet radio humour in the late 1950s was, then, an earnest affair. A lighter touch would have to wait a few more years. In 1960, another high-spirited Sunday broadcast was added to the repertoire of Soviet radio. Called simply 'Good Morning' (*S dobrym utrom*), it was rather more adventurous than 'Cheery Companion' in its use of footage from outside the studio and slightly less edificatory. At the end of the 1960s Maiak launched the even more pacey 'There We Go Again', which offered a jaunty collection of sketches and stories along with rapid-fire and playful interaction between the two presenters.[71]

A change of sensibility in the 1960s can be observed not only in satire and humour broadcasts. Another barometer of the cultural mood was broadcasting for younger listeners, who formed the single most important target group of Khrushchev-era culture. A separate department for youth radio had been a casualty of an administrative reshuffle following Stalin's death, but by 1956 the Soviet cultural establishment was registering the need to offer Soviet young people—such as the enthusiasts who had marched off to construction projects in Siberia, Kazakhstan, or the Donbass—more satisfying cultural fare.[72] It was, however, the preparations for hosting the World Youth Festival in 1957 that made the reform of Soviet broadcasting for young people seem a matter of urgency: a department for youth programming was set up in that year.

Within a few years youth radio brought profound changes to Soviet broadcasting rhetoric—not least, by adopting the practice of addressing Soviet listeners as 'friends' rather than 'comrades'. 'Friendship' was one of the key values of the post-Stalin era, and it could not have been articulated so successfully without the

[69] For the explicit agenda, see K. Voevodina, 'Radio i narodnyi kontrol'', *Sovradiotel*, no. 10 (1963): 12–13.

[70] Examples from RGALI, f. 2282, op. 2, d. 180. On the disposition of the Soviet public to 'guild readings', see Denis Kozlov, 'The Readers of *Novyi mir*, 1945–1970: Twentieth-Century Experience and Soviet Historical Consciousness', PhD dissertation (University of Toronto, 2005).

[71] For the written text of one early broadcast (from February 1968), see *VKD*, 630–2. Fragments of broadcasts can be heard on http://www.staroeradio.ru.

[72] See the correspondence in 1956 between Komsomol and the cultural apparatus in RGASPI, M-1, op. 132, d. 828.

assistance of the audiovisual media. Radio played its part by offering a form of public intimacy at the microphone that conveyed the harmonious relationship between individual and collective. In the words of a youth programme broadcast on 2 February 1957: 'the overwhelming majority of our lads and girls clearly understand that their personal happiness is inseparable from that of society'.[73]

A few days later came the first broadcast of a new 'radio journal' that was symptomatically entitled 'Friendship'. The guests offered a cross-section of Soviet society: a woman worker from a Moscow car factory; a Komsomol secretary from a Moscow district; a poet; and a physicist from an atomic research centre. The physicist, the worker, and the Komsomol man put in plugs for their respective constituencies. It was left to the poet, Nikolai Dorizo, to give voice to their common purpose:

> the possibilities of radio conform very well to the character of our Soviet way of life...you're speaking in Moscow, but your friends in Rostov or Vladivostok can hear you. The airwaves are a good home where a great number of people can get together without any fuss like a family, and you immediately sense that the Motherland is not just the unlimited expanses of our country but the friendly family of Soviet people which has gathered together.[74]

In the Stalin era, of course, radio had been celebrated precisely for its role in overcoming distance and linking 'periphery' to 'centre'. Intimacy had been a very difficult tone to strike successfully in the 1930s or 1940s. By 1957, however, it was all the rage.

The next big step forward for youth programming came when it received its own station. Launched in October 1962, Yunost provided a daily dose of 90 minutes of programming directed specifically at listeners aged 18–26. According to the initial plan, these broadcasts were to go out mainly on Channels Two and Four, but twice a week on Channel One. Almost immediately they elicited several hundred letters a day from listeners; topics like friendship and choice of profession were most prominent.[75] The aim of the new station was unambiguously to reduce the dependence of young listeners on foreign radio. By spring 1963 broadcasters were able to cite plenty of feedback to indicate that this had been achieved, even if Yunost's weekday slot of 5.30–7.00 p.m. made it hard for it to reach its target group (it could only count on a large audience on Sunday afternoons, when it was able to broadcast on the ubiquitous Channel One).[76] In 1965, a sociological survey of 860 listeners aged 14–30 in various regions of European Russia found that only 4 per cent of respondents did not listen to Yunost (even if the audience fell to less than a quarter for the 3 p.m. broadcast). More than two-thirds gave positive feedback, while a further fifth indicated that the station was 'not completely' to their

[73] GARF, f. 6903, op. 13, d. 27, l. 86.   [74] GARF, f. 6903, op. 13, d. 27, l. 154.

[75] RGASPI, f. M-1, op. 132, d. 1092, ll. 16, 20–1. For an analysis of listener's letters in 1963, see GARF, f. 6903, op. 10, d. 34.

[76] RGASPI, f. M-1, op. 132, d. 1127. A party meeting on Moscow radio of January 1965 also considered that Yunost had successfully completed its main task of taking listeners away from foreign radio: TsAOPIM, f. 2930, op. 1, d. 277, l. 8.

taste.[77] Well into the 1970s, Yunost continued to draw a substantial postbag of more than 10,000 letters per month (music and children's broadcasting were the only departments to receive more).[78]

Besides friendship, Yunost offered that other main new ingredient in post-Stalin broadcasting culture: immediacy. The style of 1962 or 1963 was far punchier than that of 1957. Syntax was now simpler and more direct. The leisurely *ocherk*, a carefully crafted written text, was replaced by what by Soviet standards counted as breathless reporting. As one practitioner noted, 'a reporter often finds out about something interesting at the very last moment. Then you take your machine, your tape recorder, and off you go to Tushino [airport].' His own report exemplified the approach: it switched rapidly from background noise (of the airport) to snippets of dialogue and finally an interview with a triumphant pilot who had broken the world record for length of flight.[79] By the late 1960s, as we can see also from the output of the satire and humour department, the style of radio presentation was altogether crisper. Several programmes took a pacey dialogue format, and there was brisk interchange between different speakers.[80]

MUSIC

No area of broadcasting was more important than music, which had always accounted for the greater part of the schedule and provided nothing less than the soundtrack of Soviet life. Yet norms were harder to establish here than in the realm of the spoken word. Even in the 1930s, there were already so many forms and genres in play: the 'classics' (Russian or non-Russian), the works of Soviet composers, 'light' music in all its varieties (including 'jazz'), folk music (whether Russian or many varieties of non-Russian), and patriotic Soviet 'mass song'. All these varieties of music had their advocates and their opponents. Towards the end of the war, the interested parties were once again jockeying for position. As usual, the crucial questions were, first, what constituted 'mass' tastes and, second, how far it was legitimate to go in order to indulge them. Perhaps, one speaker argued at a Radio Committee meeting in November 1944, it was now time to go easy with stirring wartime fare such as the Piatnitskii choir and Red Army ensembles and to think about scheduling *Boris Godunov* in one of the 'open concerts' from the Hall of Columns. Jazz was once again a bone of contention, with representatives of the classical music establishment looking askance at the wildly popular Leonid Utesov. Dmitrii Kabalevskii, for instance, found Utesov 'dubious': the quality of his programmes was uneven, and he was too inclined to indulge his daughter, the singer Edit Utesova.[81]

[77] GARF, f. 6903, op. 3, d. 284.
[78] See e.g. the data from 1973 in GARF, f. 6903, op. 42, d. 5.
[79] GARF, f. 6903, op. 13, d. 76, ll. 5–6.
[80] GARF, f. 6903, op. 12, d. 857. See also examples from Yunost in 1965 in *VKD*, 595–8, 605–14.
[81] GARF, f. 6903, op. 1, d. 96, ll. 25, 39 (stenogram of meeting on 2 November 1944).

As Kabalevskii recognized in a meeting a few weeks later, the underlying problem was that listeners had conflicting musical tastes: 'Sometimes people complain that there is too much symphonic music, sometimes that there is too little of it; some people say they're stifled by the quantity of operettas, others would like to hear more of them.' Whatever view one took of the relative merits of folk music, jazz, and 'serious' music, maintaining a varied repertoire was part of radio's mission to the Soviet listener. This view received support from no less an authority than Dmitrii Shostakovich: 'when I'm ill I keep the radio on all the time and listen to it from morning to night, and you find there all kinds of tastes—operetta, opera extracts and literary programmes'. Yet the exact balance to be struck between different musical forms remained controversial, especially given the scarcity of resources and the straitened conditions for musical performers. Shostakovich himself had recently made a recording in a venue where the ambient temperature was 8 degrees centigrade.[82] The introduction the following year of a second channel (broadcasting daily from 5.00 p.m. to 11.30 p.m.) made it possible and indeed essential to provide a greater variety of musical offerings.[83]

Music broadcasters were also affected by the introduction of more reliable recording technology. Their Achilles' heel had always been the distortions that sound underwent during transmission. The most notorious case was the new Soviet national anthem (composed in 1943), whose opening line sounded wrong to many radio listeners. One correspondent from a sanatorium in Sochi heard the word *kheruvimy* (cherubs) instead of the correct *nerushimyi* (unbreakable).[84] The introduction of magnetic tape promised to bring an end to such embarrassing cases as well as allowing Soviet radio to expand greatly its musical repertoire. It was now possible to build up a core of recordings of the major symphonies and operas and thereby release ensembles from the obligation to broadcast multiple performances. The assumption was that 'serious' music would have top priority in the recording studio, and that the share of jazz and light music would be correspondingly reduced. The keyboard would be perhaps the greatest beneficiary of the new recording technology: piano music had taken only a minor role in recording output over the previous ten to fifteen years, as it had not come across well on the *tonfil'm* of the 1930s.[85] In April 1947, the Radio Committee reported that recordings accounted for two-thirds of music broadcasting and set itself the task of increasing this figure further. Plans for 1947 included complete recordings of the songs of Glinka, Rimskii-Korsakov, and Chaikovskii. For better-known works such as the operas of Glinka and Musorgskii the ambition was to have two or three different performances on tape. Another priority was to lay down Soviet performances of major Russian works: it was time to stop relying on the composer's own recordings of the Rakhmaninov concertos, while, in the words of the conductor Evgenii

[82] GARF, f. 6903, op. 1, d. 98, ll. 1a, 15, 16.

[83] A point made in an undated memo from summer 1945: GARF, f. 6903, op. 1, d. 104, l. 44.

[84] As reported by Grinberg in a meeting of 20 November 1946: GARF, f. 6903, op. 1, d. 173, l. 40. The problem evidently did not go away. For a similar example from 1953, see Chapter 6.

[85] GARF, f. 6903, op. 1, d. 161, ll. 6–11 (meeting of Music Council, 24 January 1946).

Mravinskii, it was 'shameful' to have several foreign recordings of Shostakovich's Eighth Symphony but no Soviet performance. The bare statistics revealed just how limited Soviet capacities still were: in 1946, music recordings had amounted to 180 hours, an improvement on the 72 hours in 1945 but still a modest figure.[86] As the head of music broadcasting wrote to Molotov in June 1946, the Radio Committee badly needed better studio facilities. When the Soviets had come upon the Berlin Radiodom in 1945, they had discovered vastly better working conditions there. While the studio equipment had now been brought to the USSR, there was still nowhere to use it.[87]

Technological deficiencies could slowly be overcome, but music broadcasters also faced a more intractable problem: how to reconcile their own commitment to 'serious' repertoire with the reality—evident from any number of listeners' letters—that most Soviet people wanted fewer symphonies and more jolly, uplifting melodies. The issue of musical repertoire was discussed many times in the Radio Committee, both before the war and after, but there was never a straightforward answer to be given. One obstacle was the enduring commitment of the regime's culture-makers to a *mission civilisatrice*. But no less significant was the thorny question of what, exactly, constituted the 'popular'. What account should be taken of the fact that, for tens of millions of urbanized Soviet people, the surest source of jollity was not the *baian* (Russian accordion) but the jazz orchestra? After the turmoil of the cultural revolution, jazz had emerged stronger than ever in the Soviet Union. After 1932, it conquered musical tastes in the Soviet city; just about anything that was not 'serious' repertoire and not folk performance might call itself jazz. In the period of terror from 1936 onwards, jazz attracted fierce public criticism on predictable grounds: it was musically low-grade, apolitical, a Trojan horse of Western influence. But this was never an annihilating attack: jazz had some defenders in the political establishment, and in due course it took the stage again in a relatively tame and 'nationalized' form. Many of its leading practitioners were able, at least for a while, to continue their careers and would soon see distinguished service as wartime entertainers. From 1939 onwards, Aleksandr Tsfasman, one of the two most famous jazzmen in the Soviet Union, directed the jazz orchestra of the Radio Committee.[88]

The result was a grudging acceptance of jazz. As a contributor to one Radio Committee discussion in late 1944 noted, 'When at night I listen to waltzes by Lanner on the radio, I don't know what I should prefer: waltzes smelling of mothballs from grandma's old trunk, or good jazz? In my opinion, it's better to listen to good contemporary jazz than that kind of waltzes.'[89] Less ungraciously, a speaker at a January 1946 meeting of the music section noted that 'it must be said that light music has a very significant place in the attention of radio listeners' and should not be relegated to minor slots in the schedule. Light music was 'seasonal'

[86] GARF, f. 6903, op. 1, d. 192, ll. 12–14, 52.   [87] GARF, f. 6903, op. 1, d. 137, ll. 20–2.
[88] On jazz in the Soviet 1930s, see S. Frederick Starr, *Red and Hot: The Fate of Jazz in the Soviet Union, 1917–1980* (New York, 1983), 107–80.
[89] GARF, f. 6903, op. 1, d. 98, l. 2.

and needed to be 'up to the minute'. Broadcasting old-fashioned 1920s foxtrots would not satisfy the contemporary listener and would consign the Soviet Union to a cultural time warp relative to other countries.[90]

What this might mean in practice becomes clearer from the transcript of a Radio Committee meeting of February 1945, where prominent administrators and performers assembled to discuss a recent Central Committee resolution on radio that had placed great emphasis on music. The meeting took place on the eve of the launch of the new Channel Two, which would allow broadcasters to expand significantly the range of music programming. It remained axiomatic for most participants in the discussion that the function of music on Soviet radio was not simply to entertain: unlike, say, British radio, it was entrusted with 'major cultural tasks'.[91] Opera was not to be jettisoned; rather, there should be more of it. But the speakers also recognized that the popular stage had an important place in the schedule. Especially vociferous on the importance of *estrada* was Aleksandr Tsfasman: 'Each number should be interesting... It's a very noble task to educate the masses, but you need to please them as well.' The problem, however, was that the Soviet Union lacked talented performers: as another speaker commented, 'the tragedy of our cheerful music is that for the most part it is not cheerful and performances are extremely weak'. Aiming for the lowest common denominator would not bring satisfying results: 'Our jazz always booms out, but jazz should be intimate. The nature of its repertoire means that it will never provide the same warmth and intimacy that have made jazz a popular genre the world over.' This, presumably, was the legacy of loud and uplifting wartime popular music. Any potential shift towards the intimate was also, of course, impeded by what another speaker called the 'puritanical' attitude of the authorities to light music.[92]

Thus, although broadcasters themselves were quite receptive to the further development of jazz in the schedule, in both the late Stalin and Khrushchev periods they were constrained by official attitudes. The backlash against jazz was not long in coming. The campaign against decadent Western styles was renewed in August 1946, and several prominent popular musicians were thrown into the camps. In the Radio Committee the effects of the new puritanism were soon felt. Aleksandr Tsfasman lost his job as head of the radio orchestra in late 1947, while by 1950 all the saxophonists in this ensemble had been fired.[93] The animus against Western popular music also fed off the increasingly institutionalized anti-Semitism of the late Stalin years.[94] Wholesome Soviet song was the order of the day. Typical was the assessment of the artistic director of Estonian radio: 'The time has long since passed when listeners' letters teemed with requests for the sentimental, vulgar,

[90] GARF, f. 6903, op. 1, d. 161, ll. 33, 35.

[91] In reality, the situation on the BBC was much more complex than this speaker allowed; only with difficulty did the edificatory ethos of this institution accommodate itself to the demotic turn during the war. See Christina L. Baade, *Victory through Harmony: The BBC and Popular Music in World War II* (Oxford, 2013).

[92] GARF, f. 6903, op. 1, d. 106, ll. 3, 52, 68, 75.   [93] Starr, *Red and Hot*, 213–16.

[94] Kiril Tomoff, *Creative Union: The Professional Organization of Soviet Composers, 1939–1953* (Ithaca, NY, 2006), 291–2.

trashy songs that were our inheritance from bourgeois Estonia.'[95] The head of the Radio Committee used a familiar rhetorical manoeuvre to reconcile popular tastes and edification. In November 1946, he criticized the wording of a draft decree on popular song, which had referred disparagingly to the 'passive indulging of the tastes of the mass listener'. 'If his taste is good,' Puzin objected, 'then there is nothing bad in indulging the mass listener.' His colleagues displayed the same finesse. Genuinely popular music—such as wartime *chastushki*—was a valuable source of material, yet there was no question that popular performers had to be 'educated'.[96] Any signs of musical vulgarity fell victim to the vigilance of the time. In January 1949, Gorky radio was reprimanded by a party inspector for a *chastushka* that was risqué by the puritanical standards of late Stalinism.[97] In April 1947, even a member of the Artistic Council of the Radio Committee was prepared to declare that the rejection of light music had gone too far. Broadcasters were playing safe without attending to quality: 'we always sense the danger of giving access to the microphone to imported production in the light genre, but when we try to move instead to performing Soviet light music, these attempts don't always prove justified'. Often Soviet light music was merely a 'feeble imitation of Western composers'.[98]

The recording industry too was steered away from the popular stage (*estrada*). In September 1950, Agitprop was much concerned with the perceived underproduction of classical music gramophone records, as well as the neglect of 'songs of the peoples of the USSR' (i.e. folk music); the unworthy beneficiary was 'light music' in all its varieties (operetta, *estrada*, dance music), which had accounted for 2 million records just in the first quarter of 1950 (when the plan for the entire year projected just 27 million records of all kinds). Record production was overseen by the Committee of Radio Information, which sent a catalogue of recordings to trade organizations; the latter then made their selections. Currently, 52.5 per cent of the orders placed were for Soviet song and music of the peoples of the USSR; 13 per cent for documentary recordings (notably speeches by leaders); 29.5 per cent for light music; and a mere 3.9 per cent for classical music. Very conveniently, Agitprop was able to conclude that trade workers were incompetent and ignorant of the genuine tastes of the Soviet people; the Central Committee bureaucracy drew up a proposal for doing away with the system of placing orders.[99]

Justification for almost any music policy could be found in the voluminous postbag of the Radio Committee in the late 1940s. The listening public contained plenty of puritans who made indignant complaints about the 'amoral excesses' of *chastushki*, the 'alcoholic voice' of Leonid Utesov, or the 'talented vulgarian

[95] Lidiia Auster, 'Kak my propagandiruem sovetskuiu pesniu na rodnom iazyke', *V pomoshch' mestnomu radioveshchaniiu*, no. 5 (1952): 13. For the key Zhdanovite decree on music broadcasting (issued in late summer 1946 soon after the notorious Central Committee resolution on the journals *Zvezda* and *Leningrad*), see *VKD*, 114–16.

[96] GARF, f. 6903, op. 1, d. 173 (transcript of meeting of 20 November 1946), l. 8 (quotation from Puzin).

[97] GOPANO, f. 3, op. 1, d. 7302, l. 1.   [98] GARF, f. 6903, op. 1, d. 192, l. 8.

[99] RGASPI, f. 17, op. 132, d. 433, ll. 31–4, 40–4.

Tsfasman'.[100] In the thousands of musical requests received each month, many listeners voted enthusiastically for the rousing songs that had seen them through the war and, conversely, could see little purpose in symphonies and chamber music that did not offer 'the straightforward, joyful, accessible to everyone' music craved by millions of 'ordinary people'.[101] Music was still regarded as a means of collective mobilization. Many of the letters sent in to the Radio Committee attest to the persistence of group listening in this era: they were signed by collectives of soldiers, sailors, miners, and so on. In the more than 10,000 letters received each month by the Radio Committee there was a fundamental, and apparently unbridgeable, divide between intelligentsia and popular tastes. As one listener from Krasnodar wrote in February 1952, radio needed to 'have just a little respect for the common people' and to 'broadcast good straightforward songs, productions from the theatre, advice for doctors and agronomists. As it is we have endless *Ivan Susanin* and *Ivan Susanin*.' Or, as a listener from Moscow region wrote even more bluntly: 'You do what you want, not what millions of listeners want. You know what most people are asking for and on holidays you broadcast something good, but on ordinary days there's nothing but propaganda plus various Chuvash, Mordvinian, Chinese and Albanian music.' Yet a schoolteacher from the same Moscow region made almost the exact opposite argument: 'Listeners are no longer satisfied with popular, dance, and so-called light music. They want to go higher, to raise themselves to the dazzling peaks of the works of the great composers.'[102]

Well into the Khrushchev period, the question of what constituted legitimate 'light music' remained difficult. A published Soviet account of an international conference on broadcast music in Prague in 1959 attempted to draw a line between 'good' and 'bad' jazz: 'as soon as jazz starts resting on elements of normal music and discards its pathological features, it becomes possible and acceptable. For this reason, the issue is not whether jazz should exist at all. The issue is a particularly tendency in jazz which does not even fit aesthetic criteria, because it acts on the listener like an irritant.' At the same time, the lack of new compositions on 'contemporary, "civic" themes' gave cause for concern, as did the fact that 'tearful-sentimental' songs were displacing healthier genres.[103] Similar was a complaint voiced at a party meeting of Moscow radio staff in July 1959: major composers were not writing for the radio, which instead was regrettably acquiring works in an 'intimate-lyrical genre' (i.e. *romansy*).[104] A speaker at another meeting a few months later noted that the all-important Channel One had for a number of years directed its attention at the mass listener, serving up a large quantity of folk music, Soviet song, and light music; the classics were often presented as extracts from longer works, and symphonies had been neglected.[105]

[100] Quotations from GARF, f. 6903, op. 1, d. 246, ll. 19, 78–7 (1948, *sic*).
[101] GARF, f. 6903, op. 1, d. 246, l. 14. For similar examples from 1951, see GARF, f. 6903, op. 1, d. 382.
[102] GARF, f. 6903, op. 10, d. 3, ll. 3, 13 (summaries of listeners' letters to the music department, 1952).
[103] I. Il'in, 'Legkaia muzyka na radio', *Sovradiotel*, no. 2 (1959): 27–9.
[104] TsAOPIM, f. 2930, op. 1, d. 8, l. 138.   [105] TsAOPIM, f. 2930, op. 1, d. 17, l. 20.

Yet the passing of a generation since the war had begun to change the character of 'popular' tastes. In the 1960s, there were still letters from disgruntled *kolkhozniki* complaining of the lack of good Russian songs on the radio, but in general Soviet tastes were becoming more urbane.[106] By the early 1960s, the notorious cultural conservative in the Kremlin could do no more than thunder ineffectually on the subject of the population's musical tastes. At the party plenum of June 1963, ideology secretary L. F. Il'ichev observed that nowadays young people could take out a tape recorder, or even an adapted radio set, and blaze out their 'croaking' (*liagushech'ei muzykoi*) to the whole district. Khrushchev interjected that 'If we don't broadcast croaking, then it can't be played on radio sets'. But Il'ichev sighed that the genie could not be put back in the bottle: 'People convert radio sets and broadcast to the district or even to the region, unfortunately. We have fully mastered technology and it is very easy to do this.'[107]

The question of the acceptable parameters of light music had once again come up for extended discussion at a Radio Committee meeting of 21 February 1963. N. P. Chaplygin, head of music broadcasting, defined *estrada* as follows: 'the sphere of lyric song with a particular subject matter, particular orientation, and particular purpose'. That 'orientation' most obviously included recreation. Thus *estrada* was distinct from the broader (and, by implication, healthier) category of 'mass song'. The role of central broadcasting was, as ever, to strike the right balance between recognizing the variety of tastes while at the same time setting standards and steering the listener. This task had got considerably more difficult with the arrival of the tape recorder as a consumer item and the infiltration of non-Soviet musical norms (through the 1957 Youth Festival and various exchanges of the Khrushchev era). Attempts to create a distinctive Soviet youth music had had only limited success. Recent Komsomol investigations in dance halls had shown how little Soviet young people were following approved Soviet dance styles. A Leningrad colleague confirmed that dance rhythms from the West were by far the most popular. 'We try to create dances. We created "Evening Rhythm". Nobody is dancing it.'[108]

Efforts to police musical taste on Soviet radio continued to the end of the Soviet period. On taking over as head of Gosteleradio in 1970, Sergei Lapin stated clearly his intention to discard material that 'irritates ordinary people, without fearing that some snob will criticize us for lacking musical understanding'.[109] Even Lapin admitted, however, that he was not taking aim at jazz *in toto*; his target was merely the more outlandish forms of contemporary popular music. In general, music broadcasting in the late Soviet period seems to have been a fairly broad church. Listeners who grew up in the 1970s remember as a fixed point in the middle of the day the long-running broadcast 'A Working Lunchtime' (*V rabochii polden'*), which was above all a musical request programme, while Viktor Tatarskii's 'Encounter

---

[106] For a sample of the disgruntled *kolkhoznik* genre from 1963, see GARF, f. 6903, op. 10, d. 34, l. 27.

[107] RGANI, f. 2, op. 1, d. 635, ll. 79–80. Il'ichev's speech at the plenum was entitled 'Ocherednye zadachi ideologicheskoi raboty partii'.

[108] GARF, f. 6903, op. 1, d. 807, ll. 7–8, 11–12, 32, 80.

[109] Extract from speech of 27 April 1970, in VKD, 176.

Figure 7.1. Transistor radio in a Russian village, 1970s.
Source: © Viktor Akhlomov/Photosoyuz

with Song' (*Vstrecha s pesnei*, launched in 1967) not only offered a moderately daring selection of music but also cultivated an improvisatory, discursive style that came close to that of a Western presenter.[110] Owners of the new transistor radios of the 1960s—Spidola, Sokol, Al'pinist—did not necessarily need Voice of America to satisfy their musical cravings. They could instead tune into the jaunty offerings on Maiak, which in the 1960s and 1970s did much to launch the careers of the 'bards' Okudzhava and Vizbor, the crooner Iosif Kobzon, and the vanguard of late Soviet *estrada* Alla Pugacheva.[111] In the new sound-world of the post-Thaw, chirpy Soviet pop formed the kind of aural backdrop that once upon a time had been provided by *Carmen* and Sovinformbiuro bulletins: after the introduction of the

[110] Interview respondents (born respectively in 1968 and 1970) mention these programmes in Oxf/Lev T-04 PF19 (B), p. 13 and Oxf/Lev T-04 PF 7 (A), p. 7. For a profile of 'Vstrecha s pesnei', which was still going strong in April 2013, see http://www.radiorus.ru/section.html?rid=362.
[111] A point made by Aleksandr Tsirul'nikov in Sheveleva (ed.), *Pozyvnye trevog i nadezhd*, 15–17.

three-channel wired set, even babushkas in their kitchens could have Maiak on all day (but for a babushka with a more sophisticated piece of equipment, see Figure 7.1).

MEDIA SOCIOLOGY AND THE RECOGNITION OF AUDIENCE DIFFERENTIATION

In the post-war era, it was not just the style of broadcasting that was shifting; so was its audience. There was a vast difference between the audience of the late Stalin era, largely still of peasant origins and reliant on the single channel provided by wired networks, and the savvy, well-equipped listeners of the late 1960s and beyond. Even in the second half of the 1950s, collective listening was still the norm in many parts of rural Russia.[112] Yet, in the major cities and many not-so-major urban centres, a significantly more autonomous listening culture was emerging. In an early Thaw film like *Spring on Zarechnaia Street* (1956), the radio set gives even the priggish heroine a moment of rapturous solitude as she tunes into Rakhmaninov's Second Piano Concerto (with a male admirer reduced to spare part). By the 'high Thaw' of films such as *I Stroll Around Moscow* (1962) and *July Rain* (1966), radio provided the essential aural accompaniment to a life of open-ended self-discovery, thereby conveying the dynamism and interactivity of modern urban life. By the 1970s, it had become more mundane, if no less eloquent in its own way: in Brezhnev-era films such as Tat'iana Lioznova's *Three Poplars on Pliushchikh Street* or Vadim Abdrashitov's *Speech for the Defence* and *The Turning Point*, the burbling melodies emanating from radio sets form at times a bathetic counterpoint to the wrenching dramas of the protagonists' lives.

Although broadcasters in the Soviet Union were less well informed about audience taste than their counterparts in liberal democracies, they were far from oblivious to the changing orientations of their listeners. In the late Stalin era, listeners' letters to the Radio Committee provided the main—practically the only—feedback channel. A large proportion of letters were musical requests or factual questions arising from broadcasts, but there were also more evaluative responses. To judge by the digests in the Radio Committee archive, Soviet patriotism was prominent in listener feedback of the late 1940s and early 1950s. At times it could be literal-minded to the point of obtuseness. In 1952, one Voronezh listener wrote in to complain about a story of the rescue of fishermen who had drifted out into the open sea. Why, he wanted to know, did they not have a better boat? Why had they lost control of their vessel to this extent? And why, when the fishermen were rescued, were they not reprimanded but instead sent for a rest cure? A more sympathetic response came from a teenage girl: 'I can see them before me, lost at sea but not despairing. They are full of belief that the Motherland is thinking of them and will provide the necessary assistance.'[113]

---

[112] See e.g. A. Kanevskaia, 'Kollektivnoe radioslushanie', *Sovradiotel*, no. 1 (1957): 1–2.
[113] GARF, f. 6903, op. 10, d. 2, ll. 2–3.

Here, perhaps, the contrasting assessments could be explained by a generational difference in sensibility. Elsewhere in the postbag for 1952, however, we find clear evidence that the Soviet public was steeply stratified by education and occupation. In July of that year, a radio production of *The Skull*, a play by the Turkish-Soviet author Nazym Khikmet, drew thirty-five letters that contained wildly varying views. One listener complained that Khikmet had turned his theme—the plight of a medical researcher in the brutish capitalist world—into a mere 'fairground show' (*balagan*). His attempts at tragic pathos had completely misfired: on hearing this play, the listener was sorry 'not for the poor doctor, but for the poor listeners who are wasting their time and nerves'. As another correspondent commented, 'in his haste to condemn America, the author lost his sense of proportion: even in contemporary America the inventor of a tuberculosis vaccine could not come to such a tragic end—the issue of tuberculosis is too urgent'. Another listener, no less a figure than the head of the drama section of the Leningrad section of the Soviet Writers' Union, found that the actors had sounded false. The author also had to take some of the blame: although Khikmet had to his credit 'splendid' poems and a 'heroic' biography, this did not mean that 'what he writes is good and true'. But several other listeners took a completely different view. As an Old Bolshevik and pensioner declared with evident relish: 'This is a good spit in the face, no, not even a spit, but a proper Russian slap to the rotten mug of the bourgeoisie, which will make even Uncle Sam need to scratch himself.'[114]

The Soviet listening public of the 1950s seems to have been committed and, as a rule, serious-minded. Complaints about the excess of symphonic music remained staples of the Radio Committee's postbag well into the 1960s. As one listener wrote in 1963: 'Radio is a newspaper without paper, it should be a university of science and culture, not a Philharmonic. But what you give us is thickly covered in music.'[115] Many listeners were frustrated by the prominence in the schedule of operas and symphonies and demanded more rousing 'mass song', but plenty also wanted information and instruction—the kind of 'radio university' that was mentioned by the above listener and formally existed from 1959.[116] In the 1950s, radio might serve as a guide to propriety and *kul'turnost'* for a listening audience that consisted largely of recent migrants to the city. Leningrad broadcasters offered a (presumably) female audience advice on sexual conduct under the title 'Protect Your Virtue from Youth Onwards' (*Beregi chest' smolodu*).[117] Even in the 1960s, radio continued to play its part in countering religious belief with the verities of modern science.[118] It also offered a perfect means of reinforcing the norms of 'cultured speech' that became a matter of acute public concern in the Khrushchev era. Kornei Chukovskii, the *éminence grise* of correct usage, was among those who gave

[114] GARF, f. 6903, op. 10, d. 2, ll. 4–5.
[115] GARF, f. 6903, op. 10, d. 34, l. 12. For a similar example from 1958, see ibid., d. 15, l. 58.
[116] Sherel', *Audiokul'tura XX veka*, 92.
[117] S. I. Golod, *Chto bylo porokami, stalo nravami: Lektsii po sotsiologii seksual'nosti* (Moscow, 2005), 63.
[118] V. Uryvskii and M. Tepliakov, 'Radiozhurnal "Nauka i religiia"', *Agitator*, no. 13 (1965): 31–3.

broadcast talks on the subject.[119] Radio also went helped to satisfy the craving of many Soviet people for technical know-how. From the onset of forced industrialization in the early 1930s, Soviet culture had placed strong rhetorical emphasis on science and technology, and this orientation was only strengthened by an era of mass education, space exploration, and substantial new investment in scientific research. At least in this field, public campaigns chimed with popular interests: the radio audience in the 1960s seems to have had a healthy appetite for science and technology. A survey of the audience for the programme 'Our Time, Events and People' (*Vremia, sobytiia, liudi*, a chronicle of interesting developments in Soviet life) found that listeners were less interested in stories of exemplary workers than in information on the latest scientific discoveries and on particular branches of production.[120]

In the early 1960s, with the shift to more engaging broadcasting formats and a more conversational tone, the postbag of central radio seems to have grown significantly: from 266,000 in 1961 to 346,000 for 1962, to 300,000 just for the first three months of 1963. Although in the past listeners' letters had been taken seriously and dutifully processed by the broadcasting bureaucracy, there was little in the way of general response. In June 1963 that began to change with the launch of a new programme, 'Radio Post' (*Pochta radio*), that offered a digest of listeners' letters. As one commentator noted, it was usually a pleasure to read the postbag of central radio: one could find plenty of heart-warming stories and only very few of the anonymous denunciations that had once been staple fare.[121]

The bottom line, however, was hard to discern. By now, audience tastes were too scattered to be satisfied by a single channel, however ingeniously it balanced different interests. As one speaker noted at a meeting to discuss radio genres in November 1960, 'we get a mountain of letters saying give us more music. We start giving people more music, then we get another mountain of letters: why are you forgetting about football. There are people with different demands and different interests.' The solution, he noted, might lie in more specialized channels.[122] It was also crucial for Soviet broadcasters to accumulate more reliable information on their audience. As one commentator noted: 'In our age, journalists should be capable of persuading their audience, otherwise they turn into Don Quixotes.'[123] This was the era when Soviet radio was making its first more or less systematic attempts to assess listener response. Much as Soviet broadcasters might rail against the distortions of the capitalist media, they began to practise the audience research that had been created in capitalist conditions. This undertaking still operated on a

---

[119] Chukovskii, 'Beseda o iazyke', *VKD*, 599.

[120] See the results of a sociological survey of 1965 on the audience of this programme in GARF, f. 6903, op. 3, d. 279.

[121] A. Revenko, 'Razgovor s radioslushatelem (O peredache "Pochta radio")', *Sovradiotel*, no. 9 (1963): 4–5. Lev Markhasev recalls that Leningrad radio dutifully responded to all letters it received from listeners (a special department existed for that purpose). This was no small task: in the late 1960s, the letters arrived 'in an unending stream'. Markhasev, *Belki v kolese*, 73–4.

[122] GARF, f. 6903, op. 1, d. 663, l. 31.

[123] I. Trikkel', 'Radio v labirinte kommunikatsii', *Sovradiotel*, no. 7 (1968): 36.

shoestring. The group set up in 1962 to assess the effectiveness of Soviet broad-casting had a staff of only two people until the second half of 1965. But it none-theless managed to carry out a series of questionnaire surveys with a socially representative sample of 25,000 respondents. At this early stage, the paramount task was to show that the Soviet listening public was serious-minded and not div-ided by the social and cultural chasms found in America.[124]

In the longer run, however, something close to the opposite conclusion was in-escapable. As a published account of the new media sociology argued, 'a mass audience in the previous sense of the word does not exist today'. Instead there were at least three distinct mass audiences, ranging from the least educated (reminiscent of the listeners of the 1930s) to the most advanced (who prefigured the main-stream listening public of the 1980s).[125] At one end of the civilizational hierarchy, collective farm workers could be among the more assiduous radio listeners in the mid-1960s (as was found by a survey of Briansk region in 1965).[126] But in the urban centres television was spreading fast and media use was showing all the normal signs of class differentiation in urbanized mass society. A survey from the first four months of 1968 revealed that TV had already taken over from radio as the universal Soviet medium. Of almost 6,000 people in the Cheliabinsk region, almost all had watched TV on the days covered by the survey. However, only 76 per cent of workers and 84 per cent of pensioners and housewives had listened to radio. Engineers and intelligentsia were the only groups that showed a slight pref-erence for radio. More than two-thirds of 'engineering and technical personnel' (ITR) listened to radio for 1 hour or more daily, and almost a quarter of people in this category were listening to radio after midnight, thus putting self-improvement ahead of sleep. Soviet researchers insisted that the relationship between radio and TV was not a zero-sum game, but it was clear there was a correlation between radio listening and level of education: 'people with a higher level of development are less susceptible to emotional influence, they seek a rationalistic element in information'.[127] Radio had come full circle: having been an instrument of col-lective affect, it was now the tool of the discerning intelligentsia listener.

CONCLUSION

This chapter opened by discussing a poem by Agniia Barto that offered an emi-nently Stalinist depiction of the capacity of radio to unite individual and collective. Barto enjoyed a long and distinguished career as a children's writer both for radio and for the printed page, but she achieved her greatest success in a quite different genre—as the founding presenter of 'Find a Person' (*Naiti cheloveka*) (see Figure 7.2). Central radio had long received letters from listeners asking for help in

[124] GARF, f. 6903, op. 3, d. 277 (1965 report on results of sociological research on radio).
[125] A. Shumakov, 'Intellektual'naia vertikal'', *Sovradiotel*, no. 2 (1968): 18–20.
[126] A. Grigor'ev, *Nash drug—radio* (Tula, 1966), 6.
[127] GARF, f. 6903, op. 3, d. 505, quotation on l. 58.

Figure 7.2. Agniia Barto in the studio during a broadcast of 'Find a Person', 1969.
Source: © Nikolai Bobrov/Photosoyuz

tracking down relatives with whom they had lost touch during the war.[128] Twenty years on from the end of the war, there was still no shortage of affecting stories of displacement and separation. In 1965, accordingly, Barto launched 'Find a Person' as a monthly radio programme dedicated to reuniting Soviet families. Before long she found herself fielding hundreds of letters per month (some of them even from abroad). Many of the letters were asking for forms of assistance that went beyond the programme's remit: to search for relatives with whom contact was lost either before the war or after, to track down childhood friends, and (most commonly and poignantly) to provide information on soldiers missing in action.[129] Nonetheless, 'Find a Person' soon established itself as one of the most compelling listening experiences available on Soviet radio. By January 1970 it had reunited 520 families, and by the end of its nine-year run its tally of success stories ran to almost a thousand.[130]

As the case of 'Find a Person' suggests, by the 1960s radio was unrivalled in its capacity to build a relationship of intimacy with the listener. It had travelled a long road since the 1930s, when the microphone had been the undisguised voice of

---

[128] 'Po voprosam rozyska rodstvennikov i znakomykh' is mentioned as a category of letters in 1952: see GARF, f. 6903, op. 10, d. 1, ll. 19–22.

[129] GARF, f. 6903, op. 10, d. 71, ll. 24–5, 430ob. Even in 1973, only just over half of letters received in a typical month (519 out of 959) had a 'direct relationship' to the programme; one-third (311) were requests to track down soldiers who never came back from the war. See GARF, f. 6903, op. 42, d. 5, l. 16ob.

[130] Agniia Barto, *Naiti cheloveka* (Moscow, 1970), 299; (3rd edn., Moscow, 2005).

power. By now the rhetoric of Soviet culture had softened, listeners were 'friends' as much as they were 'comrades' or (still less) 'citizens', and the broadcasting schedule made far greater concessions to the diversity of audience taste. To be sure, large parts of the urban audience were tuning in regularly to foreign radio stations. In a 1979 survey of ITR in Gorky oblast—hardly the Soviet metropolis—the respondents surveyed were apathetic in their commitment to professional self-improvement, but more than a quarter of them admitted to listening to Voice of America 'sometimes' (once or twice a week). Nearly 30 per cent said that they had often or sometimes heard about events in the USSR from foreign sources before they were reported at home: even fifteen years after the launch of Maiak, it was clear that sluggishness of response was a defining characteristic of the Soviet media industry.[131]

Yet we should not draw from this the conclusion that the Soviet media system was 'failing'. Listening to foreign radio did not necessarily turn Soviet people into rootless cosmopolitans: just over half of the Gorky respondents thought that Western stations were biased against the USSR. Rapid response to current events was not yet the *sine qua non* of mass communications that it would become some seven or eight years later. With its well-established repertoire of children's programmes, theatre, literary adaptations, and non-controversial 'light' music, radio was playing a full part in the culture of 'developed socialism'.

---

[131] GOPANO, f. 3, op. 2, d. 4816, ll. 23–4, 26.

Epilogue
Beyond the Microphone Age

Beginnings are notoriously difficult for historians—there is an almost irresistible temptation to track the origins of a phenomenon ever further back in time—but endings can be just as problematic. I have chosen to bring my account to a close around 1970, a date that has obvious political justification. This was the year that Sergei Lapin, synonymous to the late Soviet intelligentsia with ideological rigidity, took over as head of broadcasting. Here, surely, was an end to whatever creative freedom existed in the era of de-Stalinization. In the 1970s, as various disenchanted witnesses attest, broadcasters took a full part in the artificial attempts of the Soviet propaganda industry to dress up stagnation as forward momentum.[1] They also had to conform to overbearing norms of public expression. In subsequent years, media professionals have served up any number of comic-grotesque examples of the ideological vigilance of the Lapin era. In 1976, for example, the humorous programme 'There We Go Again' (*Opiat' dvadtsat' piat'*, literally 'Once Again Twenty-Five') had to be renamed 'Morning Broadcast on Maiak' because it might otherwise have given rise to jokes about the forthcoming Twenty-Fifth Party Congress. The word 'eyebrows' was reputedly prohibited on radio in the 1970s, as this was an easily caricatured aspect of Brezhnev's anatomy.[2] Even leaving aside the baleful influence of Lapin, it has become almost axiomatic to assume that the 1970s were an era of ritualized utterance and discursive ossification.[3] The turgid character of public discourse contrasted unfavourably with the verbal fireworks of which the intelligentsia was capable in its private gatherings.[4]

Yet my periodization does not rely on the notion that the 1970s were necessarily less interesting than the preceding era. Without closer investigation of the output of that decade, it is hard to say. As before, all-union broadcasting had a large and attentive audience: central radio was still receiving half a million listeners' letters a year in the late 1970s.[5] Not all broadcasters were stuck in a late Soviet rut. According

---

[1] For example Marietta Chudakova, 'Liudskaia molv' i konskii top: Iz zapisnykh knizhek 1950–1990-kh godov', *Novyi mir*, no. 3 (2000): 134–6.

[2] Violetta Akimova, 'Iumor—delo khlopotnoe', in G. A. Sheveleva (ed.), *Pozyvnye trevog i nadezhd. K 40-letiiu radiostantsii 'Maiak'* (Moscow, 2004), 316–17.

[3] The most influential statement of this old thesis is Alexei Yurchak, *Everything Was Forever, Until It Was No More: The Last Soviet Generation* (Princeton, 2006).

[4] Geoffrey A. Hosking, *The Awakening of the Soviet Union* (London, 1990), 13. To quote: 'In my experience, the art of conversation is pursued in Moscow at a higher level than anywhere else in the world.'

[5] S. M. Gurevich, *Planirovanie raboty v redaktsii* (Moscow, 1979), 180.

to one veteran of the time, the late 1970s saw the first small experiments with a freer format for radio news; journalists would be allowed a minute or two of 'live' airtime to convey their own impressions of events. Even before Gorbachev, Maiak was 'gradually loosening the buttons on its state uniform, sometimes even taking off its tie'.[6] By the mid-1980s, a Soviet broadcasting theorist could quote Bakhtin on dialogism and fully acknowledge the emotional component in audience response: the earnest, self-improving imagined listener of the earlier Soviet period had made his exit.[7] Not all memoirists see Lapin as the source of all evil. Certainly, he had an authoritarian management style, was an inveterate anti-Semite, and disliked jazz, women in trousers, and men with beards. But he had rock-solid status as a friend and protégé of Leonid Brezhnev; for the first time in its history, Soviet broadcasting was on a stable institutional footing for an extended period. Lapin was also a man of greater cultural sophistication than many of his leading comrades (including Brezhnev): his antipathy to contemporary music was leavened by a love of silver age poetry.[8]

My decision to end at the turn of the 1960s is partly a pragmatic one: the cultural and political context of the following decade is still much less well described and understood than that of the preceding era, and the sources that might provide quick orientation on the cultural politics of broadcasting are as yet less complete than one would like. But there is also a more principled justification, which has to do with radio's relationship to other media. This book argues that it makes sense to think of a 'microphone age' of Soviet culture running from the early 1920s to about 1970. For this half-century, radio was a medium of enormous rhetorical significance. It transcended the vast distances separating different regions of the USSR and in the very act of broadcasting brought into being a national community. It provided a stable voice of authority as well as instilling cultural norms (notably those regarding the spoken word). It had a real-time immediacy that no other means of communication could match.

The 1960s were already a more sceptical age than the 1930s or even the 1950s, and the post-Thaw generation produced plenty of ironical commentary on the limited power of the mass media to bring about the ideological transfusion from leaders to led of which the Bolsheviks had dreamed in the 1920s. Perhaps the funniest example is an episode in Arkadii and Boris Strugatskii's cult novel *Monday*

---

[6] Aleksandr Ruvinskii, 'Perestroiku otkryli "Panoramy"', in Sheveleva (ed.), *Pozyvnye trevog i nadezhd*, 218–19. Ruvinskii (1944–2011) started his broadcasting career in 1969.

[7] I. Tkhagushev, 'Orientatsiia na lichnostnoe vospriiatie', in V. P. Zverev and V. N. Ruzhnikov (eds.), *V diapazone sovremennosti: Radioveshchanie 80-kh godov v nashei strane i za rubezhom* (Moscow, 1984), 59, 73.

[8] In a series on Ekho Moskvy, the liberal journalist Evgenii Kiselev chose Lapin as one of 100 outstanding Russians in the twentieth century. Although the broadcast (an interview with Aleksei Simonov, head of the Foundation for the Defence of Glasnost, who worked in broadcasting for Lapin's entire tenure at Gosteleradio) had much to say about the authoritarian conduct of this 'TV Stalin', it also betrayed a certain fascination with Lapin as a 'media magnate of the Soviet era'. See http://1001. ru/arc/issue1426/ (last checked 2 May 2013). Note also the snippets of information at http://www. forum-tvs.ru/index.php?showtopic=95328 (2 May 2013). On Lapin's credentials as an anti-Semite, see Nikolai Mitrokhin, *Russkaia partiia: Dvizhenie russkikh natsionalistov v SSSR 1953–1985 gody* (Moscow, 2003), 93–4, 106–7.

Begins on Saturday (1965), where a research institute specializing in black magic (an affectionate parody of the work environment of the post-Stalin intelligentsia) produces a kind of Frankenstein's monster and attempts in vain to inculcate in it the higher values: presented with attributes of culture such as books, radio, and TV, this creature takes no interest in them whatsoever—save for chewing the tape from a *magnitofon*.[9]

Certainly, as we saw in Chapter 7, the radio audience of the 1960s was highly differentiated, and the new listening technology of the post-Stalin era—short-wave transistor sets—gave it unprecedented opportunities to indulge its private passions. The main new development, however, was the rise of a new medium: television.[10] In 1970, the name of the main Soviet broadcasting organization was changed to recognize this shift in the balance of media power: the State Committee for Radio and Television became Gosteleradio, the State Committee for Television and Radio. By this time TV could be said to be truly national in its reach, and for the four decades since it has set the tone and the pace of public life in Russia. After forty years of serving a similar purpose, radio had to cede its role as real-time chronicle and as leading interlocutor of the Soviet people. The die was perhaps cast a few years earlier than 1970, in the early days of space exploration. Although it was exciting on 12 April 1961 to hear a radio bulletin on Gagarin's mission even as he was still in orbit, the thrill of *seeing* outer space was incomparably greater. Four years later, on 18 March 1965, Soviet radio informed listeners of the latest remarkable development: Aleksei Leonov's space walk during the Voskhod-2 mission. In the process, however, it effectively acknowledged the primacy of the visual medium: 'About half an hour ago, millions of Soviet and foreign television viewers saw on their screens an extraordinary spectacle: a man walked out of his ship into space.' The earnest interview with Leonov that Maiak broadcast three days later, eight full pages in the approved text deposited in the Gosteleradio archive, could not quite compare.[11] By now the rhetoric of Soviet culture was audiovisual more than aural— as the barely upright Brezhnev discovered to his cost in the late 1970s. Although broadcasting professionals such as Iurii Gal'perin might argue that radio and TV were not rivals but allies, there was never much doubt who was first among these equals.[12]

In the second half of the 1980s, both these fraternal media underwent revolutionary changes. Broadcasting style loosened up and became more engaging, while speech norms turned more conversational. Radio 'panoramas', extended free-form broadcasts with a strong authorial voice, were a regular feature of the schedule from early 1987. *Radiomosty*, the 1980s equivalent of the earlier *radiopereklichki*,

---

[9] The episode is in the second section of the novel, 'Sueta suet', ch. 4. The scientist creator does not, however, lose hope that 'material requirements', when satisfied, can serve as a gateway to 'spiritual requirements'.

[10] The best account of this process and its consequences is Kristin Roth-Ey, *Moscow Prime Time: How the Soviet Union Built the Media Empire That Lost the Cultural Cold War* (Ithaca, NY, 2011). An excellent new study of Soviet television in its years of maturity is Christine Evans, *Between Truth and Time: A History of Soviet Central Television* (New Haven, forthcoming).

[11] GARF, f. 6903, op. 11, d. 946 (programme transcripts for March 1965).

[12] *Shestoi s"ezd pisatelei SSSR* (Moscow, 1978), 329.

gave a voice to ordinary Soviet people without the usual studio constraints.[13] The General Secretary himself played a full part in the broadcasting component of perestroika. Although official visits were still meticulously stage-managed, radio correspondents now had to reckon with Mikhail Gorbachev's predilection for stopping his cortege and launching into impromptu chats with members of the public; whenever that happened, his media escort would leap out of their car, recording equipment at the ready. As glasnost escalated, Russia finally went the way of genuine live broadcasting. The opening of the Congress of People's Deputies in May 1989 confirmed the transformation of Soviet broadcasting style: not only were proceedings broadcast live on radio, they were accompanied by journalistic commentary rather than po-faced continuity announcements. In cars, shops, workplaces, even prisons, people were glued to their transistors for this 'theatre at the microphone'.[14]

As broadcasting norms weakened, so did the Soviet system's will to suppress dissent and its capacity to police its media empire. By September 1988, for example, the secretary of the Party committee of Estonian broadcasting wrote to the head of Gosteleradio to complain in the strongest terms about Moscow's selective editing of material sent from the Baltic republic. Coverage of recent major events—the seventieth anniversary of the creation of the 'bourgeois' Estonian republic (24 February 1988), the anniversary of Estonia's incorporation in the USSR (6 August), and the anniversary of the Molotov–Ribbentrop pact (23 August)—had been seriously distorted. Critical commentary on social and political problems in the republic had been systematically omitted, and the central media were pandering to stereotypes of Estonians as nationalists and fascists.[15] Yet, at much the same time, the Russophone population in Estonia worried that it was poorly informed compared to the locals: Estonian radio was providing only 12 hours per week of programming in Russian.[16]

In August 1991, when the Soviet system experienced what proved to be its final moment of crisis, the inability of the coup leaders to manage the mass media played at least as great a part in their downfall as their curious decision not to arrest Boris Yeltsin. This was true even of central television, ostensibly under total Kremlin control, which famously broadcast Gennadii Ianaev's trembling hands at his ill-fated press conference of 19 August.[17] But it applied much more to radio, by now a remarkably fluid and diversified medium. In St Petersburg, the half-hearted information blockade imposed by the state of emergency was soon breached. About one in seven inhabitants of the city knew about Yeltsin's defiance of the coup as early as its first morning, and of these almost half heard the news from

[13] For an account of perestroika radio in Leningrad, see Iu. V. Kliuev, 'Radioveshchanie Leningrada-Peterburga: Organizatsionnaia struktura, problematika, evoliutsiia form i zhanrov (1980–2000 gg.)', candidate's dissertation (St Petersburg, 2004), ch. 2.

[14] Ruvinskii, 'Perestroiku otkryli "Panoramy"', 220, 227, 230, 233.

[15] ERAF, f. 1, op. 42, d. 130, ll. 13–17.

[16] ERAF, f. 1, op. 43, d. 138, l. 19 (recommendations from a workplace conference, 15 November 1988).

[17] Victoria E. Bonnell and Gregory Freidin, '*Televorot*: The Role of Television Coverage in Russia's August 1991 Coup', *Slavic Review*, 52 (1993): 810–38, esp. 819–21.

Radio Liberty or from one of the independent local stations. Local television became the broadest channel of uncensored information in the second half of 19 August, while the city's wired radio network spread the word to the less media-savvy citizens on 20 August. The conclusion was clear: at a moment when access to information had been critical, the well-connected vanguard of the population had relied on a combination of radio and word of mouth.[18]

As Soviet power dissipated, broadcasting started to diversify further. The first private radio service, the Franco-Russian joint venture Europa Plus, came into being in 1990. The first American-Russian radio station, Radio Maximum, began life on 25 December 1991, a few days before the Soviet Union formally ceased to exist, and in 1994 it started broadcasting round the clock. By 1995, the number of private radio stations had reached double figures, and Russian listeners, long deprived of the music they most wanted, could gorge themselves on an endless supply of classic and contemporary rock.[19]

Meanwhile, state-owned radio was having to adjust to an uncomfortable new economic environment. Radio Moscow, the foreign-language service that had been the core of the Cold War propaganda effort, had to trim its operations severely. At its peak in the 1980s, it broadcast in eighty languages; by 1995 this had been reduced to forty-six languages, and crucial transmitter capacity in Ukraine, Kazakhstan, and Lithuania had been lost.[20] Domestic state broadcasting also suffered demotion, though there was continuity as well as rupture. The old Channel One was renamed Ostankino in December 1991. Four years later it became 'Radio-1'. In August 1997, by presidential decree, it was liquidated entirely. In the absence of state funding, the supporters of the station—foremost among them the famous crooner Iosif Kobzon and his company Moskovit—scrambled to keep it alive. Within a couple of years, however, relations between broadcasters and sponsors had soured, as the station's losses became too much to bear. Radio-1 continued to exist in various guises for another decade, but it was never a viable commercial enterprise, and in June 2010 it shut down (apparently for the last time).[21]

The mantle of the old Channel One was seized by a new state-financed station, Radio Rossii, which had started life in 1990 as a beneficiary of the struggle between Russian and Soviet institutions. In August 1991, Radio Rossii was handed the traditional prerogative of all-union radio: the crucial 'first button' on wired receivers. Demoted to the 'third button', Channel One lost its privileged access to the millions of people in the country—mainly the older and more loyal listeners—who

---

[18] Leonid Kesel'man and Mariia Matskevich, 'Sredstva massovoi informatsii v dni avgustovskogo putcha 1991 v Sankt-Peterburge', in O. N. Ansberg and A. D. Margolis (eds.), *Obshchestvennaia zhizn' Leningrada v gody perestroiki. 1985–1991: Sbornik materialov* (St Petersburg, 2009), 361–3. Originally published in *Chas Pik*, 11 September 1991, this article was based on questionnaire research conducted about ten days after the events in question. Catriona Kelly, who was staying in the city at the time, also recalls radio as playing the leading role on 19 August; it was not until 21 August that television took over (personal communication, 15 October 2013).

[19] Lynne Gross, 'Rocky Overhaul of Russian Radio', *Billboard* 107/44 (1995): 97. Radio Maximum's own account of its history is at http://www.maximum.ru/about/radio/ (checked 3 May 2013).

[20] Don Jensen, 'A Russian Radio Revolution', *Popular Electronics* 12/8 (1995): 79.

[21] The following site, put together by nostalgists for Radio-1, has a useful collection of newspaper articles on the subject: http://radio-1.narod.ru (checked 3 May 2013).

continued to rely on the *tochka*. Radio Rossii exists to this day as the only national radio station of the universal type. It remains state-funded, though it now reaches listeners not only by wire but also on a variety of frequencies and over the Internet. Of the Soviet-era channels, it was Maiak that emerged best from the wreckage of the 1990s. Although Boris Yeltsin liquidated Radio-1 in his decree of 4 August 1997, he also ordered the creation of a new national broadcasting company on the basis of the existing Maiak and Yunost; this revamped Maiak would retain the 'second button' as well as enjoying continued state funding. Fifteen years later, it has an apparently secure existence as a light entertainment channel.

DJs and chat shows were not, of course, to everyone's taste. Old-time Soviet broadcasters, as well as many listeners, grumbled about the lowering of linguistic standards.[22] The radio audience of the early twenty-first century was not limited to 30-somethings listening to music stations on digital radios as they stewed in Moscow's rush hour traffic. The homes of Russians of a certain age were still very likely to contain an old-fashioned *tochka* mounted on the kitchen wall. To be sure, this was not the one-channel 'plate' of the Stalin era but rather a post-1960s three-channel ribbed box. Yet, even in an era of iPhones and WiFi, Russia retained traces of its formative twentieth-century experience as a 'wired' society.

All the same, Russians were finding that radio, so recently a rigid state monopoly, had now broken up into a lively pluralism. Unlike television, which by the early Putin era had become a barely disguised cheerleader for the government, radio could still be lively and usefully cantankerous. Ekho Moskvy, a station formed under a different name in 1990, made its name as a centre of resistance to the August coup of 1991 and by the mid-2000s was billing itself as the only truly independent operator in the audiovisual news media. In any number of vigorous discussion programmes, it proved that the eloquent 'kitchen talk' of the 1970s intelligentsia could adapt to the era of instant news—and attract an audience in the millions. Radio's defining other was now less television than the Internet, and there were signs that this could be a relationship of complementarity, not rivalry: the Internet offered vast data resources and ease of use, while radio provided structure (through stations and rubrics) and impact (through the unadorned human voice, still hard to beat as a way of getting and holding an audience's attention). From newspaper without paper and without distances, radio had become website without screen and without search engine. The story of Russian radio's mutations as medium of public expression and political agency still has a few pages to run.

---

[22] An intelligent survey of views of this kind, which do not deserve to be dismissed out of hand, is Kliuev, 'Radioveshchanie Leningrada-Peterburga', 25–7. Note also Lev Markhasev's remarks on the *kosnoiazychie* of the post-Soviet media in his *Belki v kolese: Zapiski iz Doma radio* (St Petersburg, 2004), 200. An illuminating broader treatment is Michael S. Gorham, *After Newspeak: Language Culture and Politics in Russia from Gorbachev to Putin* (Ithaca, NY, 2014).

Note on Sources

ARCHIVES

A. S. Popov Central Museum of Communications, St Petersburg
  Collection of I. V. Brenev
  Collection of V. A. Burliand
  Radio Collection (Fond Radio)
Estonian Historical Archives (ERA.R)
  f. 1590: Estonian broadcasting committee
Gosudarstvennyi arkhiv Rossiiskoi Federatsii (GARF)
  f. 374: Worker-Peasant Inspectorate
  f. 5407: Soviet League of the Militant Godless
  f. 6903: Gosteleradio
Gosudarstvennyi arkhiv Nizhegorodskoi oblasti (GANO)
  f. 3630: Broadcasting committee for Nizhnii Novgorod/Gorky region
  f. 6924: Broadcasting network for Avtozavodskii district
Gosudarstvennyi obshchestvenno-politicheskii arkhiv Nizhegorodskoi oblasti (GOPANO)
  f. 1: Nizhegorodskii gubernskii komitet VKP(b)
  f. 2: Nizhegorodskii kraevoi komitet VKP(b)
  f. 3: Gor'kovskii obkom VKP(b)
Rossiiskii gosudarstvennyi arkhiv literatury i iskusstva (RGALI)
  f. 1038: V. V. Vishnevskii
  f. 1364: S. V. Shervinskii
  f. 1403: A. A. Ignat'ev
  f. 1448: E. A. Blaginina
  f. 1846: S. V. Bogomazov
  f. 1958: N. N. Gorich and E. A. Iuzvitskaia
  f. 2216: D. N. Orlov
  f. 2282: V. A. Dykhovichnyi
  f. 2382: V. D. Markov
  f. 2404: M. S. Narokov
  f. 2768: A. G. Koonen
  f. 2889: V. M. Kreps
  f. 2965: M. Z. Tseitlin
  f. 2979: E. P. Garin
  f. 3061: M. I. Zharov
Rossiiskii gosudarstvennyi arkhiv noveishei istorii (RGANI)
  f. 5: Apparat TsK KPSS, op. 16, op. 33 (Agitprop)
Rossiiskii gosudarstvennyi arkhiv sotsial'no-politicheskoi informatsii (RGASPI)
  f. 17 (Central Committee), op. 60 (Agitprop), op. 85 (Sekretnyi otdel), op. 125 (Agitprop),
    op. 132 (Agitprop)
  f. 135: F. Ia. Kon
  f. 495: Komintern
RGASPI, Komsomol collection (RGASPI-M)
  f. 1, op. 23, op. 32 (Agitprop)
  f. 43: N. N. Mesiatsev

Tsentral'nyi arkhiv obshchestvenno-politicheskoi istorii Moskvy (TsAOPIM)
  f. 2930: Party committee of State Broadcasting Committee, Moskvoretskii district, 1957–70
Tsentral'nyi gosudarstvennyi arkhiv istoriko-politicheskikh dokumentov Sankt-Peterburga (TsGAIPD SPb)
  f. 24: Party committee of Leningrad region, op. 8 (Agitprop)
  f. 755: Party committee of Leningrad broadcasting organization
  f. 8519: Party committee of Leningrad broadcasting organization in Kuibyshev district
Tsentral'nyi gosudarstvennyi arkhiv literatury i iskusstva Sankt-Peterburga (TsGALI SPb)
  f. 293: Leningrad broadcasting committee
Tsentral'nyi gosudarstvennyi arkhiv Moskovskoi oblasti (TsGAMO)
  f. 66: Mossovet
  f. 180: Trade union council for Moscow region

PERIODICALS

Govorit Moskva
Govorit SSSR
Literaturnaia gazeta
Miting millionov
Novosti radio
Rabotnik radio
Radio
Radiofront
Radiogazeta
Radioliubitel'
Radioprogrammy
Radioslushatel'
Radio vsem
Sovetskoe radio i televidenie

INTERVIEWS

1. Life history interviews conducted for a project sponsored by the Leverhulme Trust under grant no. F/08736/A 'Childhood in Russia, 1890–1991: A Social and Cultural History' (2003–6). The template for these semi-structured interviews contained a question on informants' memories of radio and television. The interviews are © The University of Oxford. The coding system consists of a project identifier, place code (St Petersburg (SPb.), Moscow (M.), Perm' (P), and Taganrog (T), and villages in Leningrad (2004) and Novgorod (2005) provinces (V)), a date code, a cassette number (PF), and a transcript page (e.g. 'Oxf/Lev SPb-03 PF8A, p. 38'). For further information about the project, see http://www.mod-langs.ox.ac.uk/russian/childhood and http://www.ehrc.ox.ac.uk/lifehistory/archive.htm. My thanks go to the interviewers, Aleksandra Piir (St Petersburg), Yuliya Rybina and Ekaterina Shumilova (Moscow), Svetlana Sirotinina (Perm'), Yury Ryzhov and Lyubov' Terekhova (Taganrog), Oksana Filicheva, Veronika Makarova, and Ekaterina Mel'nikova (village interviews); to the project coordinators, Professor Al'bert Baiburin and Professor Vitaly Bezrogov; and to the project leader, Professor Catriona Kelly, for making this material available to me.

2. The Harvard Project on the Soviet Social System (http://hcl.harvard.edu/collections/hpsss/index.html). An extensive collection of interviews with former Soviet citizens in the early 1950s.
3. Author's own interviews

Aleksandr Ivanovich Akhtyrskii (Moscow, 5 May 2006)
Boris Maksimovich Firsov (St Petersburg, 24 March 2006)
Iraida Fedorovna Sukhonina (Nizhnii Novgorod, 19 and 20 April 2006)
Iurii Mikhailovich Prokhorov (Nizhnii Novgorod, 20 April 2006)
Lev Solomonovich Markhasev (St Petersburg, 21 and 28 March 2006)
Liudmila Dem'ianovna Bolotova (Moscow, 6 May 2006)

Glossary

Agitprop: Department of Agitation and Propaganda, Central Committee

chastushki: rhyming folk ditties

Glavlit: the main Soviet censorship bureaucracy

Gosteleradio: State Committee for Radio and Television (from 1957)

ITR: engineering and technical personnel

magnitofon: tape recorder

MGSPS: Moscow trade union

Narkompochtel: People's Commissariat of Post and Telegraph

Narkompros: People's Commissariat of Enlightenment

NKPT: People's Commissariat of Post and Telegraph, Narkompochtel

NKVD: People's Commissariat of Internal Affairs

ODR: Society of Radio Lovers

pereklichka: live link-up

radioliubitel': radio ham, radio lover

Radioperedacha: the Soviet broadcasting company in the early years (1924–8)

radiozaitsy: radio hackers, 'free riders' who did not pay the registration fee on their sets

raion: district

RAPM: Russian Association of Proletarian Musicians

RAPP: Russian Association of Proletarian Writers

RFE: Radio Free Europe

ROSTA: Russian Telegraph Agency

RSFSR: Russian Republic

Sovinformburo: the central Soviet institution for information and propaganda during World War II

Sovnarkom: Council of People's Commissars (the main Soviet government body)

tarelka: a wired receiver point; literally 'plate'

TASS: Telegraph Agency of the Soviet Union

tochka: a wired receiver point

TRAM: Workers' Youth Theatre

VOA: Voice of America

VTsSPS: central trade union organization

vystuplenie: statement, declaration; the Stalin-era equivalent of an interview

Bibliography

Abdulova-Metel'skaia, E. M. (ed.), *Osip Naumovich Abdulov: Stat'i: Vospominaniia* (Moscow, 1969).

Adzharov, A., *Oratorskoe iskusstvo: V pomoshch' molodomu oratoru* (Moscow and Leningrad, 1925).

Afinogenov, A., *Dnevniki i zapisnye knizhki* (Moscow, 1960).

Aitken, H. G. J., *The Continuous Wave: Technology and American Radio, 1900–1932* (Princeton, 1985).

Aituganova, M. L., 'Stanovlenie sistemy radioveshchaniia v Tatarstane (1918–iiun' 1941 g.g.)', Candidate's dissertation (Kazan', 1996).

Altman, R., *Silent Film Sound* (New York, 2004).

Andrews, M., *Domesticating the Airwaves: Broadcasting, Domesticity and Femininity* (London, 2012).

Andronikov, I., *Ia khochu rasskazat' vam…* (Moscow, 1962).

Andronikov, I., *Izbrannye proizvedeniia* (Moscow, 1975).

Anduaga, A., *Wireless and Empire: Geopolitics, Radio Industry, and Ionosphere in the British Empire, 1918–1939* (Oxford, 2009).

Ansberg, O. N., and Margolis, A. D. (eds.), *Obshchestvennaia zhizn' Leningrada v gody perestroiki. 1985–1991: Sbornik materialov* (St Petersburg, 2009).

Aref'ev, V. V., *Voina v efire* (Moscow, 2006).

Arnold, K., and Classen, C. (eds.), *Zwischen Pop und Propaganda: Radio in der DDR* (Berlin, 2004).

Baade, C. L., *Victory through Harmony: The BBC and Popular Music in World War II* (Oxford, 2013).

Badenoch, A., *Voices in Ruins: West German Radio Across the 1945 Divide* (Houndmills, 2008).

Bailey, M. (ed.), *Narrating Media History* (London, 2009).

Baklanov, G., *Zhizn', podarennaia dvazhdy* (Moscow, 1999).

Barto, A., *Naiti cheloveka* (Moscow, 1970; 2nd edn., Moscow, 1975; 3rd edn., Moscow, 2005).

Barto, A., *Sobranie sochinenii v trekh tomakh* (Moscow, 1969–71).

Barto, A., *Zapiski detskogo poeta* (Moscow, 1976).

Basovskaia, E. N., *Sovetskaia pressa—za 'chistotu iazyka': 60 let bor'by* (Moscow, 2011).

Batakov, V., and Ukhin, V., *Govorit gorod Gor'kii* (Gorky, 1978).

Batrak, I., *Kolkhoznyi fort* (Moscow, 1936).

Beksonov, S., *Zhivoe slovo kak metod propagandy i agitatsii* (Samara, 1921).

Beliaev, A., *Bor'ba v efire: Nauchno-fantasticheskii roman* (Moscow and Leningrad, 1928).

Berg, A. I. (ed.), *Izobretenie radio A. S. Popovym: Sbornik dokumentov i materialov* (Moscow and Leningrad, 1945).

Berggol'ts, O., *'Govorit Leningrad'* (Leningrad, 1946).

Berggol'ts, O., *Olia: Zapretnyi dnevnik* (St Petersburg, 2010).

Bergmeier, H. J. P., and Lotz, R. E., *Hitler's Airwaves: The Inside Story of Nazi Radio Broadcasting and Propaganda Swing* (New Haven, 1997).

Berkhoff, K. C., *Motherland in Danger: Soviet Propaganda during World War II* (Cambridge, Mass., 2012).

Bidlack, R., 'The Political Mood in Leningrad during the First Year of the Soviet–German War', *Russian Review* 59 (2000): 96–113.

Binyon, M., *Life in Russia* (London, 1983).

Boglovskii, T., and L'vov, Z., *Poslednie izvestiia po radio* (Moscow, 1963).

Bonch-Bruevich, M. A., *Sobranie trudov* (Moscow and Leningrad, 1956).

Bonnell, V. E., and Freidin, G., '*Televorot*: The Role of Television Coverage in Russia's August 1991 Coup', *Slavic Review* 52 (1993): 810–38.

Bourgault, L. M., *Mass Media in Sub-Saharan Africa* (Bloomington, Ind., 1995).

Brandenberger, D., *National Bolshevism: Stalinist Mass Culture and the Formation of Modern Russian National Identity, 1931–1956* (Cambridge, Mass., 2002).

Brang, P., *Zvuchashchee slovo: Zametki po teorii i istorii deklamatsionnogo iskusstva v Rossii* (Moscow, 2010).

Braudo, E. M., *Kakim dolzhno byt' khudozhestvennoe shirokoveshchanie: Materialy k I Vsesoiuznomu S"ezdu Obshchestva Druzei Radio* (Moscow, 1926).

Bridges, B., 'A Note on the British Monitoring of Soviet Radio, 1930', *Historical Journal of Film, Radio and Television* 5 (1985): 183–9.

Brooks, J., 'Studies of the Reader in the 1920s', *Russian History* 9/2–3 (1982): 187–202.

Brooks, J., 'The Breakdown in the Production and Distribution of Printed Material', in A. Gleason et al. (eds.), *Bolshevik Culture* (Bloomington, Ind., 1985).

Brooks, J., *Thank You, Comrade Stalin! Soviet Public Culture from Revolution to Cold War* (Princeton, 2000).

Brown, R. J., *Manipulating the Ether: The Power of Broadcast Radio in Thirties America* (Jefferson, NC, 1998).

Budnitskii, O. V. (ed.), *'Svershilos'. Prishli nemtsy!': Ideinyi kollaboratsionizm v SSSR v period Velikoi Otechestvennoi voiny* (Moscow, 2012).

Bulgakova, O., *Sovetskii slukhoglaz: Kino i ego organy chuvstv* (Moscow, 2010).

Bulgakowa, O. (ed.), *Resonanz-Räume: Die Stimme und die Medien* (Berlin, 2012).

Burliand, V. A., Volodarskaia, V. E., and Iarotskii, A.V., *Sovetskaia radiotekhnika i elektros-viaz' v datakh* (Moscow, 1975).

Burshtein, R., *O gromkikh chitkakh v derevne* (Novosibirsk, 1926).

Bykhovskii, M. A., *Razvitie telekommunikatsii: na puti k informatsionnomu obshchestvu. Istoriia telegrafa, telefona i radio do nachala XX veka* (Moscow, 2012).

Carter, H., *The New Spirit in the Russian Theatre 1917–1928* (London, 1929).

Chinennaia, T. I., 'Radio v mnogonatsional'noi respublike: istoricheskii opyt, sotsial'nye funktsii, zhanrovaia spetsifika (na primere radioveshchaniia Dagestana)', Candidate's dissertation (Moscow, 2009).

Chukovskii, K. I., *Zhivoi kak zhizn': O russkom iazyke* (Moscow, 1963).

Chukovskii, K. I., *Dnevnik 1930–1969* (Moscow, 1997).

Chumakov, S. P., *Fabrichno-zavodskaia radiogazeta* (Moscow, 1932).

Comrie, B., Stone, G., and Polinsky, M., *The Russian Language in the Twentieth Century* (Oxford, 1996).

Craig, D. B., *Fireside Politics: Radio and Political Culture in the United States, 1920–1940* (Baltimore and London, 2000).

Derevianko, S. S., 'Obshchestvo druzei radio v Leningrade (1924–1933 gg.)', in A. P. Kupaigorodskaia (ed.), *Dobrovol'nye obshchestva v PetrogradeLeningrade v 1917–1937 gg.: Sbornik statei* (Leningrad, 1989).

Dobchinskii, A. A., 'Gorodskoe radioveshchanie: Retrospektiva, sovremennoe sostoianie, problemy zhurnalistskogo tvorchestva', Candidate's dissertation (Moscow, 1996).

Dobrenko, E., *Formovka sovetskogo cheloveka: Sotsial'nye i esteticheskie predposylki retseptsii sovetskoi literatury* (St Petersburg, 1997).

Douglas, S. J., *Inventing American Broadcasting 1899–1922* (Baltimore, 1987).

Douglas, S. J., *Listening In: Radio and the American Imagination, from Amos 'n' Andy and Edward R. Murrow to Wolfman Jack and Howard Stern* (New York, 1999).

Drubek-Meier, N., 'Mass-Message/Massazh mass: Sovetskie (mass-)media v 30-e gody', in M. Balina, E. Dobrenko, and Iu. Murashov (eds.), *Sovetskoe bogatstvo: Stat'i o kul'ture, literature i kino* (St Petersburg, 2002).

Dubrovin, V. B., *K istorii sovetskogo radioveshchaniia: Posobie dlia studentov-zaochnikov fakul'tetov zhurnalistiki gosudarstvennykh universitetov* (Leningrad, 1972).

Fischer, C. S., *America Calling: A Social History of the Telephone to 1940* (Berkeley and Los Angeles, 1992).

Fonshtein, A., *Gazeta bez bumagi i rasstoianii: Organizatsiia i redaktirovanie politicheskogo radioveshchaniia* (Moscow, 1935).

Frolov, M., *Reporter u mikrofona* (Leningrad, 1966).

Frolov, M., *I snova k mikrofonu vykhozhu...* (Leningrad, 1979).

Führer, K. C., 'A Medium of Modernity? Broadcasting in Weimar Germany, 1923–1932', *Journal of Modern History* 69 (1997): 722–53.

Gagarkin, A. I., 'Literaturno-dramaticheskoe radioveshchanie v dukhovnoi zhizni sotsialisticheskogo obshchestva', Candidate's dissertation (Moscow, 1981).

Gaiduchok, O. I., 'Istoriia razvitiia radio i televideniia Tiumenskoi oblasti (1946–1991 gg.)', Candidate's dissertation (Tiumen', 2006).

Gal'perin, Iu., *Vnimanie, mikrofon vkliuchen!* (Moscow, 1960).

Gati, C., *Failed Illusions: Moscow, Washington, Budapest, and the 1956 Hungarian Revolt* (Washington, 2006).

Gleizer, M., *Radio i televidenie v SSSR: Daty i fakty (1917–1986)* (Moscow, 1989).

Gleizer, M. S., and Potapov, N. M. (eds.), *Radio v dni voiny: Ocherki i vospominaniia vidnykh voenachal'nikov, izvestnykh pisatelei, zhurnalistov, deiatelei iskusstva, diktorov radioveshchaniia* (Moscow, 1982).

Glier, R., *Radioteatr i nauka: Iz opyta nauchno-khudozhestvennoi radiodramaturgii* (Moscow, 1973).

Glushchenko, A. A., *Mesto i rol' radiosviazi v modernizatsii Rossii (1900–1917 gg.)* (St Petersburg, 2005).

Gofman, V., *Slovo oratora (Ritorika i politika)* (Leningrad, 1932).

Golovchenko, E. I., 'Funktsionirovanie sredstv massovoi informatsii voronezhskoi oblasti v gody Velikoi Otechestvennoi Voiny', Candidate's dissertation (Tambov, 2002).

Golovko, V., *Ekho frontovykh radiogramm (Vospominaniia zashchitnika Leningrada)* (St Petersburg, 1999).

Gomery, D., *The Coming of Sound: A History* (New York, 2005).

Gorham, M. S., *Speaking in Soviet Tongues: Language Culture and the Politics of Voice in Revolutionary Russia* (DeKalb, Ill., 2003).

Gorham, M. S., *After Newspeak: Language Culture and Politics in Russia from Gorbachev to Putin* (Ithaca, NY, 2014).

Goriaeva, T. M. (ed.), *Istoriia sovetskoi radio-zhurnalistiki: Dokumenty. Teksty. Vospominaniia. 1917–1945* (Moscow, 1991).

Goriaeva, T. M., *Radio Rossii: Politicheskii kontrol' sovetskogo radioveshchaniia v 1920–1930-kh godakh. Dokumentirovannaia istoriia* (Moscow, 2000).

Goriaeva, T. M. (ed.), *'Velikaia kniga dnia …': Radio v SSSR. Dokumenty i materialy* (Moscow, 2007).

Goriaeva, T. M., *Politicheskaia tsenzura v SSSR. 1917–1991 gg.* (Moscow, 2009).

Granville, J., *The First Domino: International Decision Making during the Hungarian Crisis of 1956* (College Station, Tex., 2004).

Grigor'ev, A., *Nash drug—radio* (Tula, 1966).

Günther, H., and Hänsgen, S. (eds.), *Sovetskaia vlast' i media* (St Petersburg, 2006).

Gurevich, A., *Istoriia istorika* (Moscow, 2004).

Gurevich, P. S., and Kartsov, N. P. (eds.), *Lenin o radio* (Moscow, 1973).

Gurevich, P. S., and Ruzhnikov, V. N., *Sovetskoe radioveshchanie: Stranitsy istorii* (Moscow, 1976).

Gurevich, S. M. (ed.), *Planirovanie raboty v redaktsii* (Moscow, 1979).

Gutnova, E. V., *Perezhitoe* (Moscow, 2001).

Headrick, D. R., *The Invisible Weapon: Telecommunications and International Politics 1851–1945* (New York, 1991).

Hendy, D., *Life on Air: A History of Radio Four* (Oxford, 2007).

Hernandez, R. L., 'Sacred Sound and Sacred Substance: Church Bells and the Auditory Culture of Russian Villages during the Bolshevik Velikii Perelom', *American Historical Review* 109 (2004): 1475–504.

Hilmes, M., *Radio Voices: American Broadcasting, 1922–1952* (Minneapolis, 1997).

Hilmes, M., *Only Connect: A Cultural History of Broadcasting in the United States* (Belmont, Calif., 2002).

Hilmes, M., *Network Nations: A Transnational History of British and American Broadcasting* (New York, 2012).

Hirschkind, C., *The Ethical Soundscape: Cassette Sermons and Islamic Counterpublics* (New York, 2006).

Hixson, W. L., *Parting the Curtain: Propaganda, Culture and the Cold War, 1945–1961* (Basingstoke, 1997).

Hodgson, K., *Voicing the Soviet Experience: The Poetry of Ol'ga Berggol'ts* (Oxford, 2003).

Holzweissig, G., *Die schärfste Waffe der Partei: Eine Mediengeschichte der DDR* (Cologne, 2002).

Horten, G., *Radio Goes to War: The Cultural Politics of Propaganda during World War II* (Berkeley and Los Angeles, 2002).

Husband, W. B., *'Godless Communists': Atheism and Society in Soviet Russia 1917–1932* (DeKalb, Ill., 2000).

Iablonovskaia, D., and Shul'man, M., *'Odessa — Tel'-Aviv' i 'Radio — liubov' moia'* (Tel Aviv, 1985).

Iakhontov, V., *Teatr odnogo aktera* (Moscow, 1958).

Iaron, A., *Oratorskoe iskusstvo (Kak sdelat'sia khoroshim oratorom)* (Moscow, 1917).

Il'f, I., *Zapisnye knizhki 1925–1937*, ed. A. I. Il'f (Moscow, 2000).

Inkeles, A., *Public Opinion in Soviet Russia: A Study in Mass Persuasion* (Cambridge, Mass., 1950).

Inkeles, A., and Bauer, R. A., *The Soviet Citizen: Daily Life in a Totalitarian Society* (Cambridge, Mass., 1959).

Iurii Levitan: 50 let u mikrofona (Moscow, 1987).

Iurovskaia, V., *Radio-gazeta na predpriiatii* (Moscow, 1932).

James, C. V., *Soviet Socialist Realism: Origins and Theory* (London, 1973).

Jelavich, P., *Berlin Alexanderplatz: Radio, Film, and the Death of Weimar Culture* (Berkeley and Los Angeles, 2006).

Kaganovsky, L., and Salazkina, M. (eds.), *Sound, Speech, Music in Soviet and Post-Soviet Cinema* (Bloomington, Ind., 2014).

Kak provodit' gromkie chitki khudozhestvennoi literatury (Leningrad, 1936).

Kalashnikova, I. S. (ed.), *Dmitrii Nikolaevich Orlov* (Moscow, 1962).

Kalganov, I., *Pervye gody leningradskogo radio. V pervye gody sovetskogo muzykal'nogo stroitel'stva: Stat'i, vospominaniia, materialy* (Leningrad, 1959).

Kenez, P., *The Birth of the Propaganda State: Soviet Methods of Mass Mobilization, 1917– 1929* (Cambridge, 1985).

Khersonskaia, E., *Publichnye vystupleniia: Posobie dlia nachinaiushchikh* (2nd edn., Moscow, 1923).

Khersonskaia, E., *Kak besedovat' so vzroslymi po obshchestvennym voprosam* (Moscow, 1924).

Kil'chevskii, V. A., *Tekhnika obshchestvennykh organizovannykh sobranii* (Yaroslavl, 1919).

Kirschenbaum, L., *The Legacy of the Siege of Leningrad, 1941–1995: Myth, Memories, and Monuments* (Cambridge, 2006).

Klimanova, L. S. (ed.), *O partiinoi i sovetskoi pechati, radioveshchanii i televidenii* (Moscow, 1972).

Kliuev, I. V., 'Radioveshchanie Leningrada-Peterburga: Organizatsionnaia struktura, problematika, evoliutsiia form i zhanrov (1980–2000 gg.)', Candidate's dissertation (St Petersburg, 2004).

Koloskov, A. S., Dobronravov, A. S., and Strel'chuk, E. N., *Organizatsiia i planirovanie radiosviazi i veshchaniia* (Moscow, 1985).

Kopperschmidt, J. (ed.), *Hitler der Redner* (Munich, 2003).

Kostin, I. A., *Dve zhizni moego pokoleniia* (Moscow, 2006).

Kozev, N. A. (ed.), *Velenie vremeni: Obshchestvennoe nachalo v rabote sovetskoi pechati i radio* (Moscow, 1961).

Kozlova, N., *Sovetskie liudi: Stseny iz istorii* (Moscow, 2005).

Kravchenko, E. V., 'Istoriia regional'nogo radioveshchaniia (na primere Krasnodarskogo kraia)', Candidate's dissertation (Krasnodar, 2007).

Kravchenko, V., *I Chose Freedom: The Personal and Political Life of a Soviet Official* (London, 1947).

Kriukov, A., *Muzyka v efire voennogo Leningrada* (St Petersburg, 2005).

Krymova, N. A., *Vladimir Iakhontov* (Moscow, 1978).

Kudriavtsev, S., *Rozhdenie radio* (Leningrad, 1935).

Kushner, P. I. (ed.), *Selo Viriatino v proshlom i nastoiashchem: Opyt etnograficheskogo izucheniia russkoi kolkhoznoi derevni* (Moscow, 1958).

Lacey, K., *Feminine Frequencies: Gender, German Radio, and the Public Sphere, 1923–1945* (Ann Arbor, 1996).

Lahusen, T., *How Life Writes the Book: Real Socialism and Socialist Realism in Stalin's Russia* (Ithaca, NY, 1997).

Lastra, J., *Sound Technology and the American Cinema: Perception, Representation, Modernity* (New York, 2000).

Lazarova, I., *'Hier spricht Lenin': Das Telefon in der russischen Literatur der 1920er und 30er Jahre* (Cologne, 2010).

Lenoe, M., *Closer to the Masses: Stalinist Culture, Social Revolution, and Soviet Newspapers* (Cambridge, Mass., 2004).

Letunov, I., *Vremia. Liudi. Mikrofon* (Moscow, 1974).

Liaian, V. I., *Radioveshchanie v burzhuaznoi Estonii (1924–1940): Istoriia, napravleniia razvitiia i nasledstvo* (Tartu, 1968).

Liashenko, B., *Radio bez tain: Rasskaz neizvestnogo diktora* (Moscow, 1991).

Liubovich, A. M., *Nuzhno li spetsial'noe radioiskusstvo: Materialy k I Vsesoiuznomu s"ezdu ODR* (Moscow, 1926).

Liubovich, A. M., *Radio ili provoloka? Materialy k Vsesoiuznomu S"ezdu Obshchestva Druzei Radio* (Moscow, 1926).

Livshin, A. I., and Orlov, I. B. (eds.), *Sovetskaia propaganda v gody Velikoi Otechestvennoi Voiny: 'Kommunikatsionnye ubezhdeniia' i mobilizatsionnye mekhanizmy* (Moscow, 2007).

Loewenstein, K. E., 'The Thaw: Writers and the Public Sphere in the Soviet Union 1951–1957', PhD dissertation (Duke University, 1999).

Lohmus, M., *Transformation of Public Text in Totalitarian System: A Socio-Semiotic Study of Soviet Censorship Practices in Estonian Radio in the 1980s* (Turku, 2002).

London, K., *The Seven Soviet Arts* (London, 1937).

McCannon, J., *Red Arctic: Polar Exploration and the Myth of the North in the Soviet Union, 1932–1939* (New York, 1998).

McLuhan, M., *Understanding Media* (1964; London, 2001).

Magnúsdóttir, R., 'Keeping Up Appearances: How the Soviet State Failed to Control Popular Attitudes to the United States of America, 1945–1959', PhD dissertation (University of North Carolina, 2006).

Magrachev, L., *Vstrechi u mikrofona* (Moscow, 1959).

Magrachev, L., *Golosa zhizni: Iz zapisnoi knizhki radiozhurnalista* (Leningrad, 1962).

Magrachev, L., *Siuzhety, sochinennye zhizn'iu* (Moscow, 1972).

Magrachev, L., *Reportazh iz blokady* (Leningrad, 1989).

Maiakovskii, V., *Polnoe sobranie sochinenii v trinadtsati tomakh* (Moscow, 1955–61).

Malkin, I., *Gazeta v efire: Soderzhanie i tekhnika radiogazety* (Moscow, 1930).

Mal'tseva, N. A. (ed.), *Materialy po istorii sviazi v Rossii XVIII—nachalo XX vv.* (Leningrad, 1966).

Marchenko, T., *Radioteatr: Stranitsy istorii i nekotorye problemy* (Moscow, 1970).

Markhasev, L., *Belki v kolese: Zapiski iz Doma radio* (St Petersburg, 2004).

Markhasev, L., *Sled v efire: Vospominaniia i zametki* (St Petersburg, 2004).

Markov, V. D., *Zhivye doklady: Rukovodstvo dlia derevenskikh politprosvetchikov i dramaticheskikh kruzhkov* (Moscow, 1927).

Marszolek, I., and von Saldern, Adelheid, 'Mediale Durchdringung des deutschen Alltags: Radio in drei politischen Systemen (1930er bis 1960er Jahre)', in U. Daniel and Axel Schildt (eds.), *Massenmedien im Europa des 20. Jahrhunderts* (Cologne, 2010).

Martirosian, G. A. (ed.), *U mikrofona armianskoe radio* (Riazan', 1993).

Medynskii, E. P., *Kak organizovat' i vesti sel'skie prosvetitel'nye obshchestva i kruzhki* (Riazan', 1918).

Mesiatsev, N. N., *Gorizonty i labirinty moei zhizni* (Moscow, 2005).

Mirtov, A. V., *Umenie govorit' publichno* (2nd edn., Moscow and Leningrad, 1925).

Mitrokhin, N., *Russkaia partiia: Dvizhenie russkikh natsionalistov v SSSR 1953–1985 gody* (Moscow, 2003).

Moskvichev, I. I., *Iaroslav Galan v Saratove* (Saratov, 1981).

Mrazek, R., *Engineers of Happy Land: Technology and Nationalism in a Colony* (Princeton, 2002).

Murashov, I., 'Sovetskii etos i radiofikatsiia pis'ma', *Novoe literaturnoe obozrenie* 86 (2007): 47–63.

Murašov, J., 'Das elektrifizierte Wort: Das Radio in der sowjetischen Literatur und Kultur der 20er und 30er Jahre', in Murašov and G. Witte (eds.), *Die Musen der Macht: Medien in der sowjetischen Kultur der 20er und 30er Jahre* (Munich, 2003), 82–112.

Nadzhafov, D. G., and Belousova, Z. S. (eds.), *Stalin i kosmopolitizm: Dokumenty Agitpropa TsK KPSS 1945–1953* (Moscow, 2005).

Nelson, M., *War of the Black Heavens: The Battles of Western Broadcasting in the Cold War* (Syracuse, NY, 1997).

Nemnogo o radio i o nas s vami: K 75-letiiu Primorskogo radio (Vladivostok, 2001).

Novokreshchenova, T. M., *Sozdanie i razvitie radioveshchaniia v Turkmenistane* (Ashkhabad, 1991).

O'Brien, C., *Cinema's Conversion to Sound: Technology and Film Style in France and the U.S.* (Bloomington, Ind., 2005).

Ocherki istorii sovetskogo radioveshchaniia i televideniia (Moscow, 1972).

Ong, W. J., *Orality and Literacy: The Technologizing of the Word* (London, 1982).

Orlova, R., and Kopelev, L., *My zhili v Moskve, 1956–1980* (Ann Arbor, 1988).

Osinskii, V. G., and Kovtun, V. G. (eds.), *Vystoiali, pobedili (Leningrad—blokada—radio): Sbornik statei* (St Petersburg, 1994).

O sovetskom televidenii i radioveshchanii (Materialy gazet 'Pravda' i 'Sovetskaia kul'tura') (Moscow, 1975).

Ostrogorskii, V., *Radiostantsiiu nazyvali 'Marikhen' (K istorii radioveshchaniia iz Moskvy na nemetskom iazyke 1929–1945 gg.)* (Moscow, 1972).

O Valentine Aleksandrovne Sperantovoi: Stat'i i vospominaniia (Moscow, 2003).

Palladin, P. A., Zeger, M. G., and V'iunik, A. A., *Leningradskoe radio: Ot blokady do 'ottepeli'* (Moscow, 1991).

Panov, M. V., *Istoriia russkogo literaturnogo proiznosheniia XVIII–XX vv.* (Moscow, 1990).

Pelevin, V. O., *Ananasnaia voda dlia prekrasnoi damy* (Moscow, 2011).

Peresypkin, I. T., *Voennaia radiosviaz'* (Moscow, 1962).

Peters, J. D., *Speaking into the Air: A History of the Idea of Communication* (Chicago, 1999).

Pethybridge, R., *The Spread of the Russian Revolution: Essays on 1917* (London, 1972).

Petrone, K., *Life Has Become More Joyous, Comrades: Celebrations in the Time of Stalin* (Bloomington, Ind., 2000).

Plaggenborg, S., *Revoliutsiia i kul'tura: Kul'turnye orientiry v period mezhdu Oktiabr'skoi revoliutsiei i epokhoi stalinizma* (St Petersburg, 2000).

Pliatt, R., *Bez epiloga* (Moscow, 2000).

Pogartsev, V. V., 'Stanovlenie i razvitie sistemy radioveshchaniia na Dal'nem vostoke Rossii (1901–1956 gg.)', Candidate's dissertation (Khabarovsk, 2006).

Problemy televideniia i radio (Moscow, 1971).

Puddington, A., *Broadcasting Freedom: The Cold War Triumph of Radio Free Europe and Radio Liberty* (Lexington, Ky., 2000).

Pukhov, D. I. (ed.), *Govorit Iakutsk* (Iakutsk, 1980).

Radio—v derevniu: Agitsbornik (Moscow, 1926).

Radio—v kazhdyi kolkhoznyi dom (Krasnoiarsk, 1954).

Radio v rabochem klube (Leningrad, 1927).

Radio v SSSR: Otchet VII s"ezdu sovetov (Moscow, 1934).

Radio: Vremia i liudi (Syktyvkar, 2001).

Radishcheva, O. A., and Shingareva, E. A. (eds.), *Alla Konstantinovna Tarasova: Dokumenty i vospominaniia* (Moscow, 1978).

Radovskii, M., *Aleksandr Popov* (Moscow, 2009).

Raleigh, D. J., *Russia's Sputnik Generation: Soviet Baby Boomers Talk about Their Lives* (Bloomington, Ind., 2006).

Rebel'skii, I., *Vechera voprosov i otvetov* (Moscow, 1925).

Riordan, M., and Hoddeson, L., *Crystal Fire: The Birth of the Information Age* (New York, 1997).

Rodionov, V. M., *Zarozhdenie radiotekhniki* (Moscow, 1985).

Roth-Ey, K. J., *Moscow Prime Time: How the Soviet Union Built the Media Empire That Lost the Cultural Cold War* (Ithaca, NY, 2011).

Rozental', D. E. (ed.), *Iazyk i stil' sredstv massovoi informatsii i propagandy* (Moscow, 1980).

Rozhitsyn, V., *Kak vystupat' na sobraniiakh s dokladami i rechami* (Moscow, 1928).

Rubashkin, A., *Golos Leningrada: Leningradskoe radio v dni blokady* (Leningrad, 1975; rev. and expanded edn., St Petersburg, 2005).

Rudenko, I. A., 'Radioveshchanie dlia detei i iunoshestva: Stanovlenie, razvitie, problemy sovremennogo funktsionirovaniia', Candidate's dissertation (Moscow, 1986).

Ruzhnikov, V. N., *Tak nachinalos': Istoriko-teoreticheskii ocherk sovetskogo radioveshchaniia 1917–1928* (Moscow, 1987).

Ryan, H. R., *Franklin D. Roosevelt's Rhetorical Presidency* (New York, 1988).

Salagaev, E., *Do vstrechi v efire...* (Moscow, 1986).

Salisbury, H., *Moscow Journal: The End of Stalin* (Chicago, 1961).

Scannell, P. (ed.), *Broadcast Talk* (London, 1991).

Scannell, P., and Cardiff, D., *A Social History of British Broadcasting*, i. *1922–1939: Serving the Nation* (Oxford, 1991).

Schlögel, K., *Moscow, 1937* (Cambridge, 2012).

Senkevich, G., *Vadim Siniavskii—pevets futbola* (Moscow, 2002).

Shabunina, N. I., 'Muzyka v radiozhurnalistike: evoliutsiia funktsii i obraznaia sistema (1924–2004 gg.)', Candidate's dissertation (St Petersburg, 2005).

Shamshur, V. I., *Pervye gody sovetskoi radiotekhniki i radioliubitel'stva* (Moscow, 1954).

Shapkin, V. I., *Krasnye ushi: Sovetskie professional'nye lampovye radiopriemniki 1945–1970 gg.* (Moscow, 2003).

Sherel', A. A., *Rampa u mikrofona* (Moscow, 1985).

Sherel', A. A., *Tam, na nevidimykh podmostkakh ...: Radioiskusstvo: problemy istorii i teorii. 1922–1941* (Moscow, 1993).

Sherel', A. A., *Audiokul'tura XX veka. Istoriia, esteticheskie zakonomernosti, osobennosti vliianiia na auditoriiu: Ocherki* (Moscow, 2004).

Shestopalova, E. V., 'Istoriia stanovleniia i razvitiia radioveshchaniia v Irkutskoi oblasti v 1920–1930-e gody', Candidate's dissertation (Irkutsk, 2008).

Sheveleva, G. A. (ed.), *Pozyvnye trevog i nadezhd. K 40-letiiu radiostantsii 'Maiak'* (Moscow, 2004).

Shilov, L., *Golosa, zazvuchavshie vnov': Zapiski zvukoarkhivista* (Moscow, 1977).

Shpil'rein, I. N., Reitynbarg, D. I., and Netskii, G. O., *Iazyk krasnoarmeitsa: Opyt issledovaniia slovaria krasnoarmeitsa moskovskogo garnizona* (Moscow and Leningrad, 1928).

Siefert, M., ' "Chingis-Khan with the Telegraph": Communications in the Russian and Ottoman Empires', in J. Leonhard and U. von Hirschhausen (eds.), *Comparing Empires: Encounters and Transfers in the Long Nineteenth Century* (Göttingen, 2011).

Smirnov, S. E., *Govorit Tashkent: Slushaite kraevuiu radiogazetu!* (Moscow, 1932).

Smulyan, S., *Selling Radio: The Commercialization of American Broadcasting 1920–1934* (Washington and London, 1994).

Somov, V. A., 'Radio kak kommunikativnoe sredstvo formirovaniia trudovoi motivatsii v gody Velikoi Otechestvennoi voiny 1941–1945 gg. (na primere Volgo-Viatskogo regiona)', *Noveishaia istoriia Rossii*, no. 1 (2012): 132–44.

Starr, P., *The Creation of the Media: Political Origins of Modern Communications* (New York, 2004).

Starr, S. F., *Red and Hot: The Fate of Jazz in the Soviet Union, 1917–1980* (New York, 1983).

Starr, S. F., 'New Communications Technologies and Civil Society', in L. R. Graham (ed.), *Science and the Soviet Social Order* (Cambridge, Mass., 1990), 19–50.

Sterne, J., *The Audible Past: Cultural Origins of Sound Reproduction* (Durham, NC, 2003).

Stites, R., *Russian Popular Culture: Entertainment and Society since 1900* (Cambridge, 1992).

Taranova, E., *Levitan: Golos Stalina* (St Petersburg, 2010).

Taylor, R., 'A Medium for the Masses: Agitation in the Soviet Civil War', *Soviet Studies* 22 (1971): 562–74.

Taylor, R., and Christie, I. (eds.), *The Film Factory: Russian and Soviet Cinema in Documents 1896–1939* (London, 1994).

Televidenie i radioveshchanie SSSR (Moscow, 1979).

Terpugov, A. V., *Rabota u mikrofona* (Leningrad, 1933).

Tolstova, N. A., *Besedy o diktorskom masterstve* (Moscow, 1963).

Tolstova, N. A., *Vnimanie, vkliuchaiu mikrofon!* (Moscow, 1972).

Tolstova, N. A., Levitan, Iu. B., Ot"iasova, E. Ia., and Tobiash, E. M., *Sila slova: Priemy vyrazitel'nogo chteniia v agitatsionno-propagandistskoi rabote* (Moscow, 1945).

Tomoff, K., *Creative Union: The Professional Organization of Soviet Composers, 1939–1953* (Ithaca, NY, 2006).

Toye, R., *The Roar of the Lion: The Untold Story of Churchill's World War II Speeches* (Oxford, 2013).

Trikkel', I., 'Spetsifika radiokommunikatsii, ee vyrazitel'nye sredstva i zhanry', Candidate's dissertation (Tartu, 1967).

Tsukanova, M. I., 'Stanovlenie i razvitie Voronezhskogo radiovehschaniia 1925–1991 godov (na primere VGTRK)', Candidate's dissertation (Voronezh, 2007).

Tsvetova, E., *Vozrozhdennyi "Olimp": Iz istorii muzykal'noi zhizni Samary-Kuibysheva* (Samara, 1991).

U istokov sovetskoi radiotekhniki: Sbornik vospominanii rabotnikov Nizhegorodskoi radiolaboratorii imeni V. I. Lenina (Moscow, 1970).

Vakku, G. V., 'Vozniknovenie i stanvovlenie radioveshchaniia v Chuvashskoi respublike (1920–1941 gg.)', Candidate's dissertation (St Petersburg, 2002).

Vakser, A. Z., *Leningrad poslevoennyi. 1945–1982 gody* (St Petersburg, 2005).

Vasil'eva, T. V., Kovtun, V. G., and Osinskii, V. G. (eds.), *Radio. Blokada. Leningrad: Sbornik statei i vospominanii* (St Petersburg, 2005).

Vertov, D., *Stat'i. Dnevniki. Zamysly* (Moscow, 1966).

Vinogradov, G., *Ob izuchenii narodnogo oratorskogo iskusstva* (Irkutsk, 1925).

Vol'nyi syn efira: Reportazh-vospominanie (St Petersburg, 1997).

von Geldern, J., 'Radio Moscow: The Voice from the Center,' in R. Stites (ed.), *Culture and Entertainment in Wartime Russia* (Bloomington, Ind., 1995), 44–61.

Vozchikov, V. M. (ed.), *Zvuchashchii mir: Kniga o zvukovoi dokumentalistike* (Moscow, 1979).

Vstrechi u mikrofona (Rostov-on-Don, 1985).

Vysokov, M. S., *Pervye russkie radiostantsii na Dal'nem vostoke* (Iuzhno-Sakhalinsk, 1985).

Vysokov, M. S., *Elektrosviaz' v Rossiiskoi imperii ot zarozhdeniia do nachala XX veka* (Iuzhno-Sakhalinsk, 2003).

Wenzlhuemer, R., 'The Dematerialization of Telecommunication: Communication Centres and Peripheries in Europe and the World, 1850–1920', *Journal of Global History* 2 (2007): 345–72.

Werth, A., *Russia at War, 1941–1945* (New York, 1964).

Widdis, E., *Visions of a New Land: Soviet Film from the Revolution to the Second World War* (New Haven, 2003).

Wolfe, T. C., *Governing Soviet Journalism: The Press and the Socialist Person after Stalin* (Bloomington, Ind., 2005).

Woolston, H., 'Propaganda in Soviet Russia', *American Journal of Sociology* 38 (1932): 32–40.

Yurchak, A., *Everything Was Forever, Until It Was No More: The Last Soviet Generation* (Princeton, 2006).

Zakharine, D., 'Ideologiia zvukozapisi. Zvukovoi kadr v zerkale medial'noi antropologii', *Die Welt der Slaven* 54 (2009): 225–42.

Zakharine, D., 'Tonfil'ma kak zvukovoe oruzhie. Rannii opyt sovetskogo zvukovogo kino', *Die Welt der Slaven* 54 (2009): 243–60.

Zakharine, D., 'Avraamov, Vertov, Gladkov: Tri proekta rannego zvukovogo kino', *Die Welt der Slaven* 55 (2010): 148–70.

Zakharova, L., '"Le Socialisme sans poste, télégraphe et machine est un mot vide de sens": Les Bolcheviks en quête d'outils de communication (1917–1923)', *Revue historique* 660 (2011): 853–73.

Zarva, M., *Slovo v efire: O iazyke i stile radioperedach* (Moscow, 1977).

Zenzinov, V., *Vstrecha s Rossiei: Kak i chem zhivut v Sovetskom Soiuze: Pis'ma v Krasnuiu armiiu, 1939–1940* (New York, 1944).

Zherebtsov, I., *Radio i ego primenenie* (Moscow, 1937).

Zubova, A., *Znamenitosti v domashnem inter'ere* (Moscow, 2001).

Zverev, V. P., and Ruzhnikov, V. N. (eds.), *V diapazone sovremennosti: Radioveshchanie 80-kh godov v nashei strane i za rubezhom* (Moscow, 1984).

Index

Abdulov, O., 79, 94, 120, 184, 187
Afinogenov, A., 63–4, 83, 93
Agitprop, 30, 34, 37, 52, 56, 62, 138,
    139–40, 142, 151–2, 153, 154,
    171, 201
Aleksandrov, G., 136, 152, 155
Altman, R., 2
Andronikov, I., 93
anti-Semitism, 141, 153, 169, 200, 212
Ardamatskii, V., 117
Ardi, Iu., 127–8
atheism
    radio in promotion of, 50, 58, 66, 206
Avramov, A., 85
Azerbaijan, 154
Azhaev, V., 113

Babanova, M., 187
Babushkin, Ia., 116
Baklanov, G., 111
Balashkin, A. S., 48
Barto, A., 100, 181, 208–9
Batalov, A., 114
BBC, 13–14, 137, 153, 155–6
Bednyi, D., 51, 85
Beliaev, A., 43–4
Belorussia
    radio in, 23–4, 39, 54, 57, 140
Berdnikov, A., 103
Berggol'ts, O., 117, 118–19, 123
Beria, L., 189
Bespalova, N., 123
Blaginina, E. A., 182
Bliumberg, Ia., 141
Boer War, 15, 16
Bogomazov, S., 183
Bonch-Bruevich, M. A., 1–2, 21, 71, 132
Botvinnik, M., 102
Brezhnev, L., 211, 212, 213
Britain, 15, 16, 26, 62, 155
    broadcasting in, 13–14, 25, 27, 41, 47, 188
    see also BBC
Bulgakova, O., 98
Buratino, 185
Burliand, V. A., 136

Caucasus
    broadcasting in, 139
    broadcasting to, 25
censorship, 8, 30–1, 36–7, 40–1, 109, 114–15,
    117, 166, 171, 172, 174–5, 177–8, 193,
    see also Glavlit

Central Asia, 89
    broadcasting in, 139
    broadcasting to, 25, 33, 36, 79, 137
Central Committee, 27, 29, 30, 32, 77, 80, 87,
    124, 139, 141–2, 171, 189
Chaplygin, N. P., 203
Chappe, C., 15
chastushki, 75, 100, 201
Chateau, J., 15
Cheliuskin affair, 63, 95, 98
Chesnokov, D., 149, 156
children's broadcasting, 37, 43, 67, 95, 100,
    116, 129, 150, 181–6
Chukovskii, K., 91–2, 95, 100, 182, 183,
    206–7
Chuvash Autonomous Republic, 50, 68
cinema, see film
Cold War, 10, 151–8, 161, 188–9
comedy, 80, 150, 194–5
consumerism, 99–100
Crimean War, 15–16, 18
crystal receivers, 27–8, 47–9, 136

Daniel', Iu., 11
Danskii, V. G., 72
Dorizo, N., 196
Dykhovichnyi, V. A., 194

Ehrenburg, I., 119
Ekho Moskvy, 216
elections, 37, 101, 164, 170
Esperanto, 43
Estonia
    broadcasting in, 60, 149, 153, 159, 167, 177,
        190–1, 200–1, 214
estrada, 67, 101, 201, 203
Europa Plus, 215

film, 1, 83–5, 96
    radio as represented in, 46, 173, 205
    sound in, 10, 84, 90
Finin, K., 89
Finland, 155
foreign broadcasting
    into the USSR, 10, 12, 50, 60, 64,
        109, 132–3, 135, 137, 147, 151,
        155–8, 200
    out of the USSR, 130, 133, 135, 137,
        151–7, 166
formalism, 78, 87, 185
France, 15
Frolov, M., 100, 170

Gagarin, Iu., 3, 189–90, 213
Gaidar, A., 95, 182
Gal'perin, Iu., 173–4, 213
Garin, E. P., 86–7, 89
gender
  and radio audience, 49–50, 61, 99
  and radio performance, 67, 73, 120
Georgia, 46, 54–5
German, N., 185
Germany, 165, 166, 167
  broadcasting in, 9, 13–14, 25, 41, 51, 87,
    109–10, 199
glasnost, 214
Glavlit, 30–1, 109, 174–5, 177
  see also censorship
Gleizer, M. S., 125
Goebbels, J., 9
Gorbachev, M., 214
Gorbunov, N. P., 21, 71
Gordienko, M., 99
Goriaeva, T. M., 8, 36
Gorky
  broadcasting in, 7, 33–4, 40, 60, 76–7, 81,
    95, 114, 118, 129, 138, 140, 170, 174,
    191–2, 201
  listeners in, 49, 59, 62, 158, 210
Gorky, M., 26, 38, 72, 92, 93, 103
Gosteleradio, 7, 149, 213
gramophone, 41, 57, 60, 87, 118, 119 n. 58,
  136, 166, 168, 179, 201
Gus, M., 165
Gutnova, E., 111

Headrick, D., 16
Hitler, A., 9, 11–12, 116
holiday broadcasts, 54–5, 61, 69, 99, 102, 112,
  161, 162–3, 178
Hungary, 190

Iagling, B., 161
Iakhontov, V., 108, 114, 120, 121
Il'f, I., 3, 93
Il'ichev, L. F., 203
Inber, V., 123
industrialization
  as conveyed by radio, 59–60, 76, 83–4, 98,
    189, 207
Inge, Iu., 109
Internet, 7, 146, 216
interviews, 122, 169–70, 173–4, 192
Ioffe, R., 90, 129 n. 103, 141, 166, 185
Irkutsk, 19, 23, 24, 27, 37, 40, 48–9, 50, 142
Italy, 155
Iuzvitskaia, E. A., 121
Ivanov, V., 91–2

jamming, 3, 25, 26, 109, 132–3, 147, 155–6,
  157–8
Japan, 86–7

jazz, 101, 197, 199–200, 202, 203
journalism, 172

Kabalevskii, D., 197–8
Kabluchko, V., 124–6
Kachalov, V., 89, 96, 120
Kalakutskaia, M., 183
Kalganov, Iu., 96
Kamenev, L., 54
Kantsel', V., 81
Kassil', L., 39, 94, 95, 113, 120, 131,
  182, 183
Kataev, V., 46, 82, 92
Kaverin, V., 183
Kazakhstan, 154
Kazan, 21, 50, 53, 58
Kerensky, A., 19
Kerzhentsev, P., 33, 91, 96
Khabarovsk, 25, 54, 136–7, 154, 168
Khikmet, N., 206
Khlebnikov, V., 44–5
Khodynka Field
  radio station at, 2–3, 18, 19, 20, 21
Khrushchev, N., 155, 167, 172, 203
Kirgizia, 155
Kirov, S., 40, 63, 98, 102
Klub znamenitykh kapitanov, 4, 184
Knipper-Chekhova, O., 96
KOAPP, 4, 185
Kobzon, I., 204, 215
Kokkinaki, V., 99
Kolobok, 183–4
Kol'tsov, M., 101
Komintern stations, 21–2, 25–6, 79
Komi Republic, 40, 118, 168, 174
Komsomol, 35, 58, 100, 115, 147
Kon, F., 61, 77
Konsovskii, N., 187
Kopelev, L., 112
Korean War, 154
Kravchenko, V., 111–12
Krenkel', E. T., 99
Kuibyshev, 115–16, 122, 133
kul'tura rechi, 97, 104, 122, 206–7, 216
kul'turnost', 61, 69, 99, 206

Lapin, S., 178, 203, 211–12
Latvia, 117, 153
Lenin, V., 1, 19, 20, 83, 159, 178–9
  as speaker, 52, 85, 102–3, 179
  involvement in radio, 8, 21, 71
Leningrad (and region), 5
  broadcasting in, 7, 36, 40, 82, 107–10, 115,
    116, 123, 141, 169–70, 171–2, 178,
    181–2, 190, 206
  listeners in, 60, 61, 138, 143, 214–15
  Siege of, 5, 6, 107–8, 114, 119, 123, 169
Leonov, A., 213
Leonov, L., 92, 93

letters
  as used in broadcasts, 120, 123–6, 162
  sent in by listeners, 132, 187, 194–5, 196–7,
    202, 205–7, 208–9, 211
Letunov, Iu., 174, 176–7
Levenbuk, A., 186
Levitan, Iu., 5–6, 39, 91, 96, 103,
    104, 116, 120, 121, 128, 131, 141,
    159, 173
literature
  as used in broadcasts, 45, 81, 85–93, 118–20
Lithuania, 153, 155
Litovtseva, N., 95–6
Litvinov, M., 26
Litvinov, N., 185–6, 187
Livshits, A., 186
local (*raion*) broadcasting, 33, 40, 76–7, 79,
    114–15, 116, 118, 129, 139–40
Lunacharskii, A., 20, 30–1, 45, 81, 96

magnitofon, 2, 121, 132, 163–8, 169, 176,
    203, 213
Magrachev, L., 6, 123, 141, 169–70, 172
Maiak, 150, 151, 177, 178, 192–3, 195, 204,
    212, 213, 216
Maiakovskii, V., 45, 72, 82, 93, 103, 187
Malenkov, G., 139, 153, 164, 166
Mal'tsev, K. A., 39
Mandel'shtam, O., 92–3
Marconi, G., 16–18
Markhasev, L., 120
Markov, V. D., 83, 85–6
Marshak, S., 95, 100, 182, 183
McLuhan, M., 11–12
Meierkhol'd, V. 82, 89
Melaned, M. N., 171
Men'shikova, A., 185–6
Mesiatsev, N. N., 149, 189
MGSPS, 47, 54, 58–9
MGSPS station, 21–2
Mikhalkov, S., 183
Mikoian, A., 138
Mints, A. L., 25–6
Molotov, V., 25, 30, 56, 103, 152
  as broadcaster, 110–11
montage, 83–4, 88, 175
Moscow, 19
  broadcasting in, 21–2, 25, 33, 54,
    149, 171
  listening in, 61, 63, 158
Moscow Arts Theatre, 82, 94, 97
Mravinskii, E., 198–9
music
  and popular tastes, 66–8, 101, 135, 198–200,
    201–3, 207
  folk, 101, 197, 202
  on radio, 80, 89, 100–1, 197–205
  opera, 49, 54, 101

Nabutov, V., 193
Narkompochtel, 19, 21
  in administration of Soviet radio, 23, 25,
    29–32, 34, 77
Narkompros, 30, 31, 102–3
Narkomsviaz', 129
naturalism, 78, 86, 88
Nazvanov, M., 184
Nekrasov, N., 90–1
Nemchenko, N. V., 87–8, 91
news
  on radio, 72–8, 80–1, 102, 105, 150,
    188–93
newspapers, 4, 10, 71–2, 107, 118, 139–40
Nizhnii Novgorod, *see* Gorky
Nizhnii Novgorod Radio Laboratory, 1–2,
    21, 23
Novikov-Priboi, A., 86, 89, 91

ODR, 27–8, 34–5, 47–9, 73, 81–2
Olesha, Iu., 92
Opiat' 25, 186, 195, 211
Ordzhonikidze, S., 102
Orlov, D., 90–1, 103, 118
Ostrovskii, A., 85
Ostrovskii, N., 90

partisans, 108, 114
pereklichka, 37, 59, 76–7, 100, 101,
    115, 122
Perm', 143, 146–7, 186
Petrograd, 19
Petrova, M., 181–2
Piatnitsky choir, 67–8, 197
Pionerskaia zor'ka, 129, 150, 182, 183–4
Platonov, A., 183
Pliatt, R., 184
Poland, 25, 39
Polikarpov, D. A., 117
Popov, A. S., 16–18, 131, 145
Presto machine, 120, 132, 164
pronunciation, 104
propaganda, 10–11, 107, 188
public speaking, 4, 52–3, 74, 95–6
Pudovkin, V., 84
Pugacheva, A., 204
Pushkin, A., 82, 89, 91, 100
Puzin, A., 126, 133, 136, 138–9, 145, 148,
    151, 154, 156, 157, 164, 166, 167, 175,
    182, 183, 201

rabsel'kory, 170
Radio Committee, 109–10, 123–6, 129–30,
    138–9, 154, 164–6, 173, 198–9
  relationship to party and censorship agencies,
    141–2, 174–5
radiofication, 133, 136, 142–3, 162
radio films, 83, 105
Radio Free Europe, 190

radio hams, 13, 26–7, 29, 34–6, 43, 46–51, 57–8, 109, 144–7
radiogazety, 30, 72–5, 77–8, 80
radio hooliganism, 147
Radio Liberty, 147, 215
radioliubitel', *see* radio ham
radiomiting, 74–5, 115, 122
Radio Moscow, 152, 215
Radioniania, 4, 186
Radio Maximum, 215
Radioperedacha, 2, 29–32, 54, 73, 79, 103
radio plays, 81–3, 87, 187–8
Radio Rossii, 215–16
radiozaitsy, 27, 29, 51
recording, 201
    in radio broadcasts, 41, 84–5, 88, 120–1, 126–7, 154, 175–7, 198–9
    of radio broadcasts, 6
    of speeches, 21, 102–3, 179
    technologies of, 37–8, 120–1, 126, 132, 163–8, 198
Red Army, 35–6, 52, 69, 101, 104, 115, 122
Red Square, 54–5, 112–13, 121, 131
reporters, 116–17, 120–1, 127–8, 131, 167–8, 176–7
rhetoric, 11, 52–3, 96–7, 110, 132, 189, 195–6, 210, 212
Rolland, R., 87
ROSTA, 19–20, 53, 72
Russian Revolution
    communications in, 19–22, 52
    memory of, 178–9
Russo-Japanese War, 18, 145

Sadovskii, A., 30, 73–5
St Petersburg
    communications in, 15, 214–15
    see also Petrograd; Leningrad
Sakhalin, 155–6
satire, 80, 150, 194–5
scheduling, 33, 78–9, 85, 130, 148–50, 185–6, 188, 200
Schilling, P., 15
Schmidt, O., 38
Serafimovich, A., 86, 93
Sevastopol, 121, 127
Shaginian, M., 93
Shcherbakov, A., 109
Sherel', A., 7–8
Shklovskii, V., 80, 119
Schmidt, O., 96
shorinophone, 84, 85, 120–1, 127, 132, 163–4
short-wave radio, 35, 133, 136–7, 144, 146, 150–1, 152, 156–7
Shostakovich, D., 161, 198
Shub, E., 84
Shukhov Tower, 21–2, 44
Siberia, 109

broadcasting to, 33, 34, 111–12, 137, 148, 150
    see also Irkutsk; Tomsk
Siegelbaum, L., 146
Siniavskii, V., 76, 112, 121, 127–8, 164, 193
Slobodskoi, M. R., 194
socialist realism, 3, 104, 113, 131
sociology
    of listening audience, 64–6, 196–7, 205–8
sound effects, 78, 86–7, 120, 175–7, 188, 191
Soviet radio
    broadcasting profession, 39–40, 79, 93–7, 116–17, 121, 129, 139–42, 149, 152–3, 159
    failings of, 37–9, 56–8, 80–1, 128–9, 135, 140, 150–1, 156, 162, 173, 188
    genres, 78–88, 118–20, 130, 175–7, 191, 213–14
    institutional design, 26–33, 148–9, 152
    listeners, 28–9, 51–69, 73, 80, 110–14, 132, 143, 148, 205–8, *see also* letters
    memory of, 4–5, 108, 181
    outline history of, 1–4
    receiver capacity, 33–6, 41, 47–51, 54–6, 114–15, 135–7, 157–8
    significance of, 8–12, 212–13
    sources on, 6–8, 95, 108
    styles of delivery, 80–1, 96, 121–2, 128–9, 162–3, 168–75, 192, 197
    transmission capacity, 22–6, 56, 115–16, 130, 133, 137, 150–1, 152, 156–7
Sovinformburo, 109, 118, 121, 139, 168, 173
Spektor, L, 141
Sperantova, V., 184
sport, 75–6, 128, 193–4
Stakhanovites, 37, 60–1, 102, 171
Stalin, J., 41, 98, 99, 109, 135, 143, 162, 171, 188–9
    as broadcaster, 9, 61, 69, 103, 110–13, 179
Stalingrad, 121, 127–8
Stalinism, 3, 5–6, 9–11, 36–41, 89–90, 97–9, 101–2, 131, 170, 188–9
Stanislavskii, K., 89
Strugatskii brothers, 212–13
studios
    conditions in, 38, 94, 96, 118, 130, 139
Sverdlovsk, 115–16

Taganrog, 143, 186
tape recorder, *see magnitofon*
tarelka, *see* wired radio
Tashkent, 154
TASS, 29, 58, 109–10, 193
Tatarskii, V., 203–4
technology
    history of, 2, 13–14, 17–18
Telefunken, 16, 23, 25
telegraphy, 4, 14–20, 132
telephone, 4, 20

television, 186, 208, 213, 214–15
theatre, 79, 81, 94, 104
  on the radio, 81–3, 88–9, 143, 186–8
Tolstoi, A. N., 117, 131
Tolstoi, L., 103
Tolstova, N., 38, 94–5, 128
Tomsk, 48–9
tonfil'm, 37, 136, 165
transistor radios, 204, 213
Tret'iakov, S., 80, 83
Trotsky, L., 9
Tsarskoe Selo, 19
Tseitlin, M., 161
Tsfasman, A., 67, 199, 200, 201–2
Tsiolkovskii, K., 102
tube radios, 27–8, 36, 49, 136, 144
Tvardovskii, A., 118

Ugadai-ka, 183, 185
Ukraine
  broadcasting in, 37, 39, 76, 145, 147, 153–4
Union of Soviet Writers, 38, 77, 87, 93
United States, 43, 44, 50, 151–2, 154, 161
  broadcasting in, 6, 13–14, 23, 26, 41, 47, 51, 136, 137, 165, 188
Ustrialov, N., 64, 69
Utesov, L., 67, 101, 197
Utesova, E., 197

Vernadskii, V., 111–12, 113
Vertov, D., 55, 83–4, 85, 90
Veselyi sputnik, 150, 194–5

Vishnevskii, V., 118–19, 131
Vladivostok, 60, 62, 168, 174, 178
Voice of America, 137, 147, 153, 155–6, 192, 210
Volkonskii, N., 81, 86
Voronezh, 49, 93, 113
VTsSPS, 27–9
VTsSPS station, 25–6
Vysotskaia, O., 120
vystuplenie, 59, 122–3, 129, 163, 169, 170–1, 174

Weidling, H., 131
Werth, A., 112
wired radio, 3, 23, 28–9, 33–4, 36, 41, 59, 107, 114–15, 129, 135–8, 147–8, 151, 156, 204–5, 215–16
wireless radio, 114, 130, 133, 135–6, 138, 142–7, 157–8
Worker-Peasant Inspectorate, 31, 32
World War I, 2, 132
World War II, 3, 36
  Soviet broadcasting in, 104–5, 107–33, 139, 145, 164

Yeltsin, B., 214, 216
youth broadcasting, 37, 100, 195–7, 203
Yunost, 177, 196–7, 216

Zavalishin, A. I., 90
Zhdanov, A., 140–1, 155, 186
Zinov'ev, G., 31